SOCIAL STAR

*Conflict Resolution and
Community Interaction Skills
(Book 3)*

Nancy Gajewski

Polly Hirn

Patty Mayo

*Thinking Publications
Eau Claire, Wisconsin*

© **1996 Thinking Publications** ®

A Division of McKinley Companies, Inc.

Thinking Publications grants limited rights to individual professionals to reproduce and distribute pages that indicate duplication is permissible. Pages can be used for student instruction only and must include Thinking Publications' copyright notice. All rights are reserved for pages without the permission-to-reprint notice. No part of these pages may be reproduced in any form, electronic or mechanical, including photocopy, recording, or any information storage and retrieval system without permission in writing from the publisher.

05   04   03   02   01   00   99   10   9   8   7   6   5   4   3   2

Library of Congress Cataloging-in-Publication Data
(Revised for vol. 2)

Gajewski, Nancy.
    Social star.

    Contents: book 1. General interaction skills—book 2. Peer interaction skills.
    1. Social skills—Study and teaching (Elementary). 2. Social interaction—Study and teaching (Elementary). I. Hirn, Polly. II. Mayo, Patty. III. Title.
HQ783.G33   1993   372.83   92-39097
ISBN 0-930599-79-9 (v. 1)
ISBN 0-930599-91-8 (v. 2 : pbk.)

ISBN 0-930599-44-6

Illustrations by Kris Madsen and Patti Argoff

Printed in the United States of America

THINKING PUBLICATIONS®
A Division of McKinley Companies, Inc.

424 Galloway Street
Eau Claire, WI 54703
(715) 832-2488
FAX (715) 832-9082

DEDICATION

To Luke, Anna, Jenny, and Katie

NG

To Tom, Rebecca, and Matthew

PH

To Mike, Emily, and Jessica

PM

Table of Contents

Preface vii

Acknowledgments ix

Chapter 1—Getting Started 1

Chapter 2—*Social Star*: A Closer Look 15

References 37

Cognitive Planning 43

Body Talk Summary 91

Taking Charge of Feelings 93

Being Assertive 115

Being Responsible 153

Taking Charge of Anger 185

Resisting Peer Pressure 243

Settling Conflicts 287

Making an Apology 347

Responding to Criticism 363

Helping My Community 391

Appendix A—Lessons X, Y, and Z 421

Appendix B—Social Communication Skills Rating Scale 426

Appendix C—Student Social Skill Summary Form 429

Appendix D—Class Summary Form 430

Appendix E—Socialville Buildings 431

Appendix F—Socialville Characters 440

Appendix G—Parent Letter 449

Appendix H—Self-Management Sheets 450

v

Appendix I—Checking Myself 456

Appendix J—Social Gram 457

Appendix K—Great Coupon Caper 458

Appendix L—Blank T-Chart 459

Appendix M—Relaxation Scripts 460

Appendix N—Secret Formula Pages 462

Appendix O—Thought Bubble 464

Appendix P—Pairing Activities 465

Appendix Q—Roadblock Sheet 473

Appendix R—Social Super Star Badges 474

Appendix S—Thinking Skills Web 476

Appendix T—Dominoes 477

Appendix U—Numbered Heads Together Spinner 479

Appendix V—I Know.... 480

Preface

We are excited to present *Social Star: Conflict Resolution and Community Interaction Skills (Book 3)*, an elementary curriculum for teaching social communication skills. We developed *Social Star* to fill a need for a comprehensive, experiential curriculum that teaches students appropriate social skills.

We believe that an effective social skills program must provide numerous structured opportunities for students to apply and practice newly acquired skills. Teaching social skills in a traditional teacher-directed format, where students are rarely given an opportunity to interact, would be like teaching students how to use a computer but never allowing them to actually use one. *Social Star* incorporates frequent opportunities for students to interact cooperatively.

We believe that an effective educator asks, "What are my students' social skill strengths and how can those strengths be used to expand their social skill repertoire?" rather than asking, "What are my students' social skill weaknesses and how can I fix them?" In addition, the effective educator encourages students to be unique, to express their feelings, and to make their own choices rather than attempting to stifle expression of feelings to force compliance.

The social skills in *Social Star* reflect the conventions of mainstream America, which have been traditionally accepted and expected in educational and employment settings. It is critical to remember that there are marked cultural differences in social skill conventions. The intent of *Social Star* is not to strip students of their cultural beliefs or to make them feel that their beliefs are inappropriate. Rather, the intent is to provide students with the flexibility to move between their cultures and that of mainstream America.

In a world with ever-increasing violence, it is critical that our students learn how to communicate and solve problems with one another in a non-violent manner. *Social Star* is not just intended for those children with severe social skill deficits. All children can benefit and grow from direct instruction of social skills.

While writing *Social Star (Book 3)*, it has been fascinating to read the recent research on self-esteem and resiliency and to discover their link with social skills. The California Task Force to Promote Self-Esteem and Personal and Social Responsibility (1990) defines *self-esteem* as the appreciation of one's own worth and importance, and having the character to be accountable for one's self and to act responsibly towards others. According to Letts (1994), "Prosocial behavior skills and scholarship skills go hand in hand and are vital ingredients in raising children's self-esteem" (p.76). Burns (1994) defines resiliency as "the ability to bounce back, recover from, or adjust to misfortune or change" (p. 94). Bernard (1991) identifies social competence as one of the four broad traits that characterize the resilient child. This new research reaffirms our commitment to comprehensive social skill training.

We hope you enjoy using *Social Star*. Remember, you will be planting seeds that might ultimately change your students' destinies!

Acknowledgments

The authors would like to express their appreciation to all those who have helped in the completion of *Book 3*. We thank Fran Neilitz and Ann Rajek for generously devoting their time reviewing and field-testing units from *Social Star*. A very special thank you to Dr. Lynda Miller and Pattii Waldo for their many hours in reviewing *Social Star* in its entirety. An additional thank you to Pattii Waldo, who shared many creative ideas which were included in *Social Star*. We thank the D.C. Everest School District for their continuing support. We are grateful to Nancy McKinley and Linda Schreiber for their technical and editorial advice, to Kris Madsen for her artistic contributions, and to the rest of the Thinking Publications staff for making it possible for this curriculum to be shared with you.

As always, we thank our husbands, Luke Gajewski, Tom Hirn, and Mike Mayo, for their encouragement, support, and patience.

Chapter 1

Getting Started

SOCIAL SKILL INSTRUCTION—A NECESSITY!

Every educator has experienced the frustration of seeing children isolated or teased by other students. "Mandy" sits by herself at recess. No one wants to work with "Jason." "Peter" makes irrelevant comments. "Ashley" asks a question every sixty seconds. These children are in all classrooms.

Research clearly indicates that children who are unaccepted by their peers will have learning and adjustment problems both in and out of school and later in life (Parker and Asher, 1987; Putallaz and Gottman, 1981; Roff and Sells, 1978). Unpopular students often associate with other unpopular students or with younger children. This makes it difficult for them to gain the skills necessary to interact with more socially skilled children (Bullock, 1988). Children's reputations are often established early in elementary grades and become more and more stable each year (Meichenbaum, 1991). Huml (1994) stresses that life's requirements are both cognitive and social. He contends that in addressing the basic requirements for future success, social skills training is a missing link in curriculum.

Therefore, it is crucial that elementary educators address social skills. Time is of the essence for some students. Children who are rejected by their peers or who stand out negatively in some social skills, need to have the opportunity to learn acceptable social behavior. Social skills may well be the single most important subject educators teach their students! By teaching appropriate social skills, educators will have a positive impact on the lives of their students.

SOCIAL STAR: **A NEW APPROACH**

Instruction of social skills has increased rapidly over the past 15 years. While many strides have been made in the area of social skill instruction (e.g., awareness of the need for instruction, development of curriculum, program research), three major areas of concern remain.

One area of concern is that of teaching social competence as isolated skills when, in fact, any given situation requires that social skills be used in combination with each other. In addition to addressing individual social skills, *Social Star* provides numerous opportunities for students to use a combination of social skills in real-life situations through cooperative experiences.

A second concern (Neel, 1988) is over social skill instruction occurring in isolated environments, thus limiting opportunities for students to interact. *Social Star* is a unique program that provides many opportunities for students to use social skills while they are learning. As stated in the Preface, it is critical that students continually be given opportunities to interact in a positive manner with peers. According to Maag (1994), In order to integrate social skills training into existing programs, teachers must be willing to move away from traditional classroom management and instructional techniques and replace them with more participatory approaches that encourage student involvement and interaction" (p. 101). *Social Star* offers numerous activities structured to encourage cooperative interaction among students. The *Social Star* program is an ideal match for a collaborative regular education program.

A third concern (Lovitt, 1987) is that social skills are taught during a specified time period and then tend to be forgotten during the remainder of the day. *Social Star* advocates teaching a social skills class but, in addition, the program provides numerous strategies to encourage incidental teaching and reinforcement of social skills throughout the school day.

SOCIAL STAR: CULTURAL CONSIDERATIONS

Marked differences in social behavior exist among cultures. *Social Star* teaches social skills that reflect the conventions of mainstream America, which have been traditionally accepted and expected in educational and employment settings. These social skills will not match the norms and expectations within some children's home settings. This awareness of diversity is critical to the success of the program, and educators are encouraged in each unit to invite adults from various cultures to speak with children about differences in cultural conventions.

Students should never be stripped of social skills appropriate for their cultures or be made to feel that their beliefs are inappropriate or wrong. Rather, the intent of *Social Star* is to provide children with the flexibility to move between their cultures and that of mainstream America when they choose to do so.

SOCIAL STAR: GENERAL DESCRIPTION

The *Social Star* program is a series of books that emphasizes general interaction skills, peer interaction, conflict resolution, and community interaction skills. Each book includes basically the same beginning two chapters and appendices; however, the books contain different social skill units.

Social Star is a curriculum intended for use with elementary-age students (approximately grades 2–5). It is appropriate for students in general education, special education, and at-risk programs. Professionals (e.g., classroom educators, special educators, speech-language pathologists, counselors, psychologists, principals) involved with elementary-age students will find this resource valuable for providing social skill instruction.

Each unit within *Social Star* includes a goal statement, educator information (information unique to the social skill being addressed), a series of lessons for teaching the social skill, a list of related activities, a list of related literature, and suggested ways to integrate social skill instruction throughout the school day. The length of each unit varies depending on the complexity of the specific social skill.

The units incorporate a wide variety of instructional techniques (e.g., guided practice pages, scripts, cooperative teamwork, games, role-plays, cartoons, visualizations, and drill and practice). Units do not have to be taught in their entirety. Strategies for adapting units when appropriate are given on page 36. Educators are urged to choose units appropriate for specific students' needs. Most units contain lessons titled Lesson A, B, C, etc. and Lessons X, Y, and Z. Lessons X, Y, and Z follow basically the same format in every unit; therefore, a skeleton lesson for each is provided in *Appendix A*.

Each unit lesson provides an objective or objectives, a list of materials needed, a preparatory set, and a specific plan for completion of the lesson. Each unit incorporates six components. (See Figure 1.1.) These six components are described in detail in Chapter 2 and are referred to in the lesson plans within each unit.

Figure 1.1

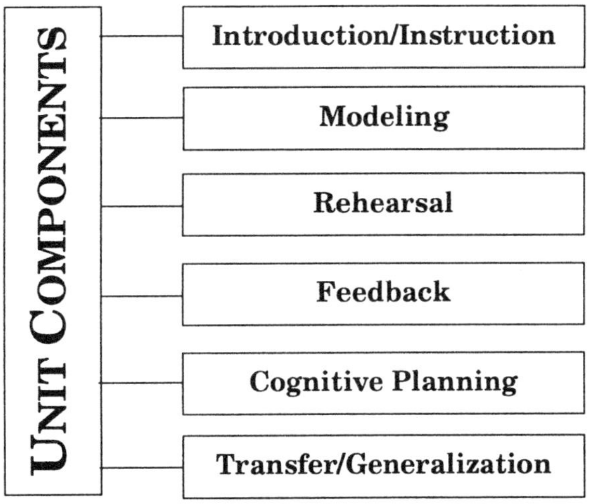

UNIT COMPONENTS
- Introduction/Instruction
- Modeling
- Rehearsal
- Feedback
- Cognitive Planning
- Transfer/Generalization

TYPES OF SOCIAL SKILL DEFICITS

Elliott and Gresham (1991) have conceptualized social skill deficits along five dimensions as summarized in Table 1.1:

Table 1.1 | **Reasons for Social Skill Deficits**

1. A lack of knowledge
2. A lack of practice or feedback
3. A lack of cues or opportunities
4. A lack of reinforcement
5. The presence of interfering problems

A lack of knowledge indicates that (1) a student has not learned the appropriate goals for social interaction (e.g., "Victor" may believe that the goal of doing a community service project is to get recognition rather than to help others in a selfless way); (2) the student has not learned the specific social skills necessary to reach appropriate social goals (e.g., "Ann" may want to stand up for her rights at school, but doesn't know assertiveness skills such as making an I-statement and using confident body language); or, (3) the student has not learned how to match social skills with appropriate situational contexts. The student may not recognize or understand cues within the environment that prompt use of specific social skills (e.g., when dealing with criticism, "Jolisa" may not recognize the difference between helpful and hurtful criticism).

A lack of practice or feedback describes the person who has the knowledge but does not perform the skill. Elliott and Gresham (1991) note that some social skill programs do not provide enough practice for newly learned skills. This can result in the student's appearing awkward or performing the skill in a rote manner (e.g., "Maria" knows how to use humor to resist negative peer pressure, but when she does, she sounds artificial).

A third deficit area involves *a lack of cues or opportunities* (Elliott and Gresham, 1991). Some people only perform social skills when specific cues are present (e.g., "Victor" may apologize only when seeing his mother's encouraging look). Stokes and Baer's (1977) "multiple exemplar strategy" of having students train with more than one person when providing social skill instruction is important to implement.

A lack of reinforcement is the fourth area for social skill deficiencies (Elliott and Gresham, 1991). Some people do not exhibit appropriate social skills because they receive no reinforcement for doing so. For example, "Mike" may not be encouraged by his parents to use anger control. He may even be reinforced for negative behaviors such as fighting (e.g., "What's wrong, aren't you tough enough?").

According to Elliott and Gresham (1991), a final reason for social skill deficiencies is *the presence of interfering problems*. Some behaviors (e.g., word-retrieval problems, hyperactivity, impulsiveness, anxiety) may prevent students from learning or performing social skills.

Social Star includes materials and ideas that will be effective for teaching social skills to students with any type or combination of social skill deficits. In addition, the reader is referred to Elliott and Gresham's (1991) *Social Skills Intervention Guide: Practical Strategies for Social Skill Training* for further information regarding specific strategies to use for each type of deficit.

IDENTIFYING A STUDENT'S SOCIAL SKILL NEEDS

A common concern of educators is determining which social skills are problematic for students. The identification of social skill deficits that cause children to have difficulties with peers is not always possible because there are usually many multiple, complex causes of peer rejection (Kauffman, 1993). Educators need to be aware of the problems associated with the exclusive use of standardized instruments when assessing social behaviors. In many respects, social competence and standardized tests are not a natural fit. Few, if any, well-standardized instruments have been developed to assess social competence. Although a comprehensive system of assessment has yet to be developed, the trend appears to be moving away from the use of standardized tests. Close attention should be paid to new research about the assessment of social skills.

Six alternatives for assessing social competence have proven valuable to date (Gresham, 1981; McGinnis and Goldstein, 1990; Schumaker and Hazel, 1984). These alternatives are listed in Table 1.2:

Table 1.2 | **Types of Social Skill Assessment**
1. Naturalistic behavioral observation
2. Analogue observation
3. Behavioral rating scales
4. Behavioral checklists
5. Sociometric devices
6. Hypothetical situations

Naturalistic behavioral observation involves observing a person socialize in real-life situations. Information obtained from naturalistic observations can be documented on the Social Communication Skills Rating Scale or the Student Social Skill Summary Form included in *Social Star* (see a description of these forms on pages 6–8; blank forms can be found in *Appendices B* and *C*).

Analogue observation involves observing a person socialize in contrived rather than naturalistic settings. The educator can purposely do something which will result in the student's having to demonstrate use of a specific social skill (e.g., offer the student constructive criticism and observe the response). Information obtained from analogue observations can also be documented on the Social Communication Skills Rating Scale or the Student Social Skill Summary Form.

Behavioral rating scales require an adult to rate on a scale a child's use of various social skills. Again, the Social Communication Skills Rating Scale could be used.

Behavioral checklists require an adult to look at a list of various social skills and check which ones a specific student needs to improve. The Student Social Skill Summary Form could be used for this purpose.

Sociometric devices involve children identifying which of their peers are most accepted and most rejected in their class or group. Reliable (albeit intrusive) data are collected about children's social impact on their peer group, but little information is gained about specific social skills or behaviors. *Social Star* skill assessment forms do not address this type of assessment.

Assessment using *hypothetical situations* involves asking a child to explain what a person should do in various social situations. Each unit in *Social Star* includes hypothetical home, school, and community situations. These situations could be used to assess a child's knowledge of various social skills.

The authors believe that a combination of several approaches will be effective for identifying the social skills to be included for instruction. An educator who has worked with a group of students for a given period of time can usually identify social skill strengths and weaknesses by using observation techniques and checklists.

SOCIAL COMMUNICATION SKILLS RATING SCALE

Social Star provides a Social Communication Skills Rating Scale which can be used for several types of skill assessment as summarized in the last section. The scale could be completed by an educator and/or a parent or another adult who has observed the student's use of social skills in a natural setting. When used as a behavioral rating scale, more than one person might complete the Social Communication Skills Rating Scale because people's perceptions vary. The scale is partially shown in Figure 1.2 and is provided in *Appendix B*.

Figure 1.2

SOCIAL COMMUNICATION SKILL	SELDOM	SOMETIMES	ALMOST ALWAYS
2. BEING ASSERTIVE—Speaks up for himself or herself in a confident and respectful way. Comments:	1	2	3
3. BEING RESPONSIBLE—Chooses to do what he or she feels is right. Comments:	1	2	3
4. TAKING CHARGE OF ANGER—Takes charge of angry feelings by dealing with them in responsible ways.	1	2	3

The Social Communication Skills Rating Scale asks the adult to rate the student on each of the social skills contained in *Social Star: Conflict Resolution and Community Interaction Skills* (*Book 3*) based on past experience with the student. Each social skill is described on the rating scale to make it as explicit as possible. The adult rates the student on a scale of 1–3: 1 if the skill is seldom used correctly, 2 if the skill is sometimes used correctly, or 3 if the skill is almost always used correctly. The educator may view a rating of 1 and possibly 2 as being problematic. The estimated readability for this rating scale is an 6.2 grade level, according to the Flesch-Kincaid Readability Scale (Readability Plus, 1988), and it is evaluated as "easy" reading using the "general purpose" scale for adults.

STUDENT SOCIAL SKILL SUMMARY FORM: DETERMINING INDIVIDUAL NEEDS

When the Social Communication Skills Rating Scale has been completed, the scores may be compiled on the Student Social Skill Summary Form, which is partially shown in Figure 1.3 and is provided in *Appendix C*.

Figure 1.3

STUDENT SOCIAL SKILL SUMMARY FORM				
STUDENT'S NAME:	Identified as a strength	Identified as problematic	Skill has been taught in class	
1. Taking Charge of Feelings				
2. Being Assertive				
3. Being Responsible				
4. Taking Charge of Anger				
5. Resisting Peer Pressure				
6. Settling Conflicts				
7. Making an Apology				
8. Responding to Criticism				
9. Helping My Community				

The summary form lists all nine social skills, with a place to mark skills identified as strengths and those identified as weaknesses. It also includes a place to mark the social skills for which the student has received instruction. Two additional blank columns have been provided for the educator to document additional information (e.g., results from naturalistic behavioral observation, analogue observation, or hypothetical situations).

There are several uses for the Student Social Skill Summary Form after its completion. A copy of the summary form may be placed in the student's file and may be attached to a student's report card. For a student in special education, a copy can be included with a specialist's report about the student or in the student's individualized education plan (IEP).

CLASS SUMMARY FORM: DETERMINING WHICH UNITS TO TEACH

The educator may wish to compile each student's data on the Class Summary Form, shown in Figure 1.4, to analyze common needs. The Class Summary Form is provided in *Appendix D*.

Figure 1.4

CLASS SUMMARY FORM

Mark social skills identified as strengths with a "+" and those identified as problematic with a "–".

STUDENTS' NAMES

SOCIAL SKILLS:
1. Taking Charge of Feelings
2. Being Assertive
3. Being Responsible
4. Taking Charge of Anger
5. Resisting Peer Pressure

To complete the form, write the name of each student across the top. For each student, mark the social skills found to be strengths and those found to be problematic areas. Thus, a profile of each student's needs is established. The Class Summary Form identifies the priority social skills and generates a sequence in which the skills may be taught. If a certain social skill is not problematic for any of the students, instruction may not be necessary for that skill. However, the educator may wish to provide a mini-lesson to promote maintenance of the skill. Suppose, conversely, a social skill is found to be a problem for several students, but not for all. When teaching that social skill, the students who are not deficient in that area can be asked to be "special assistants" (e.g., helping the educator model the social skill).

Although some skills are prerequisites for others (e.g., the *Taking Charge of Feelings* unit might be taught before the *Taking Charge of Anger* unit) there is no clear-cut hierarchy of skills. Therefore, the educator could teach the skills in the order of need or interest and not necessarily in the order presented in *Social Star*. However, the *Cognitive Planning* unit must be taught before teaching other units, because it introduces students to key strategies used throughout the program. The social skill of *body talk* (an important and more global unit from *Social Star: General Interaction Skills*) must be taught or reviewed with students first because it is incorporated into the skill steps for all social skill units within this book. Refer to the *Body Talk* unit in *Social Star (Book 1)* or refer to the *Body Talk Summary* on page 91 of this book.

SOCIAL STAR CHARACTERS

The *Social Star* program revolves around six main characters named Mike Olson, Ann Olson, Maria Parra, Victor Parra, Lee Vue, and Jolisa Walker (see Figure 1.5). They are elementary-age children going to McKinley School and living in a community called Socialville. (Major buildings in Socialville are illustrated in *Appendix E* and may be duplicated. Educators are encouraged to build a Socialville community using the building designs provided. Construction of Socialville is further explained in the *Cognitive Planning* unit.)

Figure 1.5

These six characters are also incorporated in *Communicate Junior* (Mayo, Hirn, Gajewski, and Kafka, 1991), which is an educational game board activity (see pages 35–36) to reinforce social skills taught with *Social Star*. The children, along with their parents and teachers, are referred to frequently throughout *Social Star*. The

Socialville characters (17 in all and printed in *Appendix F*) provide a common theme and continuity between units. The characters are portrayed as realistic people with social skill strengths and weaknesses. The characters interact in various home, school, and community situations and come from varied ethnic, socioeconomic, and family backgrounds as described in the next sections.

The Jackson (Olson) Family

Mike Olson, Ann Olson, Mary Jackson, and Joe Jackson

Ann and Mike live with their mother and stepfather. Their stepfather (Joe) works in a toy factory (Get Along Toy Factory) and their mother (Mary) works at a restaurant (Good Meals–Good Manners Restaurant).

The Parra Family

Maria Parra, Victor Parra, Juanita Parra, and Ricardo Parra

Maria and Victor live with their mother and father. Their mother (Juanita) is a physician at a clinic (Helping Hands Clinic) and their father (Ricardo) is an executive at the Get Along Toy Factory.

Getting Started

The Vue Family

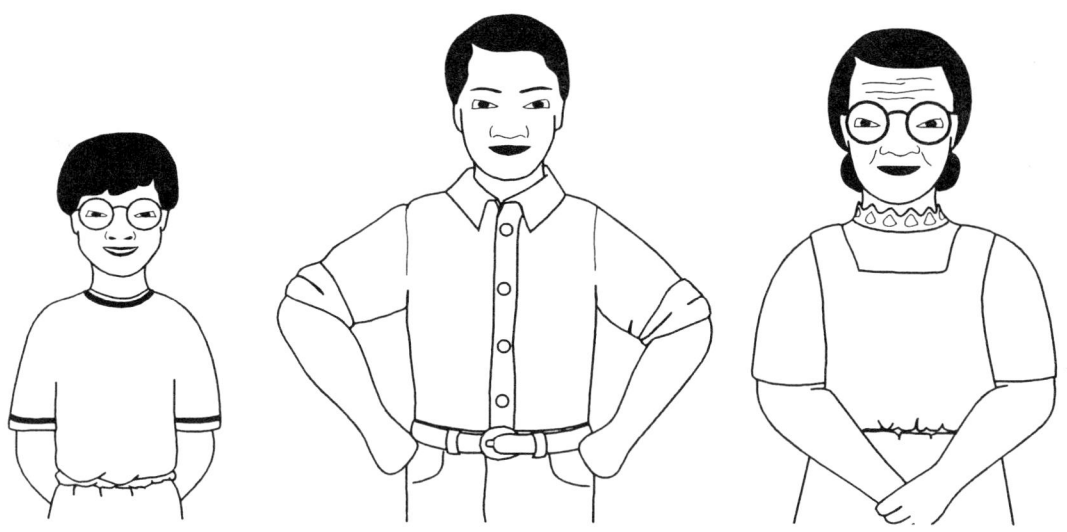

Lee Vue, Ho Vue, Mika Vue

Lee lives with his father and his grandmother. His father (Ho) is a construction worker for Happy Homes and his grandmother (Mika) is a cook at McKinley School.

The Walker Family

Jolisa Walker, Corin Walker, Jesse Walker

Jolisa lives with her mother and father. Her father (Jesse) works for the Socialville Parks Department and her mother (Corin) is a teacher's aide at McKinley School.

Social Star

McKinley School Classroom Teachers

Ms. Paula Hess, Mr. Marcus Aaron, and Mrs. Cora Marrero

SOCIAL STAR WALL CHART CONSTRUCTION

Three types of wall charts are utilized during each *Social Star* unit. They include (1) the *Cognitive Planning Formula* chart; (2) classroom posters; and (3) the *Social Super Stars* display. Directions for making these wall charts are provided in the next three sections (or preprinted color wall charts can be purchased through the publisher; see page 482).

Cognitive Planning Formula Chart

During the *Cognitive Planning* unit and in the final lesson (Lesson Z) of each social skill unit, students are taken through the four cognitive planning steps (STOP, PLOT, GO, SO). Cognitive planning, one of the six components to teaching a social skill, is explained in Chapter 2. The educator could construct a large *Cognitive Planning Formula* chart according to the pattern in Figure 1.6. The chart is used to remind students of the four steps of cognitive planning (described in the *Cognitive Planning* unit).

Figure 1.6

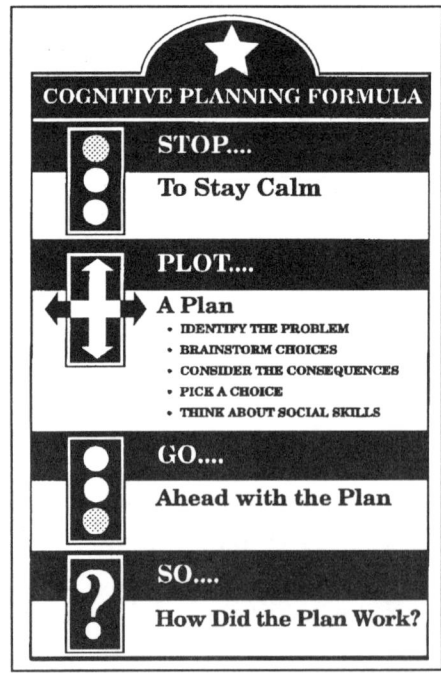

12

Classroom Posters

Lessons from each unit in the *Social Star* program call for a classroom poster. Each poster includes the skill step(s) for a specific social skill and the symbol for each step. This information is described in Lesson A within each unit and could be reproduced large enough for the whole group of students to see. An example is shown in Figure 1.7. The educator could also construct a second poster that has the Socialville characters saying "catchy" phrases reminding students to use each skill appropriately (e.g., "Settle conflicts without a fight. Learn to compromise day and night"). The posters provide an excellent resource for promoting social skills on a schoolwide basis (see page 29).

Social Super Stars Display

Lesson Z (the final lesson in each unit) calls for the use of the *Social Super Stars* display. It is used to display social skill badges that students bring back to school after their parents have signed them (see page 23). The *Social Super Stars* display could be constructed as a large chart with the heading "Social Super Stars." An example is provided in Figure 1.8.

The poster might be laminated for easy removal of the "old" badges when badges from a new unit are brought to school.

Figure 1.7

Figure 1.8

Chapter 2

Social Star: A Closer Look

Social Star provides interesting and creative ways to teach each social skill unit to students, and the variety of activities makes each social skill unit unique. As discussed in Chapter 1, however, all units have six critical components in common:

1. Social Skill Introduction/Instruction
2. Modeling
3. Rehearsal
4. Feedback
5. Cognitive Planning
6. Transfer/Generalization

This chapter describes each of these components in detail.

SOCIAL SKILL INTRODUCTION/INSTRUCTION

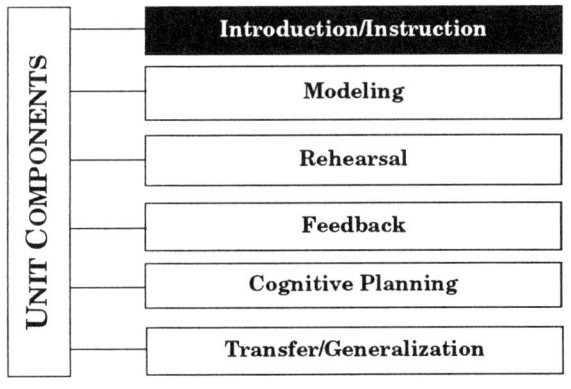

Each unit in *Social Star* includes introductory material that is critical for effective instruction and consists of these sections:

- Unit Goal
- Educator Information
- Related Activities
- Related Literature
- Social Skills All Day Long

The Unit Goal summarizes the overall focus within the chosen social skill area. Most units focus on demonstrating comprehension and use of the social skill.

Educator Information includes background information relevant to each unit that provides data or insights essential for teaching the social skill. This information may influence the way an educator teaches a unit.

Next, Related Activities are suggested that may be completed before, during, or after the lessons in the unit. They may also be used for homework (see page 24).

Similarly, Related Literature may be used at any point in the unit. Related Literature has been included so that children can hear or read stories (or excerpts) that naturally incorporate the social skills being taught. Units have both picture book and text examples of Related Literature that incorporate the target social skill.

The Related Literature books do not directly teach or discuss the target social skill. Rather, the overall theme of the books listed focuses on the particular social skill. The total number of pages for each book is included to assist educators in judging the amount of time needed to read the book.

An attempt was made to include award-winning children's literature whenever possible. Consideration was also given to accessibility; books that are commonly found in school and public libraries were chosen over alternative press titles. In general, only stories that depict realistic characters are included (e.g., folk tales were avoided because they tend to have animal or mythical characters).

The Social Skills All Day Long section provides the means for addressing social skills throughout the day. It is the last section in the introductory pages to each unit and is discussed on pages 26–29.

The lesson plans for each unit include a motivating Preparatory Set that can be used at the beginning of each class. After catching students' interest, instruction of the social skill begins. Lesson A within each unit provides students with the following:

1. A definition of the social skill
2. The skill step(s) used to execute the skill
3. A rationale for why it's important to use the social skill correctly

Other lessons within each unit involve students in hands-on, fun, experiential activities (e.g., reading scripts, performing skits, conducting interviews). Students are asked to complete these activities with a partner or in small groups. Partner and small group interactions provide opportunities for students to integrate the skills they are learning within natural social situations.

Printed materials are often included in lessons for students' use. Often, the educator is also instructed to prepare an overhead transparency and read the material along with the student. On the Flesch-Kincaid Readability Scale (*Readability Plus,* 1988), the student pages range from a 1.5 to a 5.3 grade level. Educators should use their discretion when deciding whether to read activity pages to students. The number of social skill introduction/instruction lessons within each unit varies depending on the complexity of the social skill. The lessons during the introduction and instruction component are labeled A, B, C, etc. depending on the number of lessons. The final three lessons within most units (during which modeling, rehearsal, feedback, and cognitive planning take place) are labeled X, Y, and Z.

The length of each lesson within a unit varies. Some lessons may take more than one session to complete. The average lesson length is approximately 45 minutes.

MODELING

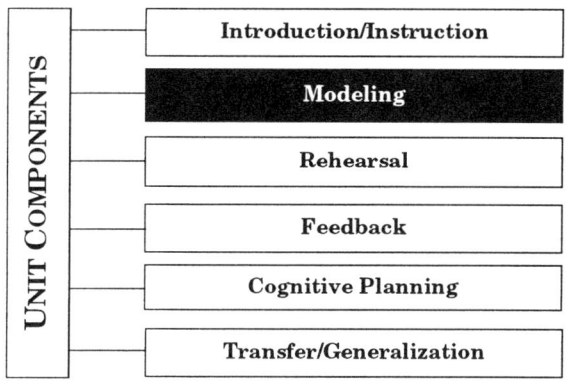

The use of modeling has been documented as an effective strategy for teaching new behaviors (Bandura, 1977; Gresham, 1981). Modeling involves having the educator demonstrate how to use a social skill appropriately. Several opportunities to model correct use of a social skill are built into each unit in *Social Star*.

When modeling, the educator should first demonstrate a social skill while verbalizing thoughts (self-talk) aloud, and then demonstrate the same social skill without verbalizing thoughts aloud. Modeling the use of self-talk for various social skills increases the likelihood that transfer/generalization will occur (Meichenbaum, 1977). Modeling scripts are provided for the educator throughout each unit. Here is an example of modeling with self-talk from the *Taking Charge of Anger* unit:

Modeling Example

Model use of the skill steps for taking charge of anger while thinking aloud. A scripted example follows:

Introduction

I am going to pretend to be someone your age who is feeling angry. I will show you how I can take charge of anger and tell you the thoughts I'm having. When I hold up this Thought Bubble, *you'll know the words I'm saying are actually what I'm thinking.*

Actual Model

While holding up the Thought Bubble *say, OK, I'm starting to feel really angry inside. I feel like I'm going to blow! I need to remind myself to stop. I am in charge of my anger.... What can I do to handle my anger? Right now, I can walk away.* Put the Thought Bubble down and walk away.

In Lesson X, the educator models the social skill in three different situations (i.e., home, school, and community). Several other tips the educator might keep in mind when modeling social skills are these:

1. Modeling is more effective when a "coping model" (Bandura, 1977) is used. For instance, when modeling the social skill of *taking charge of anger* as in the

example above, the person modeling should look and sound as though he or she is truly angry by using a loud voice and tight jaw.

2. Careful thinking and planning beforehand of the modeling display is important (McGinnis, Goldstein, Sprafkin, and Gershaw, 1984).

3. At least two examples of the skill should be modeled (McGinnis et al., 1984). For example, situations from the home, school, and/or community should be modeled.

4. Situations modeled should be realistic for the students (McGinnis et al., 1984). The educator may need to alter the role-plays included in each unit depending on the age, socioeconomic background, and ethnic heritage of the group of students being taught.

5. Students must pay attention to the modeling display being done. Cuing students that they will be asked to identify or discuss various parts of the social skill when the modeling is completed might increase the students' level of interest while observing the modeling display.

6. Negative modeling involves showing how the social skill should NOT be done (e.g., when modeling the social skill of *resisting peer pressure*, one might give in to the peer pressure). Research on the use of negative modeling examples is unclear. McGinnis et al. (1984) advocate that all modeling displays depict positive outcomes. However, Ladd and Mize (1983) state that modeling negative examples may be helpful in making the parameters of the social skill more explicit. Elliott and Gresham (1991) include examples of negative modeling for each social skill in their program.

REHEARSAL

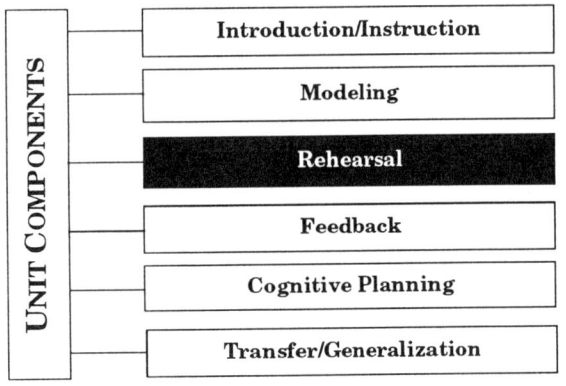

Behavioral rehearsal is an essential component when teaching children social skills. Elliott and Gresham (1991) state that repeated practice of a social skill increases retention of the skill concept and improves performance of the skill. They identify three types of rehearsal:

Covert rehearsal—thinking about and visualizing how to perform a social skill

Verbal rehearsal—reciting the components (skill steps) of a social skill

Overt rehearsal—performing (role-playing) a social skill

Covert rehearsal is incorporated in the Preparatory Set of every social skill unit in *Social Star*. A script is provided which the educator reads to guide students through a visualization of the correct use of the social skill.

Social Star emphasizes *verbal rehearsal* by having students work in pairs to tell each other the skill step(s) for the unit. The pairs verbally rehearse several times.

Each *Social Star* unit includes several opportunities for students to engage in role-playing, thereby providing *overt rehearsal* of the social skill. Many units also provide opportunities for students to drill and practice individual strategies (e.g., to practice the strategy of using an anger shrinker during the unit *Taking Charge of Anger*). In Lesson X of every unit (after students have watched the educator model correct use of the social skill in a home, school, or community situation), a student volunteer is asked to demonstrate the social skill using the following two-step approach:

1. The student demonstrates the social skill *while* verbalizing thoughts (self-talk) aloud.

2. The student demonstrates the social skill *without* verbalizing thoughts (self-talk) aloud.

In the Lesson Y *Show Time* of units in *Social Star*, each student is provided the opportunity to role-play (overtly rehearse) a home, school, and/or community situation. Situations to role-play are provided. These examples are from the *Making an Apology* unit:

> Home—Pretend you told your dad you'd clean your room after your favorite TV show but you didn't follow through. Show how to apologize sincerely to him. (What action can you take to show you are truly sorry?)
>
> School—Pretend you are at school. You accidentally run into someone when you are playing softball. Show how to apologize to the person. (What action can you take to show you are truly sorry?)
>
> Community—Pretend your dog digs a hole in your neighbor's lawn. Show how you will apologize. (What action can you take to show you are truly sorry?)

Additional role-play situations can be found in other commercially prepared programs such as *Skillstreaming the Elementary School Child* (McGinnis et al., 1984); *Skillstreaming in Early Childhood* (McGinnis and Goldstein, 1990); *Communicate Junior* (Mayo, Hirn, Gajewski, and Kafka, 1991); *Scripting* (Mayo and Waldo, 1994); and *Social Skills Intervention Guide* (Elliott and Gresham, 1991).

The role-plays in *Social Star* have been provided to decrease teacher preparation time. However, it is critical that the role-play situations be realistic and relevant for the students. The educator is encouraged to substitute relevant role-plays if the ones provided in *Social Star* are not realistic for a specific child or a group of children. The educator may wish to elicit role-play situations from the students themselves.

Other tips the educator should keep in mind when asking students to role-play are these:

1. Give students the choice of whether or not they wish to participate in the role-play (McGinnis et al., 1984); this will enhance the role-play.

2. Determine the role-play to be done, then elicit more specific information from the main actor as to the physical setting and events which might precede the role-play situation (McGinnis et al., 1984).

3. Use a multiple exemplar strategy (Stokes and Baer, 1977), which involves students role-playing with several different people instead of just one person.

4. Intervene if the student begins to do the role-play incorrectly or is not taking role-playing seriously (McGinnis et al., 1984).

5. Use role reversal by having students switch roles (Goldstein, Sprafkin, Gershaw, and Klein, 1986).

6. Focus on how the student will use the new role-play behaviors in the future rather than how the behaviors could have been used in past situations (McGinnis et al., 1984).

7. Include a variety of opportunities for the students to drill individual skill steps or strategies for a social skill as opposed to performing the entire social skill only once or twice. Georges (1988) recommends drilling each skill step to the mastery level before moving on to the next skill step.

8. Use the word "pretend" with younger children rather than "role-play" when explaining what to do.

9. Provide a box of props that can be used during role-playing. Various hats, shirts, and artifacts (e.g., eyeglasses, purses, clipboards and pens, etc.) can be available for students' use.

FEEDBACK

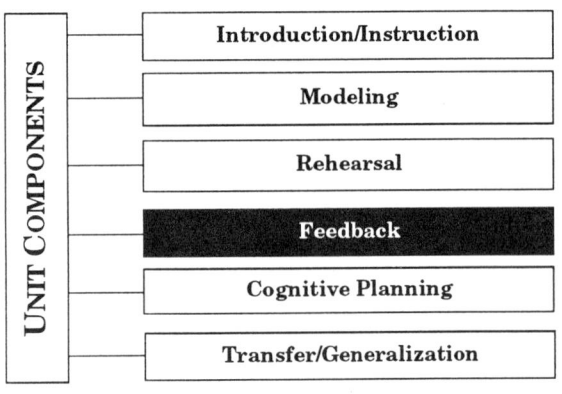

Master educators recognize the importance of providing feedback to students. Thus, it is important that students receive feedback immediately after they perform a social skill so they can make improvements. The feedback can occur formally (during class while the students are role-playing) or informally (throughout the day as appropriate or inappropriate social skill use is observed [see pages 26–29]).

When giving feedback on a student's role-play of a particular social skill, be sure to:

1. Give specific feedback on the skill steps of the social skill. Students sometimes forget skill steps or may do them inappropriately. Those students should be asked to redo the role-play (possibly with educator assistance) to ensure success.

2. Begin by pointing out the positive aspects of the role-play before giving any constructive criticism.

3. Give feedback immediately, particularly to young children. The educator should always provide oral feedback. Additional written feedback is also recommended. For example, the educator could put a smile face next to each of the skill steps the student has successfully performed.

4. Provide feedback to parents on how their children are doing on specific targeted social skills.

COGNITIVE PLANNING

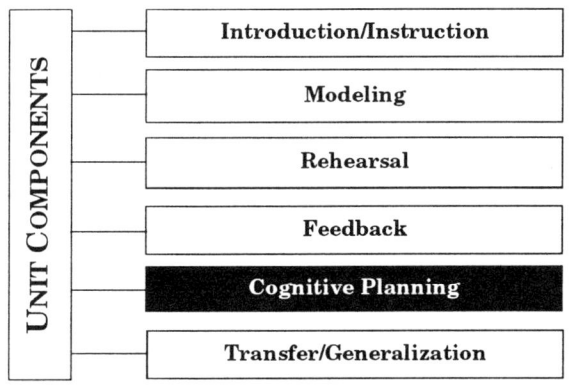

Along with learning comprehension of social skills, students need to learn and use cognitive planning. The phrase "cognitive planning strategies" refers to the independent thinking that students do about social skills.

Students need to be able to do the following:

- Keep themselves calm and in control
- Maintain a positive focus and be open-minded
- Perceive social situations accurately
- Brainstorm social skill options
- Consider consequences for each option
- Choose an option
- Develop a plan
- Carry out their plan
- Evaluate the outcomes
- Reward themselves for their successes and/or decide what to do differently the next time

Social Star has incorporated these cognitive planning strategies into a four-step "secret formula" called STOP, PLOT, GO, SO. Social skill interventions that incorporate cognitive planning strategies are described as being more effective in promoting the acquisition, transfer, and generalization of social skills than programs that do not incorporate these strategies (Hughes, 1988; Kendall and Braswell, 1982).

The first unit in *Social Star* is the *Cognitive Planning* unit. In addition to introducing students to the Socialville characters, this five-lesson unit describes the "secret formula" (the cognitive planning strategies) used by Socialville characters to solve problems and set goals. The secret formula consists of the following steps:

- STOP: Students think "stop" in their minds to stay calm by using self-control strategies.
- PLOT: Students decide what their problem is, brainstorm options, consider possible consequences for each option, and then choose the best option to use in the situation. They also think about the social skills needed to carry out their plan.
- GO: Students implement their plan.
- SO: Students ask themselves, "So, how did my plan work?" They reward themselves for their successes, and/or decide what they may want to do differently next time.

The *Cognitive Planning* unit should be taught first because it is a prerequisite for the remaining units. The four steps of the "secret formula" are reviewed in Lesson Z (Lesson Z Plot Situation) of all other social skill units by having students apply the steps to a hypothetical situation. The hypothetical situation describes a typical problem that a child might encounter and may not be specific to the particular social skill unit. For example, in the *Being Assertive* unit, students are asked to pretend they are trying to tell their mother about a problem they are having with a soccer coach and the mother is not listening. Students are encouraged to use the "secret formula" to solve the problem.

TRANSFER/GENERALIZATION

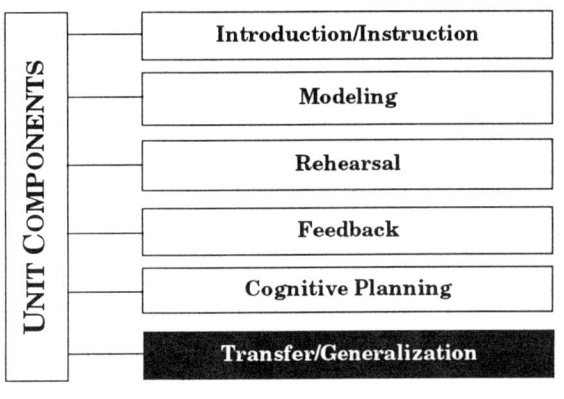

One of the major problems with any social skills training is that the skills often do not transfer/generalize to other settings. Students perform the social skill accurately while in class, yet fail to use the social skill in real-life situations. Each unit of *Social Star* has activities which increase the likelihood that transfer will occur. Some transfer ideas previously discussed are these:

- Use of cognitive planning strategies, which includes using self-control statements, developing a plan, evaluating oneself, and rewarding oneself
- Use of self-talk during modeling and role-plays
- Use of relevant role-play situations from the home, school, and community
- Use of verbal rehearsal and visualization

In addition, *Social Star* provides and/or encourages use of the transfer and generalization activities described in the remainder of this chapter.

Homework

A homework assignment is included in Lesson Z of every unit. The assignment asks students to take a *Home-A-Gram* and a social skill badge home to their parents or other significant adults. Figure 2.1 below provides an example of a *Home-A-Gram* and a badge.

The *Home-A-Gram* is a note written from a child's perspective. The note should be signed by each child during Lesson Z. The *Home-A-Gram* gives information about the social skill and provides an opportunity for the student to practice the social skill with a parent or other significant adult. The parent is asked to sign the social skill badge verifying that the activity was successfully completed. The student returns the badge to be displayed on the *Social Super Stars* display (see page 13).

Before sending home the first *Home-A-Gram* and social skill badge, supply each student's family with information about the rationale for the activity. A letter is provided in *Appendix G*.

Jackson, Jackson, and Monroe (1983) stress that homework should not be limited due to a lack of skills, time, or interest on the part of parents. Therefore, if a parent is unable or unwilling to complete the *Home-A-Gram*, it should be completed with another predetermined adult.

Figure 2.1

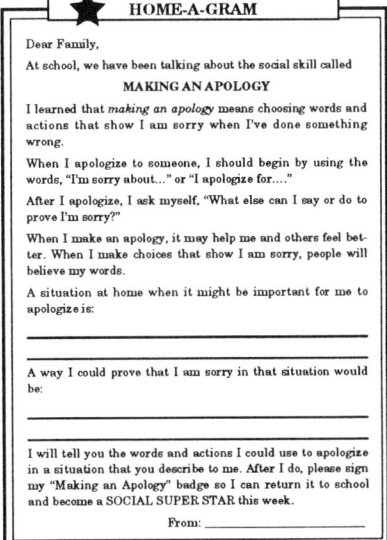

Related Activities

In addition to using the *Home-A-Gram*, the authors advocate that the educator provide motivating homework throughout each unit. The Related Activities listed at the beginning of each unit may also be utilized as homework assignments. These activities help integrate social skills into other content areas and into community settings.

Self-Management Strategies for Social Skills

The use of self-monitoring to learn self-management strategies (e.g., the SO step in the *Cognitive Planning* unit) appears to be a highly promising method for increasing the transfer and generalization of skills (Turkewitz, O'Leary, and Ironsmith, 1975). Dunlap, Dunlap, Koegel, and Koegel (1991) provide a five-step approach for designing and implementing a self-monitoring program. The approach is summarized in Table 2.1 and described in sections 1–5 that follow:

Table 2.1 | **Self-Monitoring Program**

1. Define the behavior to be monitored.
2. Develop a method for self-monitoring.
3. Teach the student how to use a self-monitoring device.
4. Allow the student to select reinforcement.
5. Fade the use of a self-monitoring device.

1. Define the behavior to be monitored. Students must understand and accurately assess themselves. For example, if children are to assess the amount of time they are "on task," they will need to understand exactly what "on task" means. In the *Social Star* program, students are asked to self-monitor in Lesson Z of every unit.

2. Develop a method for each student to monitor social skills. It is important that the educator include the student in this decision-making process. *Social Star* includes 10 *Self-Management* sheets (see *Appendix H*) which can be used with various social skill units. The educator must be careful to choose (or encourage students to choose) the type of self-management sheet that would work best for the given social skill (e.g., use a tally-sheet type shown on page 455 with a skill, such as *taking charge of feelings*, that happens frequently).

3. Teach the student to use the self-management sheets accurately. Students need to understand how to recognize the appropriate behavior and how to record when the behavior occurs. The educator should model how to use the chosen self-management device. Younger students should be asked to self-monitor relatively short, simple tasks. For example, a young child might be asked to self-monitor eye contact for a five-minute period.

4. Allow the student to assist in selecting a predetermined reinforcement for accurately performing the social skill. Students should be rewarded for accurately monitoring themselves in addition to accurately performing the social skill. At first, the educator may provide the reinforcement after the student has completed the self-management sheet. However, students should eventually learn to reward themselves, and extrinsic rewards (e.g., stickers, candy) should be replaced by intrinsic rewards (e.g., self-praise). The educator may wish to ask questions such as "When you learn to use this skill appropriately, what special feelings do you think you'll have? What can you say to praise yourself?" to assist students in moving toward being intrinsically motivated.

5. Fade the use of self-monitoring devices gradually, once the student has demonstrated mastery and generalization of the skill.

Self-Monitoring of Classroom Discussion Skills

In addition to the self-management activity during Lesson Z, students are also asked to self-monitor a classroom discussion skill within the units of *Taking Charge of Feelings, Taking Charge of Anger*, and *Making an Apology* by completing a page called *Checking Myself* (see *Appendix I*). Development of appropriate classroom discussion skills along with social skills will facilitate a positive learning environment.

The educator is provided with a script to model how the *Checking Myself* sheet should be completed. An example follows:

Introduction

I am going to pretend to be one of you completing this sheet during the discussion we will be having. I will tell you the thoughts I'm having while I'm completing the sheet. When I hold up this Thought Bubble, *you'll know the words I'm saying are actually what I'm thinking.*

Actual Model

While holding up the *Thought Bubble* say, *OK, the teacher just called on Bill. I'd better give him eye contact so he knows I'm listening to his answer. I'll draw a line between two dots on the star because I gave him eye contact.* Put the *Thought Bubble* down and draw a line between two dots on the *Checking Myself* transparency.

These classroom discussion skills could be emphasized:
- Listen to others
- Think about an answer to each question asked
- Use interested body talk
- Use appropriate eye contact

- Use a straight sitting posture
- Raise my hand

Educators may substitute other classroom discussion goals more appropriate for their students. For example, not all educators teach children to raise their hands during class discussion. The purpose of completing the *Checking Myself* activity in each unit is to reinforce the classroom discussion skills relevant to the children being taught. The specific selected content for these skills is up to the individual educator.

If the educator is concerned that a specific student may have difficulty monitoring the selected classroom discussion goal accurately, the educator can monitor the individual and compare the results with those of the student.

Social Skills All Day Long

Social skills should be addressed continually throughout the day. Each unit in *Social Star* provides suggestions in the form of encouraging, sharing a personal example, prompting students, and giving corrective feedback that educators can use to reinforce specific social skills. The authors strongly advocate that social skills be addressed throughout the day in a positive, nonthreatening manner.

Encouraging and giving corrective feedback were inspired by *The Dubuque Management System* (Keystone Area Education Agency, 1990), a highly successful social skill program that focuses on appropriate and inappropriate social skills as they occur throughout the day. The procedures for encouraging and giving corrective feedback are further explained in the next sections.

Encouraging

Educators need to reinforce students as frequently as possible when social skills are correctly used. This reinforcement is called "specific effective encouragement" in *The Dubuque Management System* (Keystone Area Education Agency, 1990). The steps involved in this encouragement are summarized in Table 2.2 and described in the next six points:

Table 2.2	**Specific Effective Encouragement**
	1. Approach the student positively.
	2. Describe the appropriate behavior.
	3. Provide a rationale for appropriate behavior.
	4. Ask for acknowledgment.
	5. Tell the consequence.
	6. Provide a transition.

1. Approach the student positively—the educator gives an initial positive greeting (e.g., smile at the student).
2. Describe the appropriate behavior—the educator describes the appropriate behavior the student used (e.g., "You offered help to Lee in such a polite way").
3. Provide a rationale for the appropriate behavior—the educator gives the reason for using the appropriate behavior (e.g., "When you offer help in such a nice way, people will want you to help them").
4. Ask for acknowledgment from the student—the educator asks the student to acknowledge (verbally or nonverbally) that there is understanding of what is said (e.g., "Do you understand?").
5. Tell the student the consequence—the educator tells the consequence the student has earned by the appropriate behavior (e.g., "When it's lunch time, you can go a minute early for offering help to Lee").
6. Provide a transition statement—the educator provides a statement that helps the student get back on task (e.g., "Why don't you spend the last five minutes reading quietly?").

Encouraging is also included at the end of each lesson in *Social Star* in the form of positive statements that are made by teachers. Children either listen to the positive statement or read it aloud in unison. The positive statements reinforce appropriate social skills and provide closure for each lesson.

Giving Corrective Feedback

The Dubuque Management System (Keystone Area Education Agency, 1990) uses a 10-step "teaching interaction" similar to that of Northrup, Wood, and Clark (1979), when inappropriate behavior occurs. "Giving corrective feedback" as modeled in *Social Star* encompasses only the first four steps of the 10-step teaching interaction process. The teaching interaction steps are summarized in Table 2.3 and are described in sections 1–10 that follow:

Table 2.3	**Teaching Interaction**
1. Approach student positively.
2. Describe inappropriate behavior.
3. Describe appropriate behavior.
4. Provide a rationale for appropriate behavior.
5. Model appropriate behavior.
6. Have student practice.
7. Give feedback to student.
8. Provide additional practice.
9. Give praise for accomplishments.
10. Give a homework assignment.

1. Approach the student positively—the educator gives an initial positive greeting (e.g., "Hi, Maria").

2. Describe the inappropriate behavior—the educator describes the inappropriate behavior to the student in specific terms (e.g., "Just now you were turned around in your desk making faces at Victor while I was talking").

3. Describe the appropriate behavior—the educator describes the appropriate behavior to be used by the student (e.g., "Maria, you could have been using your listening skills. Your body could have been facing the front and you could have been looking at me").

4. Provide a rationale for the appropriate behavior—the educator gives the reason for using the appropriate behavior (e.g., "When you face the front and look at me, you let me know you are listening. You won't miss the important things I'm saying") and/or the consequences of not behaving appropriately (e.g., "If you are turned around in your chair, not giving eye contact, your teacher or parent may become upset because you are not listening").

5. Model the appropriate behavior—the educator demonstrates the appropriate behavior (e.g., the educator sits in a desk and models body language appropriate for listening).

6. Have the student practice—the educator asks the student to practice the appropriate behavior (e.g., "Maria, show me how to sit so I'll know you are listening").

7. Give feedback to the student—the educator comments on the student's practice of the appropriate behavior. This feedback may include positive and/or negative feedback (e.g., "You're facing the front with your body. That's great! You still need to look at me when I'm talking, though").

8. Provide additional practice—the educator may request additional practice by the student (e.g., "Try that again, Maria. This time, make sure you are looking at me").

9. Give praise for accomplishments—the educator gives praise to the student for performing and participating.

10. Give a homework assignment—the educator directs the student to practice the appropriate behavior in another setting, or at a later time, or with a different person.

This model provides a positive method for changing inappropriate student behavior. While it may appear to be a time-consuming process, a teaching interaction can often be completed in a few minutes, particularly if the social skill has been previously taught. The use of teaching interactions throughout the day greatly increases the chances for skill transfer and generalization. The authors want to caution that the teaching interaction is but one small component of *The Dubuque Management*

System model. Those wishing further information about this comprehensive program should contact Management Systems Specialists, P.O. Box 3301, Dubuque, Iowa 52001-3301, 1-800-988-2861.

Schoolwide Promotion of Social Skills

Transfer and generalization of social skills will occur more readily if the use of appropriate social skills is promoted on a schoolwide basis. The school staff can jointly decide on a social skill to emphasize each week ("Social Skill of the Week"). The skill could be introduced and defined during the morning announcements. A rationale for using the skill can be given.

Educators could prepare a bulletin board which identifies a specific social skill to emphasize schoolwide. This skill could be changed periodically (weekly or monthly). For example, the elementary school cited in Figure 2.2 chose a theme and goal for each month; October's theme was football. The football was moved 10 yards each time a classroom teacher observed 10 incidents of students in his or her class "giving a compliment." The football field board could be cooperative (e.g., once a class reaches the goal, they give their additional yards to the class farthest behind; when all classes arrive at the goal line, there is an all-school reward) or competitive (e.g., the first class to get to the goal line receives a reward).

Figure 2.2

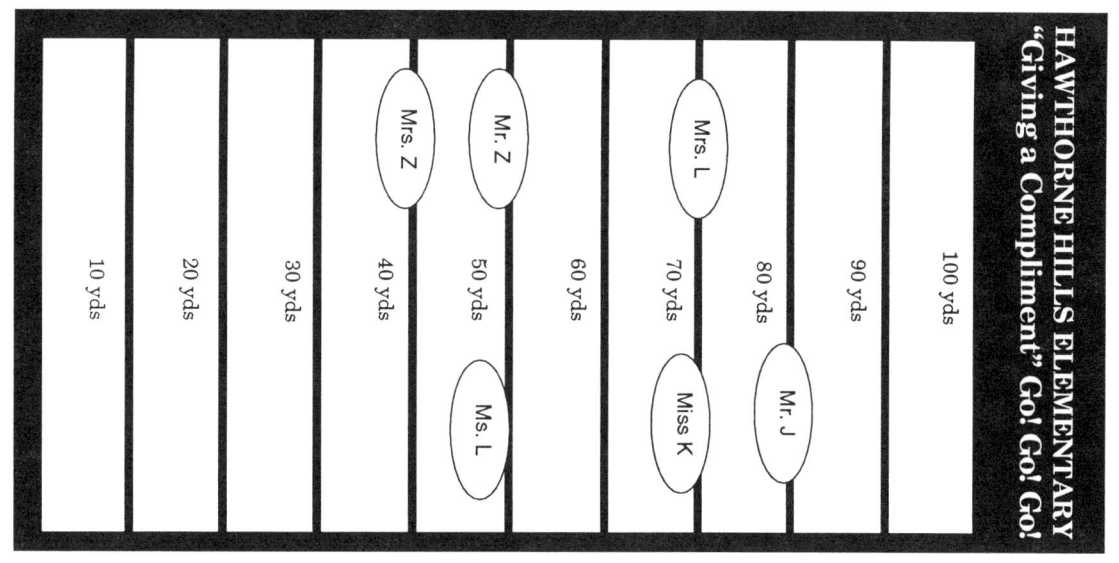

Adapted example of schoolwide promotion of social skills, compliments of Hawthorn Hills Elementary School, Wausau, WI.

Individual educators can further teach the skill using materials from *Social Star*. The "Social Skill of the Month" can be described in a school newsletter. Posters (see page 13) explaining social skills can be hung throughout the school. Students displaying appropriate social skills may be awarded coupons (see page 31), which can be turned in for a drawing. Emphasis on social skill excellence should be recognized at award presentations.

Red Flag

McGinnis, Sauerbry, and Nichols (1985) describe a "Red Flag" strategy in which the educator tells students that they will be "set up" later in the day (or the next day). *Being set up* means that the educator will purposely do something which will cause a child to demonstrate use of a particular social skill. For example, a student might be told that sometime later in the day, the educator will give (the student) constructive criticism. The student is encouraged to demonstrate the proper way to receive constructive criticism during the set up. After the "Red Flag" situation has taken place, the educator and student should discuss how the social skill situation was handled.

Parental Involvement/Training

In addition to involving parents through the *Home-A-Gram*, training should also be available for parents. Two or three parent meetings would be a start at instructing parents how to identify and praise specific appropriate behaviors in their children. Parents can be taught to view inappropriate behavior as a skill deficit that needs to be taught rather than as "naughty behavior." Parents could learn a shortened version of the teaching interaction on page 27 (such as steps 1–4) to use with their children.

Often it is difficult to get parents to attend parent-training sessions. One method of getting the message to parents is to ask the PTO/PTA organization to devote one meeting to the topic of "Communitywide Social Skills." Have the PTO/PTA brainstorm ways for their organization to get involved in this worthwhile goal.

Keep cultural diversity in mind as parent meetings are being planned and implemented. Emphasize that children are being taught flexibility in their use of social skills (see page 2).

Reward/Behavioral Programs

Many students have not reached the level at which they can self-reinforce and may need external controls to help themselves use appropriate behavior. Some ways to reinforce appropriate social behavior follow:

1. *Social Gram*

    A *Social Gram* (see *Appendix J*) can be used to reinforce the student's use of social skills. The educator fills in the student's name and appropriate information, then signs and delivers the *Social Gram* to the student. The educator may wish to describe the student's specific behavior in the blank space.

2. *Sunshine Call*

    The *Sunshine Call* is another method for reinforcing social skills. The educator keeps the names/addresses/phone numbers of all students on note cards in a card file box. Each day, the educator takes the first card from the box and either calls or writes a note to that student's family. It is important that the educator discuss only positive behaviors the child has exhibited when writing to or speaking with the family.

3. *The Great Coupon Caper*

    Each member of the class is given one coupon (see *Appendix K*) at the beginning of the day. At random, the name of a specific student is targeted. When other class members observe that student using appropriate social skills (e.g., *settling conflicts, resisting peer pressure*), they write down why they are awarding the coupon to the target student, and sign their own name. They then give it to the student. At the end of the day, the student turns the coupons in to the teacher. The next day, a different student is targeted to receive the social coupons. When the class earns a specified number of coupons, the students can earn a reward they cooperatively choose. All students should have an opportunity to be the target student.

4. *Student of the Week Graffiti Poster*

    Display a large paper with the title "Student of the Week" written on it. Choose a class member to be the "Student of the Week" and write that student's name on the graffiti poster. Class members are instructed to write times when the student has used appropriate social skills (e.g., "Lee was participating during reading today. Great job, Lee!"). At the end of the week, send the poster home with the student. Give each student the opportunity to be "Student of the Week."

5. *Bell-Ringer*

    At the beginning of the school day, identify a "Social Skill of the Day" (e.g., *being responsible*). This skill may be chosen by the teacher or the class. When the teacher observes the social skill, the teacher rings a bell in celebration!

6. *We're Hot!*

    Display a large paper thermometer with increments marked. Each time students use appropriate social skills (e.g., *making an apology*), one increment on the thermometer is colored. When the entire thermometer is filled, the class receives a special reward.

7. *Cooperative Treat*

    The educator may wish to use cooperative reward activities. These include cooperative root beer floats, tacos, cookies and cookie decorating, and pizzas. For example, when making cooperative root beer floats, one person is responsible for glasses, one for the root beer, one for the ice cream, one for the spoons, and one for the straws. The students put the floats together cooperatively. Students are allowed to consume their floats when all of the floats are ready.

Peer Reminders

Students should be encouraged to remind fellow students about using social skills (e.g., "Come on, Ann. Tell yourself to calm down. You can do it"). The educator may need to instruct students on how to give reminders in a positive manner. The *Cognitive Planning* unit uses the analogy of a stoplight to remind students to stay in control of their emotions. Students can use the word "stoplight" to remind each other to stay calm. In addition, students should encourage each other for using appropriate social skills (e.g., "Great job of making an apology").

Student Mediators

"Mediated dispute resolution" involves student conflicts being resolved by the students themselves with the help of a trained peer mediator (Koch and Miller, 1987). When a conflict arises, the students are asked if they would like to "get mediated." Students then put the disagreement "on hold" until a peer mediator is found. In a mediation session, the peer mediator first explains the ground rules. Then each student takes turns telling "his side of the story." The students then come up with a list of solutions, decide upon a solution, and sign a written agreement. This strategy, which can be used anytime throughout the school day, teaches students to compromise and negotiate. Transfer of social skills occurs when students learn to solve problems on their own rather than needing adults to intervene. This process may be appropriate for slightly older children, since it requires perspective taking and negotiating skills.

Use of Cooperative Learning

The use of cooperative learning techniques during academic classes reinforces social skills taught to students and promotes transfer and generalization of social skills. A list of Cooperative Learning Resources is provided on page 41.

The major differences between cooperative learning and traditional learning are depicted in Table 2.4.

| Table 2.4 | **Differences in Learning Groups** |
| | (Johnson, Johnson, and Johnson Holubec, 1990) |

Cooperative Learning Groups	*Traditional Learning Groups*
Positive interdependence	No interdependence
Individual accountability	No individual accountability
Heterogeneous groups	Homogeneous groups
Leadership is shared	One leader is appointed
Responsible for self and to others	Responsible for self
Task and maintenance emphasized	Only task emphasized
Social skills are directly taught	Social skills are assumed or ignored
Educator observes and intervenes	Educator ignores the groups
Group processing	No group processing

Johnson, Johnson, and Johnson Holubec (1990) describe five components necessary for cooperative learning. They are listed in Table 2.5 and elaborated upon in sections 1–5 that follow:

Table 2.5	**Cooperative Learning Components**
	1. Positive interdependence
	2. Individual accountability
	3. Face-to-face interaction
	4. Social skills
	5. Group processing

1. *Positive Interdependence*

   Johnson et al. (1990) state that one necessary component of a cooperative group is that students believe they "sink or swim together." Students have two responsibilities: learn the assigned material, and make sure that all members of their group learn the assigned material. This dual responsibility is "positive interdependence." Positive interdependence occurs when students feel they are linked with group members in a way that they cannot succeed unless their group members succeed. Positive interdependence promotes a situation in which students recognize that their work benefits group members and vice versa. When positive interdependence is clearly understood, students are aware of the following:

   - Each group member's efforts are required and indispensable for group success (i.e., there can be no "free-riders").

   - Each group member has a unique contribution to make to the joint effort because of his or her resources and/or role and task responsibilities.

   Positive interdependence can be structured in a cooperative group in several ways. Group members can work toward a "group goal" (e.g., learn the material, and make sure all group members learn the material). A "group reward" can be offered (e.g., if all group members score 85 percent on the quiz, they will receive 10 bonus points). "Dividing resources" gives each group member a necessary part of the total information to be learned so that the member must teach that part to others. Additionally, the use of "group roles" (e.g., reader, checker, timer, encourager) is yet another way to structure positive interdependence.

2. *Individual Accountability*

   According to Johnson et al. (1990), *individual accountability* means that each student's efforts are assessed and the results are given to all group members. This helps group members understand that they cannot "hitchhike" on the work of others. To structure individual accountability:

- Assess how much effort each group member is contributing to the group's work.

- Provide feedback to groups and individual students.

- Help groups avoid redundant efforts by members.

- Ensure that every member is responsible for the final outcome.

3. *Face-to-Face Interaction*

   Cooperative learning requires that face-to-face interaction takes place among students. Johnson et al. (1990) explain that this verbal and nonverbal interaction among group members promotes helping, assisting, supporting, encouraging, and praising. It allows students to pressure unmotivated group members to achieve. Students get to know each other as people.

4. *Social Skills*

   Johnson et al. (1990) warn that, oftentimes, simply placing students into a group and telling them to cooperate does not ensure that they will do so. Students need to be taught the social skills needed for positive group interaction (e.g., taking turns listening and talking, giving encouragement, having appropriate body language). These social skills are necessary if the group is to function productively. Social skills are taught by Johnson et al. (1990) through the use of *T-Charts*. *Appendix L* contains a blank *T-Chart* that can be used for any unit in *Social Star*; a completed *T-Chart* is also included in Lesson X of every unit. Use of *T-Charts* is further explained in *Appendix A*.

5. *Group Processing*

   Group processing, as described by Johnson et al. (1990), means that students discuss how well they did at achieving their goal and working together. This helps to provide for generalization of the concepts presented. During group processing, students:

- Describe what member actions were helpful and not helpful.

- Make decisions about what actions to continue or change.

The purpose of group processing is to improve each member's effectiveness in achieving the group's goals.

Kagan (1992) describes a cooperative learning structure called "Numbered Heads Together" that is useful in checking for understanding and reviewing key concepts. This structure is incorporated into some of the lessons within *Social Star* and consists of four steps: (1) team members number off; (2) educator announces a question and a time limit; (3) students put their heads together; and (4) educator calls a number.

Step 1. Team members number off.

Each student on the team numbers off. (Teams may not all have the same number of members. For example, some of the teams may have three members and some of the teams may have four members. When this happens, Person 3 from a team of three may answer when either number 3 or number 4 is called.)

Step 2. Educator announces a question and a time limit.

During this step, the educator should pose a question in the form of a directive. Instead of asking, "Why didn't Jolisa resist peer pressure?" it's better to say, "Make sure everyone on the team can explain why Jolisa didn't resist peer pressure." To keep the activity moving, the teacher may specify the amount of time teams will be given to put their heads together (e.g., "Why didn't Jolisa resist peer pressure? You have 45 seconds to make sure everyone on your team knows").

Step 3. Students put their heads together.

Students actually put their heads together to discuss the answer to the proposed question and to make certain everyone knows and can say the answer.

Step 4. Educator calls a number.

The educator calls a number at random and students with that number answer the question. An overhead spinner can be used to truly randomize the numbers being called. The educator then calls on one student to answer the question.

If only one or two students raise their hands (and there are many more than two teams), the educator can say, "Not enough two's have their hands up; I'll give you one more minute to make sure your team's number two knows the answer. Then I want to see all two's hands up." (Or use another system to identify who's ready to answer if raising hands is contrary to your philosophy and/or to the students' cultures.)

If the answer has several parts, then the educator should ask a number one to answer part one, a number two to answer part two, and so on. If a student gives a partially correct response, the educator might ask, "Is there a number three who can add to that response?"

Real-Life Outings

Some students require that social skills be isolated so that direct instruction can be provided. However, in real life, students must identify which social skills to use when and must use a combination of social skills at all times. It is important to provide real-life outings so that students can practice their social skills. Most units in *Social Star* provide a suggestion for a real-life outing in the Related Activities section. The educator could have students develop a list of social skills they feel will be necessary before going on the outing. After the outing, the educator and students might discuss the students' use of social skills.

Communicate Junior

One means of reinforcing social skill concepts previously learned is the use of educational board games, which can be effective, fun, and motivating (Cartledge and

Milburn, 1986). *Communicate Junior* (Mayo et al., 1991) is a game board activity for elementary students that focuses on 12 social skills. Each player earns an invitation to a party by responding appropriately to question or demonstration items. One by one, players earn their invitation, but the party doesn't begin until everyone is invited. Players are encouraged to help each other get to the party so they can have fun together. The original *Communicate* game (Mayo and Waldo, 1986) is appropriate for upper elementary students.

Social Skill Unit Adaptations

Educators may wish to integrate social skill instruction into content area curriculum. For example, an educator may wish to teach the social skill of *settling conflicts* as a part of a cooperative learning lesson during physical education by using the page called *Settling Conflicts* from Lesson A (the page which provides students with the definition, skill steps, and reasons for settling conflicts).

The units in *Social Star* can also be adapted for use in English-as-a-second-language classrooms. For example, educators may focus on how students can cross between their home cultures and common American cultural norms with regard to social skills when they choose to do so in response to a given situation.

Special attention was given to deleting "should" whenever possible in *Social Star*. Rather than dictating what educators *should* teach children about social skills, the focus is on what *could* be selected. When teaching from *Social Star*, educators are encouraged to honor the "could" terminology rather than lapsing into "shoulds" with children. Likewise, use of "appropriate" is recommended whenever feasible, rather than the more judgmental word "good."

SOCIAL STAR: SUMMARY OF A COMPREHENSIVE RESOURCE

The unit that follows this chapter provides the foundation for other social skills to be taught. *Cognitive Planning* teaches essential thinking strategies and should not be skipped over. The teaching sequence of the remaining 9 social skill units should be determined based upon assessment results.

Each unit contains specific information and materials for teaching a given social skill. Many times, the appendices are cited as containing necessary material to teach the unit. Any materials shared among a number of units are reproduced in an appendix section for easier accessibility.

As units are being taught, respect the diversity among your students. *Social Star* is not intended to produce carbon copies of the teacher's perception of "good" social communicators. Rather, the intent is to teach students the richness and flexibility of social communication rules and their impact on school, home, and community situations.

References

Alberti, R., and Emmons, M. (1995). *Your perfect right: A guide to assertive living*. San Luis Obispo, CA: Impact Publishers.

Alexander, K. (1990). Learning about feelings through classroom art activities. *Preventing School Failure, 29*(1) 29–31.

Arllen, N., Gable, R., and Hendrickson, J. (1996). *Beyond Behavior, 7*(1), 22–23.

Bandura, A. (1977). *Social learning theory*. Englewood Cliffs, NJ: Prentice-Hall.

Benson, P., Galbraith, J., and Espeland, P. (1995) *What kids need to succeed: Proven, practical ways to raise good kids*. Minneapolis, MN: Free Spirit Publishing.

Berman, S. (1990). Educating for social responsibility. *Educational Leadership, 48*(3), 75–80.

Bernard, B. (1991). *Fostering resiliency in kids: Protective factors in the family, school and community*. San Francisco, CA: Far West Laborator.

Bierman, K., and Wargo, J. (1995). Predicting the longitudinal course associated with aggressive-rejected, aggressive (nonrejected), and rejected (nonaggressive) status. *Development and Psychopathology, 7*, 669–682.

Buell, G., and Snyder, J. (1981). Assertiveness training with children. *Psychological Reports, 49*(1) 71–80.

Bullock, J. (1988). Encouraging the development of social competence in young children. *Early Child Development and Care, 37*, 47–54.

Burns, T. (1994). *From risk to resilience: A journey with heart for our children, our future*. Dallas, TX: Marco Polo Group.

California Task Force to Promote Self-esteem and Personal and Social Responsibility. (1990). *Toward a state of esteem*. Sacramento, CA: California Department of Education.

Campbell, J. (1992). Kids don't have to go along with the crowd. *Learning, 20*(18), 74–75.

Carter, S. (1994). *Interventions: Organizing systems to support competent social behavior in children and youth*. Washington, DC: Office of Special Education and Rehabilitation Services.

Cartledge G., and Kleefeld J. (1989). Teaching social communication skills to elementary school students with handicaps. *Teaching Exceptional Children, 22*(1) 14–17.

Cartledge, G., and Milburn, J. (Eds.). (1986). *Teaching social skills to children: Innovative approaches* (2nd ed.). Elmsford, NY: Pergamon Press.

Conari Press. (1994). *Kid's random acts of kindness*. Berkeley, CA: Author.

Cowen, E., Pederson, A., Babigan, H., Izzo, L., and Trost, M. (1973). Long term followup of early detected vulnerable children. *Journal of Consulting and Clinical Psychology, 41*, 438–446.

Duckenfield, M., and Swanson, L. (1992). *Service learning: Meeting the needs of youth at risk*. Clemson, SC: National Dropout Prevention Center.

Dunlap, L., Dunlap, G., Koegel, L., and Koegel, R. (1991). Using self-monitoring to increase independence. *Teaching Exceptional Children, 23*(3), 17–22.

Duryea, E. (1991). Principles of non-verbal communication in efforts to reduce peer and social pressure. *Journal of School Health, 61*(1), 5–9.

The Earth Works Group. (1989). *50 simple things you can do to save the earth.* Berkeley, CA: Earthworks Press.

Elliott, S., and Gresham, F. (1991). *Social skills intervention guide: Practical strategies for social skill training.* Circle Pines, MN: American Guidance Service.

Foster, E. (1989). *Energizers and icebreakers for all ages and stages.* Minneapolis, MN: Educational Media.

Freeman, S. (1989). *From peer pressure to peer support: Alcohol/drug prevention through group process.* Minneapolis, MN: Johnson Institute.

Gaylin, W. (1979). *Feelings: Our vital signs.* New York: Harper and Row.

Georges, J. (1988, April). Why soft-skill training doesn't take. *Training,* 42–47.

Gibbs, J. (1987). *Tribes: A process for social development and cooperative learning.* Santa Rosa, CA: Center Source Publications.

Goldstein, A., Sprafkin, R., Gershaw, N., and Klein, P. (1986). The adolescent: Social skills training through structured learning. In G. Cartledge and J. Milburn (Eds.), *Teaching social skills to children: Innovative approaches* (2nd ed.). Elmsford, NY: Pergamon Press.

Gresham, F. (1981). Social skills training with handicapped children: A review. *Review of Educational Research, 51,* 139–176.

Gronlund, H., and Anderson, L. (1963). Personality characteristics of socially accepted, socially neglected and socially rejected junior high school pupils. In J. Seidman (Ed.), *Educating for mental health* (pp. 87–98). New York: Crowell.

Harmin, M. (1995). *Inspiring active learning: Strategies.* Edwardsville, IL: Inspiring Strategy Institute.

Herzfeld, G., and Powell, R. (1986). *Coping for kids: A complete stress-control program for students ages 8–18.* West Nyack, NY: The Center for Applied Research in Education.

Hughes, J. (1988). *Cognitive behavior therapy with children in school.* New York: Pergamon.

Huml, F. (1994, March 16). Is social-skills training one 'missing link'? *Education Week,* p. 45.

Jackson, N., Jackson, D., and Monroe, C. (1983). Getting along with others: Teaching social effectiveness to children. Champaign, IL: Research Press.

Jakubowski, P. (1977). Assertive behavior and the clinical problems of women. In D. Carter and E. Rawlings (Eds.), *Psychotherapy with women* (pp. 147–167). Springfield, IL: Charles C. Thomas.

Johnson, D., Johnson, R., and Johnson Holubec, E. (1990). *Circles of learning* (3rd ed.). Edina, MN: Interaction Book Company.

Kagan, S. (1992). *Cooperative learning.* San Juan Capistrano, CA: Kagan Cooperative Learning.

Karnes, F.A., and Bean, S.M. (1993). *Girls and young women leading the way: 20 true stories about leadership.* Minneapolis, MN: Free Spirit Publishing.

Kauffman, A. (1993). *Characteristics of emotional and behavioral disorders of children and youth* (5th ed.). New York: Macmillan.

Kendall, P., and Braswell, L. (1982). Cognitive-behavioral self-control therapy for children: A component analysis. *Journal of Consulting and Clinical Psychology, 50,* 672–689.

Keystone Area Education Agency. (1990). *The Dubuque management system*. Dubuque, IA: Dubuque Community Schools.

Kinsley, C. (1994). What is community service learning? Children who can make a life as well as a living. *Vital Speeches of the Day, 61*(2), 40–43.

Koch, M., and Miller, S. (1987). Resolving student conflicts with student mediators. *Principal, 66*, 59–62.

Ladd, G., and Mize, J. (1983). A cognitive-social learning model of social skill training. *Psychological Review, 10*(2), 127–157.

Lang, D., and Stinson, B. (1988). *Lazy dogs and sleeping frogs*. LaCrosse, WI: Coulee Press.

Letts, N. (1994, November/December). Skills of behavior: Can they be taught? *Teaching K-8*, 76–77.

Lewis, B. (1991). Today's kids care about social action. *Educational Leadership, 49*(1), 47–49.

Lovitt, C. (1987). Social skills training: Which ones and where to do it? *Journal of Reading, Writing and Learning Disabilities International, 3*(3), 213–221.

Luhn, R. (1992). *Managing anger: Methods for a happier and healthier life*. Los Altos, CA: Crisp Publications.

Maag, J. (1994). Promoting social skills training in classrooms: Issues for school counselors. *The School Counselor, 42*, 100–112.

Mayo, P., Hirn, P., Gajewski, N., and Kafka, J. (1991). *Communicate junior*. Eau Claire, WI: Thinking Publications.

Mayo, P., and Waldo, P. (1986). *Communicate*. Eau Claire, WI: Thinking Publications.

Mayo, P., and Waldo, P. (1994). *Scripting* (2nd ed.). Eau Claire, WI: Thinking Publications.

McCarty, M., and McCarty, H. (1993). *Acts of kindness: How to create a kindness revolution*. Deerfield Beach, FL: Health Communications.

McGinnis, E., and Goldstein, A. (1990). *Skillstreaming in early childhood: Teaching prosocial skills to the preschool and kindergarten child*. Champaign, IL: Research Press.

McGinnis, E., Goldstein, A., Sprafkin, R., and Gershaw, N. (1984). *Skillstreaming the elementary school child: A guide for teaching prosocial skills*. Champaign, IL: Research Press.

McGinnis, E., Sauerbry, L., and Nichols, P. (1985). Skillstreaming: Teaching social skills to children with behavioral disorders. *Teaching Exceptional Children, 17*, 160–167.

Meichenbaum, D. (1977). *Cognitive-behavior modification: An integrative approach*. New York: Plenum Press.

Meichenbaum, D. (1991, July). Cognitive behavior therapy with adults, adolescents, and children. Workshop presentation at Egg Harbor, WI.

Morganett, R. (1990). *Skills for living: Group counseling activities for young adolescents*. Champaign, IL: Research Press.

Morse, W., Ardizzone, J., Macdonald, C., and Pasick, P. (1980). *Affective education for special education and youth*. Reston, VA: Council for Exceptional Children.

Muncsh, R. (1980). *The paper bag princess*. Toronto, Canada: Annick Press.

Neel, R. (1988). Classroom conversion kit: A teacher's guide to teaching social competency. *Severe Behavior Disorders Monograph, 11*, 25–31.

Northrup, J., Wood, R., and Clark, H. (1979). *Social skill development in children: Application of individual and group training.* Paper presented at the Fifth Annual Convention of the Association for Behavior Analysis, Dearborn, MI.

Parker, J., and Asher, S. (1987). Peer relations and later personal adjustment: Are low-accepted children at risk? *Psychological Bulletin, 102,* 357–389.

Pearl, R., Bryan, T., and Herzog, A. (1990). Resisting or acquiescing to peer pressure to engage in misconduct: Adolescents' expectations of probable consequences. *Journal of Youth and Adolescence, 19*(1), 43–55.

Putallaz, M., and Gottman, J. (1981). Social skills and group acceptance. In S. Asher and J. Gottman (Eds.), *The development of children's friendship.* New York: Cambridge University Press.

Robbins, L. (1966). *Deviant children grow up.* Baltimore, MD: Williams and Wilkins.

Roff, M., and Sells, S. (1978). Juvenile delinquency in relation to peer acceptance, rejection, and socio-economic status. *Psychology in the Schools, 3,* 3–18.

Roff, M., Sells, B., and Golden, M. (1972). *Social adjustment and personality development in children.* Minneapolis, MN: University of Minnesota Press.

Roger, J., and McWilliams, P. (1991). *You can't afford the luxury of a negative thought.* Los Angeles, CA: Prelude Press.

Salend, S., Jantzen, N., and Giek, K. (1992). Using a peer confrontation system in a group setting. *Behavioral Disorders, 17,* 211–218.

Sandler, A., Arnold, E., Gable, R., and Strain, P. (1987). Effects of peer pressure on the disruptive behavior of behaviorally disordered classmates. *Behavioral Disorders, 12,* 104–110.

Scandinavian PC Systems. (1988). *Readability plus* [Computer program]. Rockville, MD: Author.

Schumaker, J., and Hazel, J. (1984). Social skills assessment and training for the learning disabled: Who's on first and what's on second? Part I. *Journal of Learning Disabilities, 17,* 422–431.

Sparks, K., Hussey, S., Bergerson, C., Dennison, M., Cirace, C., Eubanks, T., and Simpkins, V. (1993). *Brownie girl scout handbook.* New York: First Impression.

Stokes, T., and Baer, D. (1977). An implicit technology of generalization. *Journal of Applied Behavior Analysis, 10,* 349–369.

Tavris, C. (1982). *Anger: The misunderstood emotion.* New York: Simon and Schuster.

Turkewitz, H., O'Leary, K., and Ironsmith, M. (1975). Generalization and maintenance of appropriate behavior through self-control. *Journal of Consulting and Clinical Psychology, 43,* 577–583.

U.S. Justice Department. (1994, July 18). Youths are five times more likely to be victims of violent crime. *Milwaukee Sentinel,* p. A2.

COOPERATIVE LEARNING RESOURCES

Blueprints for Thinking in the Cooperative Classroom (1990) by J. Bellanca and R. Fogarty. IRI/Skylight, 2626 S. Clearbrook Drive, Arlington Heights, IL 60005; 1-800-348-4474.

Circles of Learning: Cooperation in the Classroom (3rd ed.) (1990) by D. Johnson, R. Johnson, and E. Johnson Holubec. Interaction Book Company, 7208 Cornelia Drive, Edina, MN 55435; 1-612-831-9500.

Cooperative Learning (1992) by S. Kagan. Kagan Cooperative Learning, 27134 Paseo Espada, Suite 303, San Juan Capistrano, CA 92675; 1-800-933-2667.

Cooperative Learning, Cooperative Lives: A Sourcebook of Learning Activities for Building a Peaceful World (1987) by N. Schniedewind and E. Davidson. Brown-ROA Publishing, 1665 West Embassy Drive, Dubuque, IA 52002; 1-800-922-7696.

Cooperative Learning Lessons for Little Ones: Literature-Based Language Arts and Social Skills (1990) by L. Curran. Kagan Cooperative Learning, 27134 Paseo Espada, Suite 303, San Juan Capistrano, CA 92675; 1-800-933-2667.

The Cooperative Sports and Games Book (1978) by T. Orlick. Pantheon Books, 400 Hahn Road, Westminster, MD 21157; 1-800-733-3000.

The Cooperative Think Tank: Practical Techniques to Teach Thinking in the Cooperative Classroom (1990) by J. Bellanca. IRI/Skylight, 2626 S. Clearbrook Drive, Arlington Heights, IL 60005; 1-800-348-4474.

The Cooperative Think Tank II: More Graphic Organizers to Teach Thinking in the Cooperative Classroom (1992) by J. Bellanca. IRI/Skylight, 2626 S. Clearbrook Drive, Arlington Heights, IL 60005; 1-800-348-4474.

A Guidebook for Cooperative Learning: A Technique for Creating More Effective Schools (1984) by D. Dishon and P. Wilson-O'Leary. Learning Publications, P.O. Box 1338, Holmes Beach, FL 34218; 1-800-222-1525.

Kids Can Cooperate: A Practical Guide to Teaching Problem Solving (1984) by E. Crary. Parenting Press, 11065 5th Avenue, N.E. Suite F, Seattle, WA 98125; 1-206-364-2900.

Learning to Cooperate, Cooperating to Learn (1985) by R. Slavin, S. Sharan, S. Kagan, R. Hertz-Lazarowitz, and C. Webb, (Eds.). Plenum Press, 233 Spring Street, New York, NY 10013; 1-800-221-9369.

The Nurturing Classroom (1989) by M. McCabe and J. Rhoades. ITA Publications, 1500 W. El Camino, Suite 350, Sacramento, CA 95833; 1-916-922-1615.

Our Cooperative Classroom (1988) by D. Johnson, R. Johnson, L. Johnson, and J. Bartlett. Interaction Book Company, 7208 Cornelia Drive, Edina, MN 55435; 1-612-831-9500.

Tools for the Cooperative Classroom (1990) by M. Archibald Marcus and P. McDonald. IRI/Skylight, 2626 S. Clearbrook Drive, Arlington Heights, IL 60005; 1-800-348-4474.

Tribes: A Process for Social Development and Cooperative Learning (1987) by J. Gibbs. Center Source Publications, 305 Tesconi Circle, Santa Rosa, CA 954011; 707-577-8233.

Cognitive Planning

UNIT GOAL:

To demonstrate comprehension and use of a cognitive planning strategy called STOP, PLOT, GO, SO (a strategy that enables students to think about their behavior and its consequences before, during, and after initiating it)

EDUCATOR INFORMATION:

Cognitive planning is one of the six components involved in the instruction of social skills (see pages 21–22). These cognitive planning lessons have been provided to assist the educator in teaching the four steps of cognitive planning: STOP, PLOT, GO, SO. Within this unit, the class is instructed to construct the town of Socialville so that the *Social Star* characters might seem more realistic for students.

RELATED ACTIVITIES:

1. Ask students to run for a short time so they can practice one of the self-control strategies from the STOP step while their bodies experience the physical symptoms associated with anger (e.g., increased heart rate, heavy breathing, sweaty skin). Teach students that these are body cues that warn them of angry feelings.

2. Teach students how to do progressive relaxation (see *Appendix M*).

3. Discuss additional strategies for reducing stress (e.g., exercising, eating properly). Explain that having a high stress level can make self-control difficult to maintain.

4. Use the *Secret Formula Pages* (see *Appendix N*) to transfer use of STOP, PLOT, GO, SO to other areas of the students' lives (e.g., at home, with friends). Model the use of these pages. The page with four stars at the top is written in the present tense (e.g., "I can stay calm by..."), while the page with eight stars is written in the past tense (e.g., "I stayed calm by..."). Encourage students to use these pages to think about problems they may be facing or goals they may wish to set.

5. Inform parents of the secret formula strategy. Encourage parents to use the *Secret Formula Pages* with their children at home.

6. Discuss how the STOP, PLOT, GO, SO steps can work for academic subjects (e.g., to solve a math problem). Also, discuss how the STOP, PLOT, GO, SO steps can work for goal setting (e.g., a student could accomplish the goal of earning money to buy something special).

7. Have students work in pairs to write a story about someone using the problem-solving strategy of STOP, PLOT, GO, SO.

Social Star

Lesson A

OBJECTIVE:

To be introduced to the characters in Socialville

MATERIALS:

1. Characters from Socialville (See *Appendix F*; enlarge, color, glue on tagboard, and laminate each character for use within this and other units from *Social Star*.)

2. *Socialville and the Social Star Club* (See pages 61–66; enlarge, color, and laminate, if desired, one copy of the story for educator use; as an alternative, duplicate one copy per student and let each one color the illustrations.)

3. Buildings from Socialville (See *Appendix E*; enlarge one copy of each building.)

4. Markers or crayons for each student

PREPARATORY SET:

Have students sit in a circle. Tell them to close their eyes and put their hands behind their backs. Give each student a Socialville character. (There are 17 characters. Depending on the group size, students may need to have more than one character or students may need to share a character.) Have students open their eyes and look at their Socialville character(s). Tell students they will be showing their character(s) during a story. For older students, the educator may wish to pass out characters and have students tell if the characters remind them of someone they know and/or guess what each character's personality is like.

PLAN:

1. Read *Socialville and the Social Star Club* to students. Stop to interact directly with students when a star appears in the story. As individual characters are introduced, have the student holding that character stand and show the character.

2. After reading the story, discuss the word "social." Webster defines *social* as:

   a. Marked by or passed in pleasant companionship with one's friends or associates b. Relating to human society, the interaction of the individual and the group, or the welfare of human beings as members of society c. Tending to form cooperative and interdependent relationships with one's fellows.

A definition of *social* for students might be "getting along with other people."

Explain that a large amount of our time is spent in social situations.

3. Process this information by asking students the following questions:

- Did any of the families in Socialville remind you of your family?

- Are there any people from Socialville who you want to get to know better?

- What thoughts do you have about their Social Star Club?

4. Tell students that they will be creating a town in which the Socialville characters will live. Distribute the markers or crayons and an enlarged building to each student. (There are nine buildings. Depending on group size, students may need to have more than one building, or students may need to share a building.) Ask students to help construct Socialville by coloring their building(s). After the buildings have been colored, they could be displayed on a bulletin board or propped up in a three-dimensional manner on a table. Roads, trees, etc. can be added as desired. Socialville can be the setting when putting on skits with the characters. Socialville characters can be stored in Socialville and students can be asked to get various characters when needed. The use of Socialville will help make the characters more realistic to students.

Social Star

Lesson B

OBJECTIVE:

To practice the STOP step of the cognitive planning strategy called STOP, PLOT, GO, SO (The STOP step involves staying calm and using self-control.)

MATERIALS:

1. *STOP: Secret Formula Part 1* (See pages 67–73; enlarge, color, and laminate, if desired, one copy of the story for educator use; as an alternative, duplicate one copy per student and let each one color the illustrations.)

2. Bubble solution, a bubble blower, a soup spoon, and a bowl of water (To be used while reading the story during step 2 below.)

3. *Cognitive Planning Formula* chart (See page 12.)

4. Paper and color markers, pencils, or crayons

5. *Thought Bubble* (See *Appendix O;* one cut out for educator use.)

PREPARATORY SET:

Tell students, "I'm going to pretend to be a student in class. The teacher is handing back my corrected spelling test. Watch how I react when I get my test back and find out I got a low grade." During your role-play, become upset and respond in an out-of-control manner (e.g., pouting, ripping up the test, saying, "I hate school"). Afterwards, discuss with the class how you looked when you were out of control. Review some of the problems associated with losing control (e.g., you can hurt other people's feelings; you feel embarrassed afterwards).

PLAN:

1. Remind students of the "Social Star Club" to which the Socialville students belong. Tell students you will be reading a story about a secret formula that will help them find a solution to the problem of losing control discussed previously.

2. Read *STOP: Secret Formula Part 1* to the class. Stop to interact directly with students when a star appears in the story. (When the story asks students to practice breathing as if they are blowing bubbles or blowing on a hot spoon of soup, model first for the students using the props listed in the Materials section.)

3. Show the *Cognitive Planning Formula* chart and tell students it will be displayed in the classroom to remind them of the importance of the four steps.

4. Process this information by asking students the following questions:

    - Think about a time recently when you were angry. What did you do?

    - Which "STOP" strategy for calming down do you like best?

    - Have you ever seen your mom, dad, brother, or sister using any of these strategies? Which ones?

    - Why is it important to calm down when you're upset?

5. Point to the first stoplight symbol on the *Cognitive Planning Formula* chart. For younger students, tell them they will hear a story about the stoplight called "Sammy Stoplight." Give them paper and color markers (or pencils or crayons) and tell them to draw a picture of "Sammy Stoplight." Explain how the stoplight on the *Cognitive Planning Formula* chart might be envisioned to grow arms and legs.

    For older students, tell them they will hear a story called "Sam and the Stoplight." Give them paper and color markers (or pencils or crayons) and tell them to draw a picture of Sam, who is a boy their age. They could also include a *Thought Bubble* with a stoplight drawn inside since the story will have Sam thinking about the stoplight.

6. Read one of the stories below, depending on the age of the students.

Sammy Stoplight
(For Younger Children)

Point to the first stoplight symbol on the *Cognitive Planning Formula* chart. Tell students you will be reading a story about Sammy Stoplight. Have them look at their pictures of Sammy Stoplight while you are reading. The story follows:

Sammy Stoplight is going to Traffic School. Sammy really wants to graduate and become a stoplight at one of the intersections in town. One day, Sammy was having trouble learning a few of the traffic rules. Some of the other stoplights teased Sammy about it. Sammy lost control and broke their lights. Afterwards, Sammy felt embarrassed about losing control and sorry about hurting the others. On his way home, Sammy stopped at a very busy intersection to talk with a wise old stoplight named Sir Sidney. After hearing about Sammy's problem, Sir Sidney Stoplight said, "You already have the solution to your problem. You're just not using it." "I do? What is it?" Sammy asked. Sir Sidney said, "At traffic school, you're learning how and when to flash your red light on the outside so traffic knows when to stop. Well, you can also flash your red light on the inside, so only you can see it.

When you have a problem and feel upset, flash your red light on the inside and think 'Stop—stay calm!' You're a smart stoplight, Sammy. If you stay calm, you can think of a good way to solve any problem." Sammy was eager to try the inside red light idea. The next day in school when Sammy was feeling frustrated, Sir Sidney's idea came to mind. Sammy tried it and it worked! Sammy started using the inside red light idea more each day. It helped Sammy use self-control and stay calm. Sammy Stoplight felt very proud!

Tell students that Sammy Stoplight can be either a girl or a boy because both girls and boys need to use self-control. Tell students that whenever they feel upset or frustrated, they can think of Sammy Stoplight. They can picture a stoplight in their minds. This will help them to stop so they can use one or more of the self-control strategies mentioned in the story about the Social Star Club.

Sam and the Stoplight
(For Older Children)

Point to the first stoplight symbol on the *Cognitive Planning Formula* chart. Tell students that you will be telling them a story about a boy named "Sam." The story follows:

One day when Sam was at school, he was having problems in gym class. He felt really frustrated. Some of the other kids teased Sam. Sam lost control and got into a fight with the kids. Afterwards, Sam felt embarrassed about losing control and sorry about hurting the others. On his way home from school, Sam stopped at his grandfather's house. After hearing about Sam's problem, his grandfather said, "Sam, when I'm driving in my car and I come to a signal with a red light, I know that I'm coming to a dangerous intersection. I need to STOP my car. If I don't stop, bad things could happen." Sam couldn't figure out why his grandpa was talking about driving his car. "Grandpa, what does that have to do with my problem at school?" Sam asked. Sam's grandpa said, "Well, Sam, you can use a stoplight in your head. When the red light flashes, it means, 'Stop, dangerous situation.' When you feel angry, picture a stoplight and say to yourself, 'I need to get calm. If I don't stop, something bad might happen.'" Sam's grandpa continued, "You're a smart kid, Sam. If you stop, you can stay calm and you can think of ways to solve any problem." Sam thanked his grandpa. He was eager to try the stoplight idea. The next day in school when Sam was feeling frustrated, the stoplight idea came to mind. Sam tried it and it worked. Sam started using the stoplight idea more each day. It helped Sam use self-control and stay calm. Sam felt very proud.

Tell students that all people need to use self-control. Tell students that whenever they feel upset or frustrated, they can picture a stoplight in their minds. This will help them to stop so they can use one or more of the self-control strategies mentioned in the story about the Social Star Club.

7. Model use of the cue word "stoplight" while thinking aloud. A scripted example follows:

Introduction

I am going to pretend that someone took my favorite pencil off my desk without asking. I will show you how I stop to stay calm and tell you the thoughts I'm having. When I hold up this Thought Bubble, *you'll know the words I'm saying are actually what I'm thinking.*

Actual Model

Where is my pencil? Oh, no, it's gone. I can't believe this. I am so angry! While holding up the *Thought Bubble* say, *Stoplight! OK, stay calm. Just calm down. I'll take a deep breath. I have to think of a good way to get my pencil back.*

8. Tell students that if they see someone else from their class getting frustrated or angry, they can remind the student to stay calm by quietly saying "Stoplight" to that person. When they see a classmate successfully staying calm in a difficult situation, they can also give a compliment by saying, "Good job using stoplight!"

9. Conclude the lesson by asking students to write a letter to Sammy Stoplight (or to Sam for older children). In the letter, students could say they are proud that Sammy (Sam) is using the inside red light (or stoplight) idea so successfully.

Social Star

Lesson C

OBJECTIVE:

To practice the PLOT step of the cognitive planning strategy called STOP, PLOT, GO, SO (The PLOT step involves deciding what the problem is, brainstorming choices, thinking about consequences, deciding upon the best choice to use, and thinking about social skills to use.)

MATERIALS:

1. *Cognitive Planning Formula* chart (See page 12.)

2. *PLOT: Secret Formula Part 2* (See pages 74–78; enlarge, color, and laminate, if desired, one copy of the story for educator use; as an alternative, duplicate one copy per student and let each one color the illustrations.)

PREPARATORY SET:

Direct students' attention to the STOP step on the *Cognitive Planning Formula* chart and remind them about "Sammy Stoplight" (or "Sam and the Stoplight" for older children) and the inside red light idea. Read one of the following self-control scripts to students. Some students may have a difficult time seeing "pictures" in their heads. It may be helpful to provide them with a picture of the object to be visualized (e.g., a stoplight, the number "10") before they close their eyes so that they can visualize it more easily. (There will be additional opportunities during Lesson Z of each social skill unit to choose from and to use the scripts that follow.)

Self-Control Strategies

Script #1

When you have a problem, you need to stay in control so you can solve it. One way to stay calm is by using positive self-talk. That means you actually tell yourself to stay calm. Let's try it now. Pretend that you are being teased on the playground. First, tell yourself "stoplight" and picture a stoplight in your mind. Then tell yourself "Stay in control. Be calm. Think of a good way to solve this problem."

Script #2

When you are angry or upset, you need to be in control so you can think about how to solve your problem. When you are angry, you breathe faster. You need to slow your breathing down to stay calm. It helps to take a deep breath. Let's try it now. Pretend you are upset because something that's important to you got broken. First, tell yourself "stoplight" and picture a stoplight in your mind. Then breathe deeply and tell yourself to calm down. When you let the air out, pretend you are blowing bubbles or blowing on a spoon of hot soup.

Script #3

Have you ever been really angry at someone? When you feel yourself getting angry, you need to stay in control so that you don't do or say anything you'll feel bad about later. It might be helpful to put your hand over your mouth to stop yourself from saying something mean. Let's try that now. Pretend you are angry because a friend didn't keep a secret. First, tell yourself "stoplight" and picture a stoplight in your mind. Put your hand over your mouth before you say something mean.

Script #4

When you are frustrated about a problem, you need to help yourself stay in control. One way to give yourself time to stay in control is to count to 10. When you count to 10, you help your body relax so you can think clearly. Let's try that now. Pretend that you are frustrated with a homework assignment. First, tell yourself "stoplight" and picture a stoplight in your mind. Picture the number "10" in your head and count to 10. One, two, three, four, five, six, seven, eight, nine, ten. Take a deep breath.

Script #5

If you are disagreeing with a friend, you might help yourself calm down if you walk away. Let's try it now. First, tell yourself "stoplight" and picture a stoplight in your mind. Picture yourself walking away so you don't say or do something mean. It might be easier to calm down if you are away from the situation. After you have calmed down, you can go back and talk with your friend. Be careful, though. You might get in trouble if you walk away from a parent, teacher, or other adult.

Script #6

When you feel yourself getting upset, stay calm so you can think clearly. First, tell yourself "stoplight" and picture a stoplight in your mind. Now, think of a time when something funny happened to you and you couldn't stop laughing. When you do this, you should immediately feel less angry. This will help you stay calm so that you can solve your problem.

PLAN:

1. Tell students that they will be listening to a story about Mike and how he uses PLOT to solve a problem.

2. Read *PLOT: Secret Formula Part 2* to the class. Stop to interact directly with students when a star appears in the book.

3. After reading the story, direct students' attention to the *Cognitive Planning Formula* chart and review the five steps to PLOT. (PLOT is the most complex component of the cognitive planning strategy because it involves five steps.)

4. Lead students to understand they have more than one choice in most situations. Some students tend to view themselves as having only one choice and, unfortunately, their choice may be a negative one (e.g., when Billy is teased, he may feel that his only choice is to be physically aggressive).

   Ask students to work in pairs to brainstorm at least three choices they could make in each of the following problem situations:

   - You are told to bring a sack lunch for a field trip and you forget to bring one.
   - You spill your milk all over your pants during lunch at school.
   - Your neighbor compliments you on your bike safety and you're not sure what to say or do.
   - You are walking on the sidewalk and an older kid purposely bumps into you.

   Ask each pair to share one of their choices for each situation and record ideas where everyone can see them. Discuss possible consequences for a few of the choices listed.

5. Process the information provided in the story by asking the following questions:

   - Why is it important to know what your problem is?
   - Why is it helpful to brainstorm choices?
   - Why would you want to think ahead about what might happen after each of your choices?
   - How can you tell what your best choice is?
   - Why should you think about social skills when you go ahead and use your best choice?
   - Have you ever had a problem that you had to think about? What strategies did you use to solve your problem?
   - How do you think PLOT could help with a problem you might have?

Lesson D

OBJECTIVE:

To practice the GO step of the cognitive planning strategy called STOP, PLOT, GO, SO (The GO step means putting a plan into action.)

MATERIALS:

1. *Cognitive Planning Formula* chart (See page 12.)

2. *GO: Secret Formula Part 3* (See pages 79–81; enlarge, color, and laminate, if desired, one copy of the story for educator use; as an alternative, duplicate one copy per student and let each one color the illustrations.)

3. *Thought Bubble* (See *Appendix O;* one per pair of students.)

PREPARATORY SET:

Direct students' attention to the *Cognitive Planning Formula* chart and quickly review the STOP and PLOT steps. (Mention "Sammy Stoplight" or "Sam and the Stoplight" and the inside red light idea.) Remind students that they have a variety of choices for any given situation.

PLAN:

1. Tell students that they will be listening to a story about Mike and how he uses the GO step.

2. Read *GO: Secret Formula Part 3* to students.

3. Discuss why it is sometimes difficult to carry out the GO step (e.g., too scared, too embarrassed, it feels strange) even when one has decided on the best choice.

4. Process the information provided in the story by asking students the following questions:

    • Have you ever thought of a good idea, but had a difficult time actually doing it?

    • What are some things you can say to yourself so that you carry out your plan?

5. Read the following situation:

    One day after school, Mike saw a student throw a rock and break a school window. Mike thought "stoplight" and pictured a stoplight in his head. He stayed calm and thought about the choices he had. He decided that his best choice was to tell his teacher about what he saw. The next day, Mike got stuck on the GO step from the secret formula. When it was time to carry out his plan, he was having a difficult time actually telling his teacher.

6. Discuss why Mike might have had a difficult time with the GO step (e.g., he's afraid the other student might find out he told; he's afraid people will call him a tattletale).

7. Pair students (see *Appendix P*). Distribute a *Thought Bubble* to each pair. Ask students to work with their partners to write self-talk in their *Thought Bubbles* that Mike could have used to put his plan into action.

Cognitive Planning

Lesson E

OBJECTIVES:

1. To practice the SO step of the cognitive planning strategy called STOP, PLOT, GO, SO (The SO step means asking yourself, "So, how did my plan work?")
2. To review the four steps of cognitive planning during a game activity

MATERIALS:

1. *Cognitive Planning Formula* chart (See page 12.)
2. *SO: Secret Formula Part 4* (See pages 82–89; enlarge, color, and laminate, if desired, one copy of the story for educator use; as an alternative, duplicate one copy per student and let each one color the illustrations.)
3. *Cue Cards* (See page 58; one set cut apart.)
4. *Problem Situations* (See page 59; one set cut apart.)
5. *Score Card* (See page 60; one per student.)

PREPARATORY SET:

Students need to internalize the phrase STOP, PLOT, GO, SO so when they are actually in a problem situation, they can recall the steps. The "Beat the Clock" activities that follow review the phrase. Choose one or more to try. (There will be additional opportunities to use these activities during Lesson Z of each social skill unit.)

Beat the Clock Activities

- Have students stay seated. Go around the room in round robin fashion and have each person say in order one of the words STOP, PLOT, GO, SO. See how many times they can go around the room in one minute.

- Have students say STOP, PLOT, GO, SO quietly to themselves. Each time students finish saying the phrase, they should put a tally mark on a piece of paper. Students could see how many times they can say the words in 30 seconds.

- Have students form small groups and stand in lines facing the front of the room. When the educator says "begin," the first student from each group writes STOP on the chalkboard, runs back, and stands at the back of the line. The next member of the small group then runs up and writes PLOT on the chalkboard, and so on in relay fashion. See how many complete phrases each group can write in two minutes.

55

- Have students form a circle and then pass a ball around the circle. The first person starts out saying STOP and then passes the ball to the next person who says PLOT, etc. The group tries to pass the ball around the entire circle as many times as they can in one minute.

PLAN:

1. Read *SO: Secret Formula Part 4* to students. Stop to interact directly with students when a star appears in the story.

2. After reading the story, process the information provided by asking students the following questions:
    - Do you ever think about things after you do them? Why might it be a good idea to do this?
    - Have you ever heard the saying "Learn from your mistakes"? What does this have to do with the SO step?
    - Why is it important to tell yourself you've done a good job when you do something right?

3. Present students with the following list of reasons a person's plan may not work. Encourage students to add to the list.
    - Didn't stay calm and in control
    - Didn't use an appropriate tone of voice during GO
    - Didn't choose an appropriate time and place for GO
    - Didn't think about the possible consequences of a choice

    The list can be displayed and added to as new reasons come to mind.

4. Model phrases the students can use to praise themselves when things have gone well. Make the model exciting and somewhat exaggerated (e.g., "Hey, way to go. I did an absolutely fantastic job talking with Mr. Bill! Marvelous!").

5. Ask students to participate in several activities at which they can be successful (e.g., jumping rope, skipping around the room, drawing 10 circles). After each activity, invite students to praise themselves. Tell them that for now you'd like them to praise themselves aloud but that normally they would do it quietly inside of their heads.

6. Tell students they will be playing a game of "Problem-Solving Softball" to practice using the STOP, PLOT, GO, SO steps.

7. Ask for six volunteers to fill the following positions: batter, pitcher, first base player, second base player, third base player, and catcher. Have the volunteers stand in an actual softball formation. All volunteers, except for the batter, will be asked to read from *Cue Cards*. You may need to assist with the reading.

- Give the stack of *Problem Situations* to the pitcher.
- Give Cue Card #1 to the first base player.
- Give Cue Card #2 to the second base player.
- Give Cue Card #3 to the third base player.
- Give Cue Card #4 to the catcher.

Explain that to score a run for the class, the batter must correctly follow the secret formula to solve a problem which will be described by the pitcher.

8. Distribute *Score Cards* to the remaining students. Explain that they are the fans.

9. The pitcher draws one of the *Problem Situations* and reads it aloud to the batter. The batter waits to advance to first base.

10. The first base player reads the "STOP means..." statement and any one of the four instructions printed on Cue Card #1 to the batter. If the batter is unable to follow the instruction, other members from the class may offer help or suggestions. The batter must, however, answer in his or her own words or actions after receiving help. After the batter has followed the instruction, the fans write a "1" on the first base of their *Score Cards* (indicating that batter #1 completed that step) while the batter advances to first base.

11. The second base player reads the "PLOT means..." statement and asks the batter all four questions (one at a time) printed on Cue Card #2. After the batter has answered all four questions, the fans write a "1" on the second base of their *Score Cards* while the batter advances to second base.

12. The third base player reads the "GO means..." statement and the instruction printed on Cue Card #3 to the batter. After the batter has followed the instruction, the fans write a "1" on the third base of their *Score Cards* while the batter advances to third base.

13. The catcher reads the "SO means..." statement and asks the batter both questions (one at a time) printed on Cue Card #4. After the batter has answered the questions, the fans write a "1" on the home plate of their *Score Cards* while the batter advances to home base.

14. Depending on class size, participants can be asked to rotate positions, or six new volunteers can take the positions described in step 7. For smaller groups, you can take the role of several positions.

15. The pitcher reads a new problem situation to the second batter, and play proceeds in the same manner as above, only fans write a "2" on their *Score Cards*.

16. Continue the activity until everyone in the group has had a chance to play one or more "parts" in the softball game. You may wish to continue this activity during the next class session. In addition, students may wish to develop their own problem situations for use in the game.

CUE CARDS

Cue Card #1

STOP: Secret Formula Part 1

STOP means stay calm and use self-control.

What can you say to tell yourself to stop and stay calm.

-or-

Show how to take slow deep breaths to stay calm.

-or-

Show how to count to 10 to stay calm.

-or-

Show how to put your hand over your mouth to stay calm.

Go to First Base.

Cue Card #2

PLOT: Secret Formula Part 2

PLOT means you plan how to solve your problem.

What is your problem?

-then-

What are at least two choices you have?

-then-

What might happen after each choice?

-then-

Which choice do you think will work best?

Go to Second Base.

Cue Card #3

GO: Secret Formula Part 3

GO means go ahead and do what you decided to do.

Tell what you can say to get yourself to go ahead and do what you decided to do.

Go to Third Base.

Cue Card #4

SO: Secret Formula Part 4

SO means you ask yourself, "So, how did my plan work?"

Pretend your plan worked well. What can you say to praise yourself?

-then-

Pretend your plan didn't work well. What should you do?

*Good Job! Go to Home Plate.
You scored 1 run.*

PROBLEM SITUATIONS

Problem Situation #1

You are told to bring a sack lunch for a field trip and forget to bring one.

Start the secret formula now.

Problem Situation #2

You spill your milk all over your pants during lunch at school.

Start the secret formula now.

Problem Situation #3

Your neighbor compliments you on your bike safety and you're not sure what to say or do.

Start the secret formula now.

Problem Situation #4

You are walking on the sidewalk and an older kid purposely bumps into you.

Start the secret formula now.

Social Star

Name _____

SCORE CARD

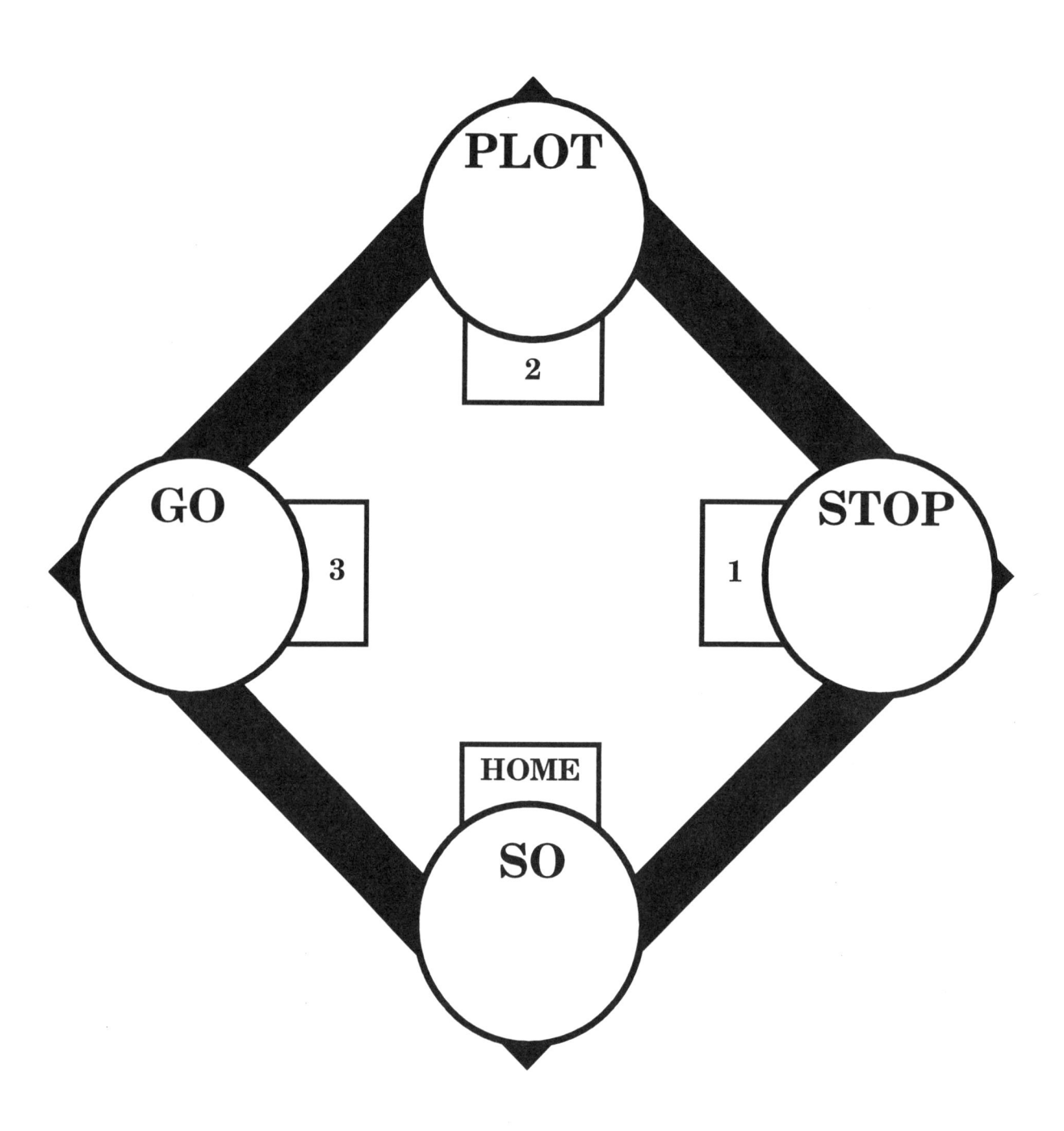

```
         PLOT
          [2]

GO                    STOP
[3]                    [1]

         [HOME]
          SO
```

© 1996 Thinking Publications   60   *Duplication permitted for educational use only.*

Socialville and the Social Star Club

Hi! Nice to meet you. We live with our mom and stepdad.

Hi! We're friends of Lee. My name is Ann Olson and this is my brother Mike.

Hi! I'm Lee Vue. I live in Socialville and I go to McKinley School. I want you to meet some friends who go to school with me.

Hello! Nice to meet you! I'm Mr. Parra. This is my wife, Mrs. Parra, and these are our children, Victor and Maria. We enjoy living in Socialville, because everyone always gets along.

And I'm Mr. Jackson. We're happy to meet you!

Hello! I'm Mrs. Jackson. I'm Mike and Ann's mom.

Our mom works at the Good Meals—Good Manners Restaurant. Our stepdad works at the Get Along Toy Factory. He works with Mr. Parra, Maria and Victor's dad. You'll meet them next.

Hi! My name is Jolisa. This is my mom and dad. My dad is the head of the Socialville Parks Department. Sometimes, I visit him at the park. My mom is a tutor at our school, so I really have to be good when she is around! Has Lee introduced you to his family yet?

Well, Mr. Parra's not totally right! We don't *always* get along, but we do our best! Mr. Parra is nice and so is Mrs. Parra! Actually, I call her Dr. Parra, because she's my doctor. She works at the Helping Hands Clinic. Next, I'd like you to meet the Walkers.

The six of us have joined a club at school called the Social Star Club. Our teachers, Ms. Hess, Mr. Aaron, and Mrs. Marrero, are the club advisors. Can you guess what we talk about in our club? ☆

I bet you've been wondering about my family! This is my dad. He builds great houses! And this is my grandmother. She lives with my dad and me. She is a cook at our school. The kids at school really like her!

Those were good guesses! In our club, we learn how to get along better with other people so our school, our town, and our whole world can be better! We talk about using appropriate manners and having appropriate behavior. Can you think of some ways to get along with other people?☆

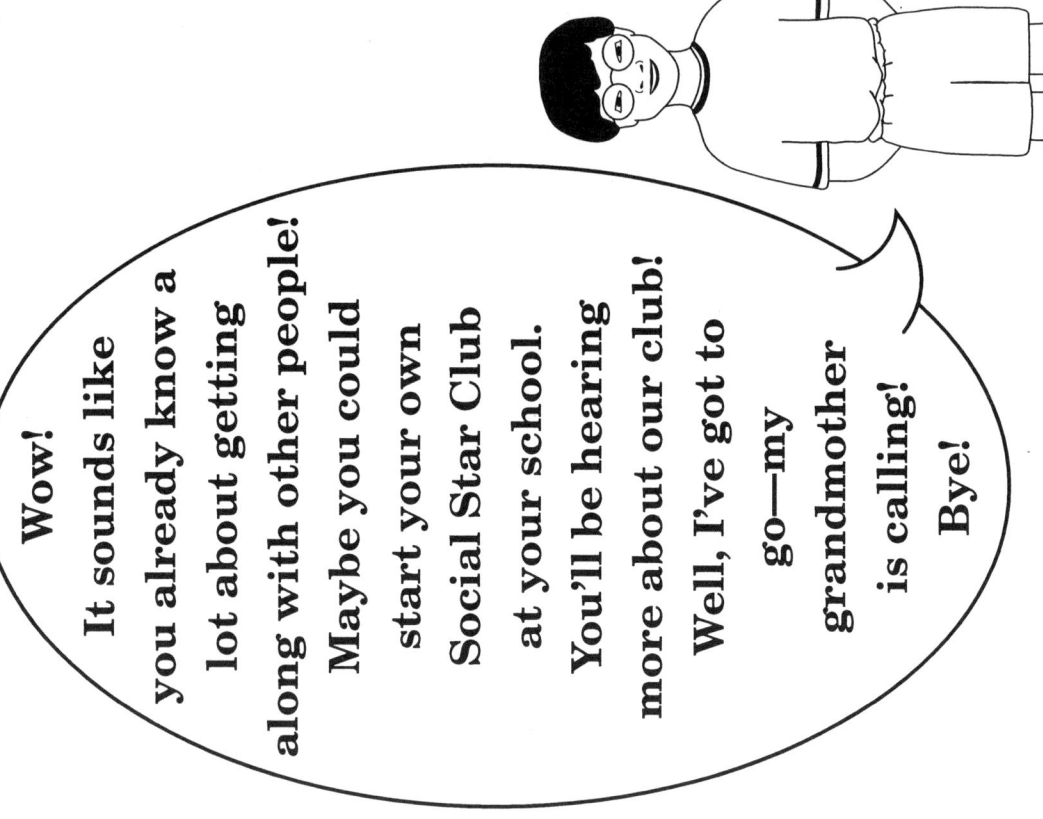

OUR CLUB

10

Wow! It sounds like you already know a lot about getting along with other people! Maybe you could start your own Social Star Club at your school. You'll be hearing more about our club! Well, I've got to go—my grandmother is calling! Bye!

11

© 1996 Thinking Publications   66   *Duplication permitted for educational use only.*

STOP: Secret Formula Part 1

© 1996 Thinking Publications — Duplication permitted for educational use only.

It's called:

SECRET FORMULA

STOP

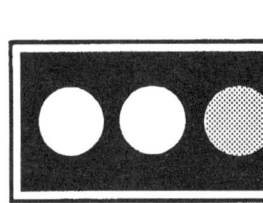

PLOT

GO

SO

Let's all say it:
STOP, PLOT, GO, SO....
STOP, PLOT, GO, SO....
It's kind of catchy!

15

Hi everybody!
Welcome to our
Social Star Club!
We talk about how to get along
with other people. It's a lot of
fun! We have a secret formula
we use to help us
solve problems. It's our
problem-solving
strategy!

14

© 1996 Thinking Publications   68   *Duplication permitted for educational use only.*

Lots of things can happen if you don't STOP to stay calm and use self-control! It's not good to be out of control! It can be embarrassing and it can get you into trouble!

You could say something mean like...

I hate you!

What other things might people do or say if they are out of control? ☆

STOP

means you STOP to stay calm and use self-control.

Do you know what *self-control* means? ☆

© 1996 Thinking Publications   69   *Duplication permitted for educational use only.*

My parents taught me how to take deep breaths to stay calm. It really works!

I breathe in deeply through my nose and I let the air out slowly through my mouth. I pretend I'm blowing bubbles or blowing on a spoon of hot soup. Try it a few times now. ☆ Taking deep breaths helps me relax my whole body so I can stay in control and get along better with people—even my brother, Victor.

19

To stay calm, the first thing I do is tell myself to STOP and I think . . . Stay calm! That helps me stay in control so I don't do something crazy!

Hey! Why don't you try it now? Think, "STOP! Stay calm!" ☆

18

© 1996 Thinking Publications 70 *Duplication permitted for educational use only.*

Sometimes I feel angry if the teacher can't help me right away. To stay calm, I take a deep breath and think "10." Then I count up to 10 in my mind. By the time I get to 10, I've calmed down and I can wait for my turn with the teacher. Try it now! Think "10," then count.... ☆ Remember, you can take deep breaths while you count.

When I'm angry, I put my hand over my mouth to stop myself from saying something mean. It works great!

Pretend you're angry at your mom or dad. Quickly put your hand over your mouth so you don't say something mean. I'm so good at it now. I just picture myself putting my hand over my mouth and I stay calm.

© 1996 Thinking Publications 71 Duplication permitted for educational use only.

"I think of funny things, too. In the movie Mary Poppins, there's a part where these people keep laughing and laughing, and floating up in the air. It's so funny! As soon as I think of it, I get the giggles, even if I'm really angry."

"When I start to feel angry, I think of something funny and goofy, like a pig riding a bicycle. That makes me start to laugh!"

"When I get upset, I stick my finger in my ear and make a goofy face. I look kind of silly but it makes me and other people laugh and then we aren't angry with each other."

"Sometimes, when I'm upset, I think "STOP." Then I walk away for awhile. If I'm angry at another kid and I feel like I'm going to lose control, I say, "I need to leave. I'm too mad to talk now." Then I walk away until I calm down. That way, I don't say or do something crazy."

"Yes, it is also a good idea to tell the person that you're leaving or walking away to work on getting in control."

"Hey, those sound like great ways to stay calm when you're angry. I'm going to use those ideas myself. Let's see . . . you just gave me six ideas. What were some of those ideas again?⭐"

To stay in control when you have a problem, you can:

1. Tell yourself to STOP and stay calm.
2. Take a deep breath and relax your body.
3. Put your hand over your mouth.
4. Think "10" and count to 10.
5. Walk away to calm down.
6. Think about something funny.

Can you think of other ways to STOP and stay calm?⭐

Keep practicing these ideas and you'll get better at using them.

PLOT: Secret Formula Part 2

Hi!
Our Social Star Club has been busy practicing our secret formula for solving problems. We already told you about STOP. (Remember, STOP means you should tell yourself to stay calm.) Now we're going to tell you about PLOT!

STOP
PLOT
GO
SO

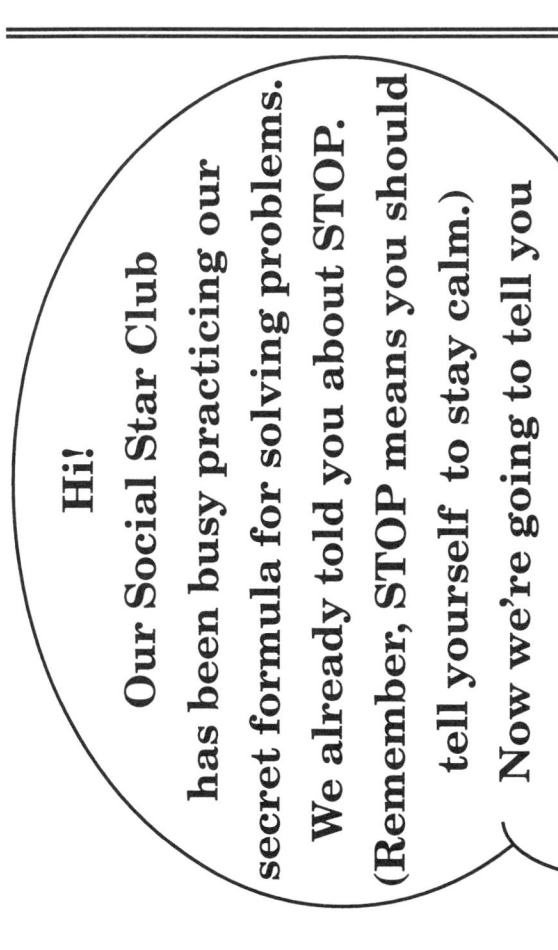

PLOT means you plot a plan to solve your problem.

When you PLOT you:

1. Decide exactly what your problem is.
2. Brainstorm the choices you have.
3. Think about what might happen after each of these choices (consequences).
4. Pick a choice you think will help solve the problem.
5. Think about the social skills you will need to use.

This is the symbol for PLOT. It reminds me that when I have a problem, I can go in different directions. (I have different choices to solve the problem.)

© 1996 Thinking Publications   75   Duplication permitted for educational use only.

PLOT

Mike knew he should use PLOT in this situation.

I used STOP to calm myself down. Now I have to PLOT.

What is my problem? I don't want to fix this paper, but I'd like to have free time.

First, Mike decided exactly what his problem was.

To help you understand PLOT, I'd like to tell you about a problem Mike had.

"Mike, you'll need to fix this paper before you can have free time!"

STOP.... Stay calm.... I'll count to 10....

Mike felt angry, but he reminded himself to STOP and stay calm.

© 1996 Thinking Publications · 76 · *Duplication permitted for educational use only.*

Second, he decided what some of his choices were.

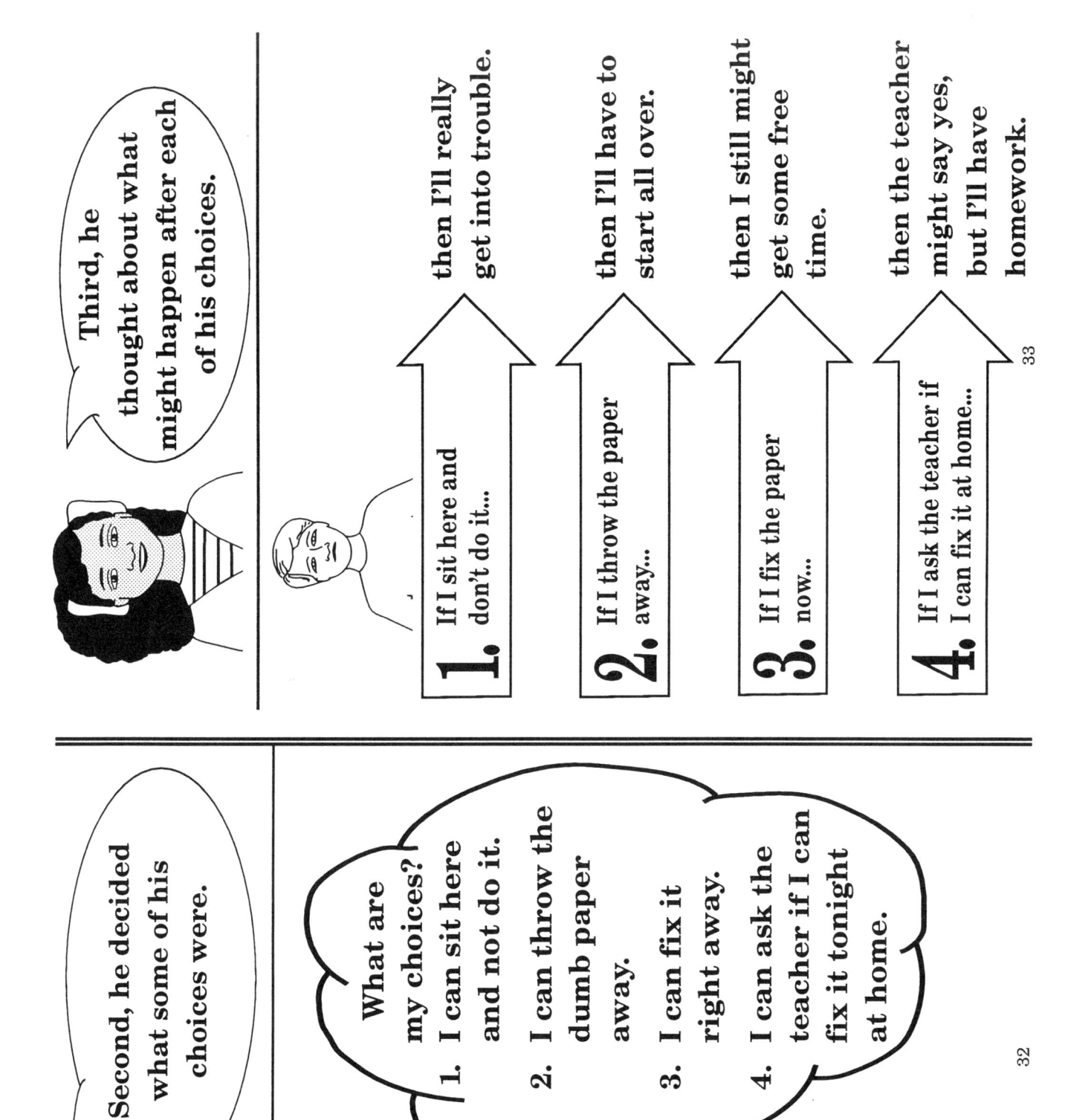

What are my choices?
1. I can sit here and not do it.
2. I can throw the dumb paper away.
3. I can fix it right away.
4. I can ask the teacher if I can fix it tonight at home.

Third, he thought about what might happen after each of his choices.

1. If I sit here and don't do it... → then I'll really get into trouble.
2. If I throw the paper away... → then I'll have to start all over.
3. If I fix the paper now... → then I still might get some free time.
4. If I ask the teacher if I can fix it at home... → then the teacher might say yes, but I'll have homework.

Fourth, Mike decided which choice was best.

I think I'll fix the paper now. Then I won't have to worry about doing it tonight. Maybe I can still have some free time.

Last, Mike thought about what social skills to use.

I won't pout while I'm working. I'll use an appropriate facial expression.

We all think Mike did a great job using the five parts of PLOT!

Can you remember what they are? ☆ You already know the first half of our secret formula. Before we teach you the second half of the formula, you can start using STOP and PLOT when you are at home, at school, and with your friends. Good luck!

© 1996 Thinking Publications

GO: Secret Formula Part 3

© 1996 Thinking Publications — 79 — Duplication permitted for educational use only.

GO

means you go ahead and do what you decided to do.

That's so you don't just think about it. You actually do it.

Can you remember our secret formula? I can! STOP, PLOT, GO, SO; STOP, PLOT, GO, SO; STOP, PLOT, GO! I'm going to tell you about GO! But first, let's review STOP and PLOT. STOP means you stay calm. PLOT means you plan what you will do.

REMEMBER....

GO means that you go ahead and carry out your plan. If you think it is going to be too hard, tell yourself, "I can do it!"

You only have one more part of the secret formula to learn. It's called SO. We'll talk about SO next time.

STOP | PLOT
GO | SO

41

Remember when Ms. Hess asked me to fix my paper before I could have free time at school? I used STOP and told myself to calm down. I used PLOT and decided to fix my paper.

When I followed the GO step of the secret formula, I actually did what I decided to do. Here's a picture of me fixing my paper.

40

© 1996 Thinking Publications   81   *Duplication permitted for educational use only.*

SO: Secret Formula Part 4

SO

means you ask yourself, "So, how did my plan work?"

A question mark is used for this step, because during SO, you ask yourself a question.

What question do you ask yourself? ☆

STOP ✛ PLOT ❓ GO ★ SO

Hi! Let's all whisper our secret formula for solving problems five times.... ☆
Can you remember what STOP, PLOT, and GO mean? ☆
Now we're going to tell you about the last step called SO.
Later you can come to an awards ceremony at our Social Star Club.

© 1996 Thinking Publications 83 Duplication permitted for educational use only.

Praising yourself means telling yourself you did a good job. You could say, "I did great solving my problem." What are some other things you could say to yourself when you make a plan that works well? ☆

47

When you ask yourself, "So, how did my plan work?" you'll either decide that it worked well or that it didn't work well. If you decide your plan worked well, you made a good choice. That's a good time to praise yourself.

SO?

Plan worked well → Praise Yourself

Plan didn't work well

46

© 1996 Thinking Publications 84 *Duplication permitted for educational use only.*

STOP, PLOT, GO, SO. SO is SO, SO, SO important!

It's time for the awards ceremony at our Social Star Club. Mike and Maria are receiving awards today, because they used the secret formula in a real-life situation. You'll find out how they used STOP, PLOT, GO, and SO.

49

When I first learned about SO, I asked, "Why should I praise myself? Shouldn't I just wait for someone else to praise me for making a good plan?"

I like it when someone else praises me, but I found out I can't always count on other people to notice my good choice or to remember to praise me. I can count on myself though . . . and besides, it feels good when I say something nice to myself!

48

© 1996 Thinking Publications   85   *Duplication permitted for educational use only.*

Excellent, Mike! On behalf of the Social Star Club, we'd like to present you with this Social Super Star badge for successfully using the secret formula in your life.

Social Super Star
Mike Olson

Mike, you told us about using STOP, PLOT, and GO when Ms. Hess asked you to fix your paper before getting free time. Your plan was to fix your paper right away. Please tell us how you used SO in this situation.

When I asked myself, "So, how did my plan work?" I decided it worked great! I fixed my paper right away and still had a few minutes left for free time.

During GO, I went ahead and asked my mom using a nice tone of voice. **During SO,** I decided my choice worked well because my mom said OK. I told myself, "Great job, Maria!"

Maria, I'm glad you praised yourself during SO. Our Social Star Club would like you to keep this Social Super Star badge as a reminder of how well you used STOP, PLOT, GO, and SO.

53

Maria, can you tell us how you used STOP, PLOT, GO, and SO?

Sure! Yesterday, I was leaving to go to Jolisa's house when my mom told me to clean my room first. **During STOP,** I took three deep breaths. **When I PLOTTED,** I decided to ask if I could pick up my room right away but wait to dust and vacuum until after I got home.

52

© 1996 Thinking Publications • 87 • *Duplication permitted for educational use only.*

"One of my plans didn't work very well for me last week. I borrowed Lee's video game and accidentally broke it. I used the secret formula to solve the problem. During PLOT, I decided to keep telling Lee I left it at home. But then Lee said he would come over to my house to get it. My plan didn't work very well. I think I should have picked a different choice. I should have told the truth right away!"

"That concludes our awards ceremony. Do you have anything you want to ask or talk about?"

"During the SO step, what if you decide your plan didn't work very well?"

"Good question, Jolisa! If you decide your plan didn't work very well, you may need to use STOP again so you don't get upset. When your choice doesn't work well, you need to decide what you'll do differently next time."

Plan went well → Praise

SO?

Plan didn't work well → What can I do differently next time?

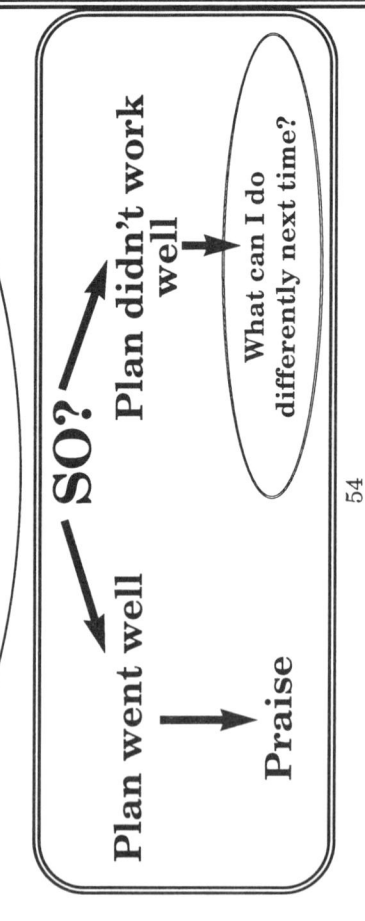

© 1996 Thinking Publications — 88 — Duplication permitted for educational use only.

STOP, PLOT, GO, SO...

Use it when you're in a bind, and hopefully you will find that things are easier every day when you pick the best to do and say!

Let's hear it for the secret formula.

Hip, Hip, Hooray!

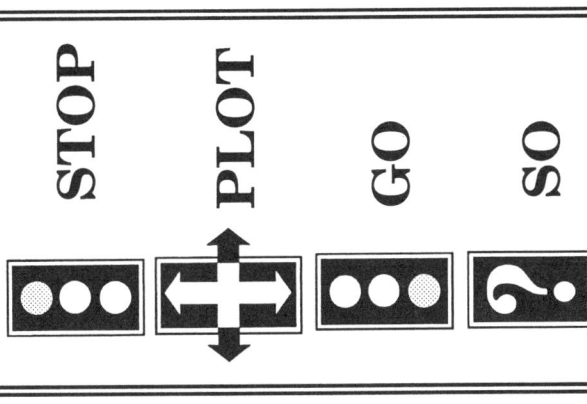

SECRET FORMULA

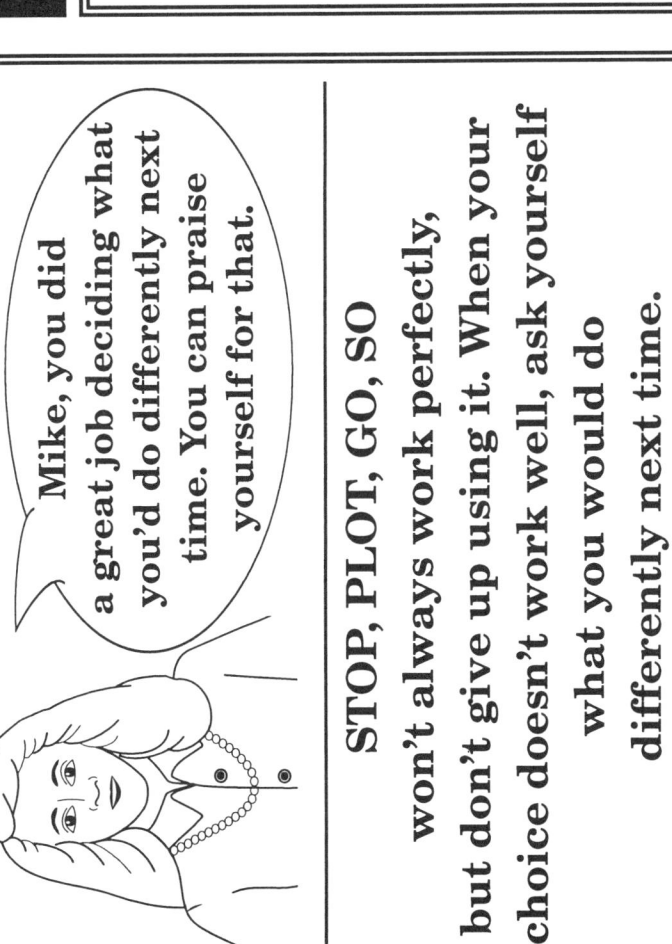

STOP	::
PLOT	✛
GO	::
SO	?

Mike, you did a great job deciding what you'd do differently next time. You can praise yourself for that.

STOP, PLOT, GO, SO won't always work perfectly, but don't give up using it. When your choice doesn't work well, ask yourself what you would do differently next time.

Body Talk Summary

In each unit of *Social Star,* the symbol for the skill called *body talk* is incorporated in the skill step section. "Body talk" is a term used to describe various components of the human body which can be used in different ways to communicate a variety of messages. The students are reminded that it is important to demonstrate appropriate body talk in conjunction with each individual skill.

Body Talk is addressed in detail as an individual unit in *Social Star: General Interaction Skills (Book 1)*. It emphasizes that students have control over their own bodies and helps students recognize that there are times when they need to demonstrate self-control with their bodies. The unit emphasizes the following body-talk components: eye contact, facial expression, posture, personal space, hygiene, volume, tone of voice, body movements, breathing, and speed of movements. These components (except for body movements, breathing, and speed of movements) are also units in and of themselves within *Social Star (Book 1)*. Though it is not necessary that the *Body Talk* unit be taught in its entirety before teaching the units in *Social Star (Book 3),* the educator should ensure that students have a basic understanding of the term and its components. The educator is reminded to exert sensitivity and care in generalizing rules about body talk into the children's home cultures.

Taking Charge of Feelings

Social Star

UNIT GOAL:

To demonstrate comprehension and use of strategies for taking charge of feelings

EDUCATOR INFORMATION:

1. This unit teaches that people have a wide variety of feelings and that all feelings are OK. As the unit title suggests, children learn that they are in charge of how they feel. No situation or person can "make" them feel a specific feeling. This unit also emphasizes that feelings need to be expressed in a responsible manner. It is not acceptable to express feelings in a way that can hurt oneself, others, or property.

2. It is important for educators to realize that children vary in their ability to verbally express their feelings. Often, it is through their actions that they express what's going on inside. Adults can learn to cut through offensive behavior and respond to the underlying feelings. For example, a child who shouts, "I hate you," may truly mean, "I hate being told I can't do something!" or "I have no say in this family and that's not fair!" The adult's response may be to tell the child why he or she should not feel that way. A more effective response might include, "Sometimes you feel frustrated when I tell you what to do," or "It seems that you don't like that." This allows the child a "right" to his feelings. A nonopinionated, nonjudgmental response will encourage a child to reveal feelings so that he or she can be understood (Carter, 1994).

3. The term "feelings" will be used throughout this unit. However, experts in the field use the following related terms (Gaylin, 1979):

   Emotion—a general term that means the feeling tone, the biophysiological state, and chemical changes experienced.

   Affect—the dominant emotional tone of a person.

   Feeling—our awareness of our emotional state.

4. Children with emotional challenges frequently have difficulty with social interaction as well as written and oral expression. Art activities can assist them in finding words for their feelings (Alexander, 1990). Some of the "healing techniques" from art therapy may be helpful in getting students to reveal feelings. Alexander (1990) states that "students may find artmaking the only safe way to communicate about suicidal tendencies" (p. 30). Educators may sometimes feel that "angry"

students exhibit too much emotion. However, their behavior may be the only way they have to reveal their feelings (Morse, Ardizzone, Macdonald, and Pasick, 1980).

5. An excellent resource that addresses feelings is:
   The Feelings Book: Expressing Emotions Creatively.
   A Guide for Children and Grownups (1988)
   by Caryn Frye Boddie
   Cardillera Press
   P.O. Box 3699
   Evergreen, CO 80439

RELATED ACTIVITIES:

1. Have children try to imagine the feelings that the following people may be experiencing:

   - An elderly man has just been moved into a nursing home. His mind is intact, but his physical capabilities are deteriorating.

   - A friend's family just got a new baby.

   - A preschooler is hit and pushed by another child.

   - A father goes to use his tool set and finds that several parts are missing.

   - A friend's parent is being sent to an active war zone on military assignment.

   - A 12 year old whose parent is being sent to an active war zone on military assignment.

2. Share poetry, music, and works of art that express emotions. Discuss how poets, songwriters, and artists express feelings in their works.

3. Have students create a movable bar graph showing the level of happiness they are feeling each day.

4. Have students take on the roles of inanimate objects (e.g., furniture, food) and tell or write about the feelings those objects might have if they came to life.

5. Ask students to imagine that everyone in the world knows how to take charge of their feelings. Discuss what effect that increase would have on society (e.g., a decrease in domestic abuse and community violence).

6. Invite adults from different cultures to talk to the students about how their cultures' conventions for taking charge of feelings compare with the strategies presented in this unit.

It is important for educators to provide opportunities for students to work in groups, so they can experience social skills in contexts where social communication is needed. Therefore, educators are encouraged to have students complete the Related

Activities in small groups whenever possible. Educators trained in cooperative learning could incorporate the five components (see pages 33–34) into the group activity. An excellent resource for teaching students cooperative skills and building a sense of community is *Tribes: A Process for Social Development and Cooperative Learning* (1987) by Jeanne Gibbs.

RELATED LITERATURE:

Sometimes I Get So Mad (1980) by Paula Z. Hoban, Ill. by Karen Shapiro, Raintree. (31 pages)

Aldo Applesauce (1979) by Johanna Hurwitz, Ill. by John Wallner, William Morrow. (127 pages)

Spinky Sulks (1988) by William Steig; Farrar, Straus, and Giroux. (32 pages)

Free to Be a Family...A Book About All Kinds of Belonging (1987) by Marlo Thomas, Bantam. (176 pages)

SOCIAL SKILLS ALL DAY LONG:

Look for opportunities to teach social skills throughout the day (incidental teaching). Four ways to reinforce appropriate social skills and an example of each follow:

Encouragement

Jolisa, I know you used to feel angry when Maria teased you. I notice that you've taken charge of your feelings. You remained calm. You must have decided not to let her comments upset you.

Personal Example

I was feeling jealous yesterday because a friend of mine moved into a brand new home. When she phoned and asked me to come over to see it, I almost said no. Then I realized that I needed to take charge of my feelings. I went to visit and reminded myself to be happy when good things happen to my friends.

Prompting

Lee, you might choose to take charge of your feelings. You can say, "I feel frustrated because I can't do this math problem" to let others know how you feel.

Corrective Feedback (must be positive, private, specific, and nonthreatening)

Ann, you just kicked Peter. It seems like you're feeling angry. When you show your feelings, it is not OK to hurt someone else. You need to tell him with words in a responsible way. You could say, "Peter, I'm angry because you gave me a putdown. Please stop doing that."

Fear is the most devastating of all emotions.

Paul Parker

Taking Charge of Feelings

Lesson A

OBJECTIVES:

1. To brainstorm feelings

2. To state the meaning of *taking charge of feelings* and tell why it's important

3. To listen to the self-talk associated with appropriate use of the skill

MATERIALS:

1. A large body cut-out (Made out of tagboard or butcher paper for use during step 2 of this Plan)

2. A dark, thick marker (For educator use)

3. *Taking Charge of Feelings* (See page 100; one per student and one transparency.)

4. *Thought Bubble* (See *Appendix O*; one for educator use.)

PREPARATORY SET:

Pair students using *Inside-Outside Circle* (see *Appendix P*). Ask one pair of students to help you attach the body cut-out to a wall or bulletin board where you can write on it and all students can see it.

PLAN:

1. Tell students that this unit will be about taking charge of feelings. Explain that feelings are the way people react to the things they experience. Ask students to work with their partners to think of five or more feelings that a person may have. Encourage them to use words other than "sad," "mad," or "happy" in order to develop vocabulary.

2. Call on pairs to share feelings they thought of. As each new feeling is named, have a student write the word inside the body cut-out. As an option, ask students to think of a way to write the word so it portrays the feeling (e.g., if angry is the feeling, it is written in bold letters; if scared is the feeling, it is written with wavy letters).

3. Being able to name a feeling helps to manage the feeling. To expand students' "feelings" vocabulary, choose a few of the feelings listed on page 98, define them, and then have students add them to the body cut-out. (As a way to assess students' knowledge of the names of feelings, you may also wish to have students complete open-ended sentences about the feelings you select [e.g., I feel grateful when..., I felt depressed the day...].)

Social Star

accepted	dissatisfied	misunderstood
affectionate	disturbed	naughty
afraid	elated	neglected
angry	embarrassed	nervous
annoyed	encouraged	obnoxious
anxious	enthusiastic	outraged
appreciated	envious	overwhelmed
ashamed	frantic	peaceful
astonished	frustrated	pleased
attacked	furious	positive
belittled	grateful	protected
betrayed	guilty	proud
blamed	hateful	put down
bored	hopeful	rejected
challenged	humbled	relieved
concerned	hurt	ridiculous
confident	hysterical	satisfied
confused	ignored	surprised
content	important	suspicious
courageous	intimidated	tempted
daring	irritated	terrific
delighted	jealous	terrified
depressed	joyful	tired
desperate	lonely	understood
disappointed	loved	unimportant
discouraged	marvelous	willing
disgusted	miserable	worried

4. Make the following five points about feelings:

   - Your feelings are real and important.

   - All feelings are OK. (There are no right or wrong ways to feel.)

   - Your feelings can help you learn what you like and don't like.

   - Your feelings can help you understand yourself and others better.

   - Your feelings can help you stay safe and grow as a person.

   (The points above are critical. Find ways to review them throughout the remainder of the unit.)

5. Using the examples written in the body cut-out, go to each pair and whisper the name of a feeling. Assign each pair a different feeling. Ask student pairs not to tell any other pairs the feeling you whispered to them. Give students a few

minutes to work with their partners to write down two or more situations in which a person may experience the feeling they were assigned.

6. Ask student pairs to take turns telling their situations to the whole group while the remaining class members guess what feeling the student pair was assigned.

7. Distribute and display *Taking Charge of Feelings*. Discuss the definition. Explain the skill steps and the symbols next to them. Remind students that the symbols are there to help them visualize and remember the skill steps. Refer to the body-talk symbol in the left-hand margin. Remind students that appropriate body talk is important when taking charge of feelings. Discuss and model the body parts that help to show feelings. Discuss the reasons for taking charge of feelings.

8. Model use of the skill steps for taking charge of feelings while thinking aloud. A scripted example follows:

Introduction

I am going to pretend to be someone your age who is feeling unhappy. I will show you how I take charge of my feelings. When I hold up this Thought Bubble, *you'll know the words I'm saying are actually what I'm thinking.*

Actual Model

While holding up the *Thought Bubble* say, *I'm feeling really unhappy. I've spent all recess looking for the money my dad gave me to buy popcorn at the school sale today. I know it's OK to feel unhappy. But I'm in control of my feelings, so I'm not going to pout about this. I don't want my friends to think I'm acting like a baby. I think I'll talk to my teacher.*

9. Read the story at the bottom of *Taking Charge of Feelings*. Discuss what Victor did to follow the three skill steps.

10. Ask student pairs to take turns telling each other the meaning of *taking charge of feelings* and why it's important to use the skill. Students could be reminded that the information they are to say is printed on *Taking Charge of Feelings*.

As an option to add structure to this activity, ask partners to come to an agreement about which person will be called "A" and which person will be called "B." After students have made their decisions, ask "A" to tell "B" the definition of *taking charge of feelings*. Next, ask "B" to tell "A" the definition. Ask students to use the same procedure to tell each other the reasons for taking charge of feelings.

───────────★★★───────────

I'm happier...guess I made up my mind to be that way.

Merle Haggard

Social Star

Name _____

Taking Charge of Feelings

MEANING OF TAKING CHARGE OF FEELINGS:

Knowing you have control over how to express your feelings

SKILL STEPS:

1. Ask myself: What am I feeling?

2. Remind myself:
   I'm in charge of my feelings

3. Tell myself:
   I can express my feelings responsibly

REASONS FOR USING THIS SKILL:

Knowing that you are in charge of your feelings gives you confidence. You can feel proud when you express your feelings in ways that do not harm yourself, other people, or property. You're healthier when you express your feelings responsibly and others may feel more comfortable around you.

DIRECTIONS:

Listen to the story below. Look at the picture of Victor while you listen.

Victor did not understand his science assignment. After slamming his pencil down, he knew he felt frustrated. Victor told himself that he could take charge of his feelings and decided that slamming his pencil would not help. Victor decided to talk to his teacher. He picked up his pencil and raised his hand. When the teacher got to his table, Victor said, "I'm getting really frustrated about this science assignment. Could you please help me?"

© 1996 Thinking Publications   Duplication permitted for educational use only.

Lesson B

OBJECTIVE:

To understand that people are in charge of their own feelings

MATERIALS:

1. A judge's gavel (A real or homemade one)

2. *Taking Charge of Feelings* classroom poster (See page 13.)

3. *I'm in Charge Gavel* (See page 104; one per student.)

4. Scissors (One per student)

PREPARATORY SET:

Call the class to order by pounding the gavel and announcing, "Order in the classroom! Order in the classroom!" Ask if students can name what you are pounding (a gavel), who usually pounds a gavel (a judge), what purpose a gavel has (it's used to command attention), and why a judge uses a gavel (it helps the judge be in charge of the court). Ask students to name other people who are in charge of things (e.g., parents are in charge of a family, teachers are in charge of the classroom, a boss is in charge of the employees, a baby-sitter is in charge of the children). Ask students what it means to be "in charge" (the person in charge gets to decide how things are done). Tell students, "In today's lesson, we'll talk about skill step 2 for taking charge of feelings. We'll talk about how you are just like a judge with a gavel when it comes to your own feelings because you are in charge of them. You are the only person who can decide what to do, or not to do, with your feelings. No one can make you feel anything if you don't let them."

PLAN:

1. Review the definition and skill steps for *taking charge of feelings* by referring the class to the *Taking Charge of Feelings* classroom poster.

2. Pair students (see *Appendix P*). Ask student pairs to take turns telling each other the skill steps for taking charge of feelings. Follow the procedure described in step 10 of Lesson A. Next, ask students to work with their partners to think of a situation when it's important to take charge of one's feelings. Tell students that one or more pairs will be called on to share their situations.

3. Ask students to listen carefully to a story you'll read, so they can answer questions about what they hear. Tell the following story:

Social Star

Billy Blamer was mad. He was mad because he didn't have his baseball glove to use for the baseball game during recess. When he got to school, he went straight to the office and said to the secretary, "My mom forgot to give me my baseball glove. I need to call home so she can bring it to me before recess. She makes me so mad!" The secretary reminded Billy, "I'm sorry, but you can't call home unless you have an emergency." Billy Blamer became even more angry and left the office. A friend saw Billy and asked, "What's wrong with you?" Billy said, "Everyone is really burning me up. First my mom forgot to put my baseball glove in my backpack and now the secretary in the office won't let me call home to tell mom to bring it over. I wish people would quit making me so mad!"

Ask students the following:

- What feelings might describe how Billy felt in the story? (Ask students to name several possible feelings [e.g., angry, mad, furious, upset, outraged].)

- Is it OK to feel anger? (Yes)

- Why do you think Billy's nickname is "Billy Blamer"?

- What words did Billy use to show that he was not taking charge of his own feelings, but instead was blaming his mother and the secretary for his anger? (Answers might include "She makes me so mad," "Everyone is really burning me up," and "I wish people would quit making me so mad." Point out the key words "I wish," "making me," and "everyone is.")

- If Billy had taken charge of his feelings, what might he have said differently to the secretary and his friend? (E.g., "I'm feeling angry because I didn't bring my glove to school.")

- What self-talk could Billy have used to remind himself of skill step 2?

4. Distribute *I'm in Charge Gavel* and scissors. Ask students to cut out their gavels and write "I'm in charge of my feelings" on the back side and then place them on their desks. Explain that you will be describing several different situations. After you read each situation, ask students to decide if the person in the situation took charge of his or her feelings or not. Tell students to pick up their gavels from their desks when they have made up their minds, so you know when they are ready to answer.

Read the following situations (to make this exercise more relevant to the group, you might also develop situations that have actually happened in class, omitting student names) and have students use their gavels as directed; when most students are holding up their gavels, call on one or more to answer):

- Jolisa got a poor grade on her writing assignment and was upset. She told Ann, "Mr. Aaron gave me a bad grade on my paper. He really makes me mad!"

- Lee was feeling disappointed. Play practice was cancelled due to a blizzard. He said to his mother, "I'm really disappointed that practice is cancelled. I hope the weather is better tomorrow."

- Victor was feeling sad. His mother just scolded him for getting home late. He said to his sister, "I wish Mom would quit making me feel so bad."

- Ann was angry. Some kids on the playground called her a mean name. She told her friend, "I'm not going to let what those kids say ruin my day."

- Mike was frustrated. He could not understand his reading assignment. He said to himself, "I'm really frustrated. Who can I ask for help?"

- Maria was feeling crabby. When her mother asked her why she was being so crabby she said, "I can't help it. I'm feeling crabby because everyone makes me feel that way."

- Jolisa was feeling afraid. She stayed too late at her friend's house and it was dark. Jolisa said to herself, "I'm scared so I'm going to call home for a ride."

5. Pair students (see *Appendix P*). Ask student pairs to take turns telling each other the skill steps for taking charge of feelings. Follow the procedure described in step 10 of Lesson A. Next, ask students to work with their partners to think of a situation when it's important to take charge of one's feelings. Tell students that one or more pairs will be called on to share their situations.

———— ★★★ ————

Ninety percent of the way you feel is determined by how you want to feel.

John Kozak

Social Star

I'm in Charge Gavel

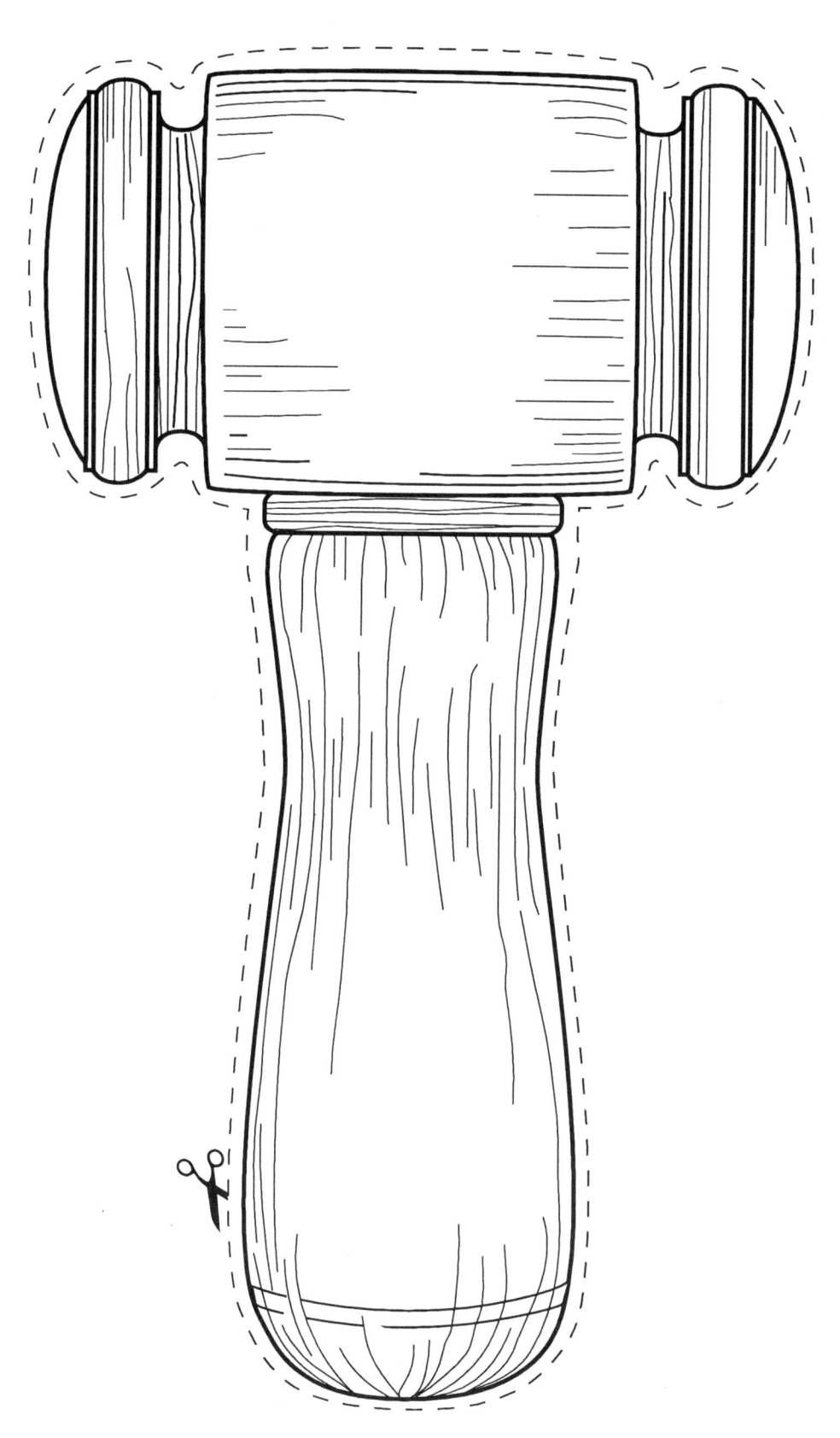

104

Lesson C

Social Star

OBJECTIVE:

To understand the importance of expressing feelings in ways that show responsibility toward yourself, other people, and property

MATERIALS:

1. *Taking Charge of Feelings* classroom poster (See page 13.)

2. *How Ann Expresses Her Anger* (See page 108; one transparency.)

3. *Checking Myself* (See *Appendix I*; one per student and one transparency.)

4. *Thought Bubble* (See *Appendix O*; one for educator use.)

5. Large sheets of paper (One per student)

6. An assortment of crayons or markers

PREPARATORY SET:

Play "Feeling Rumors." Have students sit in a circle with their right shoulders facing the center of the circle. (Each person will be facing another person's back.) Instruct students to keep their eyes closed or keep looking down until a tap on the shoulder is felt. Designate a starter. Ask the starter to secretly decide on a feeling to pantomime while sitting and then to tap the shoulder of the person in front of him or her. The person in front should turn around and observe what feeling the starter is expressing through gestures and facial expression. Have each student continue to pass the same feeling around the circle in the same format using body language. The last person in the circle should pantomime the feeling while everyone watches and then the person who started the process should tell whether or not the feeling demonstrated was the same feeling that he or she started. After two rounds, say to the students, "We just passed two feelings around the circle. Can anyone remember two skill steps for taking charge of feelings? "After calling on students, say, "Today we'll practice skill step 3."

(This activity is adapted from *Energizers and Icebreakers for All Ages and Stages* [1989] by Elizabeth Sabrinski Foster.)

PLAN:

1. Review skill step 3 for taking charge of feelings by referring the class to the *Taking Charge of Feelings* classroom poster.

2. Display *How Ann Expresses Her Anger*. Tell students you will be having a whole class discussion about how Ann expresses her anger.

3. Distribute and display the discussion guideline sheet called *Checking Myself*. Ask students to complete the statement by the top megaphone with the words "use interested body talk," or use another classroom discussion goal more appropriate for your group (see pages 25–26). Encourage students to demonstrate body talk that shows they are interested in the discussion (e.g., sitting up, leaning slightly forward, nodding, giving eye contact). Tell students that during the discussion, they should ask themselves if their body talk says, "I'm interested in this discussion." Instruct students to draw a line between two dots on the star each time a new person begins to speak and they are using interested body talk.

4. Model use of the *Checking Myself* sheet while thinking aloud. A scripted example follows:

Introduction

I am going to pretend to be one of you completing this sheet during the discussion we will be having. I will tell you the thoughts I'm having while completing the sheet. When I hold up this Thought Bubble, *you'll know the words I'm saying are actually what I'm thinking.*

Actual Model

While holding up the Thought Bubble say, *A different person just started talking. Am I using interested body talk? Yes, I am sitting up straight and giving her eye contact. I'll draw a line between two dots on the star.* Put the Thought Bubble down and draw a line between two dots on the transparency.

During the discussion, periodically remind students to draw a line between two dots on the guideline sheets whenever they find themselves using body talk that shows they are interested.

5. Proceed with the discussion by asking these questions:

- Look at the top scene. Why is the manner in which Ann expresses her anger not responsible?

- Why is it important not to hurt other people when you're feeling angry?

- Look at the middle scene. Why is the manner in which Ann expresses her anger not responsible?

- Why is it important not to hurt property when you're feeling angry?

- Look at the bottom scene. Why is the manner in which Ann expresses her anger not responsible?

- Why is it important not to hurt yourself when you're angry?

- What could Ann do or say to express her anger responsibly in the first situation? In the second situation? And in the third situation?

- Is anger the only feeling that should be expressed in a responsible way? Explain your answer.

After the discussion, ask students to complete the bottom of *Checking Myself*.

6. Process use of the sheet by asking the following question or another one more appropriate for your group:

    - Why do you think it is important to use appropriate body talk during a discussion?

    Process further by asking the students who volunteered to speak during the discussion to share their answers to the following questions:

    - You shared one of your answers during the discussion. How could you tell if someone was using interested body talk?

    - How did you feel when others used interested body talk when you were talking?

7. Distribute a large piece of paper and markers or crayons to each student. Ask students to draw a picture about a time when someone did **not** express feelings in a responsible way.

8. As students finish their drawings, ask each student to explain what the drawing is about. (Use discretion when asking students about their pictures in front of others.) Some possible questions to ask individual students include:

    - Why might this person have expressed feelings in this way?

    - What might have been a more appropriate way for this person to express those feelings?

———— ★★★ ————

Most powerful is he who has himself in his own power.

Seneca

How Ann Expresses Her Anger

Lessons X, Y, and Z

Taking Charge of Feelings

Due to similarities in format, the final three lesson plans for each unit in *Social Star* are provided in *Appendix A*. Substitute the words "taking charge of feelings" whenever a "____" appears in the lesson plans. Information specific to this unit follows.

LESSON X PREPARATORY SET:

Before class, create a banner or poster that says "I am in charge of my feelings." Roll up the banner. Say the following while holding the hidden banner or poster:

I am holding something very powerful. It is a magical phrase that can help you be powerful tomorrow, next month, five years from now, and when you are 90 years old. (Slowly unroll the banner and read it aloud to the students.) *I hope you will take this phrase and tuck it deep down inside yourself to keep forever, so you will have it whenever you need it. Any time you want to express your feelings, you can pull out your magical phrase, repeat it to yourself over and over, and you will have the strength to express your feelings in a responsible way.*

LESSON Y PREPARATORY SET:

Darken the room, if you prefer, and ask students to visualize themselves correctly using this social skill by reading the following script:

Let's take a few moments to relax.... Make sure you are in a comfortable position.... Close your eyes if you feel like it.... On the count of three, take a very slow, deep breath. Remember to breathe in quietly through your nose. One...two...three.... Breathe in deeply.... Now breathe out slowly and quietly through your mouth. Let your entire body relax.... Now imagine yourself feeling happy. Tell yourself how good it is to feel happy. Tell yourself that when you take charge of your feelings, you may be happy more often.

LESSON Z PLOT SITUATION:

Ask students to pretend they have a habit of eating too much when they feel sad, afraid, or mad.

LESSON Z ROADBLOCK EXAMPLES:

- Believing that other people control you and your feelings
- Having parents or others become upset when you express how you really feel
- Thinking that a person shouldn't feel too happy
- Believing that some feelings are bad to have

Taking Charge of Feelings T-Chart

LOOKS LIKE...	SOUNDS LIKE...
using appropriate body talk • body talk that matches what you're feeling responsible actions that don't hurt you, others, or property • talking to someone instead of hitting • drawing a picture about how you feel instead of breaking something • taking deep breaths to calm down • writing about how you feel instead of shouting	an appropriate tone of voice an appropriate volume saying aloud • "I'm sad because…" • "I feel great today!" • "I need to be by yourself for a while to calm down." saying to yourself • "Why do I feel this way?" • "I'm in control of how I feel." • "I feel like hitting, but if I do…"

SHOW TIME

HOME

Pretend you're really hungry and your mom says you can't have anything else to eat until dinner. How might you feel? Show how you could take charge of that feeling and express it responsibly.

SCHOOL

Pretend you'll be getting a new teacher for the rest of the school year. How might you feel? Show how you could take charge of that feeling and express it responsibly.

COMMUNITY

Pretend your clarinet teacher makes you do the same things over and over again during your lessons. How might you feel? Show how you could take charge of that feeling and express it responsibly.

Social Star

I'm in Control of My Feelings

HOME-A-GRAM

Social Star

Dear Family,

At school, we have been talking about the social skill called

TAKING CHARGE OF FEELINGS

I learned that *taking charge of feelings* means I have control over how I express my feelings.

I learned it's important to think about how I'm feeling (all of my feelings are OK and I can trust them). I also learned that I'm in charge of my feelings and I can express my feelings responsibly.

Being in charge of my feelings gives me confidence. I can feel proud when I express my feelings in ways that do not harm myself, other people, or property.

Below I have drawn how my face might look when I'm feeling angry, sad, and afraid.

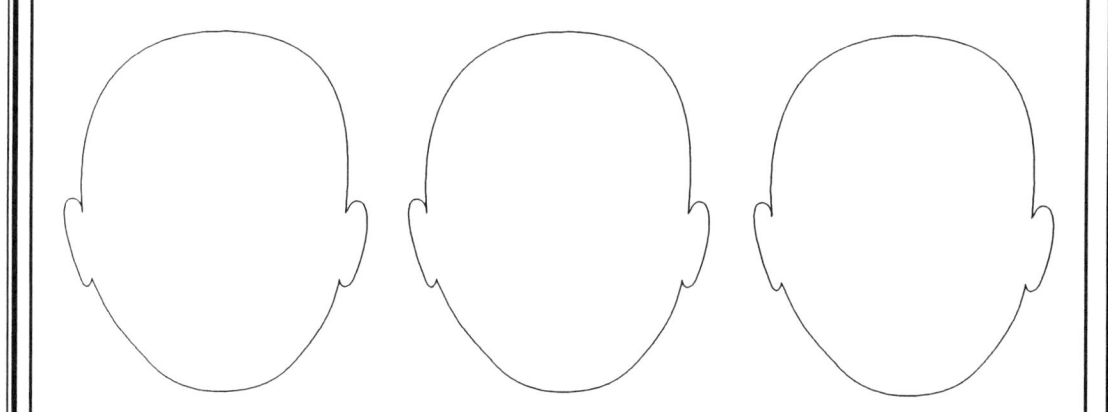

After I tell you a responsible way I could express each of the feelings shown above, please sign my "Taking Charge of Feelings" badge so I can return it to school and become a SOCIAL SUPER STAR this week.

From: _____

Being Assertive

Social Star

UNIT GOAL:

To demonstrate comprehension and use of strategies for being assertive

EDUCATOR INFORMATION:

1. This unit teaches that all people have basic human rights (e.g., the right to be treated fairly, the right to make a mistake and learn from it, the right to make decisions, the right to express your feelings, the right to judge your own actions). In this unit, students develop their own "Kids' Bill of Rights." The remainder of the unit deals with how one can respond assertively when rights are violated. Students become aware of the rights of others and understand that being assertive is not the same as being aggressive.

2. There is little recognition of the value of assertiveness skills for children. Yet, children often experience situations which call for assertive behavior (Buell and Snyder, 1981). Research indicates that children who are on opposite ends of the assertiveness continuum (e.g., withdrawn or aggressive) experience more school maladjustment (Bierman and Wargo, 1995; Gronlund and Anderson, 1963), more mental health problems as adults (Cowen, Pederson, Babigan, Izzo, and Trost, 1973), more delinquency (Roff, Sells, and Golden, 1972), and marginal employment records as adults (Robbins, 1966). Additionally, a high percentage of people who develop stress-related symptoms are rated low on assertiveness skills (Alberti and Emmons, 1995; Herzfeld and Powell, 1986).

3. Society often sends mixed messages about assertiveness (Herzfeld and Powell, 1986). People are taught to be polite, kind, considerate, and unselfish. Yet, success and winning (behaviors which may conflict with these behaviors) are highly desirable. Women are taught to be passive and children are taught to obey their elders. Educators appreciate the quiet, well-behaved, nonaggressive child. Jakubowski (1977) provides several specific examples of how these socialization messages impact our ability to be assertive; for instance, one societal message is that we are not to hurt other people's feelings. This message may cause people to believe they have no right to do something that might hurt another's feelings so they often do not choose to say what they truly think or feel. Jakubowski contends that while it is not desirable to purposely hurt others, each of us has a right to express our thoughts and feelings even if someone else's feelings might get hurt. To do otherwise would result in our being phoney and we would be denying other people an opportunity to learn how to handle their own feelings.

4. Herzfeld and Powell (1986) warn educators to be prepared to accept students' newly learned assertive behaviors and to help students understand that being

assertive every minute of one's life will alienate others. There are situations when it may be best to harbor one's thoughts.

5. The following information by Jakubowski (1977) describes how socialization messages may negatively affect assertion.

Negative Affects of Socialization Messages on Assertion			
Socialization Message	**Effect on Rights**	**Effect on Assertive Behavior**	**Healthy Message**
Think of others first; give to others even if you're hurting. Don't be selfish.	I have no right to place my needs above those of other people's.	When I have a conflict with someone else, I will give in and satisfy the other person's needs and forget about my own.	To be selfish means that a person places his desires before practically everyone else's desires. This is undesirable human behavior. However, all healthy people have needs and strive to fulfill these as much as possible. Your needs are as important as other people's. When there is a conflict over need satisfaction, compromise is often a useful way to handle the conflict.
Be modest and humble. Don't act superior to other people.	I have no right to do anything which would imply that I am better than other people.	I will discontinue my accomplishments and any compliments I receive. When I'm in a meeting, I will encourage people's contributions and keep silent about my own. When I have an opinion which is different from someone else's, I won't express it; who am I to say that my opinion is better than theirs?	It is undesirable to build yourself up at the expense of another person. However, you have as much right as other people to show your abilities and take pride in yourself. It is healthy to enjoy one's accomplishments.

(continued)

Negative Affects—*Continued*

Socialization Message	Effect on Rights	Effect on Assertive Behavior	Healthy Message
Be understanding and overlook trivial irritations. Don't be a complainer [sic].	I have no right to feel angry or to express my anger.	When I'm in a line and someone cuts in front of me, I will say nothing. I will not tell my girlfriend that I don't like her constantly interrupting me when I speak.	It is undesirable to deliberately nit-pick. However, life is made up of trivial incidents and it is normal to be occasionally irritated by seemingly small events. You have a right to your angry feelings, and if you express them at the time they occur, your feelings won't build up and explode. It is important however to express your feelings assertively rather than aggressively.
Help other people. Don't be demanding.	I have no right to make requests of other people.	I will not ask my girlfriend to reciprocate babysitting favors. I will not ask for a pay increase from my employer.	It is undesirable to incessantly make demands on others. You have a right to ask other people to change their behavior if their behavior affects your life in a concrete way. A request is not the same as a demand. However, if your rights are being violated and your requests for a change are being ignored, you have a right to make demands.

(continued)

Negative Affects—*Continued*

Socialization Message	Effect on Rights	Effect on Assertive Behavior	Healthy Message
Be sensitive to other people's feelings. Don't hurt other people.	I have no right to do anything which might hurt someone else's feelings or deflate someone else's ego.	I will not say what I really think or feel because that might hurt someone else. I will inhibit my spontaneity so that I don't impulsively say something that would accidentally hurt someone else.	It is undesirable to deliberately try to hurt others. However, it is impossible as well as undesirable to try to govern your life so as to *never* hurt *anyone*. You have a right to express your thoughts and feelings, even if someone else's feelings get occasionally hurt. To do otherwise would result in your being phoney and in denying other people an opportunity to learn how to handle their own feelings. Remember that some people get hurt because they're unreasonably sensitive and others use their hurt to manipulate you. If you accidentally hurt someone else, you can generally repair the damage.

From "Assertive Behavior and the Clinical Problems of Women," by P.A. Jakubowski, 1977, in D. Carter and E. Rawlings (Eds.), *Psychotherapy with Women*, pp. 149–151, Springfield, IL: Charles C. Thomas. © 1977 by Charles C. Thomas. Reprinted with permission.

RELATED ACTIVITIES:

1. Discuss a television show, movie, or a comic strip that is familiar to your students. Discuss which characters tend to be passive, assertive, or aggressive. View a clipping that depicts examples of these behaviors.

2. Have students make a "choose your own ending book" to demonstrate how various situations can turn out differently depending on whether a character acts

passively, assertively, or aggressively. Begin a story and ask students to write an ending for it, if desired.

3. To involve bodily/kinesthetic learners, have students spell the word ASSERTIVE by forming letters of the alphabet with their bodies (e.g., three students combine to form the A, two students wind around to form each S, etc.)

4. Have students create a cheer about being assertive.

5. Invite adults from different countries and cultures to talk to the students about how their country's rights differ from those of the students and how their cultures' conventions for being assertive compare with the strategies presented in this unit.

It is important for educators to provide opportunities for students to work in groups, so they can experience social skills in contexts where social communication is needed. Therefore, educators are encouraged to have students complete the Related Activities in small groups whenever possible. Educators trained in cooperative learning could incorporate the five components (see pages 33–34) into the group activity. An excellent resource for teaching students cooperative skills and building a sense of community is *Tribes: A Process for Social Development and Cooperative Learning* (1987) by Jeanne Gibbs.

RELATED LITERATURE:

My Name Is Maria Isabel (1993) by Alma Flor Ada, Ill. by K. Dyble Thompson, Atheneum. (57 pages)

Owen (1993) by Kevin Henkes, Greenwillow. (24 pages)

Amazing Grace (1991) by Mary Hoffman, Ill. by Caroline Binch, Dial. (28 pages)

Wendy and the Bullies (1980) by Nancy K. Robinson, Ill. by Ingrid Fetz, Hastings House. (128 pages)

SOCIAL SKILLS ALL DAY LONG:

Look for opportunities to teach social skills throughout the day (incidental teaching). Four ways to reinforce appropriate social skills and an example of each follow:

Encouragement

Mike, you spoke up and let me know your opinion in an assertive manner. I was impressed by your confident tone of voice.

Personal Example

It's sometimes difficult for me to be assertive, but I try to remember that I have a right to speak up for myself.

Prompting

If there is something that is happening to you in this classroom that you do not like and it's really bothering you, I hope that you will use your assertiveness skills and state your opinion.

Corrective Feedback (must be positive, private, specific, and nonthreatening)

Jolisa, just now you gave Lee a put-down. You might have gotten your message across better by being assertive and expressing your feelings in a calm way.

---★★★---

By standing up for ourselves and letting ourselves be known to others, we gain self-respect and respect from other people.

Arthur Lange and
Patricia Jakubowski

Lesson A

OBJECTIVES:

1. To state the meaning of *being assertive* and tell why it's important

2. To listen to the self-talk associated with appropriate use of the skill

MATERIALS:

1. A bag (Or some other container)

2. *Being Assertive* (See page 123; one per student and one transparency.)

3. *Thought Bubble* (See *Appendix O;* one for educator use.)

PREPARATORY SET:

Tell students they will be given a few minutes to write about things that other people do or say to them that they don't like. Ask students to write their ideas on a piece of paper without naming specific people. Share a few examples (e.g., "I don't like getting pushed when I'm standing in line"). Ask students to place their responses in a bag or some other container. Pull several of the examples out and read them aloud. Tell students that when these things happen there is a way to stand up for themselves in a confident and respectful way. Explain that being assertive is the skill they will be learning about in this unit.

PLAN:

1. Distribute and display *Being Assertive*. Discuss the definition. Explain the skill step and the symbol next to it. Remind students that the symbol is there to help them visualize and remember the skill step. Tell students that they will learn more about the "I" in the next lesson. Refer to the body-talk symbol in the left-hand margin. Remind students that appropriate body talk is important when being assertive. Discuss the reasons for using this social skill.

2. Model use of the skill step for being assertive while thinking aloud. A scripted example follows:

   Introduction

   I am going to pretend to be someone your age. I will show you how I can be assertive in a confident and respectful way. I'll tell you the thoughts I am having. When I hold up this Thought Bubble, *you'll know the words that I'm saying are actually what I'm thinking.*

Social Star

Actual Model

While holding up the *Thought Bubble* say, *Everyone else has had a chance to use the new calculator except me and I would like to try it too. I need to move in closer and speak up for myself in a confident and respectful way.* Put the *Thought Bubble* down and politely say, *I've been waiting. It's my turn now.*

(If desired, model the difference between a respectful and a disrespectful tone of voice while making the assertive statement in the model above.)

3. Read the story at the bottom of *Being Assertive* aloud to students.

4. Ask students to process the story using the *Question, All Write* strategy (Harmin, 1995). This strategy maximizes the number of students who actually think about questions by asking students to write answers to questions before calling on them. Ask all students to write answers to the following questions before calling on them to answer.

   - Why was it important for Jolisa to be assertive in all three situations?

   - Why was it important that Jolisa used a calm voice when she told her father that she needed him to listen?

   - What assertive words did Jolisa use when someone called her a name?

   - Jolisa was assertive when someone tried to pressure her into doing something she did not want to do. Tell about another situation in which it would be important to be assertive and say "no."

   (If all answers are shared, this procedure may be time-consuming. As an alternative, some of the questions may be saved for discussion during another lesson.)

5. Pair students (see *Appendix P*). Ask student pairs to take turns telling each other the meaning of *being assertive* and why it's important to use the skill. Students could be reminded that the information they are to say is printed on *Being Assertive*.

   As an option to add structure to this activity, ask partners to come to an agreement about which person will be called "A" and which person will be called "B." After students have made their decisions, ask "A" to tell "B" the definition of *being assertive*. Next, ask "B" to tell "A" the definition. Ask students to use the same procedure to tell each other the reasons for being assertive.

———————— ★★★ ————————

To know oneself, one should assert oneself.

Albert Camus

Name _____

Being Assertive

MEANING OF BEING ASSERTIVE:

Speaking up for yourself in a confident and respectful way

SKILL STEP:

1. Ask myself: Is this a time to tell about my rights, feelings, or beliefs?

I think...
feel...
want...
need...
believe...
don't...
won't...

REASONS FOR USING THIS SKILL:

Being assertive helps you feel confident when someone doesn't respect your rights. You show others that your feelings and beliefs are important too. You give the message that you believe in yourself.

DIRECTIONS: Listen to the story below. Look at the picture of Jolisa while you listen.

Jolisa knows a lot about being assertive. On Wednesday, she chose to be assertive three times. Before she went to school, she kept asking her dad a question and he didn't listen. She calmly and respectfully said, "I want you to listen to me. I need to ask you a question." When someone called her "stupid" at school, she said with a firm voice, "I'm not stupid. I don't like being called stupid!" That afternoon, Jolisa went to the park. A kid tried to pressure Jolisa into carving her name on a bench. She assertively said, "No. I don't destroy property."

© 1996 Thinking Publications   123   *Duplication permitted for educational use only.*

Social Star

Lesson B

OBJECTIVE:

To identify basic interpersonal rights that form the basis for assertiveness

MATERIALS:

1. *Kids' Bill of Rights* (See page 127; one per student and one transparency.)

2. *Wait a Minute #1–6* (See pages 128–133; one transparency of each page.)

3. *Wait a Minute #__* (See page 134; one transparency for optional use in step 4 of this Plan.)

4. *Being Assertive* classroom poster (See page 13.)

PREPARATORY SET:

Briefly introduce students to the United States Bill of Rights by saying:

You and I, and every other person in our country, the United States of America, have special freedoms that people in some other countries don't have. (Note: Delete this opening sentence, or modify it, if your students are not U.S. citizens.) *When the United States of America was very young, the country's leaders wrote down how they thought the government could best be organized. What they wrote in 1787 is called the Constitution of the United States. A few years later, in 1791, they decided that some important rules were left out, so they wrote 10 amendments (or changes) to the constitution. Those 10 amendments are called the Bill of Rights. The Bill of Rights explains some of the freedoms and rights that Americans have.*

Refer to the easy version of the Bill of Rights that follows and consider sharing a few examples with students. Conclude this discussion by saying, "I bet some of you are wondering why we are talking about the Constitution and the Bill of Rights when we are supposed to be talking about being assertive!"

- *1st Amendment*—Congress cannot pass laws that take away:

    Freedom of Religion (you can believe and worship as you wish)

    Freedom of Speech (you can express your ideas)

    Freedom of the Press (you can write what you want)

    Freedom to Assemble (you can get together with people peacefully)

    Freedom to Petition (you can ask the government to correct wrongs)

- *2nd Amendment*—States have a right to allow people to keep weapons in their homes because, in an emergency, citizens may be needed to fight.

- *3rd Amendment*—People don't have to let soldiers stay in their homes during peacetime.

- *4th Amendment*—People (their homes and their things) cannot be searched or taken away unless the government has a good reason to do so. Police usually have to get permission from a judge to arrest someone or to make a search.

- *5th Amendment*—People don't have to give evidence against themselves in court. If they have been found innocent of a crime, they can't be tried again for the same crime. People must be treated fairly by the law and cannot have their lives, liberty, or property taken from them unfairly.

- *6th Amendment*—People accused of a crime can have a lawyer and a trial by jury. They have to be told what they are accused of and they can ask questions about it.

- *7th Amendment*—If a disagreement between people is about something that costs more than $20, they can have a jury trial.

- *8th Amendment*—People who have been arrested can be free while they wait for their trial if they post bail (money paid to the court as a way of promising they will return for their trial). If they show up, they get this money back. Fines have to be fair and people found guilty cannot be punished in a cruel or unusual way.

- *9th Amendment*—The rights listed above are not the only ones people have. Any rights not mentioned in the Bill of Rights belong automatically to people.

- *10th Amendment*—Any powers that do not belong to the national government belong to the states. The United States government has only those powers listed in the Constitution.

PLAN:

1. Write the following six sentence-completion phrases where all students can see them: be treated in a nice way, say what we think and how we feel, ask for what we need, say "no", make honest mistakes, be the best that we can be. Tell students they will be learning about rights that all kids have. (The phrases you just wrote will help them learn what those rights are.)

2. Distribute *Kids' Bill of Rights*. Ask students to take notes on this sheet as you discuss each "right" during step 3.

3. Display *Wait A Minute #1*. Tell students that both people shown on the page are having one of their *Kids' Bill of Rights* broken or violated. After reading both cartoons, ask students to complete the sentence at the bottom of the page by choosing the correct sentence-completion phrase from the list written in step 1 of this Plan. Write the phrase the students select on the transparency and ask students

to write the phrase on their *Kids' Bill of Rights* sheets. As a group, identify at least one other situation when the identified right might be broken or violated. (If students want to discuss what they can say when their rights are violated, let them know that will be the focus in Lesson D.)

4. Continue the same procedure for *Wait A Minute #2–6*. *Wait A Minute #__* can be used if you and the students want to brainstorm additional rights (e.g., the right to change your mind, begin and end a conversation, say "I don't know").

5. Review the definition and skill step for *being assertive* by referring the class to the *Being Assertive* classroom poster.

6. Pair students (see *Appendix P*). Ask student pairs to take turns telling each other the skill step for being assertive. Follow the procedure described in step 5 of Lesson A. Next, ask students to work with their partners to think of a place to keep their *Kids' Bill of Rights*. Tell students that one or more pairs will be called on to share their ideas.

———————— ★ ★ ★ ————————

A secure individual...knows that the responsibility for anything concerning his life remains with himself...and he accepts that responsibility.

Harry Brown

Being Assertive

Name _____

KIDS' BILL OF RIGHTS

★ #1 We all have the right to...

★ #2 We all have the right to...

★ #3 We all have the right to...

★ #4 We all have the right to...

★ #5 We all have the right to...

★ #6 We all have the right to...

Social Star

Wait a Minute #1

You can't ask that question. It's stupid!

I really need a tissue. But, I can't get one—the teacher said to stay in our seats.

Wait a minute...

KIDS' BILL OF RIGHTS

#1 We all have the right to...

© 1996 Thinking Publications   128   *Duplication permitted for educational use only.*

Wait a Minute #2

You have to give me a cookie or I won't be your friend.

You have to be mean to Joe at recess. We're all going to do it.

Wait a minute...

KIDS' BILL OF RIGHTS

★#2 We all have the right to...

Wait a Minute #3

I can't tell them this movie scares me!

You're wrong—that's not the best color.

Wait a minute...

KIDS' BILL OF RIGHTS

#3 We all have the right to...

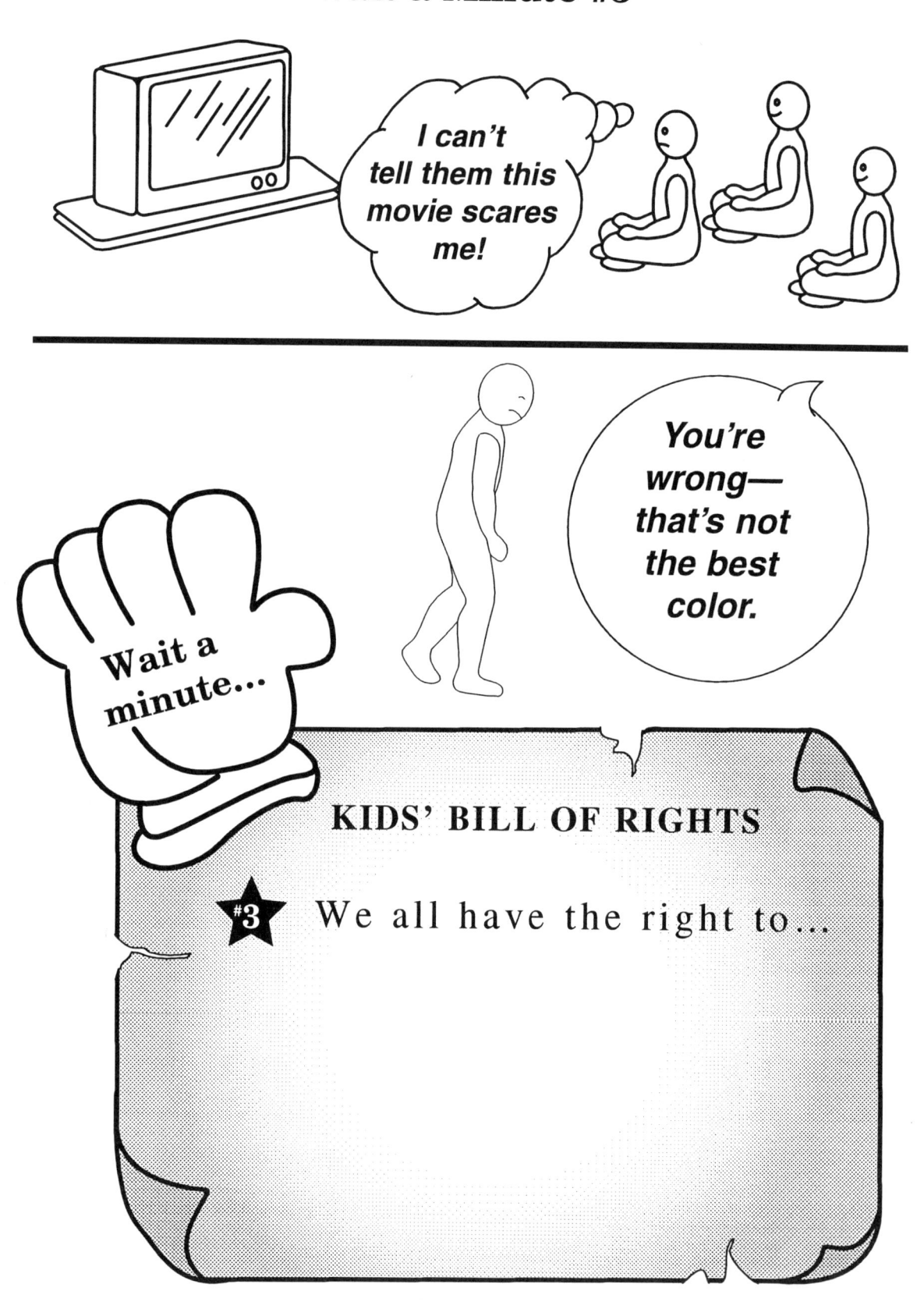

Wait a Minute #4

Don't bother practicing. You'll never be a good reader!

You probably won't be any good at math. Your dad never was.

Wait a minute...

KIDS' BILL OF RIGHTS

★ #4   We all have the right to...

Social Star

Wait a Minute #5

You can't jump rope! Yesterday, you tripped and fell.

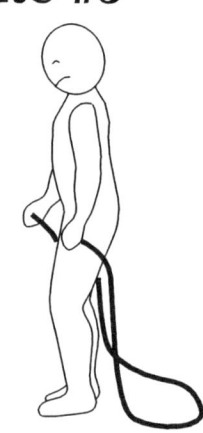

I can't volunteer to read aloud. I might say a word wrong and some kids will laugh.

Wait a minute...

KIDS' BILL OF RIGHTS

★#5 We all have the right to...

© 1996 Thinking Publications 132 *Duplication permitted for educational use only.*

Being Assertive

Wait a Minute #6

You're so stupid! And your shoes are ugly too.

You can't play on the jungle gym— we were here first, so we get to use it all day long!

Wait a minute...

KIDS' BILL OF RIGHTS

#6 We all have the right to...

Wait a Minute #__

KIDS' BILL OF RIGHTS

★ We all have the right to...

Lesson C

EDUCATOR INFORMATION:

During this lesson, students learn three ways to respond (i.e., passively, assertively, and aggressively) when one's rights are violated. Substitute terminology if you feel other terms would be more appropriate for your students. For example, Cartledge and Kleefeld (1989) use the terms "weak talk," "straight talk," and "mean talk" to describe passive, assertive, and aggressive responses.

OBJECTIVES:

1. To identify three ways people respond when their rights are violated (i.e., passively, assertively, and aggressively)

2. To tell reasons why it's important to respond assertively instead of passively or aggressively

MATERIALS:

1. *I Would...* (See page 137; one per student and one transparency.)

2. *Three Responses* (See page 138; one per student and one transparency.)

3. *Wait a Minute #1–6* (See pages 128–133; use the transparencies from Lesson B.)

PREPARATORY SET:

Say to the students:

Let's play Beat the Clock. When I say "go", I want you to tell me as many things as you can remember about our country's Bill of Rights and the Kids' Bill of Rights. We'll start with one person and keep going around the room until the time is up (specify an appropriate amount of time). *If you can't think of anything to say when it is your turn, it's fine to say "I pass." Get ready. Go!*

PLAN:

1. Distribute *I Would...* Have students complete the activity as directed and hand it in. (Looking at each student's response may provide useful information about how they view themselves.)

2. Explain that even though everyone has rights, some people don't know how to speak up for themselves in a confident and respectful way when their rights are violated. Some people feel afraid, so they keep quiet and don't say anything. Other people feel so angry that they yell or hit.

3. Distribute and display *Three Responses*. Complete the page as a group.

4. Pair students (see *Appendix P*). Display the first *Wait a Minute* transparency. Ask students to discuss with their partners what might happen or how the characters may feel if they act passively. Call on a few pairs to share their thoughts. Next, ask students to discuss with their partners what might happen or how the characters may feel if they act aggressively. Call on a few pairs to share their thoughts. Tell students they'll discuss how to be assertive in the next lesson.

5. Follow the same procedure for the remaining *Wait a Minute* transparencies. (You may want to complete this activity over a couple of sessions.)

───────── ★★★ ─────────

In assertiveness, style is all-important.

Arnold Lazarus

Being Assertive

Name _____

I Would...

DIRECTIONS: Put an "X" next to the way you would probably respond in each of the situations below.

1. If a student told me I couldn't be friends with someone, I would probably...

   _____ not say anything.

   _____ tell my opinion.

   _____ yell at the person.

2. If a student shoved me in a mean way at recess, I would probably...

   _____ not do anything.

   _____ tell the person to stop.

   _____ shove the person.

3. If our teacher asks for our opinion about which art activity we want to do, I would probably...

   _____ keep quiet and not tell my idea.

   _____ tell my idea.

   _____ tell the teacher we have to do my idea or I won't do the activity.

© 1996 Thinking Publications — Duplication permitted for educational use only.

Social Star

Three Responses

DIRECTIONS: Read each cartoon below to learn three different ways people can react when their rights are violated. Discuss what you think might happen in each situation and how each person might feel.

PASSIVE "Hold-It-in Harry"

- "You're a fat pig!"
- *I'm not saying anything. Why am I such a chicken?*

AGGRESSIVE "Exploding Ed"

- "You're a fat pig!"
- "You're the fat pig! I'm gonna smash your face in!"

ASSERTIVE "Say-It-Straight Sam"

- "You're a fat pig!"
- "That's a put-down. I want you to stop."

Lesson D

OBJECTIVES:

1. To tell what an *I-statement* is
2. To explain the reason for using I-statements
3. To demonstrate use of I-statements

MATERIALS:

1. *I-Statements Help!* (See page 142; one per student and one transparency.)
2. *I-Statement Cards* (See pages 143–144; one copy cut apart)
3. *Being Assertive* (See page 123 from Lesson A; one transparency.)
4. *Pencil Toppers* (See pages 145–146; one set per student.)

PREPARATORY SET:

Ask students: "What is the 9th letter of the alphabet?" Once students have identified the letter "I," say, "In this lesson, you'll be learning about something called an I-statement which can be helpful to use when being assertive."

PLAN:

1. Remind students that *being assertive* means telling about your rights, feelings, and beliefs in a confident, respectful way. Say, "When you choose to be assertive with someone, they may feel angry or hurt and not listen to what you have to say. If you use an I-statement, you show others that your feelings and beliefs are important without making threats toward them. An I-statement uses the word 'I' and tells how you feel, think, or believe. It doesn't blame others or make them feel that their ideas are bad."

   Draw an "eye" where everyone can see it and tell students, "When you use an I-statement it helps others to see (point to your eye) what your real thoughts and feelings are." Examples of I-statements are:

   - I feel hurt when you call me names.
   - I think the red flag looks the best.
   - I believe it would be good to have four people in the group.

   Tell students, "When making an I-statement, it's important that your body talk does not look or sound mean or weak." Ask students to describe specifically what body talk would be important to use when making an I-statement (answers could include: eye contact, serious but respectful tone of voice, appropriate voice volume, confident body posture, etc.).

Social Star

2. Distribute and display *I-Statements Help!* Have the students complete the sheet as directed. Call on students to share their answers and the reasons for their answers. Discuss the fact that putting an "I" at the beginning of a sentence doesn't always make it assertive (e.g., "I hate you," "I think you stink").

3. Write the sentences, "I feel _____ when _____. I need _____." where everyone can see them. Demonstrate to the students how to fill in the blanks to make an assertive statement (e.g., I feel angry when I get pushed in line. I need you to stop pushing.)

4. Pair students using *Line-up–Fold-up* (see *Appendix P*). Ask students to work with their partners to think of several more ways to fill the blanks to form an I-statement appropriately. Call on one or more pairs to share their answers.

5. Ask student pairs to come to an agreement about which person will be called "A" and which person will be called "B." After students have made their decisions, ask all of the "A's" to form a circle, facing outward. Next ask all of the "B's" to make a circle outside the "A's" with each student now facing their partner. Pass out one *I-Statement Card* to each of the students in the outer circle. Explain that the students in the outer circle will read only the top part of the card to their partner. The partner should respond by making an I-statement appropriate for the situation on the card. Remind students that they should use assertive body talk, and a respectful tone of voice when making their I-statement. (If the student cannot come up with an I-statement, the person on the outer circle can read the example I-statement and have his or her partner repeat it.) The outer circle should then rotate clockwise one person which would give them a new partner to read the situation on the card to. After several rotations, ask the outside person to give the *I-Statement Card* to his or her partner in the inside circle. The partners on the inside then read the card to their partners on the outside of the circle. Repeat the process described until the students are again facing their original partners.

6. Display *Being Assertive*. Remind students of the phrases that can be used to make I-statements (I think, I feel, I want, I need, I believe, I don't, I won't). Distribute *Pencil Toppers*. Explain the procedure you would like the students to follow for coloring and attaching the pencil toppers (e.g., students could color one pencil topper per day for seven consecutive days; students could choose their favorite pencil topper to keep and distribute the remainder to kids from other classes or to siblings, etc.).

7. Before ending this lesson, ask students, "Besides making an I-statement, what else might you say or do to be assertive?" (Accept all reasonable answers, but lead students to an understanding that there are other ways to be assertive.)

Ask students, "Do you always need to be assertive and speak up whenever you feel that someone has violated your rights?" (Accept all reasonable answers, but lead students to the conclusion that for small things, they may decide to walk away, ignore, or not respond at all. It's important for them to be assertive in situations in which they really feel angry or violated.)

———————————— ★★★ ————————————

Two types of respect are involved in assertion: respect for oneself, that is expressing one's needs and defending one's rights, as well as respect for the other person's needs and rights.

Arthur Lange
Patricia Jakubowski

Social Star

Name _____

I-STATEMENTS HELP!

DIRECTIONS: Circle the statement that an assertive person would choose to say.

A   B

A		B
I felt sad when I heard what you said. I need you to stop saying mean things about me.	*or*	Why did you talk about me behind my back?
I feel frustrated with all of the noise. I need it to be really quiet when I read.	*or*	It's too noisy. Be quiet!
I'm going to punch you if you call me that again.	*or*	I feel hurt when you call me names. I want you to stop calling me names.
You are such a big mouth.	*or*	I feel upset when you tell everyone what I say. I need you to keep things I tell you private.
I feel left out when I raise my hand and never get called on. I would like to share some answers.	*or*	You never call on me.

I-Statement Cards

1. Your brother calls you a "brat." Make an I-statement.

("I feel angry when you call me names.")

2. A classmate takes your pencil. Make an I-statement.

("I need to get my pencil back right away.")

3. You feel that your parent lets your sister have more privileges than you. Make an I-statement.

("I feel hurt when you let ___ do more than I can.")

4. You feel sick at school. Make an I-statement.

("I feel sick. I need to go to the health aide.")

5. Another kid cuts in front of you at the waterslide. Make an I-statement.

("I was in line first. I think you should go behind me.")

6. A friend wants you to be mean to the new girl in class. Make an I-statement.

("I don't want to be mean to her. I want to make her feel welcome here.")

7. Your parent's friend asks what you like best about your school. Make an I-statement.

("I believe the best thing about my school is....")

8. You want to ask your parent to help you with your homework. Make an I-statement.

("Dad, I really need some help on my reading homework.")

I-Statement Cards

9. A friend wants to borrow your shirt. You don't want to lend it out. Make an I-statement.

("I don't want to lend my shirt to anyone.")

10. The person next to you at lunch says, "I won't be your friend anymore unless you let me have your sandwich." Make an I-statement.

("No. If I give you my sandwich, I'll be hungry.")

11. You accidentally broke your grandfather's fishing pole. Make an I-statement.

("I'm really sorry, Grandpa. I accidentally broke your fishing pole.")

12. You forgot to return your library book to school. Make an I-statement.

("I'm sorry I forgot my library book. Will there be a fine?")

13. The people sitting next to you at the movie theatre are talking loudly. Make an I-statement.

("I can't hear the movie. Could you please be quiet?")

14. The others in your group have not let you share your idea. Make an I-statement.

("I have an idea that I want to share.")

15. A person in your club laughs at you when you make a mistake. Make an I-statement.

("I feel hurt when you laugh at my mistakes. Please stop.")

16. A friend borrowed a tape from you. When he returned it, the tape was broken. Your friend didn't mention it. Make an I-statement.

("I feel angry that my tape is broken. I want to know how it happened.")

PENCIL TOPPERS

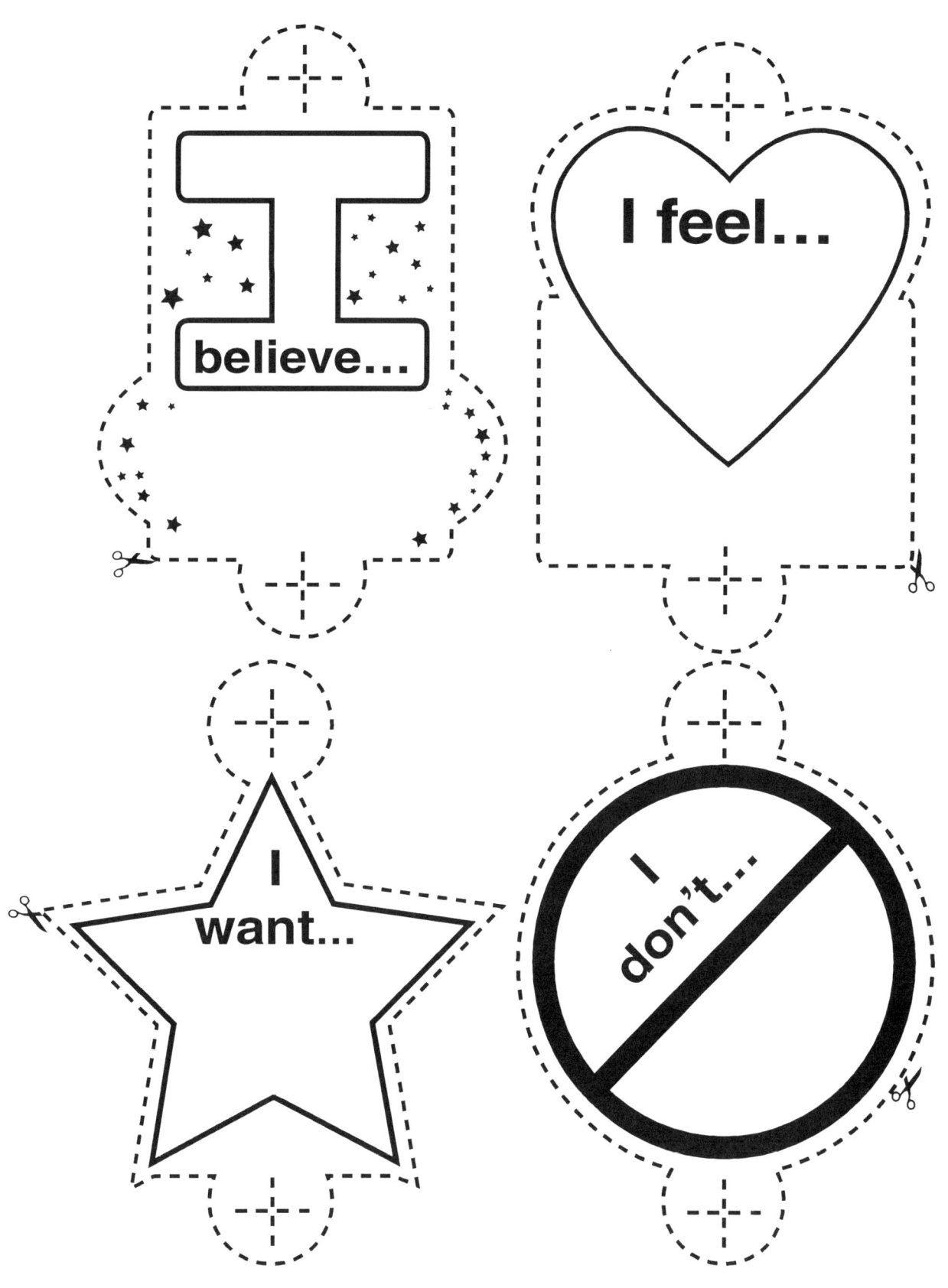

I believe...

I feel...

I want...

I don't...

Social Star

PENCIL TOPPERS

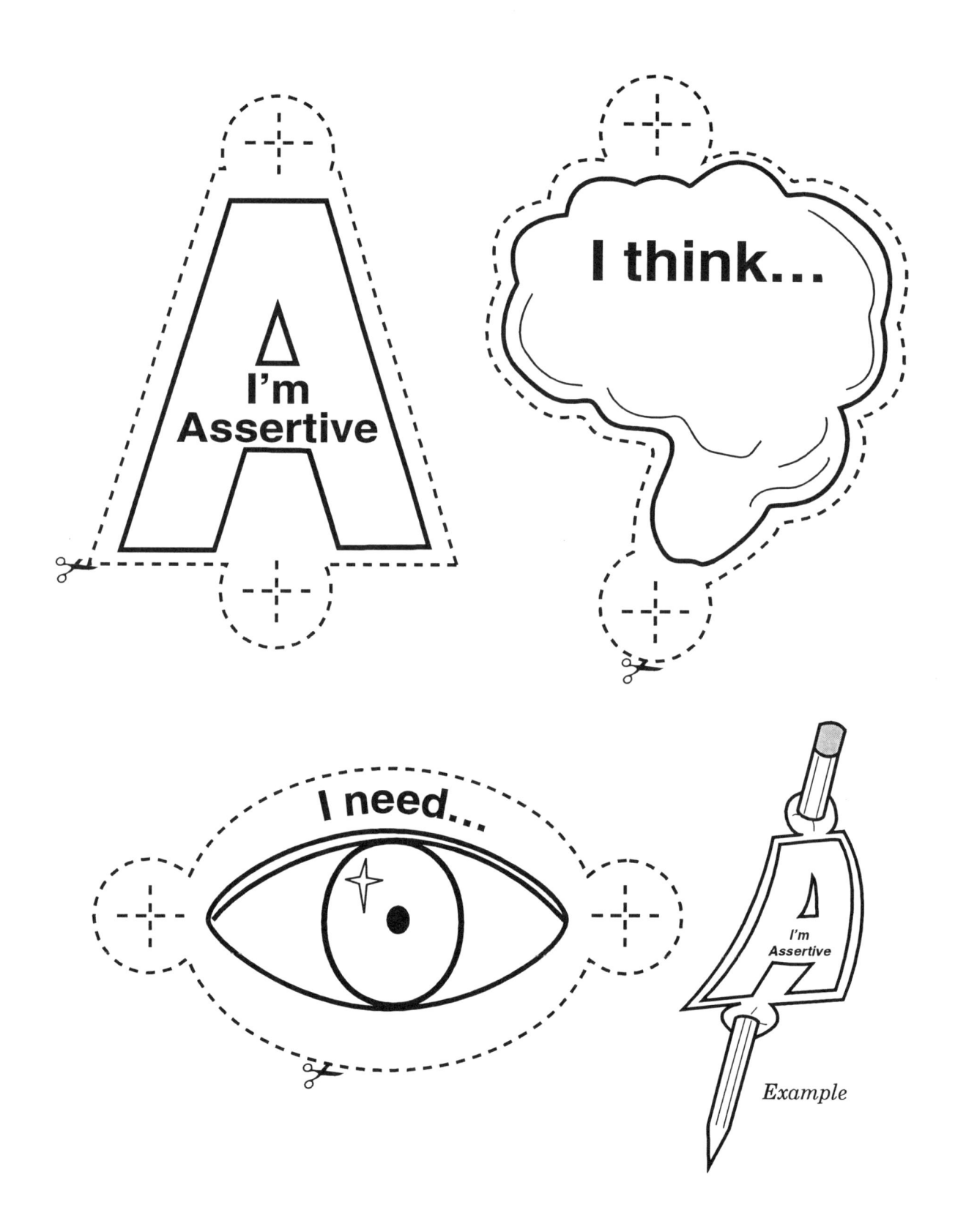

I'm Assertive

I think...

I need...

I'm Assertive

Example

© 1996 Thinking Publications · Duplication permitted for educational use only.

Lessons X, Y, and Z

Due to similarities in format, the final three lesson plans for each unit in *Social Star* are provided in *Appendix A*. Substitute the words "being assertive" whenever a "_____" appears in the lesson plans. Information specific to this unit follows.

LESSON X PREPARATORY SET:

Before class, cut a large letter "I" out of poster paper. Display the "I" on a wall or a bulletin board. Have students write an assertive I-statement that they have made recently or are going to make soon. Attach those I-statements to the large "I."

LESSON Y PREPARATORY SET:

Darken the room, if you prefer, and ask the students to visualize themselves correctly using this social skill by reading the following script:

Let's take a few moments.... Make sure you are in a comfortable position.... Close your eyes if you feel like it.... On the count of three, take a very slow, deep breath. Remember to breathe in quietly through your nose. One...two...three.... Breathe in deeply.... Now breathe out slowly.... Remember to breathe out quietly through your mouth. Let your entire body relax.... Now imagine yourself using confident body language in your small group at school. You express your beliefs even though some other people disagree with you. Think about how proud you feel because you expressed your opinion in an assertive manner.

LESSON Z PLOT SITUATION:

You have been trying to tell your mom about a problem you are having with your soccer coach and she doesn't listen to you.

LESSON Z ROADBLOCK EXAMPLES:

- Making an assertive I-statement to an adult and having them think you are being sassy

- Thinking assertive thoughts but not having the courage to say what you think

- Making an assertive statement that causes the person to get angry with you

Being Assertive T-Chart

LOOKS LIKE...

using appropriate body talk

- looking at the person
- having a confident body posture
- showing a serious facial expression

SOUNDS LIKE...

a serious, respectful tone of voice

a medium volume

stating your feelings, opinions, and beliefs

- "I think…"
- "I feel…"
- "I want…"
- "I need…"
- "I believe…"

telling what you won't do

- "I won't…"
- "I don't want to…"

SHOW TIME

HOME

Pretend your older sister hits you whenever your parents leave. Demonstrate an assertive statement you could make to your sister (or to your parents) about your feelings.

SCHOOL

Pretend a boy at school has been taking "cuts" in front of you. Demonstrate an assertive statement you could make to let him know you'd like him to stop taking "cuts."

COMMUNITY

Pretend you are at a swimming pool and a girl keeps trying to dunk you. Demonstrate an assertive statement you could make so she stops.

SPEAK UP!

For Your Rights, Feelings, and Beliefs

HOME-A-GRAM

Social Star

Dear Family,

At school, we have been talking about the skill called

BEING ASSERTIVE

I learned that *being assertive* means speaking up for myself in a confident and respectful way.

I learned that it's important to ask myself, "Is this the right time to tell about my rights, feelings, or beliefs?"

If I choose to be assertive when others are not respecting my rights, it sends the message that my feelings and beliefs are important.

I learned that each of us has rights. One of the rights that we talked about is:

_____

I practiced using I-statements to help me send the message that I believe in myself without making threats to others. Below I have written words I can use to be assertive next time someone is not respecting my rights:

_____

_____

_____

After I share the I-statement I have written with the people in my family, please sign my "Being Assertive" badge so I can return it to school and become a SOCIAL SUPER STAR this week.

From: _____

© 1996 Thinking Publications — *Duplication permitted for educational use only.*

Being Responsible

Social Star

UNIT GOAL:

To demonstrate comprehension and use of strategies for being responsible

EDUCATOR INFORMATION:

This unit teaches students that they have a responsibility for themselves and to the world. *Being responsible* means a variety of things (e.g., accepting consequences, following rules and directions, making appropriate choices, taking care of your body, asking permission, doing something without being told, being honest, following through and doing what you say you'll do). Students are encouraged to consider that there are often several responsible choices one can make in any given situation.

RELATED ACTIVITIES:

1. Read parts of the book *50 Simple Things You Can Do to Save the Earth* (The Earth Works Group, 1989).

2. Have each student create a drawing that demonstrates their connection to the world to show they are responsible for themselves and to the world in general.

3. Use fabric paints to make T-shirts that show examples of being responsible.

4. Have students identify people they know (e.g., themselves, their parents, their teachers) and brainstorm the various responsibilities each person has.

5. Discuss people who have exhibited a high level of social responsibility. Include historical as well as more contemporary examples (e.g., Harriet Tubman, Martin Luther King, Jr., Eleanor Roosevelt, Jonas Salk, Jimmy Carter, Betty Ford).

6. Have students make a class scrapbook containing articles about people who are currently demonstrating responsibility for themselves and to the world.

7. Have students discuss the social responsibility that television network producers need to consider when deciding which shows to air.

8. Have the class raise money to have signs about responsibility put on the outside of city buses. An example created by children in Wausau, Wisconsin is:

   For Adults Only—We learn our behaviors from you; you are our role models.

9. Have students interview an older acquaintance (e.g., a grandparent) to discuss ways in which responsibilities for children have changed over the years.

10. Spotlight a "Responsible Student of the Week." Draw a picture or write a paragraph about something someone in the class did to act responsibly. Create a permanent bulletin board that highlights the responsible behavior of students.

11. Invite adults from different cultures to talk to the students about how their cultures' conventions for being responsible compare with the strategies presented in this unit.

It is important for educators to provide opportunities for students to work in groups, so they can experience social skills in contexts where social communication is needed. Therefore, educators are encouraged to have students complete the Related Activities in small groups whenever possible. Educators trained in cooperative learning could incorporate the five components (see pages 33–34) into the group activity. An excellent resource for teaching students cooperative skills and building a sense of community is *Tribes: A Process for Social Development and Cooperative Learning* (1987) by Jeanne Gibbs.

RELATED LITERATURE:

The Girl Who Knew It All (1979) by Patricia Reilly Giff, Delacorte. (118 pages)

The Gift Giver (1980) by Joyce Hansen, Houghton. (118 pages)

Jamaica's Find (1985) by Juanita Havill, Ill. by Anne Sibley O'Brien, Houghton Mifflin. (32 pages)

Eddie, Incorporated (1980) by Phyllis Reynolds Naylor, Ill. by Blanche Sims, Atheneum. (101 pages)

Home Lovely (1995) by Lynne Rae Perkins, Greenwillow. (32 pages)

SOCIAL SKILLS ALL DAY LONG:

Look for opportunities to teach social skills throughout the day (incidental teaching). Four ways to reinforce appropriate social skills and an example of each follow:

Encouragement

Ann, you have been very responsible about getting your homework done on time every day this week. That's a skill you'll need all through school and when you get a job.

Personal Example

I'm going to take my children to the neighborhood playground to pick up paper. We do that every Earth Day because we all have a responsibility for our community.

Prompting

*Remember, responsible people think about the consequences of their actions **before** they act.*

Corrective Feedback (must be positive, private, specific, and nonthreatening)

Maria, I noticed that when you spilled paint by the back table you walked away. There were a few responsible choices you might have made. You could have told me or you could have wiped it up yourself. Can you think of any other responsible ways to handle that situation?

———————— ★★★ ————————

No man will succeed unless he is ready to face and overcome difficulties and is prepared to assume responsibilities.

William J.H. Boetcher

Social Star

Lesson A

OBJECTIVES:

1. To state the meaning of *being responsible* and tell why it's important

2. To listen to the self-talk associated with appropriate use of the skill

3. To identify various ways to demonstrate responsibility toward oneself and toward the world

MATERIALS:

1. *The ABC's of ___* (See page 159; one transparency.)

2. *Being Responsible* (See page 160; one per student and one transparency.)

3. *Thought Bubble* (See *Appendix O*; one for educator use.)

4. *Responsibility Hunt* (See page 161; one per student and one transparency.)

PREPARATORY SET:

Display *The ABC's of ___*. Say:

I'm going to go through the first six letters of the alphabet and tell you what each letter stands for. Write each phrase next to the appropriate letter on the transparency as you go. After I am finished, I want you to guess which word is missing from the title. That word is what this new unit is all about. Are you ready? OK! "A" is for asking permission. "B" is for brushing your teeth without being asked. "C" is for coming home on time. "D" is for doing the dishes. "E" is for eating healthy food. "F" is for finding ways to recycle. Can anyone guess what word fits in the blank?

If no one offers the word "responsibility," write the letter "R" in the first blank of the title. Keep adding letters after every incorrect guess, until someone guesses the word "responsibility." Save this transparency to complete in Lessons B, C, D, and X.

PLAN:

1. Distribute and display *Being Responsible*. Discuss the definition of *being responsible*. Explain the skill step and the symbol next to it. Remind students that the symbol is there to help them visualize and remember the skill step. Refer to the body-talk symbol in the left-hand margin. Remind students that appropriate body talk is important when being responsible. Discuss the reasons for being responsible.

2. Model use of the skill step for being responsible while thinking aloud. A scripted example follows:

Introduction

I am going to pretend to be a student your age. My family has a dog. Before we got the dog, I agreed that it would be my job to take care of it. I will show you how I can be responsible when I get home from school and tell you the thoughts that I'm having. When I hold up this Thought Bubble, *you'll know the words that I'm saying are actually what I'm thinking.*

Actual Model

While holding up the *Thought Bubble* say, *Before I go outside to play, I need to check on the dog. How can I be responsible? I can take the dog for a walk. I can brush its fur. I can pick up the droppings from the yard. I can wash out its pen. I think I'll pick up the droppings now and then take the dog for a walk before dinner.*

3. Read the story at the bottom of *Being Responsible* aloud to the students.

4. Ask students to process the story using the *Sharing Pairs* strategy (Harmin, 1995). This strategy maximizes the number of students who talk about their ideas and hear the ideas of others by asking them to discuss answers to questions with their partners before calling on them. Ask students to discuss answers with their partners to the following questions before you call on one pair to share their ideas with the whole class:

   - Why might it be helpful to think about your day before you go to sleep, like Mike did in the story?
   - Why did Mike feel proud when he thought about choices he made during his day?
   - Why was it responsible for Mike to throw out his gum before entering the library?
   - Why was it responsible for Mike to admit what he did to Mr. Walter's flowers?
   - Why did Mr. Walters call Mike's dad?
   - Can you think of a time when you were responsible? How did you feel?

5. Distribute and display *Responsibility Hunt*. Read the directions and the example provided. Tell students that during the next lesson, they will be sharing the examples of responsibility they found. Explain that examples can be from home or school. Examples could also come from current events featured on the nightly news broadcast or from the newspaper.

6. Pair students (see *Appendix P*). Ask student pairs to take turns telling each other the meaning of *being responsible* and why it's important to use the skill. Students could be reminded that the information they are to say is printed on *Being Responsible*.

As an option to add structure to this activity, ask partners to come to an agreement about which person will be called "A" and which person will be called "B." After students have made their decisions, ask "A" to tell "B" the definition of *being responsible*. Next, ask "B" to tell "A" the definition. Ask students to use the same procedure to tell each other the reasons for being responsible.

───────── ★★★ ─────────

The price of greatness is responsibility.

Winston Churchill

Being Responsible

The ABC's of
_____

A _____
B _____
C _____
D _____
E _____
F _____
G _____
H _____
I _____
J _____
K _____
L _____
M _____
N _____
O _____
P _____
Q _____
R _____
S _____
T _____
U _____
V _____
W _____
X _____
Y _____
Z _____

© 1996 Thinking Publications — *Duplication permitted for educational use only.*

Social Star

Being Responsible

MEANING OF BEING RESPONSIBLE:

Choosing to do what is right

SKILL STEP:

1. Ask myself: How can I be responsible?

REASONS FOR USING THIS SKILL:

When you show responsibility, people will view you as being trustworthy and dependable. You feel proud making choices that will help you and will help the world be a better place to live.

DIRECTIONS: Listen to the story below. Look at the picture of Mike while you listen.

Mike crawled into bed. He thought about his day while he waited to fall asleep. He felt proud remembering some of the responsible choices he had made. He thought about how he followed the "no gum chewing" rule in the school's library. He threw out his gum without being reminded. He also thought about how honest he was with his neighbor. After school, he accidentally kicked a ball into his neighbor's garden and a few plants got broken. Mike knocked on the door and apologized to Mr. Walters right away. Just then, Mike's dad came into his bedroom and said, "Mike, Mr. Walters just called to say how impressed he is with your honesty. I'm really proud of the responsibility you showed."

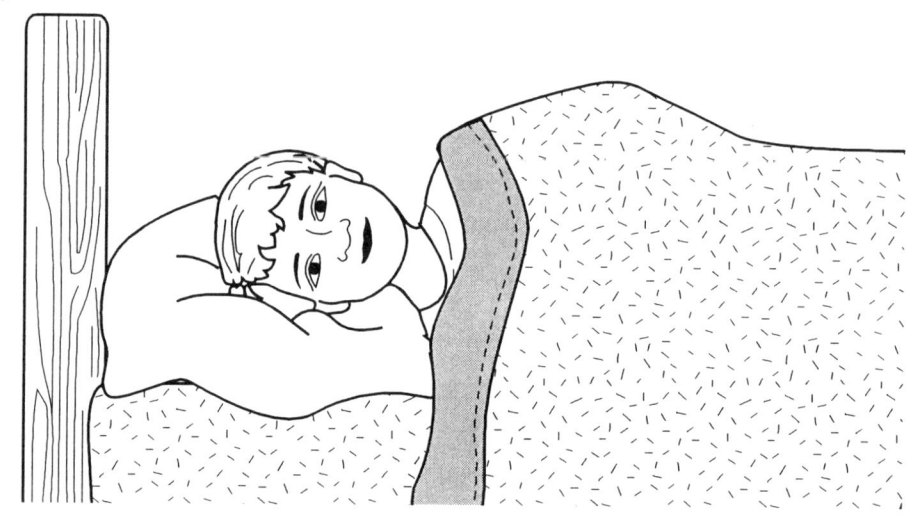

Name _____

Responsibility Hunt

DIRECTIONS: Be on the lookout for people being responsible. When you notice someone being responsible, write the information on the chart below. Look at the example.

WHO	WAS RESPONSIBLE BY:
★ 1 Howie	*Picking up the paper that accidentally blew on the neighbor's lawn while he was setting the garbage out for pickup.*
★ 2	
★ 3	
★ 4	

Social Star

Lesson B

OBJECTIVE:

To identify a variety of ways to be responsible

MATERIALS:

1. *The ABC's of* ____ (One transparency saved from Lesson A)

2. *Responsibility Hunt* (Begun in step 5 of Lesson A)

3. Props to simulate a game show (E.g., upbeat music, a bell, a decorated contestants' table with four chairs, an emcee costume, a microphone)

4. *The Really Responsible Game Show Questions* (See pages 164–166; one for educator use.)

5. *Responsibility Badges* (Optional) (See page 167; one per student.)

6. *Being Responsible* classroom poster (See page 13.)

PREPARATORY SET:

Display *The ABC's of* ____ . Challenge students to complete five of the remaining 21 letters with examples of responsibility described during the Preparatory Set in Lesson A. Save for use in Lesson C.

PLAN:

1. Display *Responsibility Hunt*. Ask students to share examples of responsibility they observed and recorded on their copies of *Responsibility Hunt* assigned in Lesson A. After the examples have been shared, thank the students and say in a theatrical voice, "And now, let's play a game show called 'Really Responsible'!"

2. Ask students if they have ever seen a TV game show and ask for examples. Tell students that today they will be contestants on a game show called "Really Responsible." Before the game begins, divide students into groups of three or four. Ask students to number off from one to three (or one to four) within their groups. Check to be certain that everyone remembers his or her number by saying something like, "All the one's raise your hands," etc.

3. Explain the purpose of the game by saying, "During the game, I will be describing a situation to you. Your job is to decide if the person in the situation is being responsible. You may be asked to explain your answer."

4. Put on the emcee costume, hold the microphone, turn on the music, and say in a theatrical voice, "Welcome to 'Really Responsible,' the game show filled with

fun and excitement! Without further ado, would all the three's please raise your hands? Congratulations and COME ON DOWN, three's. You're our first contestants on the 'Really Responsible' show. Take a seat at our contestants' table."

5. While the three's are being seated, write a number between 1 and 50 on a piece of paper so no one can see it. Ask each three to quickly pick a number between 1 and 50. Say to whoever comes closest to your number, "____, congratulations! You get to answer the first question on the show."

6. Read the first situation from *The Really Responsible Game Show Questions*. Allow a comfortable period of time for the student to answer. The student can consult with the other three's before answering. You might ring a bell after the answer is completed to signal a transition if desired.

7. Ask all the three's to go back to their seats, and then ask all the two's (or one's or four's) to COME ON DOWN! Continue playing using the same procedure as described above as long as time allows. A scoring system may be implemented (e.g., when the total score reaches a predetermined number, give the entire class a responsibility badge from the *Responsibility Badges* on page 167).

8. Review the definition and skill step for *being responsible* by referring the class to the *Being Responsible* classroom poster.

9. Pair students (see *Appendix P*). Ask student pairs to take turns telling each other the skill step for being responsible. Follow the procedure described in step 6 of Lesson A. Next ask students to work with their partners to think of a situation when it's important to be responsible. Tell students that one or more pairs will be called on to share their situations.

─────── ★ ★ ★ ───────

Failures become the seeds of future success when we acknowledge our responsibility for them and learn from our mistakes.

Martial Arts of America

Social Star

The Really Responsible Game Show Questions

1. Jolisa promised to clean her room as soon as she was done reading her magazine. When she finished reading, Jolisa went to her friend's house, thinking she'd clean her room when she got home. Was Jolisa being responsible? Explain your answer.

2. Victor got his assignment done on time, but he rushed through it and there were several errors. Was Victor being responsible? Explain your answer.

3. Mike helped sell tickets for the homeless shelter fund-raiser. Was Mike being responsible? Explain your answer.

4. Lee's dad gave him money for hot lunch at school. He skipped lunch and used the money to buy candy instead. Was Lee being responsible? Explain your answer.

5. Ann left a mess on the kitchen table. She thought to herself, "Dad will clean it up." Was Ann being responsible? Explain your answer.

6. When some other kids were teasing her friend, Jolisa asked them to stop. Was Jolisa being responsible? Explain your answer.

7. Victor broke a switch on his friend's headset. When he gave the headset back, he never mentioned the broken switch. Was Victor being responsible? Explain your answer.

8. When Mike's library book was overdue, he told his mother it was her fault for not reminding him to take it back to school. Was Mike being responsible? Explain your answer.

9. Maria saw some kids writing on a neighbor's garage. She told her mother what she saw. Was Maria being responsible? Explain your answer. (If desired, add the following after the student has responded: "It's important to remember that we each have a responsibility to keep our communities safe and free from crime. If you see someone doing something they shouldn't be doing, you have a responsibility to let someone know.")

© 1996 Thinking Publications — Duplication permitted for educational use only.

Being Responsible

10. Ann received a gift in the mail from her aunt. The next day she wrote her aunt a thank-you note. Was Ann being responsible? Explain your answer.

11. Victor was unsure about how to do his assignment. Instead of reading the directions, he shouted to the teacher that he needed help. Was Victor being responsible? Explain your answer.

12. Lee left his coat, shoes, and backpack scattered in the living room. Was Lee being responsible? Explain your answer.

13. Maria and her brother picked up litter at the park by their house. Were Maria and her brother being responsible? Explain your answer.

14. Jolisa saved some of her allowance to donate to the animal shelter in her town. Was Jolisa being responsible? Explain your answer.

15. Mike set the table without being told to do it. Was Mike being responsible? Explain your answer.

16. Victor found a dollar on the kitchen table. He knew it wasn't his so he left it there. Was Victor being responsible? Explain your answer.

17. When Ann left the fast food restaurant, she didn't look to see if there was a place for customers to put their garbage and trays. She just left everything sitting on her table. Was Ann being responsible? Explain your answer.

18. Lee told the teacher that another boy was stealing supplies from kids in the class. Was Lee being responsible? Explain your answer. (If desired, add the following after the student has responded: "It's important to remember that we each have a responsibility to keep our communities safe and free from crime. If you see someone doing something they shouldn't be doing, you have a responsibility to let someone know.")

19. Maria accidentally spilled milk on the floor and no one saw her doing it. When the teacher said, "Would whoever spilled this milk please clean it up?" Maria did nothing. Was Maria being responsible? Explain your answer.

20. Jolisa and some friends helped to plant flowers at an older neighbor's house. Were they being responsible? Explain your answer.

21. Victor listened very carefully while the teacher explained the directions for the art project. Was Victor being responsible? Explain your answer.

22. When Lee's cousins were visiting, they snuck upstairs and started jumping on Grandma Vue's bed. Lee joined in even though he knew that was not allowed in his home. Was Lee being responsible? Explain your answer.

23. Maria remembered to ask permission from her parents before going to play softball. Was Maria being responsible? Explain your answer.

24. Mike had agreed to practice if he could take drum lessons. After the first week, he never practiced. Was Mike being responsible? Explain your answer.

25. When Grandma Vue's friend phoned, Lee wrote down the message so his grandmother would be sure to see it when she got home. Was Lee being responsible? Explain your answer.

26. Ann was supposed to give a note from her parent to her teacher. Ann left it in her desk. Was Ann being responsible? Explain your answer.

ID-DEL
RESPONSIBILITY BADGES

RESPONSIBILITY

BE RESPONSIBLE

BE RESPONSIBLE

BE REALLY RESPONSIBLE

I KNOW HOW TO BE RESPONSIBLE

RESPONSIBILITY

Lesson C

OBJECTIVE:

1. To answer questions about the social skill of being responsible
2. To demonstrate responsible behavior

MATERIALS:

1. *The ABC's of ____* (One transparency saved from Lessons A and B)
2. *Responsibility Rainforest Cards* (See pages 171–172; one set for educator use and one set per student.)
3. *Responsibility Rainforest Questions* (See pages 173–174; one for educator use.)
4. *Responsibility Rainforest* game board (See page 175; one per student.)
5. Light-colored markers or crayons (An assortment for each pair of students)
6. Scissors and paper clips (One of each per student)
7. *Responsibility Rainforest Game Pieces* (See page 176; one per student.)
8. Business-size or larger envelopes (One per student)

PREPARATORY SET:

Display *The ABC's of ____*. Challenge students to complete five of the remaining 16 letters with examples of responsibility described during the Preparatory Set in Lesson A. Save for use in Lesson D.

PLAN:

1. Tell students they are going to be making a game called "Responsibility Rainforest" to play with a partner at school and to take home to play with their families. (As an alternative to using the game board provided, allow students to work in small groups to create one of their own.)

2. Pair students (see *Appendix P*). Tell students you will be reading through the *Responsibility Rainforest Cards* with them so that when they play the game during the next lesson, they will already have some experience with the cards. Read the first statement (card A) from the *Responsibility Rainforest Cards,* omitting the consequence statement at the end (e.g., "Flip the coin again"). Have students put their thumbs up if the statement shows an example of "being responsible" and their thumbs down if the statement shows an example of "not being responsible." Ask the corresponding question from the *Responsibility Rainforest*

Questions and ask students to discuss their answers with their partners. Call on one pair of students to share their answer.

3. Follow the same procedure for cards B, C, and D.

4. Tell students, "Let's take a break from these game cards, so you can make the game board for 'Responsibility Rainforest.' I will be giving each of you a copy of the game board and markers to color it. Be sure to write your name on your game board. I will be watching for people having responsible behavior while you are coloring. What are some examples of things you might say or do to show responsible behavior while you are working?" Encourage the students to share examples.

5. Distribute markers and the *Responsibility Rainforest* game board. Allow five minutes for students to complete their coloring task.

6. Follow the same procedure described in step 2 of this Plan for cards E, F, G, and H.

7. Tell students, "Let's take another break from these game cards so you can continue preparing your game. I will be giving each of you a copy of the game cards, a pair of scissors to cut them apart, and a paper clip to clip the cards together. I will be watching for people being responsible to others while you are cutting."

8. Distribute scissors, paper clips, and the *Responsibility Rainforest Cards*. Allow five minutes for students to complete their cutting task.

9. Follow the same procedure as described in step 2 of this Plan for cards I, J, K, and L.

10. Tell students, "Let's take another break from these game cards so you can continue preparing your game. I will be giving you each a copy of the game pieces to color and cut apart. When you are finished cutting them apart, fold the playing pieces in half on the dotted lines so they form tents. I'll be watching for people being responsible."

11. Distribute the *Responsibility Rainforest Game Pieces*. Allow five minutes for students to cut them apart and fold them.

12. Follow the same procedure as described in step 2 of this Plan for cards M, N, O, and P.

13. Tell students, "Now we are finished going through all of the game cards. I will be giving each of you an envelope. Please write your name on it. Next, put your game cards that are paper clipped together and your folded playing pieces inside the envelope."

14. Distribute one envelope to each student. Collect the envelopes and the game boards after students have finished.

15. Discuss examples of being responsible that have been observed during this lesson. Ask students to share their observations also.

———————— ★★★ ————————

Along with...rights and freedoms come responsibilities.

Martial Arts America

Responsibility Rainforest Cards

A — You separated the recyclables in your family's garbage. Great!

Flip the coin again.

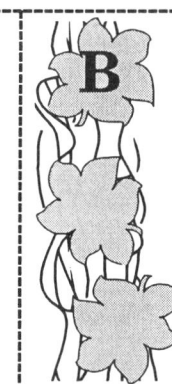

B — You politely asked your mom if you could play at your friend's house. How nice!

Stay on your space.

C — You forgot your backpack at home for the third time this week. Oh no!

Lose 1 turn.

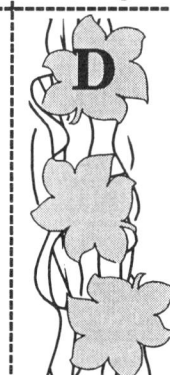

D — You told the teacher the truth about your inappropriate behavior at recess. Super!

Move ahead 1 space.

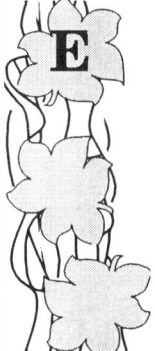

E — You yelled at your dad when he said you could not play outside until your chores are done. Oh my!

Lose 1 turn.

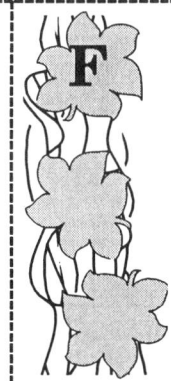

F — You do two things to help other people in your community. Wonderful!

Move ahead 2 spaces.

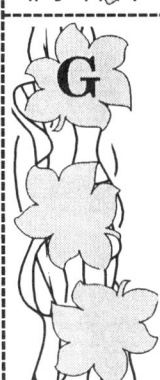

G — You accept the blame for a mistake you've made. Impressive!

Move ahead 2 spaces.

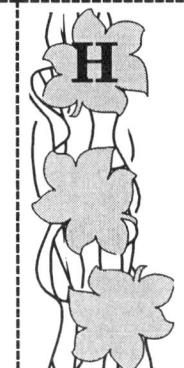

H — You lost your second baseball glove. Not good!

Lose 1 turn.

Social Star

Responsibility Rainforest Cards

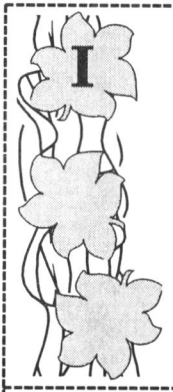

I You forgot to hang up your jacket when you came home. Oops! Stay on your space.	**J** Your dad told you not to snack before dinner. You ate a candy bar anyway. Yuck! Move back 3 spaces.
K You chose to eat an apple instead of candy and cookies. Super! Flip the coin again.	**L** You treat all students respectfully even if they're not your friends. Way to go! Move ahead 3 spaces.
M You always wash your hands after using the restroom. Okay! Flip the coin again.	**N** You threw a rock and dented a mailbox. You never told anyone. Not good! Stay on your space.
O You always stop at stop signs and you use hand signals when riding your bike. Careful citizen! Stay on your space.	**P** You returned your library books to the public library on time. Good citizen! Move ahead 2 spaces.

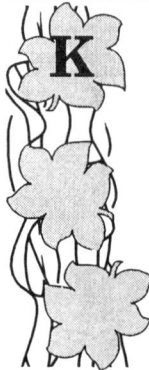

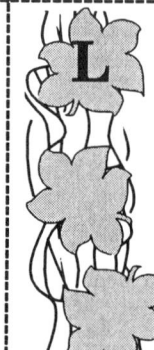

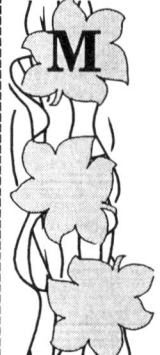

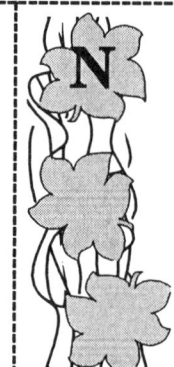

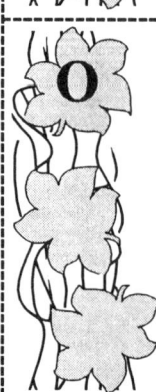

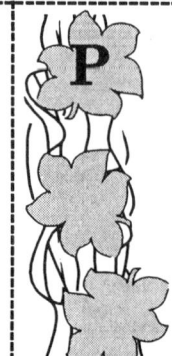

© 1996 Thinking Publications — *Duplication permitted for educational use only.*

Responsibility Rainforest Questions

A. How might you go about recycling garbage?

Why is recycling good for the environment?

B. How might your mom feel because you asked politely?

What words could you say to ask politely?

C. What might be some consequences for forgetting your backpack?

What are two strategies you could use to remember your backpack?

D. What might have happened if you had lied?

Explain how you were a role model for other students.

E. Why would yelling at your dad not be responsible?

How could you show responsibility in this situation?

F. What are two ways to help people in your community?

Why is it important to help people in your community?

G. Why is it sometimes difficult to admit your mistakes?

How do you feel about people who don't admit their mistakes?

H. What are two strategies you could use to keep track of your baseball glove?

How might your parents feel if you keep losing things?

I. What positive thoughts could you have if you start hanging up your jacket?

How does not hanging up your jacket affect the others in your house?

J. Why is it important for you to be responsible for your eating, instead of relying on your parents?

Why is it not responsible to eat candy right before a meal?

K. Why is it responsible to eat fruits?

What other foods are considered responsible to eat?

L. Why do all people deserve respect?

How do you show respect to others even if they are not your friends?

M. How does washing your hands show responsibility to yourself and others?

What are the possible consequences of not washing your hands?

N. What is your conscience? How can it help you to be responsible?

How might you feel if you tell the truth even when you don't have to?

O. What effect does being responsible when riding your bike have on other people?

What are other ways of showing responsibility on your bike?

P. What strategies might you use to remember to return books on time?

How else might you show responsibility to library books?

Being Responsible

Name: _____

Responsibility Rainforest

- Give an example of responsibility.
- Draw a card.
- Give an example of responsibility.
- Draw a card.
- Draw a card.
- Give an example of responsibility.
- Give an example of responsibility.
- Draw a card.
- Give an example of responsibility.
- Draw a card.
- Give an example of responsibility.
- Draw a card.
- Give an example of responsibility.

CARDS

START

Responsibility Rainforest

FINISH

© 1996 Thinking Publications 175 *Duplication permitted for educational use only.*

Social Star

Responsibility Rainforest Game Pieces

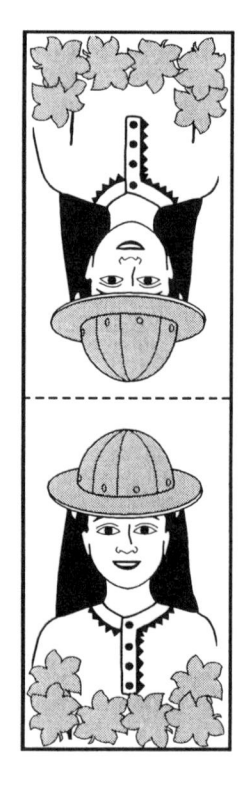

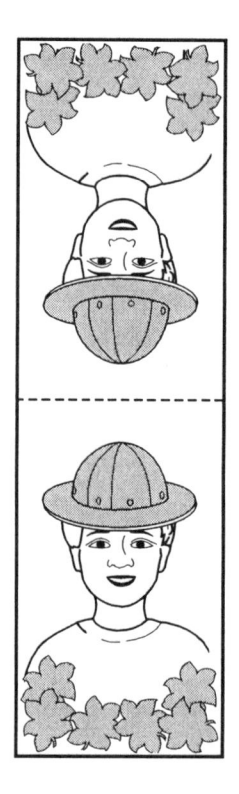

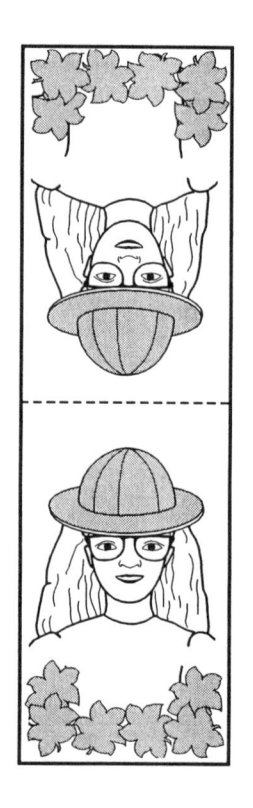

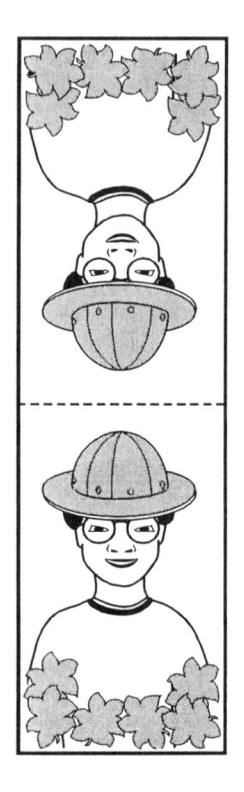

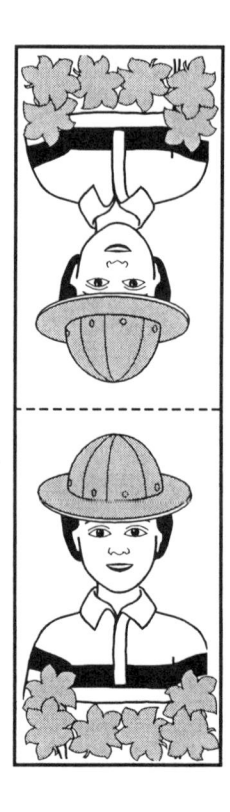

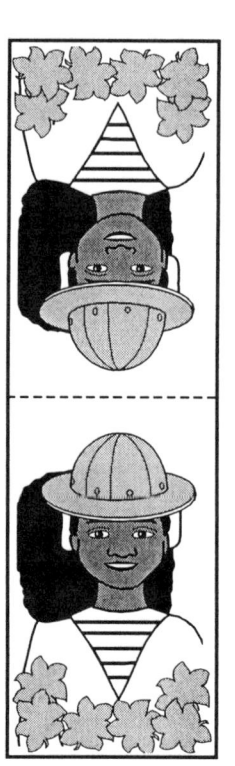

176 © 1996 Thinking Publications — Duplication permitted for educational use only.

Being Responsible

Lesson D

OBJECTIVE:

To play a game about being responsible

MATERIALS:

1. *The ABC's of ___* (One transparency saved from Lessons A, B, and C)
2. *Responsibility Rainforest* game boards (From previous lesson)
3. Envelopes from previous lesson filled with game cards and game pieces
4. *Responsibility Rainforest Game Rules* (See page 178; one per student.)
5. *Picture Puzzle* (See *Appendix P*; one per pair of students.)
6. Coins (One per pair of students)

PREPARATORY SET:

Display *The ABC's of ___*. Challenge students to complete five of the remaining 11 letters with examples of responsibility described during the Preparatory Set in Lesson A. Save for use in Lesson X.

PLAN:

1. Distribute *Responsibility Rainforest Game Rules* and, as a class, read and discuss them. Ask students to tell things they can do to be a friend while playing the game with a partner (e.g., taking turns, following the game rules, showing appropriate reactions to winning and losing, making positive comments to each other).

2. Pair students using the *Picture Puzzle* activity (see *Appendix P*).

3. Ask partners to determine which person's game board and game pieces will be used to play the game. (There may be time for the game to be played twice and in that case both games could be used.)

4. Have students play the game as directed with their partners and when they finish, have them fold their game boards and place them, as well as the game pieces and game cards, in their envelopes.

5. Collect the students' games and save them to be redistributed to students to take home with the Home-A-Gram during Lesson Z.

★★★

You can't escape the responsibility of tomorrow by evading it today.

Abraham Lincoln

Responsibility Rainforest Game Rules

1. Place the game cards on the space indicated on the game board. Choose one of the Socialville characters as your game piece and place it on the start space.

2. Get a coin and place it near the game board.

3. The player who is youngest goes first.

4. Player #1 flips the coin. *Heads* means to move 1 space on the game board and *tails* means to move 2 spaces (i.e., players should move from one leaf to the next). If "Give an example of responsibility" is written on the space, the player tells any example of being responsible. Then play advances to the next player. If the player lands on a "Draw a card" space, the player reads the top card aloud and follows the direction given on the card (e.g., "Move ahead 1 space," "Lose 1 turn," etc.). Reshuffle the game cards, if needed.

5. To enter the Responsibility Rainforest, a player must flip the exact number needed (e.g., if a player has 1 space to go, a *heads* must be flipped on the coin).

6. The first player to get to Responsibility Rainforest is the winner.

Lessons X, Y, and Z

Due to similarities in format, the final three lesson plans for each unit in *Social Star* are provided in *Appendix A*. Substitute the words "being responsible" whenever a "_____" appears in the lesson plans. Information specific to this unit follows.

LESSON X PREPARATORY SET:

Display *The ABC's of ____*. Challenge students to complete the remaining letters with examples of responsibility described during the Preparatory Set in Lesson A.

LESSON Y PREPARATORY SET:

Darken the room, if you prefer, and ask the students to visualize themselves correctly using this social skill by reading the following script:

Let's take a few moments.... Make sure you are in a comfortable position.... Close your eyes if you feel like it.... On the count of three, take a very slow, deep breath. Remember to breathe in quietly through your nose. One...two... three.... Breathe in deeply.... Now breathe out slowly.... Remember to breathe out quietly through your mouth. Let your entire body relax.... Now imagine yourself being responsible and telling your parents the truth about something inappropriate you have done .... You know you have a responsibility to be honest. Think about how proud you feel for being a responsible person.

LESSON Z PLOT SITUATION:

You agreed to care for your friend's pet cat while she or he is out of town for the weekend. Now you've been invited to go camping with your aunt on the same weekend you promised to "cat-sit."

LESSON Z ROADBLOCK EXAMPLES:

- Forgetting about your responsibilities
- Worrying about the trouble you will get into for being honest
- Feeling you're too busy to be responsible
- Thinking you might get teased for being a goody-goody or a tattletale

Being Responsible T-Chart

LOOKS LIKE...

using appropriate body talk
- looking at the person you are talking to

being where you said you would be

doing your chores

helping to keep your environment clean and safe

SOUNDS LIKE...

a polite tone of voice

an appropriate volume

telling the truth

expressing your opinion

sticking up for a friend

using self-talk
- "It's important to think about other people."
- "How can I be responsible in this situation?"

Being Responsible

SHOW TIME

HOME

Pretend you accidentally dialed a long distance wrong number. You did not realize your parents would be billed for the call. When the phone bill arrives, your parents are puzzled about the charge. Tell what you could say or do to be responsible.

SCHOOL

Pretend you forgot to bring a prop that you promised to bring for your group's puppet show. Tell what you could say or do to be responsible.

COMMUNITY

The kids on your team often throw aluminum soda cans in the park on the way home from practice. Tell what you could say or do to be responsible.

RESPONSIBILITY RULES!

Social Star | **HOME-A-GRAM**

Dear Family,

At school, we have been talking about the skill called

BEING RESPONSIBLE

I learned that *being responsible* means choosing to do what is right.

When I show responsibility, people are likely to view me as trustworthy and dependable. I can feel proud when I make choices that will help me or will help the world be a better place.

I have written down one way I can be responsible in each of the following places:

At home: _____

_____

At school: _____

_____

In my community: _____

_____

I am bringing home a game about responsibility for us to play. After I respond to the situations on the game cards while we play the game, please sign my "Being Responsible" badge so I can return it to school and become a SOCIAL SUPER STAR this week.

From: _____

Taking Charge of Anger

Social Star

UNIT GOAL:

To demonstrate comprehension and use of strategies for taking charge of anger

EDUCATOR INFORMATION:

1. The unit titled *Taking Charge of Feelings* should be taught before teaching this unit.

2. This unit emphasizes the importance of recognizing anger as a legitimate feeling for all people to experience and express. It teaches students to take charge of their anger. When angry, students are encouraged to "stop and think" to avoid expressing their anger in an inappropriate manner. The unit is built on the premise that people can use their anger constructively. It is assumed that additional activities and strategies will be used to reinforce students' continued development of anger management.

3. Each student starts a "collection" of strategies (called *anger shrinkers*) for reducing anger. Thirty-nine strategies are included in this unit. Each one is described and illustrated on a separate page. The educator can choose to teach any or all of the strategies to students. A blank *Anger Shrinker* page is also included so students can create their own anger shrinker if they wish.

4. Some of the anger shrinkers are adapted from neurolinguistic programming (NLP) techniques (e.g., "Turn Off" Your Angry Thoughts, Make Funny People Pictures, Think of a Role Model, Use Positive Self-Talk—Part 2). For additional information about NLP, contact:

   NLP Comprehensive
   4895 Riverbend Rd., Suite A
   Boulder, CO 80301
   (800) 233-1657

5. Much attention has been given to the physical/medical results of anger. According to Luhn (1992), it has been established that if anger is suppressed or handled incorrectly, it can cause cardiovascular disease, headaches, depression, relationship abuse, poor self-esteem, addictions, and other diseases. Luhn categorizes anger as "good" and "bad" and describes results of each.

   - "Good" anger can:
   Energize you.
   Help you communicate when you are upset.
   Resolve your hidden conflicts.

Give you new thoughts.
Alert you to threats.
Provide you with information.

- "Bad" anger can:
Disrupt your life.
Control your thinking.
Ruin your relationships.
Cause pain.
Cause health problems.
Cause other emotional problems.
Leave a negative impression.

6. Anger may be a confusing feeling, particularly for children. It's important for adults to recognize the variety of feelings and behaviors that may be rooted in anger. Roger and McWilliams (1991) list the negative emotions often associated with anger:

   hostility
   resentment
   guilt (anger at oneself)
   rage
   seething
   depression
   hurt (you're usually upset with someone else, yourself, or both)

7. Educators may wish to share the following folktale with students, if it is appropriate to their level of understanding (it provides a strong rationale for viewing anger as a legitimate feeling):

   On a train, a Swami sat beside a man who asked him if he had attained self-mastery as the name "Swami" suggests.

   "I have," said the Swami.

   "And do you have control of your anger?"

   "I do."

   "Do you mean to say you have mastered anger?"

   "I have."

   "Do you mean you can control your anger?"

   "Yes."

   "And you don't feel anger?"

   "I do not."

"Is this the truth, Swami?" the man asked.

The Swami said, "It is."

The man was silent for a while then asked again, "Do you really feel that you can control your anger?"

As I told you, I can," the Swami answered.

"Then are you saying you never feel anger, ever?"

"Why are you going on and on? What do you want?" the Swami shouted. "Aren't you listening? When I have told you…"

"Oh, Swami, you are angry. You have not mastered anger."

"Oh, but I have," the Swami replied. "Haven't you heard the story of the abused snake? Let me tell it to you.

A cobra lived on a path that went to the village. The cobra would bite people on their way to worship at the temple. As the biting increased, people became fearful, and many refused to go to the temple. The Swami, who was the master at the temple, recognized the problem and took it upon himself to solve it. He went to the path where the snake lived. He used a mantra to call the snake to him and bring it into submission. The Swami reminded the snake that it was wrong to bite the people who walked along the path on their way to worship. The Swami made the snake promise he would never bite people again. Soon a passerby walked the path. The snake made no move to bite him. It became known that the snake had become passive and people grew unafraid. It was not long before the village children were dragging the poor snake along behind them as they ran laughing and playing. When the Swami passed the path again, he called to the snake to see if he had kept his promise. The snake, looking miserable, humbly slithered to the Swami who cried, 'You are bleeding. Tell me how this happened.' The snake was near tears and cried out that he had been abused ever since he made his promise to the Swami.

'I told you not to bite,' said the Swami, 'but I did not tell you not to hiss.'"

8. Tavris (1982) offers a perspective about anger that varies from popular views. She examines the current "anger business" in which a variety of therapies promote venting one's anger, based on the assumption that it is unhealthy to bottle it up. This "ventilationist" view has become a widespread philosophy in which people are encouraged to "let their feelings out." Tavris refutes this viewpoint by stating that sometimes the best thing to do with anger is nothing at all. She maintains that 50 percent of the time it will turn out to be unimportant and soon forgotten. The other half of the time, keeping quiet gives you time to calm

down and decide whether the matter is worth pursuing or not. Tavris advises that expressing anger while you feel angry almost always causes anger to increase.

9. The U.S. Justice Department (1994) reports that young people ages 12–17 are the most common victims of violent crime in America, being raped, robbed, or assaulted at five times the rate for adults 35 and older. This statistic should cause us to examine how we can better teach preventative measures, including methods for dealing with the anger that victims typically experience and the anger that causes the perpetrator to commit the crime.

RELATED ACTIVITIES:

1. Have students contact local counselors/psychologists to gather statistics about the number of clients they see who have trouble managing anger. Ask what strategies the therapists recommend.

2. Have students write an article for the school newspaper or a letter to a local newspaper describing what they've learned about taking charge of their anger.

3. Invite a speaker from a domestic violence center to talk with students about some of the problems that occur when people use their anger to control and intimidate others.

4. Have students meet with the mayor or another city representative to brainstorm ways their class can send out a message to the community about taking charge of anger.

5. Have students create nicknames for each classmate. The nicknames should have calm, peaceful, connotations (e.g., "Nice Nadia," "Polite Percy," "Peaceful Parker," "Likable Lisha," "Calm Carmen").

6. As a science/health extension, review the physiological responses that occur as a person's anger builds (e.g., muscles tighten, blood glucose is increased, heart rate increases, blood pressure increases, breathing becomes shallow and more difficult, body sweat increases, adrenaline flows faster).

7. Invite students to keep an anger diary noting times of anger and strategies used to manage it.

8. Invite adults from different cultures to talk to the students about how their cultures' conventions for taking charge of anger compare with the strategies presented in this unit. For example, Tavris (1982) reports the Japanese are expected to smile and be polite even when feeling very angry inside.

It is important for educators to provide opportunities for students to work in groups, so they can experience social skills in contexts where social communication is needed. Therefore, educators are encouraged to have students complete the Related Activities in small groups whenever possible. Educators trained in cooperative learning could incorporate the five components (see pages 33–34) into the group activity. An excellent resource for teaching students cooperative skills and building a sense of community is *Tribes: A Process for Social Development and Cooperative Learning* (1987) by Jeanne Gibbs.

RELATED LITERATURE:

Dinah's Mad Bad Wishes (1989) by Barbara Joosse, Ill. by Emily Arnold McCully, Harper. (32 pages)

Don't Make Me Smile (1981) by Barbara Park, Knopf. (114 pages)

Rollo and Juliet, Forever! (1981) by Marjorie Sharmat, Ill. by Marylinn Hafner, Doubleday. (32 pages)

Carnival and Kopeck and More About Hannah (1979) by Minday Warshaw Skolsky, Harper. (74 pages)

SOCIAL SKILLS ALL DAY LONG:

Look for opportunities to teach social skills throughout the day (incidental teaching). Four ways to reinforce appropriate social skills and an example of each follow:

Encouragement

You used one of the anger-shrinking strategies when you were frustrated. I saw you close your eyes and take a slow, deep breath.

Personal Example

It's been helpful for me to talk about these anger-shrinking strategies with this class. The other night I was angry with my daughter. I decided to use the strategy of "waiting a while" before I talked with her. After waiting, I realized that what I was angry about wasn't a big deal. I'm glad I waited so I was able to talk calmly about the problem with her.

Prompting

If you start to feel angry at someone this week, remember to think about the skill steps for taking charge of anger.

Corrective Feedback (must be positive, private, specific, and nonthreatening)

Right now you are yelling and making a threatening face at Tom. Remember the skill steps for taking charge of anger. Stop and think! You are in charge of your feelings. Decide on a way to deal with the anger. What are some other possible strategies you might use?

———————————★★★———————————

Keep cool; anger is not an argument.

Daniel Webster

Lesson A

OBJECTIVES:

1. To state the meaning of *taking charge of anger* and tell why it's important

2. To listen to the self-talk associated with appropriate use of the skill

MATERIALS:

1. Two small balloons

2. A bouncing ball

3. *Taking Charge of Anger* (See page 195; one per student and one transparency.)

4. *Thought Bubble* (See *Appendix O;* one for educator use.)

5. *Checking Myself* (See *Appendix I;* one per student and one transparency.)

PREPARATORY SET:

Hold up an uninflated balloon and tell the following story:

One day, Brugie Bannister was outside. An older boy drove by and yelled something mean to Brugie. Brugie felt angry (blow up the balloon a little). *Brugie kept thinking about the older boy and got even more angry* (blow up the balloon more). *She went in the house. Her brother, Brussel Bannister said he had accidentally lost her best baseball. Now Brugie really felt angry* (blow up the balloon more). *Brugie started bellowing at her brother, called him a beast, and got even angrier* (blow up the balloon more). *Brugie's father, Brumpy Bannister told Brugie to be quiet. Brugie told herself, "He never understands," and guess what...she got angrier* (blow up the balloon more). *Mrs. Bannister reminded Brugie that she needed to make her bed before she went to play baseball. Brugie thought about how she hated to make her bed* (blow up the balloon more). Ask students, *What is going to happen if Brugie continues to let her anger grow?* (Continue to add situations to the story until the balloon pops.)

Discuss how Brugie let her anger build up. She didn't do anything to help herself take charge of her anger.

PLAN:

1. Blow up another balloon. (Do not let it pop.) Slowly let the air out of the balloon. Ask the students what is happening to the balloon. (It's "shrinking.") Tell students that they will be learning some strategies they can use to help "shrink" their anger so that it doesn't get out of control and they can take charge of it.

Discuss other items that shrink (e.g., the witch on the *Wizard of Oz*, the children from the movie *Honey, I Shrunk the Kids,* a wool sweater in a dryer, a bar of soap as it gets used up).

2. Ask students to form a large circle. Tell students they will be bouncing a ball to one another. Explain that the first person to bounce the ball should tell about a time they felt angry (a current or past situation) before passing the ball to someone in the circle. The next person who has the ball should continue in the same manner. The game should proceed until all students have had an opportunity to bounce the ball. Give students the opportunity to "pass" if they want to. Tell students, "Anger is something we all experience. It's OK to feel angry. We'll be learning about many responsible ways to express anger."

3. Distribute and display *Taking Charge of Anger*. Discuss the definition of *taking charge of anger*. Explain the skill steps for taking charge of anger and the symbols next to them. Remind students that the symbols are there to help them visualize and remember the skill steps. Refer students to the body-talk symbol in the left-hand margin. Remind students that appropriate body talk is important when taking charge of anger. Discuss the reasons for taking charge of anger.

4. Model use of the skill steps for taking charge of anger while thinking aloud. A scripted example follows:

Introduction

I am going to pretend to be someone your age who is feeling angry. I will show you how I take charge of anger and tell you the thoughts I'm having. When I hold up this Thought Bubble, *you'll know the words I'm saying are actually what I'm thinking.*

Actual Model

While holding up the *Thought Bubble* say, *OK, I'm starting to feel really angry inside. I feel like I'm going to blow! I need to remind myself to stop. I am in charge of my anger.... What can I do to handle my anger? Right now, I can walk away.* Put the *Thought Bubble* down and walk away.

5. Read the story at the bottom of *Taking Charge of Anger*.

6. Distribute and display the discussion guideline sheet called *Checking Myself*. Ask students to complete the statement by the top megaphone with the words "listen to others" or use another classroom discussion goal more appropriate for your group (see pages 25–26). Tell students that you will be leading a discussion about the story they just heard. Explain that when a student is answering a question or making a comment during the discussion, it's important for everyone

to be polite by listening to that student. Tell students that they can show they are interested by giving eye contact, nodding their heads, asking relevant questions, or making relevant comments. Instruct them to draw a line between two dots on the star each time a person talks and they are listening.

7. Model use of the *Checking Myself* sheet while thinking aloud. A scripted example follows:

Introduction

I am going to pretend to be one of you completing this sheet during the discussion we will be having. I will tell you the thoughts I'm having while completing this sheet. When I hold up this Thought Bubble, *you'll know the words I'm saying are actually what I'm thinking.*

Actual Model

While holding up the *Thought Bubble* say, *Jeremy is telling one of his answers. I'll be polite by looking at him when he's talking and smiling at him so he knows I'm listening. I'll draw a line between two dots on the star because I listened to Jeremy.* Put the *Thought Bubble* down and draw a line between two dots on the transparency.

8. Proceed with the discussion by asking the following questions (the story may need to be reread first):

- How did Victor respond when Maria asked him to wait a few minutes for the newspaper?

- Why did Victor get angry?

- Was it OK for Victor to feel angry? (Yes, all feelings are OK, but not all actions are.)

- Would most people have felt angry in Victor's situation?

- Would you have been angry if you were Victor?

- How did Victor express his anger?

- Did he express his anger responsibly?

- Why did Maria get angry?

- Was it OK for Maria to feel angry? (Yes, all feelings are OK, but not all actions are.)

- Would you feel angry if you were in Maria's situation?

- Did Maria follow the skill steps for taking charge of anger? Why or why not?

- What might have happened if Maria had hit Victor back?
- Are there times when your anger can hurt you? Are there times when your anger can help you? (E.g., feeling angry when you see someone getting teased in a mean way may cause you to offer support to the person.)

9. After the discussion, have students complete the bottom of *Checking Myself.*

10. Process use of the sheet by asking the following question or another more appropriate for your group:

    - Why do you think it's important to listen to others while they are talking?

    Process further by asking the students who volunteered to speak during the discussion to share their answers to the following questions:

    - You shared one of your answers during the discussion. How could you tell that people were listening to you? How did you feel knowing others were listening?

11. Say to students, "Earlier we talked about everyone having angry feelings. We said that it's OK to feel angry, but that it's important to deal with anger in a responsible way. Some people get in trouble because they say or do inappropriate things when they are angry, just like Victor. They don't worry about how they hurt other people. Tomorrow we will learn how responsible people deal with their anger. You will learn many different strategies you can use to 'shrink' your own anger."

12. Pair students (see *Appendix P*). Ask student pairs to take turns telling each other the meaning of *taking charge of anger* and why it's important to use the skill. Students could be reminded that the information they are to share is printed on *Taking Charge of Anger.*

    As an option to add structure to this activity, ask partners to come to an agreement about which person will be called "A" and which person will be called "B." After students have made their decisions, ask "A" to tell "B" the definition of *taking charge of anger.* Next, ask "B" to tell "A" the definition. Ask students to use the same procedure to tell each other the reasons for taking charge of anger.

———————★★★———————

People who fly into a rage always make a bad landing.

Will Rogers

Name _____

Taking Charge of Anger

MEANING OF TAKING CHARGE OF ANGER:

Knowing you have control over how to deal with your anger

SKILL STEPS:

1. Stop! Remind myself that I'm in charge of my anger

2. Ask myself: What can I do to deal with my anger?

REASONS FOR USING THIS SKILL:

Knowing that you are in charge of your anger may help you get along better with others. You can avoid getting into trouble when you express your anger responsibly. You can feel proud when you stay in control.

DIRECTIONS: Listen to the story below. Look at the pictures of Maria and Victor while you listen.

Maria was reading the sports section from the newspaper. Victor came in and said, "I want to see that paper! Give it to me!" Maria said, "You can have it in a few minutes. I'm almost done." Victor slugged Maria in the arm, took the paper, and left the room. Maria felt so angry she wanted to scream. She was just about ready to run after Victor and pound him back when she stopped. She said to herself, "I'm in charge of my anger. I'm not going to do something stupid." Later during supper, Maria said in a calm but firm way, "You've got a problem, Victor! You're going to lose friends if you hit when you are angry."

Social Star

Lesson B

EDUCATOR INFORMATION:

During this lesson, students are first introduced to the concept of a collection (e.g., a collection of stamps, coins, pins, dolls, baseball cards). Next students are provided with a means of starting a collection of "anger shrinkers" (strategies used to reduce anger). There are 39 anger shrinkers and a blank anger shrinker page supplied in this lesson. The educator should decide which of the anger shrinkers to present to the students and the manner in which those chosen strategies will be introduced. Some examples include:

- introducing one a day;
- introducing one a week and focusing on it the entire week; or
- introducing a few at each grade level (e.g., 10 strategies in first grade, 10 in second grade) and making it a schoolwide activity.

Students who have great difficulty with anger control may have more success if fewer strategies are presented and reinforced over long periods of time.

The educator could also create an attractive and motivating way for students to "store" the anger shrinker pages in their collections.

OBJECTIVE:

To learn and practice several strategies for reducing anger

MATERIALS:

1. A collection that can be shown to students (e.g., coins, stamps, sports cards)
2. *Taking Charge of Anger* classroom poster (See page 13.)
3. *Numbered Stones* (See *Appendix P*; one set per pair of students.)
4. Preselected *Anger Shrinker* pages (See pages 198–237; one set per student, printed single-sided.)

PREPARATORY SET:

Display and explain your collection. Ask if any of the students have collections at home. (Make arrangements for interested students to bring in their collections and share them with the group.)

PLAN:

1. Review the definition and skill steps for *taking charge of anger* by referring the class to the *Taking Charge of Anger* classroom poster.

2. Pair students using *Numbered Stones* (see *Appendix P*). Ask students to take turns telling each other the skill steps for taking charge of anger. Follow the procedure described in step 12 of Lesson A. Next ask students to work with their partners to think of a situation when it's important to take charge of anger. Tell students that one or more pairs will be called on to share their situations.

3. Remind students that it's OK to feel angry as long as we deal with anger in a responsible manner. It's sometimes difficult to think clearly when angry. That's why it's a good idea to learn and practice as many ways of reducing anger as possible. Then when we are angry, we'll have several strategies that we can pick from.

4. Tell students they will be starting their own collection of strategies for reducing anger called *anger shrinkers*. Explain how the students can accumulate and organize their collection (or elicit ideas from students).

5. Begin with the *Anger Shrinkers* you feel are appropriate for your students, one at a time. Consider the following options when presenting each *Anger Shrinker*:

   - First model and then ask students to practice the anger strategy.

   - Look for ways that students can personalize their *Anger Shrinker* pages (e.g., ask them to actually practice the strategies or give more examples on the backs of the pages).

   - Ask students to identify situations when a certain anger shrinker may work well or may not work well and explain why.

   - After reading the thought bubble at the bottom of the *Anger Shrinker* page, ask students to share other thoughts they may have while using the strategy.

   - Have students relate the anger strategy to personal situations, then write the situations on the back side of the *Anger Shrinker* page.

   - Send (or have students take a copy of) the *Anger Shrinker* home for parents' signatures.

6. A blank *Anger Shrinker* page is provided on page 237, if students wish to develop their own strategy.

---★★★---

Anger is only one letter short of danger.

Anonymous

Social Star

KNOW YOUR OUTSIDE TRIGGERS

Anger Shrinker #

Outside triggers are things that happen outside your body that "spark" your anger. Some examples include:

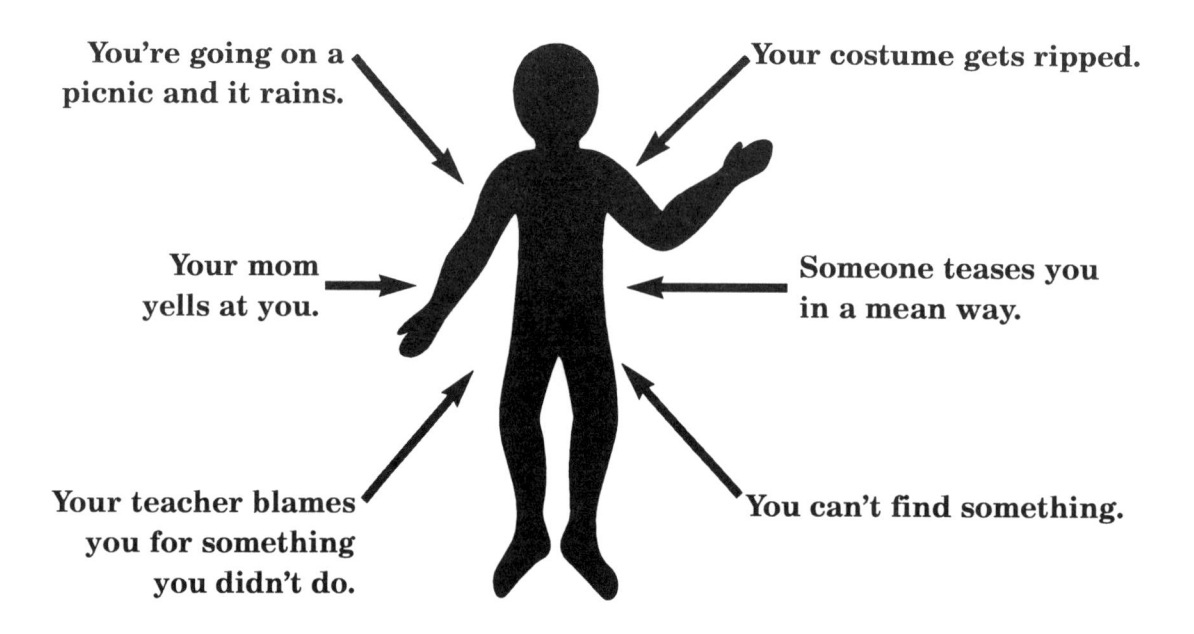

- You're going on a picnic and it rains.
- Your costume gets ripped.
- Your mom yells at you.
- Someone teases you in a mean way.
- Your teacher blames you for something you didn't do.
- You can't find something.

Your outside triggers might be different from someone else's. If you know your outside triggers, you can plan ways to stay in control.

> Oh, oh! He's teasing me. That's one of my outside triggers. I need to stay calm!

© 1996 Thinking Publications — Duplication permitted for educational use only.

Taking Charge of Anger

Anger Shrinker #

CHANGE YOUR INSIDE TRIGGERS

Inside triggers are things you say to yourself that "spark" your anger. Some examples include:

- Things never go right!
- Why did I do that? I'm so stupid!
- I know he's saying mean things about me!
- I feel like kicking him!
- I hate her—she never plays fair!

Your inside triggers might be different from someone else's. If you find yourself using inside triggers, you can choose to change your thoughts to help shrink your anger.

Thinking these things is making me more angry. I'm going to change my thoughts.

© 1996 Thinking Publications — Duplication permitted for educational use only.

Social Star

KNOW YOUR BODY SIGNALS

Anger Shrinker #

When you start to feel angry, changes start to happen to your body. Some examples include:

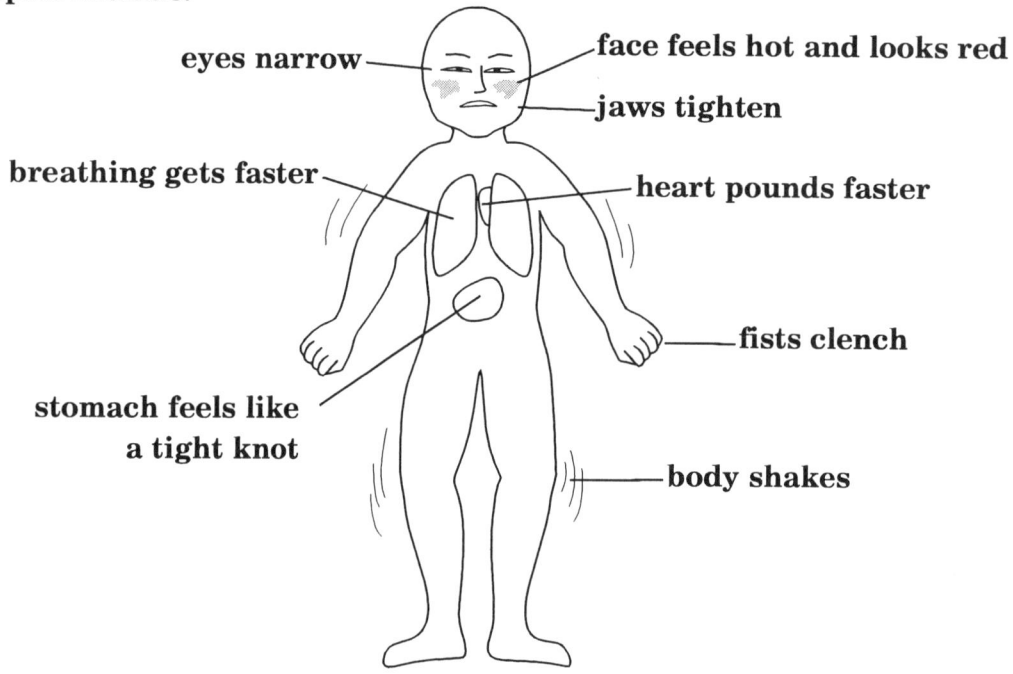

- eyes narrow
- face feels hot and looks red
- jaws tighten
- breathing gets faster
- heart pounds faster
- fists clench
- stomach feels like a tight knot
- body shakes

These changes can be important signals that you are angry. If you know the signals, you can help yourself stay in control!

I know I'm angry because my body is...

© 1996 Thinking Publications   *Duplication permitted for educational use only.*

USE POSITIVE SELF-TALK—Part 1

Anger Shrinker #

When you use positive self-talk, you tell yourself helpful things to stay calm. Some examples include:

- Be calm!
- I'm going to stop and think!
- I can stay in control!
- I can take charge of my anger.
- I'll be calm and think about my choices.

When you use positive self-talk, it keeps away inside triggers that make you more angry. Positive self-talk can help you take charge of your anger.

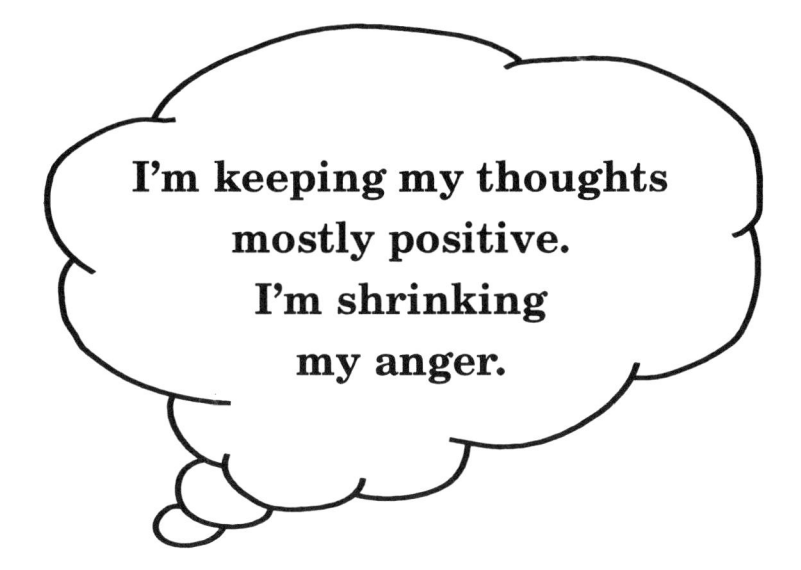

> I'm keeping my thoughts mostly positive. I'm shrinking my anger.

Taking Charge of Anger

© 1996 Thinking Publications — Duplication permitted for educational use only.

Social Star

Anger Shrinker #

TAKE DEEP BREATHS

To take deep breaths, breathe in quietly and deeply through your nose. Then, breathe out slowly and quietly through your mouth (pretend you are blowing on a hot spoonful of soup). You can even count to yourself as you breathe in and out. For example:

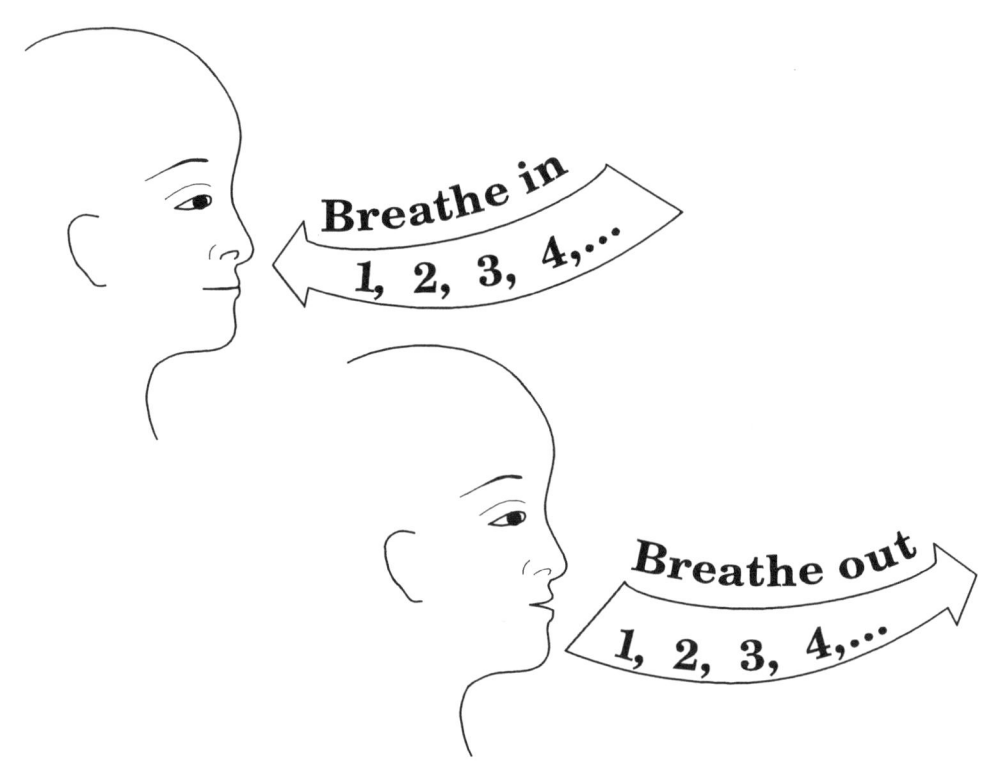

Breathe in 1, 2, 3, 4,...

Breathe out 1, 2, 3, 4,...

When you are angry, you breathe faster. By slowing your breathing down, you can shrink your anger.

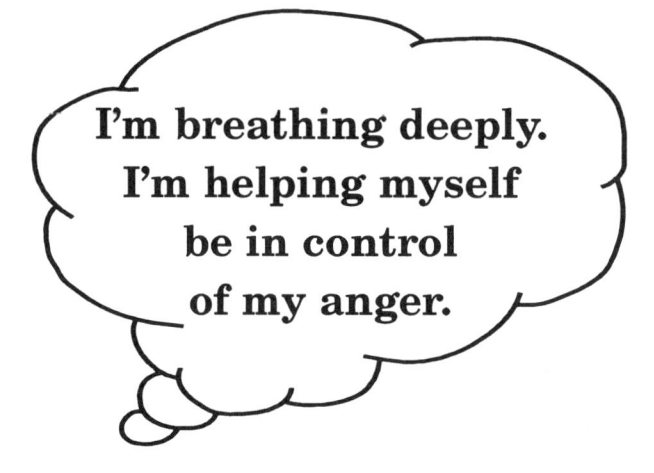

I'm breathing deeply. I'm helping myself be in control of my anger.

© 1996 Thinking Publications — Duplication permitted for educational use only.

Taking Charge of Anger

Anger Shrinker #

THINK OF THE CONSEQUENCES

When you get too angry, you may say or do something that can hurt others, hurt yourself, or hurt property.

When you think of the consequences, you are considering what might happen if you lose control.

If I lose control...

- **and say to my sister, "I hate you!", then** ➡
- **and hit her, then** ➡
- **and tear up this book, then** ➡

When you get angry, think of the consequences before you say or do something that might cause trouble.

I'm not going to _____, because if I do I'll feel bad later.

© 1996 Thinking Publications   Duplication permitted for educational use only.

Social Star

THINK OF SOMETHING FUNNY

Anger Shrinker #

Find something really funny that makes you laugh or gives you the giggles whenever you think about it. It might be a joke or a time when you couldn't stop laughing.

> Ha Ha Ha!
>
> That's so funny!
>
> Ha Ha Ha!

If you are angry and you want to feel better, you can think about your funny situation.

> I'm tired of feeling so angry! I'm going to think about that really funny time when...

© 1996 Thinking Publications — *Duplication permitted for educational use only.*

Taking Charge of Anger

"TURN OFF" YOUR ANGRY THOUGHTS

Anger Shrinker #

Sometimes you keep thinking about things over and over again in your mind and you get even angrier. You can pretend your angry brain voice is like a radio that keeps broadcasting how angry you are.

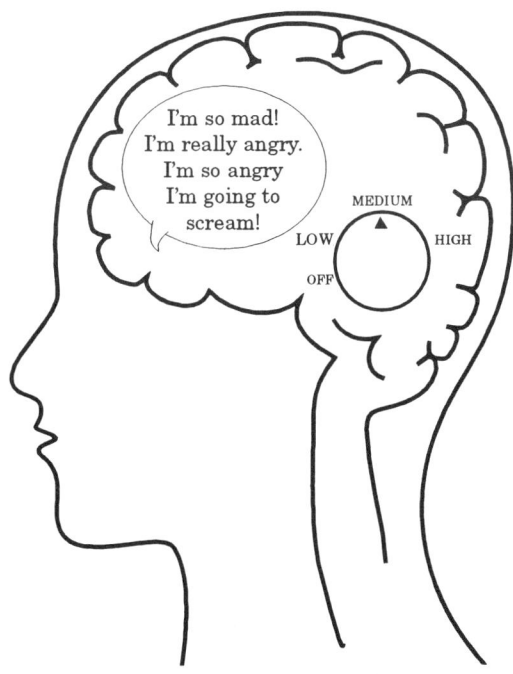

I'm so mad! I'm really angry. I'm so angry I'm going to scream!

OFF LOW MEDIUM HIGH

If you want, you can pretend to "turn off" your angry brain voice. Or you can pretend to "turn down its volume," or "change its channel."

I'm in control of my thoughts! I can turn off my angry brain voice!

click OFF

© 1996 Thinking Publications 205 Duplication permitted for educational use only.

Social Star

LEAVE FOR A WHILE

Anger Shrinker #

Sometimes when you are really angry, it's a good idea to leave for a while. For example:

- If you are angry with your brother and you think you might hit him, go into another room for a while.

- If you get really angry while playing with your friend, maybe it's best to go to your house for a while.

I'm too angry! I need to leave for a while!

When you leave, you give yourself time to calm down before you hurt yourself, hurt others, or hurt property. You may still need to discuss things later, but you'll be more calm.

I'm really angry! I'd better get out of here and calm down.

© 1996 Thinking Publications   *Duplication permitted for educational use only.*

Taking Charge of Anger

MAKE A MIND MOVIE

Anger Shrinker #

When you make a "mind movie," you think of a fun and happy situation, for example, swimming at the beach or riding your bike.

Ready...
Action...
Roll 'em!

If you are angry, you can make a mind movie to stay calm. Pretend you are really in your fun mind movie situation and your anger will shrink.

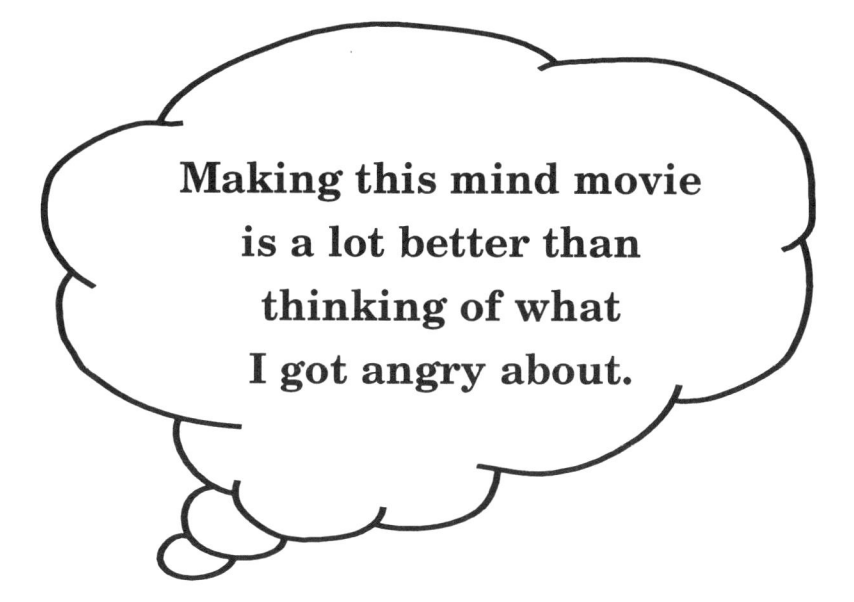

Making this mind movie is a lot better than thinking of what I got angry about.

© 1996 Thinking Publications — Duplication permitted for educational use only.

Social Star

Anger Shrinker #

TALK TO A FRIEND

Talking about your feelings can help you feel better. Next time you feel angry, try talking to a friend. Remember, an adult can be a friend too (e.g., teacher, parent, relative, neighbor).

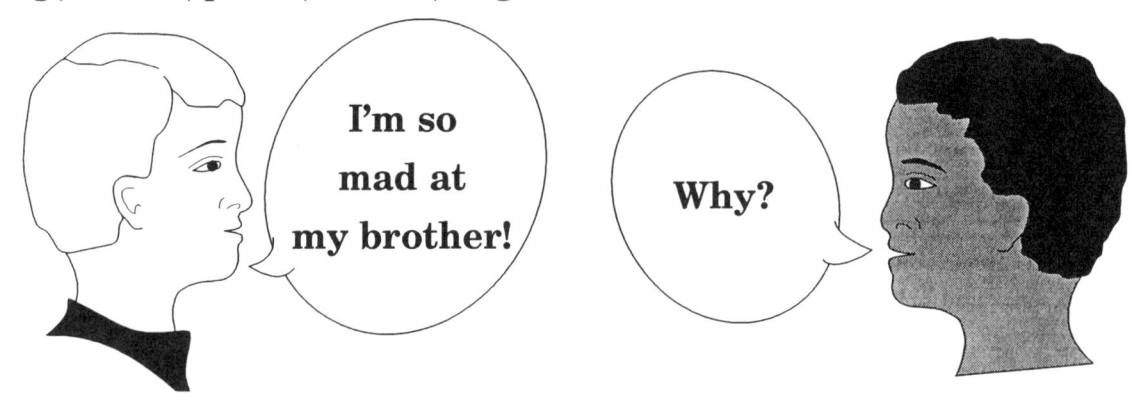

I'm so mad at my brother!

Why?

Choose a friend who will not say things to make you even angrier.

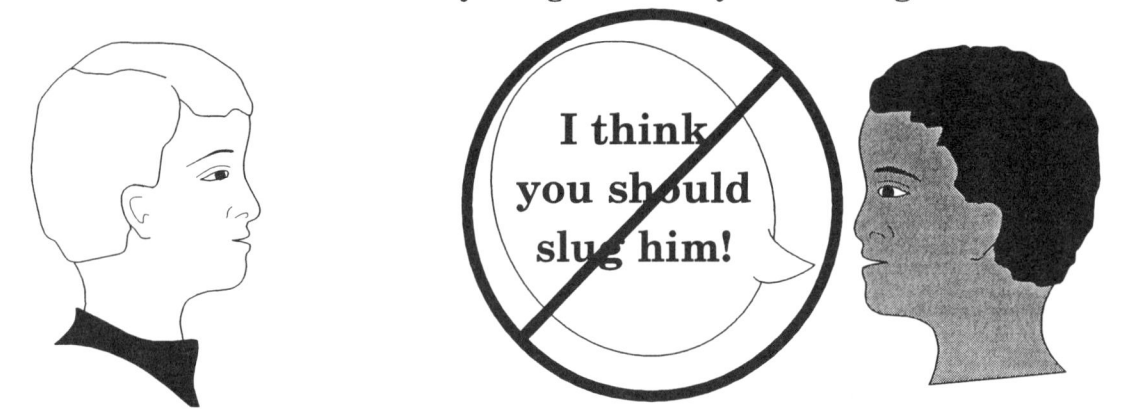

I think you should slug him!

If one of your friends wants to talk about angry feelings with you someday, be a good listener!

I want to talk to someone. I know I'll feel better if I talk to...

© 1996 Thinking Publications *Duplication permitted for educational use only.*

Taking Charge of Anger

Anger Shrinker #

LISTEN TO FUN MUSIC

When you feel angry, turn on some fun, cheerful music.

Have you ever noticed that when you hear a fun song, your body starts moving along with the beat of the music? The right kind of music can really shrink your anger and help you feel happier.

I love this song! I'll get a copy so I can listen to it whenever I want.

© 1996 Thinking Publications   Duplication permitted for educational use only.

Social Star

Anger Shrinker #

HIT SOMETHING SOFT

If you're so angry that you feel like hitting, choose something soft to punch.

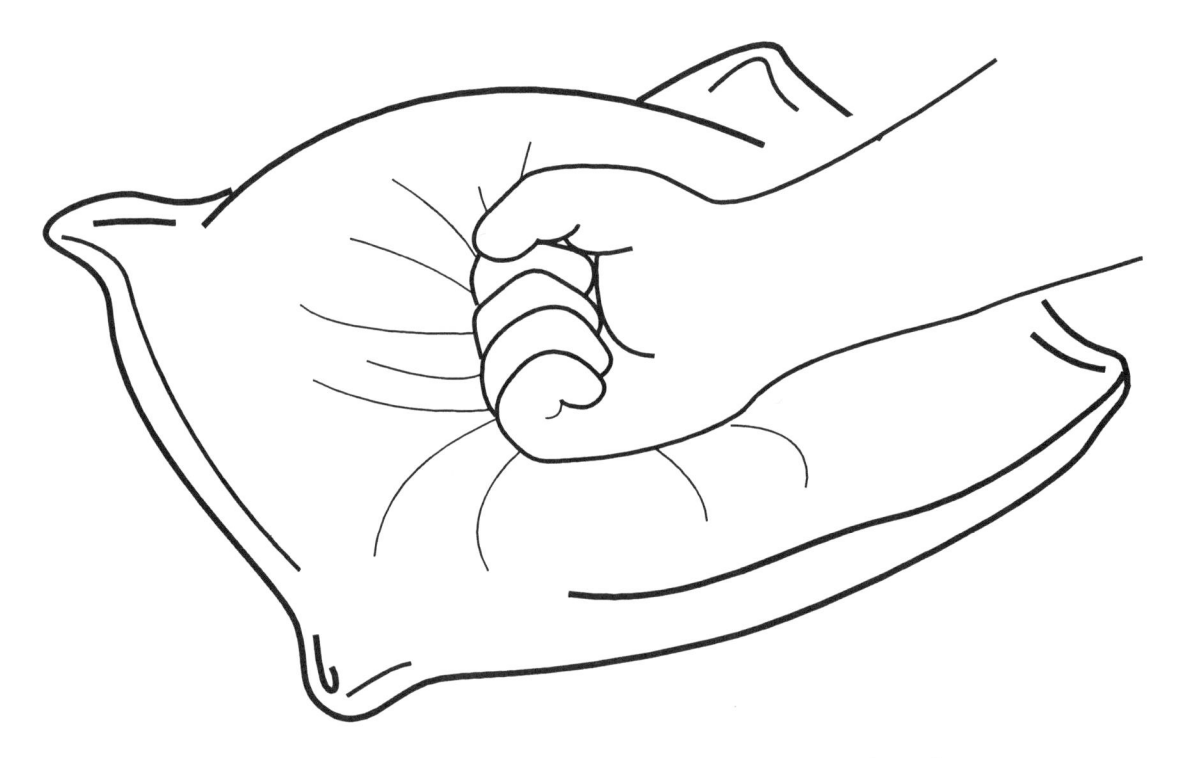

Punching something soft can shrink your anger without hurting you, someone else, or property. Remember, most pillows won't feel a thing if hit!

I know it's not OK to punch a person! It is OK to punch a pillow if I need to.

Taking Charge of Anger

MAKE AN I-STATEMENT

Anger Shrinker #

Sometimes it helps to talk about your feelings with the person you are angry with. When you do this, start with the word "I" instead of the word "you."

> I feel angry about being pushed!

NOT

> You make me so mad! Stop pushing.

If you start with the word "you," the other person may get upset and not listen. When you start with the word "I," the other person is more likely to listen.

> I want to tell how I feel. It would be better if I start with the word "I."

© 1996 Thinking Publications — Duplication permitted for educational use only.

Social Star

Anger Shrinker #

GET PHYSICAL

Getting physical means doing something active with your body. Some examples include:

Doing something physical helps shrink tension that builds up in your body when you feel angry. Remember, the physical activity you choose should not hurt yourself, others, or property.

I think I'll feel better if I do something physical. I'll ride my bike.

© 1996 Thinking Publications　　　　*Duplication permitted for educational use only.*

Taking Charge of Anger

Anger Shrinker #

DRAW A PICTURE

When you feel angry, sometimes it helps to draw a picture that shows how you are feeling. You can keep the picture to yourself or you can show it to someone else.

Drawing your feelings in a picture can help shrink your angry feelings.

I feel really mad right now! I'm going to draw a picture...

© 1996 Thinking Publications   213   *Duplication permitted for educational use only.*

Social Star

COUNT TO YOURSELF

Anger Shrinker #

When you feel really angry, stop and count to yourself! You can count to 10, count by 5's, or even count backwards from 100.

1, 2, 3, 4, 5, 6, 7, 8...

5, 10, 15, 20, 25, 30...

100, 99, 98, let's see, what comes next? Oh yeah, 97, 96...

By counting, you give yourself time to calm down. When you are calmer, you can deal with your anger in a responsible way.

I am so mad right now! I'm going to count before I say or do anything else...

© 1996 Thinking Publications — 214 — Duplication permitted for educational use only.

Taking Charge of Anger

Anger Shrinker #

WRITE TO SOMEONE

Sometimes when you're angry, you might not feel comfortable talking about it. Another great way to share your feelings is to write a letter to someone.

Jessy,

I'm really mad about my gum.

I don't want you to take my gum without asking first!

Pat

Dear Mrs. Walker,

I feel angry!

Jessy took my gum without asking me. I don't like it when Jessy does that!

from Pat

Give the letter to the person you are angry with (or to another person who cares about your feelings.)

I'm angry. I think I'll write to _____ about what happened.

© 1996 Thinking Publications — Duplication permitted for educational use only.

Social Star

Anger Shrinker #

WRITE TO YOURSELF

Write to yourself about your anger. Start a journal (a small notebook or diary) and write about your feelings and ideas.

Dear Diary, I got so mad at my sister today! When I was talking on the phone, she was listening in on the other line. I

Your journal can be like a trusted friend you can talk to any time you want.

I usually feel better after I write in my journal.

© 1996 Thinking Publications　　216　　*Duplication permitted for educational use only.*

Taking Charge of Anger

Anger Shrinker #

TAKE A SHOWER OR A BATH

Warm water can really help to relax your body. Next time you feel angry, take some time for a warm shower or bath.

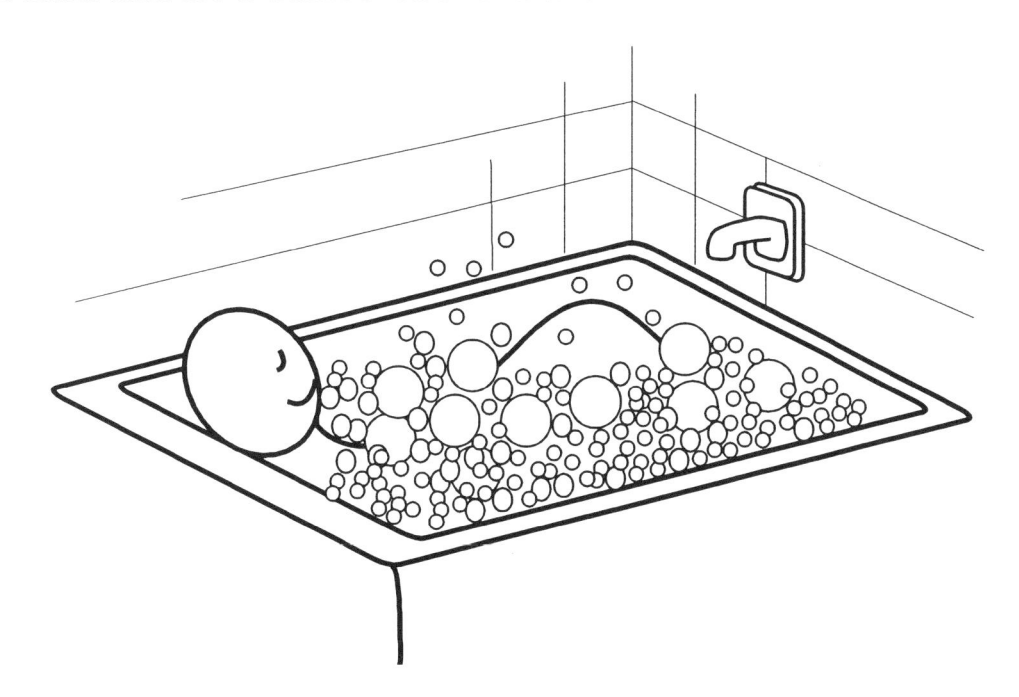

You might even want to share your feelings with a rubber ducky!

Oh... this feels so-o-o-o good!

© 1996 Thinking Publications   *Duplication permitted for educational use only.*

Social Star

RELAX TIGHT MUSCLES

Anger Shrinker #

Practice this anger shrinker exercise as often as you can:

1 Pick a body part (like your hands).

2 Tighten it up as much as you can. Hold it for a few seconds.

Squeeze!!

3 Slowly let the tightness out. Enjoy the relaxed feeling.

Relax!!

4 Do the same thing with different body parts (e.g., arms, legs, stomach).

When you feel angry, your muscles might get tight. If that happens, remember your anger shrinker exercises and let that tightness go.

When I relax, my anger melts away!

© 1996 Thinking Publications — Duplication permitted for educational use only.

Taking Charge of Anger

Anger Shrinker #

MAKE FUNNY PEOPLE PICTURES

When you make a funny "person picture," you visualize the person you are angry with in a goofy way. For example, draw your person picture with big Mickey Mouse ears or dressed like a duck.

This anger shrinker should not be used to be mean to the person you are angry with. If you keep your picture to yourself, you can get a little giggle inside and shrink your anger.

> Those funny people pictures really do make me giggle.

© 1996 Thinking Publications   *Duplication permitted for educational use only.*

Social Star

Anger Shrinker #

THINK OF A ROLE MODEL

A *role model* is a person you "look up to" and admire. Next time you get so angry that you think you might lose control, think of someone who is a role model for you. Pretend your role model is standing right next to you.

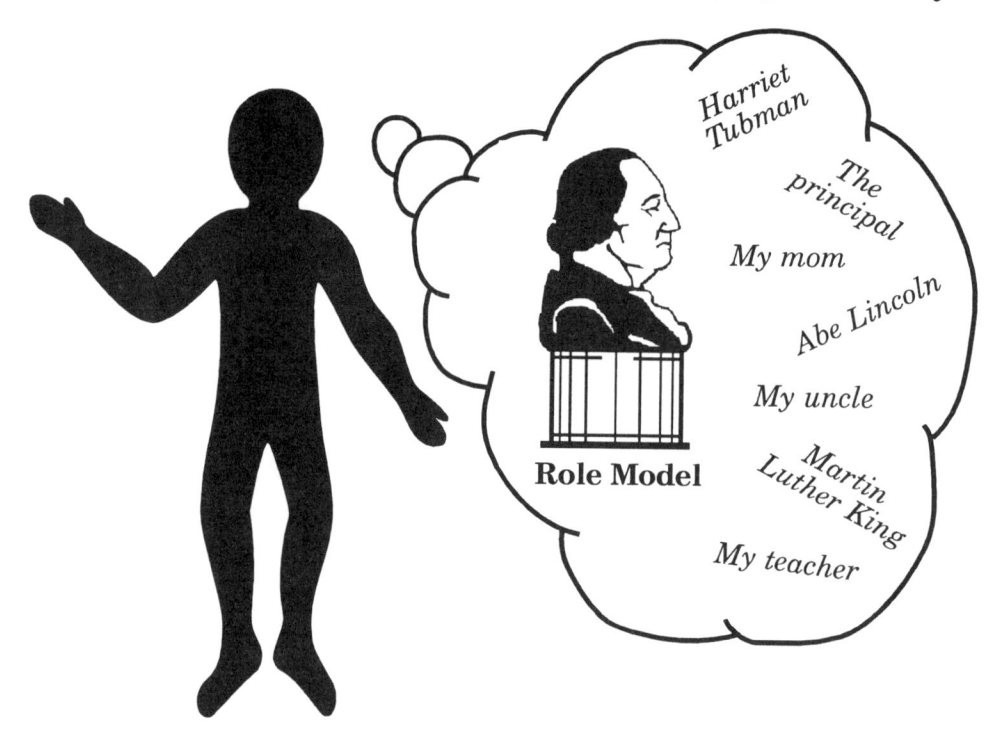

Role Model

Harriet Tubman
The principal
My mom
Abe Lincoln
My uncle
Martin Luther King
My teacher

If you really were with your role model, you'd probably behave the best that you could, because you'd want the person to view you in a good way. So, if you pretend your role model is with you, it's a little trick you can play to help yourself deal with your anger in the best way you can.

I'd never lose control and hit someone in front of my role model!

© 1996 Thinking Publications — Duplication permitted for educational use only.

Taking Charge of Anger

FORM HEALTHY HABITS

Anger Shrinker #

Form healthy habits like: eating nutritious foods, getting enough sleep, and exercising. It is a fact that people who are healthy can deal with challenges (like being angry) easier than people who are unhealthy.

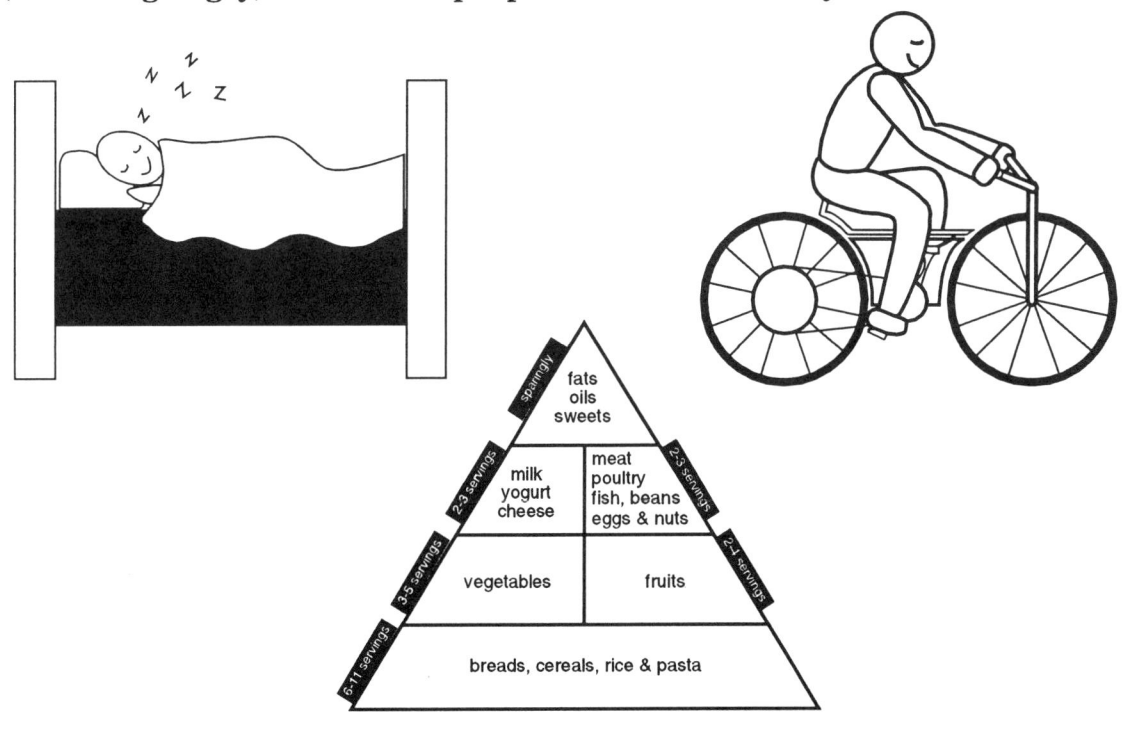

A bicycle that isn't taken care of won't ride very well and a body that isn't taken care of won't deal with anger very well either!

I know that when I'm tired, I get angry faster.

© 1996 Thinking Publications   221   *Duplication permitted for educational use only.*

Social Star

WAIT UNTIL TOMORROW

Anger Shrinker #

Sometimes when you feel angry, it's a good idea not to say or do anything for a while. Try saying to yourself, "I'm going to wait and think about what to do with my anger tomorrow."

| MON | TUES | WED | THURS | FRI | SAT | SUN |

After a night's sleep, it will be easier to come up with a positive plan for dealing with your anger. In fact, you may wake up not even feeling angry at all anymore!

I feel better today. Now what choices can I make about what happened yesterday?

© 1996 Thinking Publications — Duplication permitted for educational use only.

Taking Charge of Anger

Anger Shrinker #

CRY

If you think that it's bad to cry, think again! Crying can be a helpful way to deal with angry feelings without hurting anyone or anything. We use water to clean the outside of our bodies and crying can help "clean" the feelings on the inside of our bodies.

Most adults feel like crying from time to time, so it has nothing to do with being a "baby." Find a private place if you think you'll feel embarrassed by crying.

It's OK for me to cry! It doesn't mean I'm a wimp.

© 1996 Thinking Publications *Duplication permitted for educational use only.*

Social Star

TALK TO A PET

Anger Shrinker #

Tell your pet (if you have one) or stuffed animal all about why you feel angry.

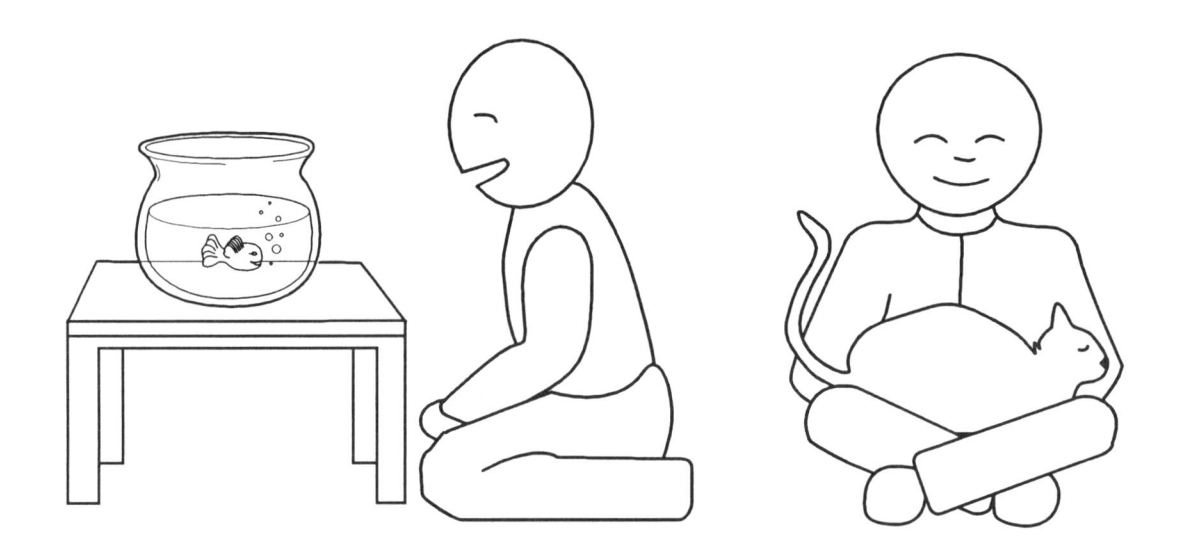

Pets can be great to talk to because they are usually happy to spend time with you and they listen without interrupting!

Rover, you're always here when I need you.

© 1996 Thinking Publications · *Duplication permitted for educational use only.*

Taking Charge of Anger

Anger Shrinker #

FIND A DISTRACTION

Finding a distraction means getting involved in a positive activity to help you think about something else besides your anger for awhile. A distraction could be something like watching a funny movie or reading a good book.

If you "take a break" from your anger for awhile, you'll relax and find it easier to deal with your anger in a positive way when you come back to it.

I didn't even think about being angry while I was reading.

© 1996 Thinking Publications   Duplication permitted for educational use only.

Social Star

USE POSITIVE SELF-TALK—Part 2

Anger Shrinker #

Did you know that your self-talk voice can have different speeds, volumes, and tones? You can talk to yourself really fast, loud, and harsh, or you can talk to yourself really slow, quiet, and calm. Practice *thinking* the phrases below (first fast, loud, and harsh, and then slow, quiet, and calm).

- Stay calm.
- I can shrink anger.
- I won't lose control.

If you tell yourself to stay calm, but your self-talk voice is fast, loud, and harsh, the anger shrinker may not work!

- My self-talk voice sure sounds nice!

© 1996 Thinking Publications — Duplication permitted for educational use only.

Taking Charge of Anger

Anger Shrinker #

IMAGINE AN ANGER SHIELD

When you feel angry at someone, you can picture yourself standing behind an anger shield. By doing that, you can imagine that you're protected and blocked from whatever the person is saying or doing.

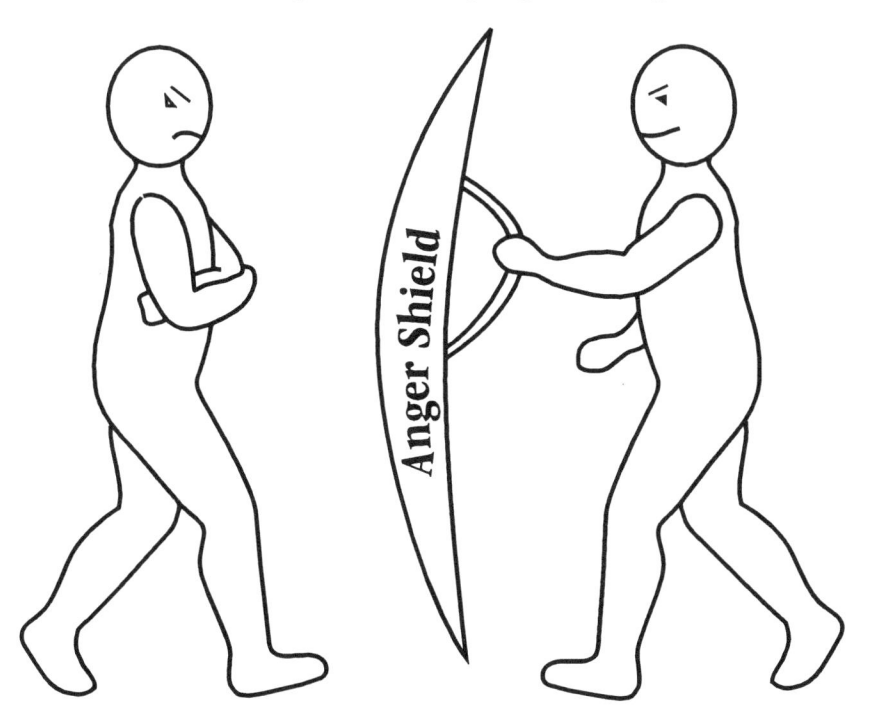

Putting up a pretend anger shield is a reminder that you choose your feelings. You don't have to feel angry!

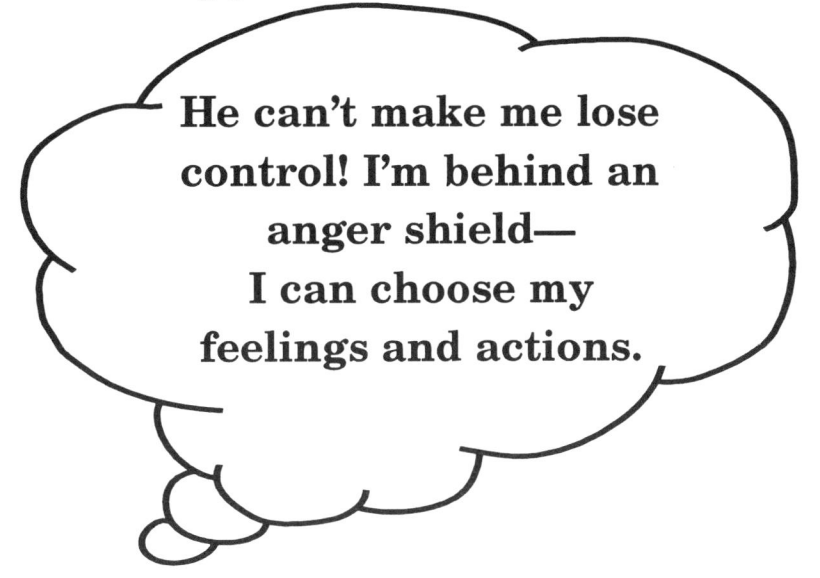

> He can't make me lose control! I'm behind an anger shield—
> I can choose my feelings and actions.

Social Star

Anger Shrinker #

SIGN A CONTRACT

When you feel angry, do you sometimes lose control and hurt people or things? If you do, and you want to stop, find a piece of paper and a pen. Write a contract stating that you agree not to hurt yourself, someone else, or property when you are angry. Make sure to sign your name at the end (you can even find someone else to co-sign their name too).

> I, Jane Doe, agree not to hurt myself, someone else, or property (even when I am angry!). I will keep my hands and feet to myself and I won't say mean things.
>
> Jane Doe

Writing and signing contracts helps many people keep their promises! When you follow your contract, celebrate! Tell yourself you feel proud knowing that you can stay in control even when you are angry.

> I did it!
> I followed my contract!
> I wanted to sock her,
> but I stayed in control.
> **YES!**

© 1996 Thinking Publications — *Duplication permitted for educational use only.*

Taking Charge of Anger

Anger Shrinker #

TOTALLY IGNORE

Is there someone who knows just how to get you angry? That person probably keeps doing the same thing over and over because he or she enjoys controlling you. Next time, be smart and totally ignore. That means don't look at and don't say anything to the person. Don't even let yourself look like you're angry. Walk away if you can.

Hey! Fish breath!

Smart ignoring takes the fun away from the other person. That person will probably start bugging someone else who doesn't have the self-control to ignore. Remember—this anger shrinker works best if you totally ignore every time.

I'm doing a great job ignoring. I'm not saying anything to him and I don't even look like I'm angry.

© 1996 Thinking Publications · Duplication permitted for educational use only.

ASK YOURSELF HELPFUL QUESTIONS

Anger Shrinker #

Asking yourself questions can make you feel more angry or less angry. It all depends on what types of questions you ask. You'll feel more angry if you ask yourself questions like:

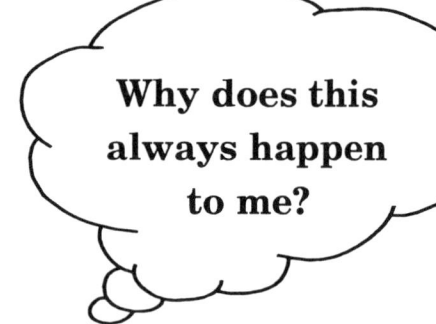

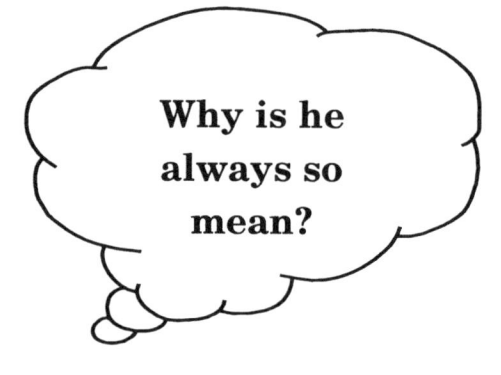

> Why does this always happen to me?

> Why is he always so mean?

You'll feel less angry if you ask yourself questions like this:

> I know there has to be something good about this situation! What is it?

> How would I feel if I were him?

One interesting thing about your brain is that when you ask it a question, it will search to find an answer. So remember to ask questions that will shrink your anger!

> Why am I so great at dealing with my anger?

Taking Charge of Anger

USE THE 20-YEAR RULE

Anger Shrinker #

Have you ever heard people say things like "Don't sweat the small stuff" or "Don't make a mountain out of a mole hill"? What they mean is, don't let yourself get really angry or upset about small problems. Next time you feel angry, ask yourself the following question:

20 years from now, will this make a difference in my life? Will this matter?

If the answer is no, then you are probably in a situation where you don't need to let yourself get so upset or angry!

I'm angry because I spilled ketchup on my pants, but 20 years from now, will this matter? NO!

© 1996 Thinking Publications   231   Duplication permitted for educational use only.

Social Star

Anger Shrinker #

GET THE FACTS FIRST

Sometimes when people get angry, they find out later that what they were angry about really didn't happen. Has something like this ever happened to you?

Oh that Marty— I hate him! He wrecked my tape.	*Marty, you jerk! How many times have I told you to stay out of my room. You better buy me a new tape.*
Before you go "flying off the handle," go talk to mom.	*I'm sorry. I forgot to close the gate and Rover got into your room.*

When you jump to conclusions, it means you believe something before you have all the information. Don't jump to conclusions. Get the facts first!

Before I get angry, I'd better check the facts!

© 1996 Thinking Publications — Duplication permitted for educational use only.

Taking Charge of Anger

Anger Shrinker #

PLAN AHEAD AND PRACTICE

Sometimes a situation that triggers your anger happens over and over again.

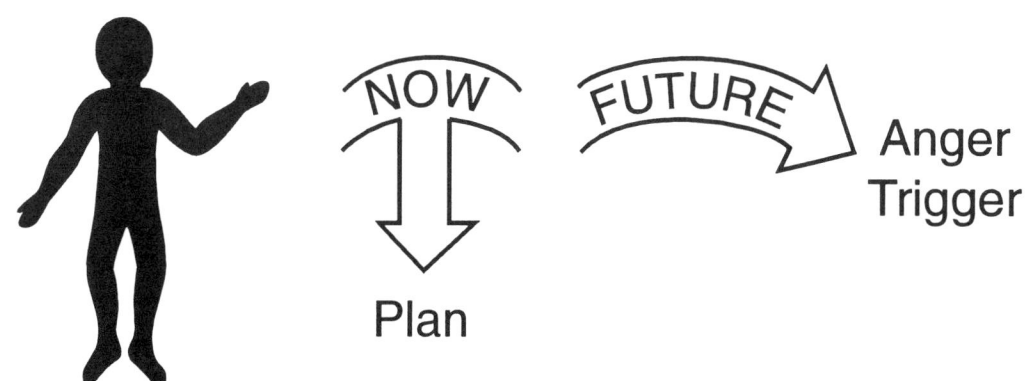

NOW → Plan

FUTURE → Anger Trigger

If you can predict ahead of time that something will make you angry, then you can come up with a plan to avoid getting angry and practice that plan.

> Oh no, we're going to Aunt Maggie's house again! Every time I go there, I get mad at my cousin Kim. What can I do? I know, I'll take a good book and read while I'm there. What will I say to Kim? I know, I'll say, "This is such a good book, I just can't put it down."

© 1996 Thinking Publications — Duplication permitted for educational use only.

Social Star

Anger Shrinker #

THINK OF A BALLOON

When you're angry, you might feel like a balloon being blown up—getting bigger and tighter and ready to explode! But remember, when a balloon is untied, the air comes rushing out and it shrinks. Next time you're angry, shrink the feeling by thinking of an untied balloon.

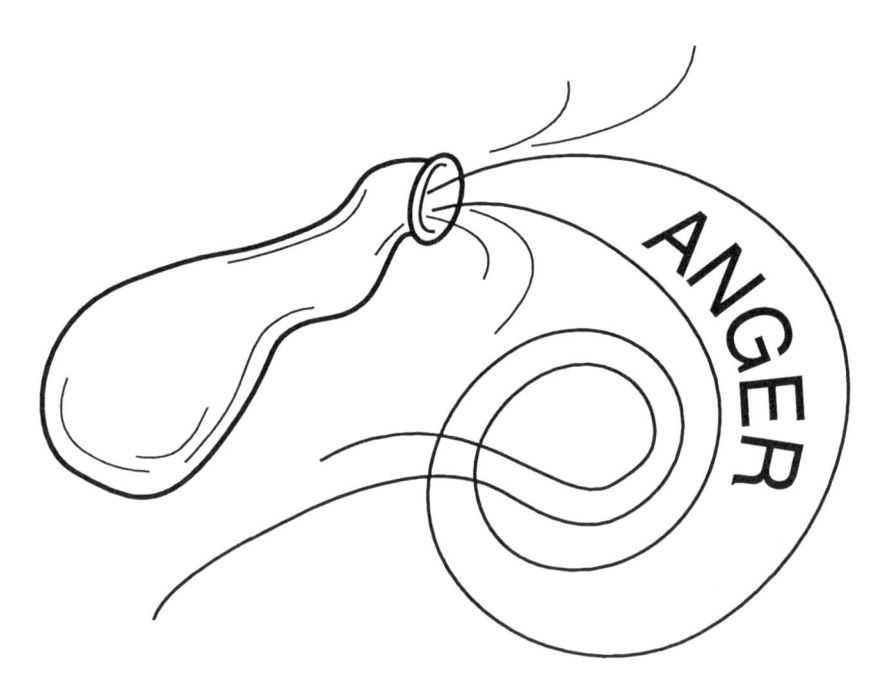

If you don't shrink your anger, you could end up exploding like an overblown balloon and hurt someone, something, or yourself.

I'll let this anger rush right out of me— just like air rushing out of a balloon!

© 1996 Thinking Publications — Duplication permitted for educational use only.

Taking Charge of Anger

Anger Shrinker #

BE FORGIVING

Sometimes when you feel angry at someone, it's best to forgive the person and forget the situation ever happened.

"Forgive and Forget!"

Forgiving someone means you tell yourself, "That's OK! No one is perfect and we all make mistakes from time to time."

OK, I'll forgive her— no one's perfect.

© 1996 Thinking Publications — *Duplication permitted for educational use only.*

Social Star

PUT YOURSELF IN THE OTHER PERSON'S SHOES

Anger Shrinker #

When you feel angry at another person, you can shrink your anger by "putting yourself in the other person's shoes." That means you think about how you would feel if you were the other person.

other person's shoes

Putting yourself in the other person's shoes will help you understand why that person may have said or done the things that led to you feeling angry.

If I were as tired as she was, I might have yelled too!

© 1996 Thinking Publications   Duplication permitted for educational use only.

Taking Charge of Anger

Anger Shrinker #

Lessons X, Y, and Z

Due to similarities in format, the final three lesson plans for each unit in *Social Star* are provided in *Appendix A*. Substitute the words "taking charge of anger" whenever a "_____" appears in the lesson plans. Information specific to this unit follows.

LESSON X PREPARATORY SET:

Distribute one balloon to each student. Tell students that on the count of three, they can blow their balloons up, but that they should not tie them or pop them. Then to show how they can be in charge of their anger, have them let the air out of their balloons (either slowly or quickly so the balloons fly about the room).

LESSON Y PREPARATORY SET:

Darken the room, if you prefer, and ask the students to visualize themselves correctly using this social skill by reading the following script:

Let's take a few moments.... Make sure you are in a comfortable position.... Close your eyes if you feel like it.... On the count of three, take a very slow, deep breath. Remember to breathe in quietly through your nose. One...two...three.... Breathe in deeply.... Now breathe out slowly and quietly through your mouth. Let your entire body relax.... Now imagine yourself starting to feel angry because your mom said she would not help you and you asked her nicely twice. Picture yourself using one of the anger control strategies to deal with your anger in a responsible manner. Imagine how relieved you feel because you are in control of your anger.

LESSON Z PLOT SITUATION:

Ask students to pretend that someone in their family doesn't deal with anger responsibly and often loses control by yelling.

LESSON Z ROADBLOCK EXAMPLES:

- Trying to use an anger strategy, but having the anger control you anyway and then doing something stupid

- Being in the habit of "exploding" or "losing control" and finding it's hard to break that habit

- Hiding your anger and acting like everything is fine

Taking Charge of Anger T-Chart

LOOKS LIKE...

actions that are responsible and calming

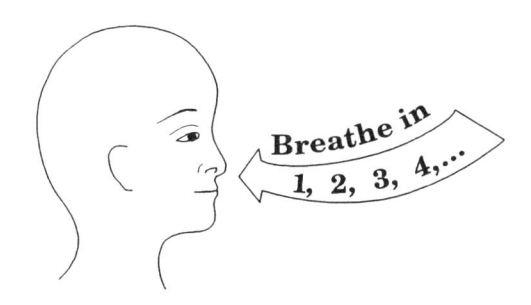

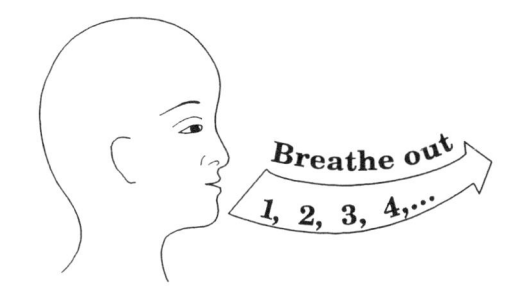

Breathe in 1, 2, 3, 4,...

Breathe out 1, 2, 3, 4,...

leaving to calm down

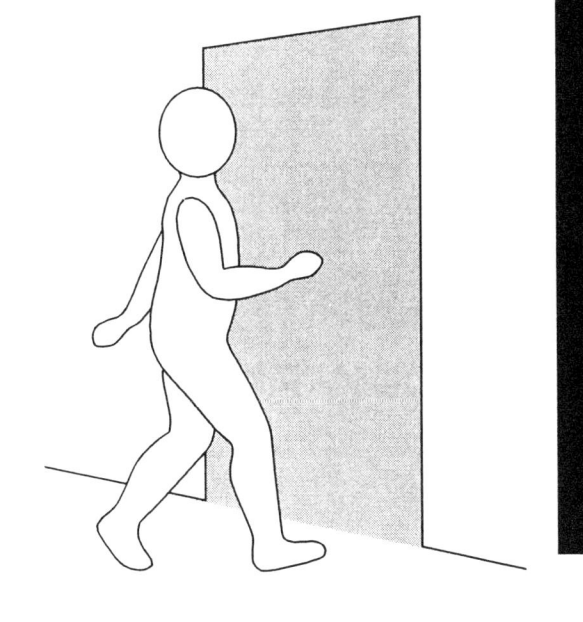

SOUNDS LIKE...

saying

- "I'm angry because..."
- "I'm too angry right now. I need to be by myself for awhile."

SHOW TIME

HOME

Pretend you are angry because your brother is trying to get you into trouble. Demonstrate an anger shrinker you can use to take charge of your anger.

SCHOOL

Pretend a lunchroom helper gives you a put-down and you're feeling angry. Demonstrate an anger shrinker you can use to take charge of your anger.

COMMUNITY

Pretend you are at a basketball game and your parent says you have to leave before it's over. Demonstrate an anger shrinker you can use to take charge of your anger.

ANGER is OK

If You Handle It RESPONSIBLY

Social Star

HOME-A-GRAM

Dear Family,

At school, we have been talking about the social skill called

TAKING CHARGE OF ANGER

I learned that *taking charge of anger* means I have control over how to deal with my anger. When I'm angry, I will:

1. Think "stop" and remind myself that I'm in charge of my anger.
2. Ask myself, "What can I do to deal with my anger?"
3. Choose an anger shrinker to use.

An *anger shrinker* is something that helps me take charge of my anger. I've started a collection of anger shrinkers. One anger shrinker that works well for me is called:

_____

Here is a picture of me using this anger shrinker.

I'm going to tell you about this anger shrinker. After I do, please sign my "Taking Charge of Anger" badge so I can return it to school and become a SOCIAL SUPER STAR this week.

From: _____

© 1996 Thinking Publications — Duplication permitted for educational use only.

Resisting Peer Pressure

Social Star

UNIT GOAL:

To demonstrate comprehension and use of strategies for resisting peer pressure

EDUCATOR INFORMATION:

1. In this unit, students differentiate between positive and negative peer pressure. They learn that they are likely to encounter situations in which people exert pressure on them to do things they feel they should not do. This unit was developed to help students understand that they are responsible for their actions, even if pressured into an activity. They learn that except in extreme cases, peers cannot force them to do things they know they should not do. They explore tactics ("tricks") that people might use to exert pressure on them. This unit uses a "peers teaching peers" approach. Students work in small groups to become knowledgeable about specific tactics and share their knowledge with other groups. Students have the opportunity to identify and role-play strategies for resisting peer pressure.

2. Duryea (1991) examined the role that nonverbal communication plays in pressuring peers and resisting peer pressure. Most school health curricula do not train students how to recognize or resist nonverbal peer pressure. Duryea examined four major areas of nonverbal communication.

   - *Gaze*—Children who gaze or stare at someone give the impression of being confident. Staring is a tactic that is sometimes used to pressure people. However, students who are being pressured can be taught to return the gaze to neutralize the gaze they are receiving.

   - *Stance*—This refers to the position of the body, legs, and arms during communication. People who communicate frontally (looking and speaking directly to people as opposed to at an angle) are viewed as more self-assured. The "Akimbo" position (standing with hands on hips) sends a message of assertiveness and confidence. Students can be taught to use these confident body stances.

   - *Gestures and emblems*—Forceful gestures (e.g., pounding the table while talking) can be used to send messages of resistance when people are feeling pressured. Emblems are gestures that have exact meanings for specific groups. One emblem is that of putting hands in armpits and flapping them up and down to send the message, "You're chicken." Students can be taught how to ignore these emblems or use a return emblem of pointing a finger at the person and saying, "Don't even **think** about asking me to do that with you!" Students could brainstorm other emblems that might be used to give a message of disapproval to those who try to pressure them. Having a nonverbal strategy would be helpful to those children less verbally skilled.

- *Facial expression*—Sometimes children who pressure others use *facial falsification* which can include one of three forms: (1) *simulation*—giving an expression you do not feel (e.g., looking confident, to imply there is no way of getting caught); (2) *neutralization*—not expressing what you actually feel (e.g., not looking impatient when you actually are in a hurry to convince the other person); and (3) *masking*—using one expression to hide another (e.g., looking amused to cover feeling afraid). If students learn that facial falsification is a tactic used to pressure people, they can more easily resist it. In a slightly different twist, shy students often use facial falsification (e.g., smiling when they are actually upset or fearful) when dealing with peers.

3. As students get older, their need to belong increases. Campbell (1992) states that at age eight or nine, peers become the most important part of a child's world. Therefore, it is critical that students understand they will sometimes need to go against their peers to do what is right. While students may want to do what is right, they sometimes lack the skills necessary for resisting peer pressure. Campbell advocates a three-step approach called *peer pressure reversal*.

   - *Check out the situation*—Students are encouraged to ask themselves, "Is this trouble?"

   - *Make a good decision about what to do*—Students must weigh possible positive consequences against possible negative consequences. They should keep in mind that peers generally point out the positive and ignore the negative.

   - *Act to avoid trouble*—Students need to have a comeback when they are being pressured. Some examples include coming up with a better idea or making an excuse.

4. Additional strategies for resisting peer pressure include using avoidance and creative extrication (Duryea, 1991). In avoidance, students predict the degree of peer pressure in various situations and then choose which situations to avoid altogether. In creative extrication, a person removes oneself from an uncomfortable situation by walking away from the event.

5. Information regarding students with learning disabilities and peer pressure suggests that they expect peer pressure requests to be brief and direct (e.g., "Let's steal this car") while nondisabled students expect the request to be trickier (e.g., "Let's borrow this car and we'll bring it right back" or "Let's go for a ride; it'll be fun") (Pearl, Bryan, and Herzog, 1990). This suggests that students with learning disabilities may not be prepared to resist less direct forms of peer pressure.

RELATED ACTIVITIES:

1. Have students survey older students to determine strategies they have used to resist peer pressure.

2. Ask students to keep a scrapbook of news articles in which people may have gotten into trouble by not resisting peer pressure (e.g., drinking and driving, shoplifting).

3. Have students create and distribute a student newsletter about resisting peer pressure. If a school newspaper exists, have students submit articles about resisting peer pressure.

4. Have a "Tip of the Day" read on the announcements or posted in hallways, emphasizing strategies to resist peer pressure.

5. Elicit parental involvement by encouraging the formation of a grass-roots citizens' group that would develop community programs to assist students in resisting peer pressure.

6. Create or learn new lyrics to familiar melodies for each of the strategies presented in the unit (e.g., for the strategy of walking away, teach new lyrics to the melody of "These Boots Are Made For Walking" by Nancy Sinatra—*These boots are made for walking and walking's what they'll do! If you try to pressure me, I'll walk away from you!*).

It is important for educators to provide opportunities for students to work in groups so they can experience social skills in contexts where social communication is needed. Therefore, educators are encouraged to have students complete the Related Activities in small groups whenever possible. Educators trained in cooperative learning could incorporate the five components (see pages 33–34) into the group activity. An excellent resource for teaching students cooperative skills and building a sense of community is *Tribes: A Process for Social Development and Cooperative Learning* (1987) by Jeanne Gibbs.

RELATED LITERATURE:

Ida Early Comes Over the Mountain (1980) by Robert Joseph Burch, Viking. (145 pages)

Get on Out of Here, Phillip Hall (1981) by Bette Greene, Dial Press. (150 pages)

Joshua's Masai Mask (1993) by Dakari Hru, Ill. by Anna Rich, Lee and Low. (32 pages)

Don't Ask Miranda (1979) by Lila Perl, Seabury. (164 pages)

SOCIAL SKILLS ALL DAY LONG:

Look for opportunities to teach social skills throughout the day (incidental teaching). Four ways to reinforce appropriate social skills and an example of each follow:

Encouragement

Lee, I just heard Tommy tell you to throw your bowling ball down the wrong lane and you didn't do it. Resisting peer pressure is not always easy to do. It takes a strong person. You can be proud that you resisted Tommy's pressure!

Personal Example

I think that everyone sometimes worries about having friends. You want to do things to please them. When I was younger, there was a time when I received pressure to...and I....

Prompting

When you attend the Community Fest this weekend, remember the strategies you can use to resist pressure if people try to convince you to do something you know you should not do. Think about the tricks they are using and tell yourself, "I'm not going to fall for these tricks."

Corrective Feedback (must be positive, private, specific, and nonthreatening)

Maria, I heard you've been getting involved in some trouble with other kids at a store after school. Remember, you know ways to resist peer pressure. It's hard to do, but you'll feel better about yourself and keep out of trouble if you do.

―――――― ★★★ ――――――

This above all: to thine own self be true.

William Shakespeare

Lesson A

OBJECTIVES:

1. To state the meaning of *resisting peer pressure* and tell why it's important

2. To listen to the self-talk associated with appropriate use of the skill

MATERIALS:

1. Candy (For use during step 3 of this Plan)

2. *Resisting Peer Pressure* (See page 250; one per student and one transparency.)

3. *Thought Bubble* (See *Appendix O*; one for educator use.)

PREPARATORY SET:

Ask for your students' attention, then turn and have a conversation with an imaginary person standing next to you. Say:

> *Oh come on, please.... I'll give you a pack of gum if you do.... If you don't, I won't be your friend any more.... But everyone does it.... What's the matter, are you stupid or what?.... You have to because I helped you last week.... Why not? You've done it before.... Oh come on, it will be so much fun.... We won't get caught, I promise.... There is no way we can get hurt.... I'll hit you if you don't.... Fine, I just won't talk to you anymore....*

Turn back to your students and ask what they think you were trying to do. Next, ask what the imaginary person was probably saying or trying to do. Use this activity to introduce this unit called *Resisting Peer Pressure*.

PLAN:

1. Pair students (see *Appendix P)*. Ask student pairs to quickly agree on who will be Person "A" and who will be Person "B."

2. Ask the A's to wait quietly outside the classroom door until you join them in the hallway. Make certain the door is closed so the students waiting in the hallway (the A's) cannot hear what is being said to those remaining in the classroom (the B's).

3. Place candy on a table in the room. Explain to the B's that their job will be to try to convince their partners to take some of the candy without permission. Tell them to try a variety of ways to convince their partners to take the candy.

4. Exit the classroom and explain to the A's that their job will be to say "no" to whatever their partners ask them to do.

5. Have the A's join with their B partners and allow them a brief amount of time to follow the directions they have been given. Consider waiting outside the classroom while the B's are pressuring the A's (negative peer pressure is more likely to happen in real life when authority figures are not present).

6. Ask the A's to respond to the following question:

   - What thoughts/feelings did you have when your partner was trying to convince you to take the candy?

   Ask the B's to respond to the following question:

   - What thoughts/feelings did you have when you were trying to convince your partner to take the candy?

   Ask all of the students to respond to the following question:

   - Have you ever been in a situation when someone tried to convince you to do something you didn't want to do or you knew you shouldn't do? (Have students describe the situations.)

7. Distribute and display *Resisting Peer Pressure*. Discuss the definition. Discuss the difference between positive peer pressure (e.g., a classmate encourages a friend to study for a big test instead of watch TV) and negative peer pressure (e.g., a classmate pressures a friend to watch TV instead of studying for a big test). Tell students this unit will focus on negative peer pressure. Explain the skill step and the symbol next to it. Remind students that the symbol is there to help them visualize and remember the skill step. Refer students to the body-talk symbol in the left-hand margin. Remind students that appropriate body talk is important when resisting peer pressure. Discuss the reasons for resisting peer pressure.

8. Model use of the skill step for resisting peer pressure while thinking aloud. A scripted example follows:

Introduction

I am going to pretend to be someone your age at recess. A girl is trying to convince me and other kids in class to pull a prank on a substitute teacher. I will show you how I resist peer pressure and tell you the thoughts I'm having. When I hold up this Thought Bubble, *you'll know the words I'm saying are actually what I'm thinking.*

Actual Model

While holding up the *Thought Bubble* say, *I'm being pressured to do something that I know I shouldn't do. She's going to think I'm chicken if I don't go along with the prank, but I really don't want to play a trick on the "sub." I don't think it's right. I need to choose a way to resist the pressure. I think I'll say, "No way!" and walk away.* Put the *Thought Bubble* down and using assertive body talk say, *No way,* and walk away.

9. Read the story and the talk bubbles in the illustration at the bottom of *Resisting Peer Pressure*.

10. Ask students to process the story using the *Sharing Pairs* strategy (Harmin, 1995). This strategy maximizes the number of students who talk about their ideas and hear the ideas of others. The strategy asks students to discuss answers to questions with their partners before they are called on to share their ideas with the whole class. Ask students to discuss answers to the following questions with their partners, then call on one pair to share their ideas with the whole class:

    - Can anyone force Victor to smoke?
    - What did Victor do to resist the pressure?
    - What else could Victor have done to resist pressure?
    - Why do you think the girl tried to get Victor to smoke?
    - What might have happened to Victor if he had smoked?
    - Do you agree or disagree with the statement, "No one can make you do something you don't want to do"?
    - Are there situations when you really might be forced to do something you don't think you should do?
    - Do you think the girl will try to pressure Victor again? Why or why not?

11. Ask student pairs to take turns telling each other the meaning of *resisting peer pressure* and why it's important to use the skill. Students could be reminded that the information they are to say is printed on *Resisting Peer Pressure*.

    As an option to add structure to this activity, ask partners to come to an agreement about which person will be called "A" and which person will be called "B." After students have made their decisions, ask "A" to tell "B" the definition of *resisting peer pressure*. Next ask "B" to tell "A" the definition. Ask students to use the same procedure to tell each other the reasons for resisting peer pressure.

———————— ★★★ ————————

Let me listen to me and not to them.

Gertrude Stein

Social Star

Name _____

Resisting Peer Pressure

MEANING OF RESISTING PEER PRESSURE:

Knowing you have control over how to express your feelings

SKILL STEP:

1. Ask myself: "How can I resist this pressure?"

NEGATIVE PEER PRESSURE

REASONS FOR USING THIS SKILL:

If I resist peer pressure I can feel proud about making a positive choice for myself. I can be a positive role model for people. I can avoid getting into trouble or getting hurt.

DIRECTIONS: Listen to the story below.

Victor stayed after school to get some extra help from his teacher. When they were finished, he waited for his parents to pick him up in the school's parking lot. While he was waiting, an older girl tried to pressure him into smoking. Here's what they said to each other:

"Hey, kid, those boys over there want you to smoke this cigarette. It'll make you look cool."

"You've got to be kidding. NOT ME!"

© 1996 Thinking Publications — Duplication permitted for educational use only.

Lesson B

EDUCATOR INFORMATION:

During this lesson, students will be learning about and teaching each other the many tactics ("tricks") people use to pressure others in a negative way and why those tactics often work. The emphasis of this lesson is about the numerous tactics that people often "cave-in" to; Lesson C emphasizes ways to resist the pressure. Therefore, when students complete the *Trick Presentation Sheet* and the *Pressure Script* during steps 4, 5, and 8 of this Plan, they may want to include characters that "fall for" the tricks and give in to the negative pressure.

OBJECTIVE:

To identify "tricks" commonly used to exert pressure on others

MATERIALS:

1. *Trick #1—Begging* (See page 254; one transparency.)

2. *Trick Presentation Sheet* (See page 255; one transparency and one per group of students.)

3. *Pressure Script* (See page 256; one transparency and one per group of students.)

4. *Pressuring Tricks* (See page 257; one transparency.)

5. *Tricks #2–#14* (See pages 258–270; one transparency and one copy of each page.)

6. *Peer Pressure Tricks Word Search* (See page 271; one per student.) (*A Peer Pressure Tricks Word Search Key* is provided on page 272 for educator use.)

PREPARATORY SET:

Tell students, "Pretend that you want me to let you leave school five minutes early today. I know I should not let you leave early, so I am going to say 'no.' I will, however, give you three minutes to try to pressure me to let you leave early. Only one person can speak at a time during those three minutes." Allow time for students to pressure you.

PLAN:

1. Tell students that all of the things they said and did were "tricks" to try to pressure you into doing something you knew you shouldn't do. Briefly discuss the various ways students tried to convince you to let them leave early. Tell students that in this lesson they will be working in groups to become experts at recognizing the tricks that people might use to pressure them. Explain that each group will have an opportunity to share their expertise with the rest of the class.

2. Divide students into groups of three or four. Ask students to sit with their group but call for everyone's attention while you work as a class to discuss the first trick people might use to pressure someone.

3. Display *Trick #1—Begging*. Read the information about the trick called *begging* to the class. Disregard the bottom half of the sheet; it is referred to during step 7 of this Plan. Ask students:

    - Can anyone think of a time when someone might use (or has used) the trick of begging to pressure you?

    - If you were going to teach someone else about this trick, what things would you tell them?

4. Display *Trick Presentation Sheet*. Ask students to help you create illustrations (with talk bubbles and/or thought bubbles) showing someone using the trick of begging. Using stick figures is fine. (Four frames are provided on the sheet in case you want the illustrations to be like a cartoon strip, but not all four frames have to be filled in.) Provide assistance in creating illustrations that appropriately demonstrate the trick. Tell students that for this activity, it is permissible for the character being pressured to fall for the trick and to give in to the pressure. Assure them that during Lesson C, they will learn five great ways to resist tricks.

5. Display *Pressure Script*. Ask students to help you write a short script that would be useful to teach others about the trick. Provide assistance to ensure that the skit appropriately demonstrates the trick. Again, let students know that it is fine for the character being pressured to fall for the trick and give in to the pressure. Remind them that during Lesson C, they will learn several very effective strategies for "standing up" to the pressure so they don't get tricked.

6. Tell students they will become experts on other tricks people might use to pressure others. Display *Pressuring Tricks* and read the list of tricks to the class. Tell students that each group will be receiving a sheet similar to *Trick #1—Begging* about one of the tricks listed on *Pressuring Tricks*. Explain that their jobs are to work with their groups to read the information on their sheets and then to create illustrations, similar to those they created for the begging trick in step 4. Remind them to show someone using the trick. Finally, explain that each group will write and present a short script, similar to the one written for the begging trick in step 5, to help their classmates understand the trick.

7. Divide *Tricks #2–#14* among the groups. (Use all of the tricks, or select only those most appropriate for the age and level of the class.) Ask student groups to refer to the "notes or questions about this trick" section at the bottom of their sheets. Explain that they should use that section to jot down notes or questions

they might have while becoming experts about their tricks. (This is especially important considering you will be able to help only one group at a time.) Model this step by completing the bottom half of *Trick #1—Begging*. Tell students that when each group presents their trick to the rest of the class, they will show a transparency of their assigned tricks.

8. Distribute one *Trick Presentation Sheet* and one *Pressure Script* to each group. Provide students with the time needed to read the information about their assigned trick, complete their *Trick Presentation Sheet* (inform students that the illustrations and writing should be neatly done because it will be made into an overhead transparency for them to use when teaching their tricks to the class), and develop and prepare their *Pressure Script*. (Ask students to write neatly on their scripts. Let them know you'll make copies of the scripts so that each group member has his or her own copy to use when presenting the script to the whole class.) Closely monitor progress to ensure that when the groups present their information to the whole class they are providing accurate and understandable information. Provide alternate activities for groups who finish early or who are waiting for your assistance (e.g., *Peer Pressure Tricks Word Search*).

9. When groups are ready, make overhead transparencies of the completed *Trick Presentation Sheets* and sufficient copies of the completed *Pressure Scripts*. Distribute the transparencies and the copies to each group. Provide students with precise directions about the procedures you would like them to follow for sharing their transparencies and scripts with each other. The presentations may take place over a period of several sessions.

———————— ★★★ ————————

Rise above principle and do what's right!

Walter Heller
(In a speech to Congress, 1985)

Social Star

Trick #1—Begging

One trick people might use to pressure you into doing something you don't think you should do is called

Begging

When people beg you:

- They have a pleading tone in their voice (e.g., "Please, come on, oh please...pretty please!")

- They ask you over and over and over. They want you to give in.

When people use this trick, they hope you will either feel sorry for them or that you will get tired of the begging. They think that if they beg long enough, you will do what they want you to do.

Notes or Questions About This Trick

Resisting Peer Pressure

Trick Presentation Sheet

Names _____

_____

If anyone tries to pressure me with this trick, I won't fall for it!

Name of Trick:

_____

The illustrations below show a person using this trick to pressure someone.

© 1996 Thinking Publications   255   *Duplication permitted for educational use only.*

Social Star

Names _____
_____

Pressure Script

DIRECTIONS: Use the spaces provided below to fill in the script for the skit your group is presenting.

Name of Trick: _____

Setting: _____
_____

Characters: _____
_____

_____: _____
_____

_____: _____
_____

_____: _____
_____

_____: _____
_____

_____: _____
_____

_____: _____
_____

(Use the back side of this sheet if more script space is needed.)

© 1996 Thinking Publications   *Duplication permitted for educational use only.*

PRESSURING TRICKS

Begging

Offering Something

Making Threats

Giving Put-Downs

Giving the Silent Treatment

Sensationalizing

Getting You "Hooked"

Saying, "Everyone Does It!"

Saying, "You Owe Me!"

Saying, "You've Done It Before!"

Saying, "You Won't Get Caught!"

Saying, "You Won't Get Hurt!"

Saying, "But You Promised!"

Saying, "I Dare You!"

Beware—the Pressure Can Be Great!

Social Star

Trick #2—Offering Something

One trick people might use to pressure you into doing something you don't think you should do is called

Offering Something

When people offer you something:

- They say they will give you something they know you want if you will do what they want (e.g., "I'll give you candy if you let me copy your homework").

- If you still say "no," don't be surprised if they offer you something different or something more.

When people use this trick, they hope that what they are offering will be so tempting to you that you will decide to do what they are pressuring you to do.

Notes or Questions About This Trick

Trick #3—Making Threats

One trick people might use to pressure you into doing something you don't think you should do is called

Making Threats

When people make threats:

- They say they will do something mean if you don't do what they want you to do. They might say:

    "I won't be your friend anymore."

    "I'll hurt you if you don't."

    "I won't sit with you on the bus."

    "I'll tell your mom that..."

You never really know for sure if they will follow through with their threat. The people using this trick hope you will get scared and do what they are pressuring you to do.

If someone uses this trick, and you are worried about what they might do, it is important to let an adult know about the threat.

Notes or Questions About This Trick

Social Star

Trick #4—Giving Put-Downs

One trick people might use to pressure you into doing something you don't think you should do is called

Giving Put-Downs

When people give put-downs:

- They may call you mean names (e.g., "You're a chicken!").

- They may say something unkind about you to try to hurt your feelings.

When people use this trick, they want you to forget you can ignore put-downs. They hope the put-downs will make you feel bad enough that you will give in to their pressure.

Notes or Questions About This Trick

© 1996 Thinking Publications — Duplication permitted for educational use only.

Trick #5—Giving the Silent Treatment

One trick people might use to pressure you into doing something you don't think you should do is called

Giving the Silent Treatment

When people give you the silent treatment:

- They totally ignore you after you say "no" to their pressure. And they may keep ignoring you for quite a while.

- They don't look at you or talk to you (even if you try to talk to them).

When people use this trick, they hope that you'll hate being ignored. They think you'll feel so badly about being ignored that you'll do what they are pressuring you to do.

Notes or Questions About This Trick

Trick #6—Sensationalizing

One trick people might use to pressure you into doing something you don't think you should do is called

Sensationalizing

When people sensationalize:

- They make it sound like the activity they want you to do is the best thing in the whole world.

- They may say things like, "Come on, it's great! You'll love it!" or "It's awesome! You just have to try it!"

When people use this trick, they hope you'll give in to their pressure because you're afraid of missing out on something really great.

Notes or Questions About This Trick

Trick #7—Getting You "Hooked"

One trick people might use to pressure you into doing something you don't think you should do is called

Getting You "Hooked"

When people get you hooked:

- They pretend to be your friend. They give you an addictive substance (e.g., cigarettes, alcohol, chewing tobacco, marijuana) for free until your body starts feeling like it has to have more.

- They start making you pay once you're addicted. They ask for money or valuable items that belong to you or your family. They may ask you to steal things to "pay."

People use this trick either because they want company (someone to use the substance with) or because they want to make money. It can be very difficult to get "unhooked," so don't be afraid to talk to a trusted adult if you need help!

Notes or Questions About This Trick

Trick #8—Saying, "Everyone Does It!"

One trick people might use to pressure you into doing something you don't think you should do is called

Saying, "Everyone Does It!"

When people say, "Everyone does it!":

- They want you to think you're the only one who isn't doing what they're pressuring you to do (e.g., "You must be the only person in the whole world who doesn't want to do this!").

- They think you'll believe their lie. (It's not true that everyone is doing it.)

When people use this trick, they hope you'll feel like a "weirdo" and give in to the pressure.

Notes or Questions About This Trick

Trick #9—Saying, "You Owe Me!"

One trick people might use to pressure you into doing something you don't think you should do is called

Saying, "You Owe Me!"

When people say, "You owe me!":

- They talk about nice things they've done for you in the past (e.g., "Remember last week when I stuck up for you in the lunch line?").

- They say that, in return, you have to do what they're pressuring you to do.

When people use this trick, they hope you won't have the courage to say, "I'm still not going to do it!"

Notes or Questions About This Trick

Social Star

Trick #10— Saying, "You've Done It Before!"

One trick people might use to pressure you into doing something you don't think you should do is called

Saying, "You've Done It Before!"

When people say, "You've done it before!":

- They remind you of past situations when you gave in to their pressure.

- They want you to feel like you have to give in to their pressure again (e.g., "You lied to your mom last week. What's the big deal? You can do it again!").

When people use this trick, they hope you don't know that you have the right to change your mind and the right to change it whenever you want to.

Notes or Questions About This Trick

© 1996 Thinking Publications — Duplication permitted for educational use only.

Trick #11—Saying, "You Won't Get Caught!"

One trick people might use to pressure you into doing something you don't think you should do is called

Saying, "You Won't Get Caught!"

When people say, "You won't get caught!":

- They want you to believe that it is perfectly OK to do what they are pressuring you to do because you won't get caught.

- They want you to believe a promise they can't keep. (There's always the possibility of being caught.)

Even if you don't get caught, your conscience will probably bother you because you'll know what you did was wrong.

Notes or Questions About This Trick

Trick #12—Saying, "You Won't Get Hurt!"

One trick people might use to pressure you into doing something you don't think you should do is called

Saying, "You Won't Get Hurt!"

When people say, "You won't get hurt!":

- They want you to believe there's no danger in what they are pressuring you to do (e.g., "Come on, let's climb up there. We won't get hurt").

- They want you to believe that accidents only happen to other people, never to you.

When people use this trick, they hope that you'll ignore the sensible voice inside your mind that says, "I shouldn't do this. It's dangerous."

Notes or Questions About This Trick

Trick #13—Saying, "But You Promised!"

One trick people might use to pressure you into doing something you don't think you should do is called

Saying, "But You Promised!"

When people say, "But you promised!":

- They want you to think it's wrong to change your mind (e.g., "You have to steal this. You promised me yesterday that you would!").

- They want to make you feel guilty about breaking your promise.

When people use this trick, they hope you don't know that people always have the right to change their minds. It is important to be honest and keep your promises, but not when you have promised to do something that doesn't feel right to you.

Notes or Questions About This Trick

Social Star

Trick #14— Saying, "I Dare You!"

One trick people might use to pressure you into doing something you don't think you should do is called:

Saying, "I Dare You!"

When people say, "I dare you!":

- They are hoping you won't be able to resist the challenge.

- They want you to feel you can "prove yourself" and be more important if you take the dare.

When people use this trick, they are trying to turn the situation into a game so you'll do what they want.

Notes or Questions About This Trick

PEER PRESSURE TRICKS WORD SEARCH

DIRECTIONS: Find and circle the phrases listed at the bottom of this page. They are all things people might say to trick you into doing something you don't think you should do. The phrases are hidden in the puzzle vertically, horizontally, and diagonally. (No spaces or apostrophes are included.)

Y	Y	O	E	R	C	S	D	V	B	Y	I	W	C	L	H	A	O	G	C	I
O	O	Y	O	U	W	O	N	T	G	E	T	H	U	R	T	J	F	M	D	T
U	U	I	P	E	N	L	H	J	T	D	R	G	Q	I	K	P	D	I	N	L
W	V	T	I	W	O	N	T	B	E	Y	O	U	R	F	R	I	E	N	D	L
O	E	L	O	A	J	P	B	Q	A	T	D	I	J	M	F	N	B	M	R	B
N	D	P	G	S	C	E	K	D	R	J	B	P	Y	O	U	O	W	E	M	E
T	O	Q	L	J	F	O	A	M	F	L	N	F	Q	C	P	E	O	H	L	G
G	N	G	K	E	N	H	D	R	R	G	A	Y	I	G	H	T	U	R	S	R
E	E	S	H	W	A	U	E	S	B	Z	O	J	C	P	K	O	V	D	M	E
T	I	A	T	E	N	S	C	G	H	S	D	M	J	O	Y	M	F	G	N	A
C	T	M	C	R	F	L	E	V	E	R	Y	O	N	E	D	O	E	S	I	T
A	B	D	P	A	M	I	J	O	F	Q	K	P	R	X	I	W	F	S	M	H
U	E	G	L	J	Q	C	P	B	R	H	N	A	U	E	N	A	T	B	V	I
G	F	P	B	O	F	R	J	R	L	O	D	R	K	D	L	I	Z	J	Q	F
H	O	Y	O	U	R	E	A	C	H	I	C	K	E	N	T	M	E	K	Z	L
T	R	H	L	E	R	K	F	L	S	J	M	B	J	P	G	S	H	Y	C	U
P	E	C	N	I	L	L	G	I	V	E	Y	O	U	M	O	N	E	Y	P	Q
Y	O	U	C	A	N	T	C	H	A	N	G	E	Y	O	U	R	M	I	N	D

PLEASE	YOU'RE A CHICKEN	I WON'T BE YOUR FRIEND
I DARE YOU	EVERYONE DOES IT	YOU WON'T GET CAUGHT
YOU OWE ME	I'LL GIVE YOU MONEY	YOU'VE DONE IT BEFORE
IT'LL BE GREAT	YOU WON'T GET HURT	YOU CAN'T CHANGE YOUR MIND

© 1996 Thinking Publications — *Duplication permitted for educational use only.*

Social Star

PEER PRESSURE TRICKS WORD SEARCH KEY

DIRECTIONS: Find and circle the phrases listed at the bottom of this page. They are all things people might say to trick you into doing something you don't think you should do. The phrases are hidden in the puzzle vertically, horizontally, and diagonally. (No spaces or apostrophes are included.)

Y	Y															I
O	O	Y	O	U	W	O	N	T	G	E	T	H	U	R	T	T
U	U															L
W	V		I	W	O	N	T	B	E	Y	O	U	R	F	R	I	E	N	D	L
O	E															B
N	D	P								Y	O	U	O	W	E	M	E
T	O		L													G
G	N			E										U		R
E	E			A								O			E
T	I				S						Y			A
C	T					E	V	E	R	Y	O	N	E	D	O	E	S	I	T
A	B									R					
U	E								A						
G	F						D								
H	O	Y	O	U	R	E	A	C	H	I	C	K	E	N		
T	R														
	E		I	L	L	G	I	V	E	Y	O	U	M	O	N	E	Y		
Y	O	U	C	A	N	T	C	H	A	N	G	E	Y	O	U	R	M	I	N	D

PLEASE	YOU'RE A CHICKEN	I WON'T BE YOUR FRIEND
I DARE YOU	EVERYONE DOES IT	YOU WON'T GET CAUGHT
YOU OWE ME	I'LL GIVE YOU MONEY	YOU'VE DONE IT BEFORE
IT'LL BE GREAT	YOU WON'T GET HURT	YOU CAN'T CHANGE YOUR MIND

Lesson C

EDUCATOR INFORMATION:

During this lesson, students are presented with five strategies that are appropriate for resisting peer pressure. These strategies provide a manageable repertoire of choices for students. *The Big Five* memory technique is also provided to help students remember the five strategies. In addition to the five strategies included in this unit, other ways to appropriately resist peer pressure exist. These include, but are not limited to:

- *Repeat*—Keep repeating your "no" statement.

- *Ignore*—Don't look at the person and don't say anything to the person.

- *Suggest alternative actions*—Suggest an appropriate activity that you would be willing to participate in.

- *Tell the consequences*—Remind yourself and people what might happen.

- Use *assertive body language*—Put your hands on your hips, face the person, and stare at him or her when you resist the pressure.

Embed these strategies in this lesson if appropriate to the age and level of the students.

OBJECTIVES:

1. To identify strategies for resisting peer pressure
2. To choose and practice strategies for resisting peer pressure

MATERIALS:

1. *The Big Five* (See page 277; one transparency.)
2. *Finger Bands* (See page 278; one transparency and one per student.)
3. *Scissors and tape* (For student use)
4. *Partner Practice* (See page 279; one transparency and one per pair of students.)
5. *Resisting Peer Pressure* classroom poster (See page 13.)

PREPARATORY SET:

Walk around the room and give a "high five" to each student in the class. Afterwards, hold up a hand and wiggle all five fingers. Tell students that in today's lesson, they will be learning about *The Big Five* technique to resist peer pressure.

PLAN:

1. Tell students that before learning *The Big Five,* you want to review the tricks they taught each other in Lesson B by using the *Whip Around–Pass Option*

strategy (Harmin, 1995). (This strategy increases the number of students who process and then volunteer answers.) "Whip" around your classroom by asking each student to either share one of the fourteen peer pressure tricks or to say, "I pass."

2. Display *The Big Five*. Introduce and practice each of the following strategies (scripts are provided as examples):

The "No"

The first strategy is called The "No." *It means you actually say "no" to the person pressuring you. When someone tries using any of the 14 pressure tricks on you, just say the word "no." You've got to say "no" like you mean it.* (Demonstrate saying "no" with a serious, confident tone of voice and facial expression.) *Sometimes you have to say "no" several times. Everyone please stand up. I want you to practice saying "no" five times. Walk around the room and say "no" to different people and say it like you really mean it.* (Participate and model a firm "no" yourself as you walk around with the students.)

The Getaway

The second strategy is called The Getaway. *It means you leave or walk away when someone is pressuring you. When someone uses tricks to pressure you, sometimes getting away is the best thing you can do. I want everyone to practice "The Getaway." First, get in a circle. Now turn to a person next to you, say "no," and practice getting away by walking out of the circle.* Emphasize that pushing or shoving is not allowed!

The "Because"

The third strategy is called The "Because." *It means you give a reason to the person pressuring you. When someone uses tricks to pressure you, you can just explain why you don't want to do it. You can say something like, "I don't want to smoke because my Grandpa died from smoking." We can remember this strategy by singing a phrase from the movie* The Wizard of Oz. (Sing the lyrics, *Because, because, because, because, becaauusse, because I can choose what's right for me,* to the tune of the song from *The Wizard of Oz.) I want everyone to practice "The Because" strategy by singing with me. Let's sing...Because, because...*

The SOS

The fourth strategy is called The SOS. *It means you get help when someone is pressuring you. We'll call it the SOS because in code called the Morse code, SOS means "help." When someone uses tricks to pressure you, you can try to resist the pressure yourself. However, sometimes it's hard to resist the pressure without telling a friend or an adult. When someone tries to trick you, get help. I would like everyone to practice "The SOS" by using sign language for the letters SOS. The letter "S" is formed this way...(following is an example). The "O" is formed this way...(following is an example). And then the "S" is made again. Practice signing SOS and remember it means* I need help!

The "Ha Ha Ha"

The fifth strategy is called The "Ha Ha Ha." *It means you respond with humor when someone is pressuring you by saying the words, "You've got to be kidding!" When someone uses tricks to pressure you, you can catch them off guard by responding with a humorous comment. I want everyone to practice "The 'Ha Ha Ha'" by saying, "You've got to be kidding! Ha Ha Ha!"*

3. Ask the students if they know of other ways to appropriately resist peer pressure. Discuss their ideas.

4. Tell the students they will need to remember *The Big Five* technique and you have a helpful way for them to do it. Display and distribute *Finger Bands*, scissors, and tape. Tell students to cut out each of the finger bands and then tape them onto each of their fingers, as reminders of "The Big Five."

5. Pair students (see *Appendix P*). Ask students to sit with their partners.

6. Display and distribute *Partner Practice*. As a class, read Situation #1. Ask students to decide which strategy they would choose to respond to Situation #1 and then mark the strategy on their sheets. Then have students practice the strategy chosen by demonstrating it to their partners. (For example, if a partner chooses to respond by using "The 'No,'" they should practice saying "no" in a confident manner.)

7. As a class, identify four more pressure situations that students their age might face. Write the situations (with tricks) on the transparency *Partner Practice* and instruct each pair of students to write them on their copies of *Partner Practice*.

8. Ask students to complete *Partner Practice* by deciding which strategy they might use to resist the pressure in each situation, mark it on their sheets in the corresponding column, and practice the strategy chosen. Walk around the classroom and check student pairs as they complete this activity.

9. Review the definition and skill step for *resisting peer pressure* by referring the class to the *Resisting Peer Pressure* classroom poster.

10. Ask student pairs to take turns telling each other the skill step for resisting peer pressure. Follow the procedure described in step **11** of Lesson A. Next, ask students to think of a situation when it would be important to resist peer pressure. Tell students that one or more pairs will be called on to share their situations.

———————★★★———————

It is better to be alone than in bad company.

George Washington

The Big Five

Five great ways to resist peer pressure

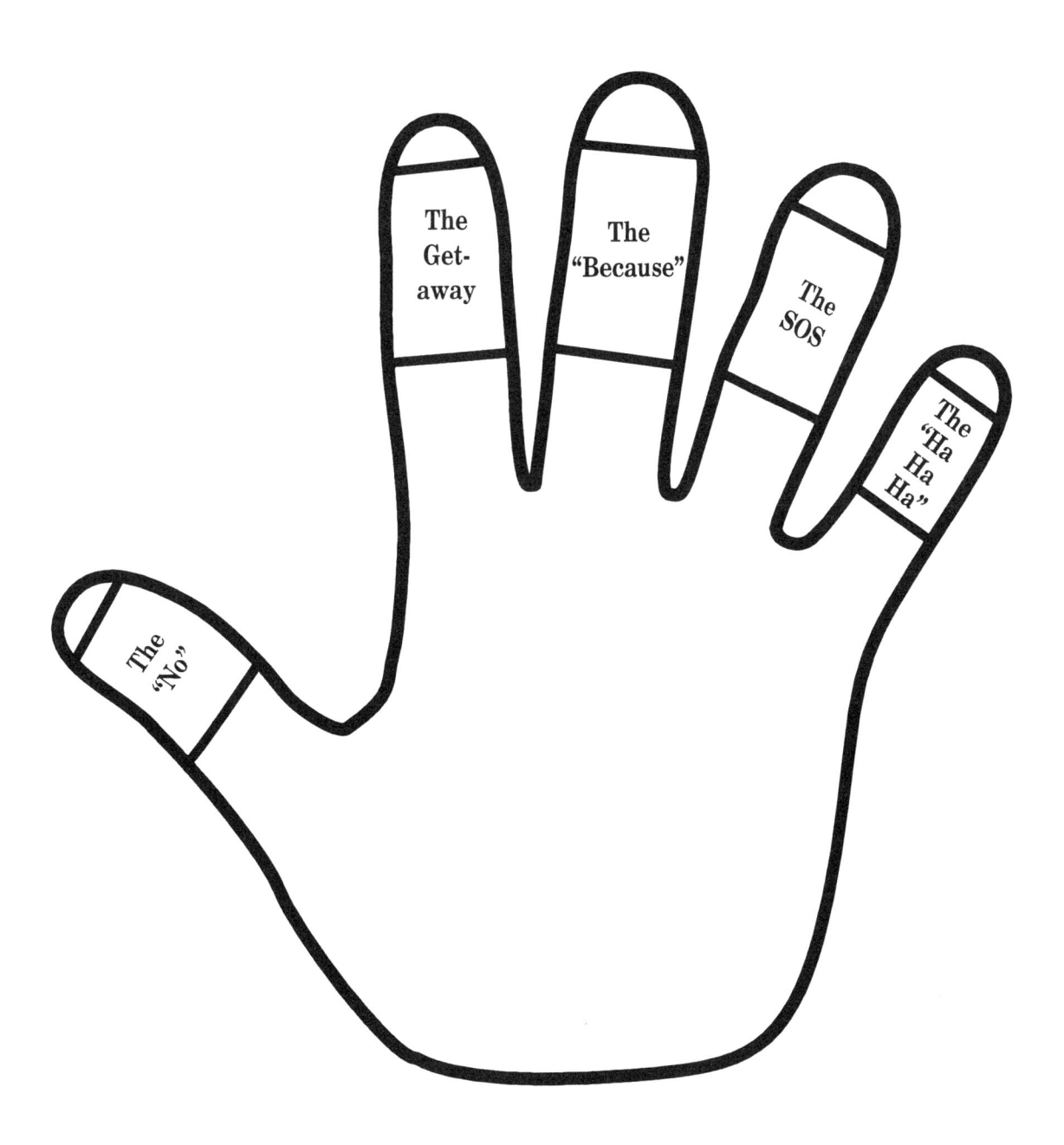

- The Get-away
- The "Because"
- The SOS
- The "Ha Ha Ha"
- The "No"

FINGER BANDS

| | The "No" | |

| | The Get-away | |

| | The "Because" | |

| | The SOS | |

| | The "Ha Ha Ha" | |

Names _____

Partner Practice

DIRECTIONS: Read Situation #1 as a class. Mark the strategy you choose to use to respond to the situation. Copy other situations from the transparency as your class creates them. Mark the strategy you choose to respond to the situation. Then practice the strategy for resisting the pressure.

	The "No"	The Getaway	The "Because"	The SOS	The "Ha Ha Ha"
Situation #1 Your brother wants you to lie and tell your parents that he's in his room. Really, he wants to sneak out to a friend's house. He says, "You owe me a favor!"					
Situation #2					
Situation #3					
Situation #4					
Situation #5					

Social Star

Lessons X, Y, and Z

Due to similarities in format, the final three lesson plans for each unit in *Social Star* are provided in *Appendix A*. Substitute the words "resisting peer pressure" whenever a "_____" appears in the lesson plans. Information specific to this unit follows.

LESSON X PREPARATORY SET:

Use the *Whip Around–Pass Option* strategy (Harmin, 1995) to have students describe a situation in the future in which they will be able to resist peer pressure. (The *Whip Around–Pass Option* strategy involves starting on one end of the class and having each student share an answer. A student may pass if unable to think of a response.)

LESSON Y PREPARATORY SET:

Darken the room, if you prefer, and ask the students to visualize themselves correctly using this social skill by reading the following script:

Let's take a few moments.... Make sure you are in a comfortable position.... Close your eyes if you feel like it.... On the count of three, take a very slow, deep breath. Remember to breathe in quietly through your nose. One...two... three.... Breathe in deeply.... Now breathe out slowly.... Remember to breathe out quietly through your mouth. Let your entire body relax.... Now imagine yourself listening to your friend who's trying to talk you into going to the bowling alley when your dad said you couldn't go. Your friend uses many tricks to try to convince you to go. First, your friend begs. Next, your friends offers you money. Then your friend says, "You owe me." You keep saying "No," like you really mean it. You feel proud that you are able to resist peer pressure.

LESSON Z PLOT SITUATION:

Two kids with whom you really want to be friends, want you to put a mean note in another student's desk.

LESSON Z ROADBLOCK EXAMPLES:

- Thinking the thing you're being pressured to do sounds fun and you'd like to try it
- Feeling scared of what will happen if you don't do what the other kids want you to do
- Feeling angry with your parents, so you're tempted to go along with the gang just to "show your parents"

- Going along with things and not really realizing what you're getting yourself into until it seems too late
- Feeling afraid you'll hurt someone's feelings if you say "no"
- Being afraid you'll get into trouble because someone will tell about something you did wrong in the past

Resisting Peer Pressure T-Chart

LOOKS LIKE...

using appropriate body talk

- having a serious facial expression
- looking directly at the person
- standing up straight

walking away

going to find an adult

SOUNDS LIKE...

an assertive tone of voice

an appropriate volume

saying

- "No"
- "You've got to be kidding!"

telling a reason why you don't want to do something

laughing at the pressure trick

SHOW TIME

HOME
Pretend your friend tries to talk you into having people over to your house when your parents are gone. Your friend says, "They'll never find out!" Demonstrate a strategy you could use to resist peer pressure.

SCHOOL
Pretend a student is pressuring you into letting him copy your homework. The student says, "If you don't let me copy, I'll tell the teacher what you did last month!" Demonstrate a strategy you could use to resist peer pressure.

COMMUNITY
Pretend a kid walks up to you at the mall and demands that you give him money. He threatens to hurt you if you won't give him any. Demonstrate a strategy you could use to resist peer pressure.

NEGATIVE PEER PRESSURE

DON'T BE TRICKED BY IT!

HOME-A-GRAM

Dear Family,

At school, we have been talking about the social skill called

RESISTING PEER PRESSURE

I learned that *resisting peer pressure* means not letting people talk me into doing what I think I should not do.

I learned about "tricks" that people might use when trying to pressure me.

I learned *The Big Five* strategies I can use to resist peer pressure. On the hand below, I have written the names of those strategies.

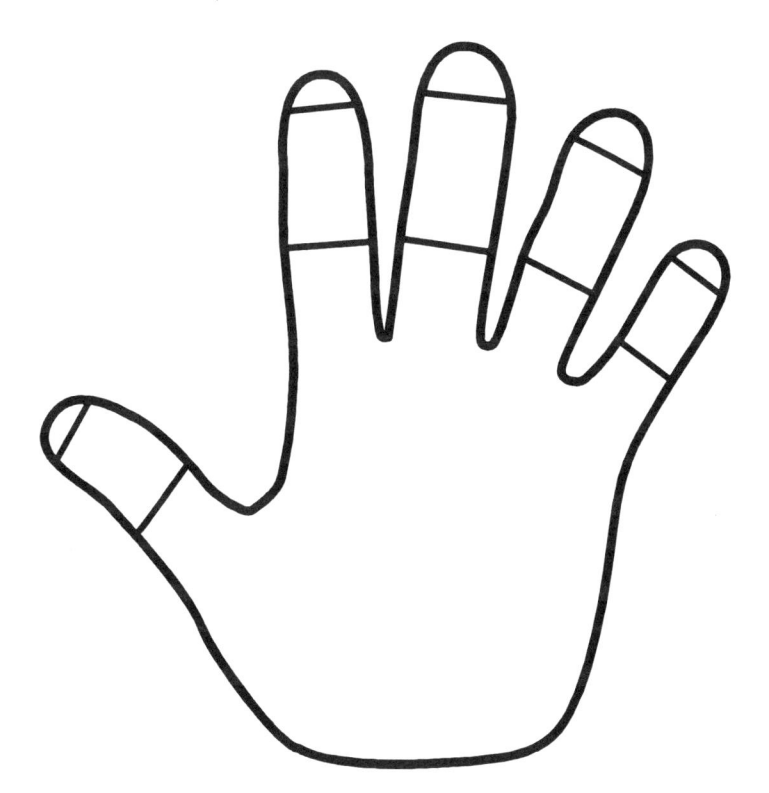

After I tell you about these five strategies at home tonight, and about some of the tricks people use to try to pressure others, please sign my "Resisting Peer Pressure" badge so I can return it to school and become a SOCIAL SUPER STAR this week.

From: _____

Settling Conflicts

Social Star

UNIT GOAL:

To demonstrate comprehension and use of strategies for settling conflicts

EDUCATOR INFORMATION:

1. Students are taught that conflicts are a natural part of life and that they can be positive experiences for several reasons. When a conflict occurs:

   - It means that people are willing to be honest and share their varying viewpoints.

   - It allows people to discover new perspectives.

   - It provides an opportunity for people to polish their skills of problem solving, negotiating, and compromising.

   In this unit, students are taught to seek win-win solutions to conflict.

2. Freeman (1989) describes the following five behavior styles which usually occur in conflict situations.

   Avoiding—One or both people withdraw from the conflict situation. They do not acknowledge the conflict or they refuse to deal with it.

   Smoothing—One person wants to preserve the relationship and does so by emphasizing common interests or areas of agreement rather than confronting the disagreement. This usually means "giving in." (People using this style are often taken advantage of.)

   Compromising—Both people bargain so that each side gets part of what it wants and gives up part of what it wants. Compromising is sometimes the best solution to a problem, but often people compromise without truly examining all the alternatives because they think that "splitting the difference" is the only solution.

   Forcing—One person makes the other person give in and gets what he or she wants at the other's expense.

   Problem solving—Both people agree to cooperate in finding a solution that will meet the needs of each person. Problem solving is difficult, but rewarding.

   Educators are encouraged to assist students in identifying problem-solving styles in conflict situations.

3. For more information about conflict resolution programs, contact:

National Institute for
Dispute Resolution
1726 M Street, NW, Suite 500
Washington, DC 20036
(202) 466-4764

Center for Conflict Resolution
200 N. Michigan Avenue
Suite 500
Chicago, IL 60601
(312) 372-6420

4. *Peer confrontation* is a concept similar to conflict resolution that can be used as inappropriate conflict resolution behavior occurs (Arllen, Gable, Hendrickson, 1996). Peer confrontation means students are taught how to challenge a peer's inappropriate behavior, identify the effects of the behavior on others, and assist the peer in selecting an alternative response. Peer confrontation has been successful in decreasing inappropriate verbalizations (Salend, Jantzen, and Giek, 1992), reducing noncompliant behaviors, insults, gestures, and threats, and increasing on-task behavior (Sandler, Arnold, Gable, and Strain, 1987). Steps for implementing a modified version of peer confrontation in the regular classroom are as follows:

- Teach all students to identify appropriate and inappropriate behaviors of peers.

- Teach all students to recognize the consequences of inappropriate behavior. Students can be taught to categorize consequences in the following manner.

  Tangible consequences (e.g., The desk will look terrible if you carve on it.)

  Intangible consequences (e.g., The teacher won't trust you anymore.)

  Short-term consequences (e.g., You'll get a detention.)

  Long-term consequences (e.g., The desk will be ruined for the next students.)

- Peers conduct problem solving that involves precisely describing the inappropriate behavior, discussing consequences, brainstorming alternatives, and challenging the target student to use alternative responses. (This process may initially need to be modeled to assist student problem solving.)

- Provide periodic retraining to peers to ensure success of the strategy.

- Continually monitor the use of the strategy by peers and the effects of the strategy on targeted students.

5. Sunburst Communications produces and sells videotapes geared to four different grade levels (Pre–K to 2, 2–4, 5–9, and 7–12) on the topics of character education, self-esteem, family life, health, and conflict resolution. To obtain a catalog, call 1-800-431-1934 or write to Sunburst Communications, 39 Washington Ave., P. O. Box 40, Pleasantville, NY 10570-0040.

RELATED ACTIVITIES:

1. Create a bulletin board entitled "Working It Out" that includes photographs of students shaking hands, putting their arms around each other, etc.

2. Have students interview a personnel director from an area corporation that's unionized to discuss ways employee disputes (conflicts) are handled and how contract negotiations are handled between management and the union. Help students understand that contract negotiations can be a time of many conflicts.

3. Have students identify several conflicts that are making headlines in the news. Discuss options (alternatives) the people could use (or could have used) to "work it out."

4. Discuss how words can hurt people. Have students interview a partner about a past conflict when hurtful words were said to them and the conflict didn't get worked out. Have students make a list of words or phrases that can hurt other people or draw posters about common themes underlying conflicts.

5. Explain what a continuum is. Have students identify conflicts or disagreements that fall on all points of the continuum (less severe conflicts such as disagreeing on what type of snack to eat compared to very severe conflicts such as one country invading another country).

6. Have students create a "Work It Out Invention" that would solve any problem. Have students develop problems and put them into the machine to see what solution the machine comes up with.

7. Have students bring in an old pair of shoes (or boots) from home. Line up the shoes in the front of the room. Discuss the phrase, "Put yourself in the other person's shoes." Give a conflict situation, go down the line of shoes and discuss various perspectives that people in the situation may have. As a related art activity, have each student draw a pair of shoes. Display the shoe drawings on a bulletin board and have students create a talk or thought bubble to represent what the person in the shoes would say or think in a given situation.

8. Discuss the idea of peace talks, especially if and when they are in the news.

9. Invite adults from different cultures to talk to the students about how their cultures' conventions for solving conflicts compare with the strategies presented in this unit.

It is important for educators to provide opportunities for students to work in groups, so they can experience social skills in contexts where social communication is needed. Therefore, educators are encouraged to have students complete the Related Activities in small groups whenever possible. Educators trained in cooperative learning could incorporate the five components (see pages 33–34) into the group activity. An excellent resource for teaching students cooperative skills and building a sense of community is *Tribes: A Process for Social Development and Cooperative Learning* (1987) by Jeanne Gibbs.

RELATED LITERATURE:

Big Book for Peace (1990) edited by Ann Durell and Marilyn Sachs, Dutton. (119 pages)

The Bridge Across (1980) by Max Bolliger, Andersen Press. (26 pages)

Smoky Night (1994) by Eve Bunting, Ill. by David Diaz, Harcourt. (32 pages)

Give Us a Great Big Smile, Rosie Cole (1981) by Sheila Greenwald, Little Brown. (76 pages)

Scooter (1993) by Vera B. Williams, Greenwillow. (147 pages)

SOCIAL SKILLS ALL DAY LONG:

Look for opportunities to teach social skills throughout the day (incidental teaching). Four ways to reinforce appropriate social skills and an example of each follow:

Encouragement

Ann, I admire the way you and Mike worked it out when you had a disagreement about how to end your story.

Personal Example

Last night, my daughter and I were disagreeing about which television show to watch. We settled our conflict by talking it over and by totally changing the activity and agreeing to read a book together instead.

Prompting

When you have a disagreement at home this week, remember to think of one of the ways to work it out.

Corrective Feedback (must be positive, private, specific, and nonthreatening)

Ann and Maria, just now I saw some pushing and shoving going on. The two of you might have used one of the strategies for settling conflicts. Which strategy could you have used?

———— ★★★ ————

In adversity, remember to keep an even mind.

Horace

Lesson A

OBJECTIVES:

1. To state the meaning of *settling conflicts* and tell why it's important
2. To listen to the self-talk associated with appropriate use of the skill

MATERIALS:

1. *I Know....* (See *Appendix V*; one per student and one transparency.)
2. *Settling Conflicts* (See page 294; one per student and one transparency.)
3. *Thought Bubble* (See *Appendix O*; one for educator use.)

PREPARATORY SET:

Write the following letter sequence where all students can easily see it:

QCRRJGLE AMLDJGARQ

Tell students that you have just written the title for the new *Social Star* unit they will be starting today. Explain you have written the title using a secret code. Challenge students to crack the code (Settling Conflicts). Explain that each letter you have written is really supposed to be two letters later in the alphabet. For example, the first letter, "Q," is really supposed to be the letter "S."

PLAN:

1. After introducing the title of the unit, work with students to define the term "conflict." Distribute and display *I Know....* to each student. Instruct students to write "Settling Conflicts" on the line above "I Know...." and on the line above "I Learned...." Ask them to write down what they already know about settling conflicts in the "I Know...." column. Model this by saying, "I know it's important to stay calm when settling conflicts so I might write, 'stay calm.'" Have students leave the "I Learned...." column blank. Collect the sheets to be completed during Lesson X. (As an alternative, the *I Know....* activity could be completed as a class with ideas written on a large sheet of butcher paper or it could be completed in pairs to increase sharing of ideas.)

2. Distribute and display *Settling Conflicts*. Discuss the definition of *settling conflicts*. Explain the skill steps for settling conflicts and the symbols next to them. Remind students that the symbols are there to help them visualize and remember the skill steps. Refer students to the body-talk symbol in the left-hand margin. Remind students that appropriate body talk is important when working out conflicts. Ask students to identify the specific body talk that is important when using this skill. Discuss the reasons for settling conflicts.

3. Model use of the skill steps for settling conflicts while thinking aloud. A scripted example follows:

   Introduction

   I am going to pretend to be someone your age who is settling a conflict. I will show you how I settle conflicts and tell you the thoughts I'm having. When I hold up this Thought Bubble, *you'll know the words I'm saying are actually what I'm thinking.*

   Actual Model

   While holding up the *Thought Bubble* say, *My sister and I are going to have popsicles for a snack. We both want an orange one, but there is only one orange popsicle left. How can we work this out? Some ways I can think of that could be fair for both of us are:*

   - *We could split the orange one in half.*

   - *She could have the orange one this time, if she agrees to let me pick first next time.*

   - *We could both choose a different flavor and save the orange one for Dad. That's his favorite flavor too.*

   Put the *Thought Bubble* down and say, *How about if we both choose a different flavor and save the orange for Dad, that's his favorite flavor too.*

4. Read the story at the bottom of *Settling Conflicts* aloud to students.

5. Ask students to process the story using the *Question, All Write* strategy (Harmin, 1995). This strategy maximizes the number of students who actually think about questions by asking students to write answers to questions before calling on them. Ask all students to write answers to the following questions before calling on students to answer them.

   - What was the conflict between Jolisa and Maria?
   - What did Jolisa and Maria do to "work it out"?
   - Did both girls listen to each other's ideas? Why or why not?
   - Can you think of another way they could have settled their conflict?
   - What might have happened if the girls had not worked together to come up with a solution they were happy with?

6. Pair students (see *Appendix P*). Ask student pairs to take turns telling each other the meaning of *settling conflicts* and why it's important to use the skill.

Students could be reminded that the information they are to say is printed on *Settling Conflicts*.

As an option to add structure to this activity, ask partners to come to an agreement about which person will be called "A," and which person will be called "B." After students have made their decisions, ask "A" to tell "B" the definition of *settling conflicts*. Next, ask "B" to tell "A" the definition. Ask students to use the same procedure to tell each other the reasons for settling conflicts.

---★★★---

Adversity introduces a man to himself.

Unknown

Social Star

Name _____

Settling Conflicts

MEANING OF SETTLING CONFLICTS:

Finding a way to work out disagreements so that everyone involved feels OK

SKILL STEPS:

1. Ask myself: What are ways we can settle this conflict?

2. Share ideas and listen to others

3. Choose an idea everyone agrees to

REASONS FOR USING THIS SKILL:

When you know how to work out disagreements, you will have a lifelong skill to use when working with others. People will respect your ability to promote peace. You can be proud when you do your part to settle conflicts.

DIRECTIONS: Listen to the story below. Look at the pictures while you are listening.

Jolisa and Maria were having a disagreement. They both wanted to be the recorder for the group they were working in at school. Jolisa said, "Well, we both want to be the recorder, so what are we going to do?" The girls thought about ways to settle the conflict. Maria said, "We could share the job. You could be the recorder during the first half of the project and I could be the recorder for the second half." Jolisa said, "That would work! Another thing we could do is let Lee be the recorder and we could both pick other jobs." Maria said, "Yeah. That would work too." After a short discussion, Jolisa and Maria both agreed to share the recording job.

© 1996 Thinking Publications   Duplication permitted for educational use only.

Lesson B

EDUCATOR INFORMATION:

During this lesson, students read a "choose your own ending book" called *Conflict in the Congo*. The story helps students learn six strategies for settling conflicts. The class reads the book together and decides which pages to turn to. Because there are various strands to the book (see *Flowchart* on page 324), it may take several days for students to read it and to learn the six strategies for solving conflicts.

OBJECTIVE:

To identify six ways to settle a conflict

MATERIALS:

1. *Conflict in the Congo* (See pages 297–322; duplicate pages back to back and assemble one storybook per student.)

2. *Six Ways to Settle a Conflict* (See page 323; one per student and one transparency.)

3. *Flowchart* (See page 324; one transparency.)

PREPARATORY SET:

Ask students if they have ever read a choose-your-own-ending book before. Ask students who are familiar with that type of book to explain how they work. If no one volunteers, explain that a choose-your-own-ending book allows the reader to make decisions about what should happen next in the story. Tell students that during today's lesson about settling conflicts, they will be reading a choose-your-own-ending book that teaches six ways to solve a conflict. Write the following sequence where all students can easily see it:

EQPHNKEV KP VJG EQPIQ

Tell students that you have just written the title for the choose-your-own-ending book. Explain that you have written the title using a secret code. Challenge students to crack the code (Conflict in the Congo). Explain that each letter you have written stands for two letters earlier in the alphabet. For example, the first letter, "E," is really supposed to be the letter "C".

PLAN:

1. Remind students that the book called *Conflict in the Congo* will teach six strategies people can use to settle a conflict. Ask students if they can guess what any of those six strategies might be. Respond to all guesses by saying, "We'll find out if your guess is correct when we read the story."

Social Star

2. Distribute *Conflict in the Congo*. Ask students to identify where the Congo is. Before beginning, it is important that students understand that the Congo is in a jungle setting.

3. Distribute and display *Six Ways to Settle a Conflict*. Explain that each time one of the strategies for settling a conflict is explained in the book, they will be stopping to write the name of the strategy next to one of the six arrows.

4. As a class, read *Conflict in the Congo*. Have the class vote on which decisions to make. Each time you come to a page in the story that describes one of the six strategies, **the page number will be marked with an ***. When you finish reading one of those pages, stop to display *Six Ways to Settle a Conflict*. Write the title for the strategy (the titles are bold printed in the story) next to one of the arrows on the transparency and ask students to write the same thing on their sheets.

5. After completing each strand of the story, stop to display *Flowchart*. Highlight the lines on the flowchart that follow the completed story strand. This will help students in two ways. First, they can get a picture of how the choose-your-own-ending book is organized. Second, it will be a good record of which strands have been completed. Continue reading the book until all strands have been read.

6. After students have discovered the six ways to solve a conflict, discuss them as a class. Collect their completed *Six Ways to Settle a Conflict* sheets. Save them, as well as the completed transparency, for use during step 2 of Lesson C.

(If desired, adapt the above plan so that it fits the level of the class. A different lesson plan may involve having students work in cooperative groups to discover as many different strategies as they can. To shorten the amount of time spent on the story, small groups could be given certain pages to read and then come back to the large group to share. As an extension, have students develop their own flowchart that shows the layout of the book. The flowchart could be used as a way to show students how to "analyze" any kind of story or it could be used as a transition into story mapping. Students may also enjoy drawing additional features on each page. Encourage students to create their own story using a computer writing program.)

———————— ★★★ ————————

He that wrestles with us strengthens our nerves and sharpens our skill.
Our antagonist is our helper.

Edmund Burke

Conflict in the Congo

It's a summer morning. You are riding bikes with your friends, Curly, Shep, and Mo. You feel happy to be outside with them. You really don't care where you ride. But, your three friends are disagreeing about where to go. Each one wants to go to a different place. Curly wants to go to the carnival, Shep wants to ride to the shopping mall, and Mo insists on going to the movie theater. Before you know it, everyone is upset. You are thinking to yourself, "Oh, come on! Why don't they work this out so we can enjoy the day." Before you have a chance to say anything, your bikes suddenly go flying into the sky. You can't believe your eyes! You keep flying higher and higher into the air. First you go over the treetops. Then, you go even higher. You and your friends are almost to the clouds!

Go to page 5.

1

You find some twigs and start a fire with your expert survival skills. You hear something in the far-off distance. It sounds like a plane. It's coming closer and closer. You start to fan the fire so the airplane will see the smoke. Your plan works! The plane lands and flies you back to your homes. On the way home, you eat lots of peanuts.

THE END

Curly says, "How is that going to help? We are friends and look how we are fighting!" You say, "Have you ever tried to **find a mediator**?" They look at you with confusion written all over their faces. Finally Mo asks, "What's a meteor?" You say, "Not a meteor, a mediator. A mediator is someone who helps people settle their arguments." Larry wants to know where you learned that fancy word. You reply, "I just learned how to be a peer mediator at school." You go on to explain that a mediator is not like a judge who makes a final decision. A good mediator asks each person in a conflict to tell his or her side of the story. Then the mediator encourages them to work together to find a solution. You say, "So, do you want me to be your mediator?"

If they all nod their heads in agreement, go to page 6.

If they say, "Let's find out how to get home first," go to page 10.

3*

Boo kila may, zimbo zay means, "Hey, you guys, we're not very tasty. Let's see if you can agree on a totally different idea for what to eat." The creatures keep licking their chops and rubbing their bellies. You keep talking. "You don't want to eat us! Have you ever tried coconuts? Or how about bananas?" You throw a few bananas and coconuts to the creatures. They don't seem to know what to do with them.

You crack open a coconut and show them how to drink the milk and eat the coconut meat. You peel a banana and demonstrate how to eat that, too. The creatures look puzzled. Finally, one of them tries a banana. A big smile spreads across her face. The others try the bananas and coconuts. They love them! Suddenly they run toward you and hug you. They pick you up and put you on their shoulders. (They also pick up your friends who are still laying on the ground.) They carry you to a cave at the top of a mountainside.

If you suddenly sit up in bed, go to page 11.

If you see a huge glowing crystal ball, go to page 24.

4

When you reach the clouds you all start falling very quickly to the ground. Everyone is screaming and yelling. You are falling, falling, falling. Suddenly, you start floating very slowly and you land on top of a palm tree. You look around and see that your friends are in the palm tree with you. Everyone looks relieved and starts to laugh. Finally you say, "I think we're in a jungle in the Congo. How will we get down from this tree?" That was a big mistake! Curly yells, "Let's try to slide down the tree trunk." Larry argues, "No, let's break off some palm branches and make feathers for ourselves." Mo angrily disagrees, "Don't be foolish. We'll just jump!" Once again, your friends are having a conflict and none of them seem willing to work it out.

If you decide to whistle loudly, go to page 16.

If you decide to use your rope skills, go to page 8.

5

You say, "We don't need to solve how to get down from the palm tree, because we're already down. So, let's work out the disagreement about what to do on our bikes when we get home. Remember I'm the mediator, so I'm not going to take sides. I just want to help you three find a way to solve your conflict in a way that you can all agree to. Mo, where did you want to go?" Mo says, "Well, I certainly didn't want to come here! I was hoping we could all go to the movie theater." Next you say, "Curly, what was your idea?" Curly says, "I kind of like it here, but I thought going to the carnival at home would be fun." Next Shep explains, "I really wanted to go to the shopping mall." You ask, "Can any of you think of a way to work out this disagreement?" After a long pause, Mo says, "Hey, I've got an idea!" Before Mo has a chance to share his idea, you all realize the area has been surrounded by large rodents in ninja costumes. They look like they might want to play. You try to tiptoe away and motion for your friends to follow. You notice a red flashing button on a nearby tree. You sneak over to the button. It says, "Press me." You don't have a lot to lose at this point because when you all move toward the tree, the rodents move closer!

Go to page 19.

Liko, biko, siko, gum noto pob means "Humans don't digest well!" The creatures don't believe you, so you try a different approach. You say, "Let's have a race to that huge boulder. I'll race your fastest runner. If I win, you release us and help us get out of the Congo. If you win, I guess we're chopped liver. Does that sound fair?" All of the creatures nod their heads yes. You revive your friends and tell them about the race. The fastest creature steps forward and you both take your places at the starting line. Your heart is pounding. Can you really win? One of the creatures makes a strange noise to signal the start of the race. You are off to a slow start as the creature speeds way ahead of you.

If you catch up to the creature, go to page 12.

If your legs are lead and the creature is way ahead of you, go to page 14.

While everyone is yelling and arguing, you grab a vine and make a lasso. You swing the lasso around and around and lasso your friends together. After tying the lasso vine onto the top of your tree, you lower them to the ground. Then you slide down the lasso vine only to find that your friends are still upset with each other. Finally, you say, "I thought this was supposed to be a fun day together! Do you realize this is your second conflict in less than 15 minutes? That's probably why we ended up in the Congo. You're acting like animals!"

If the next thing you say is..."Do you remember the story about the three little pigs?" turn to page 23.

If the next thing you say is..."Maybe you just need a little help from a friend," turn to page 3.

If the next thing you say is..."Haven't you ever heard of the song that says, 'We can work it out'"? turn to page 18.

8

You are all laughing and cannot stop. You try to stop but everything seems funny. After an hour of laughter, you feel exhausted and sit down. You say, "You know, we could solve our conflict about where to go on our bikes if we **take turns**. If we find our way home, we could go to the shopping mall today, to the carnival tomorrow, and to the movie theater the next day." Your friends agree to take turns. Mo asks, "Are any of you hungry? I'm starving!" You all think that eating something would be a good idea.

If you decide to build a fire to warm some food, turn to page 2.

If you decide to look around for some food, turn to page 15.

9*

THERE'S NO PLACE LIKE HOME

Shep says, "Now I know how Dorothy and ToTo must have felt when they were in Oz." Mo says, "Hey, she clicked her heels together. But what did she keep saying to get home?" Curly argues, "No way, she went home in a hot air balloon!" You say, "Before this turns into another fight, quickly close your eyes and repeat after me. 'There's no place like home. There's no place like home.'" When you all open your eyes, you are back home on your bikes again. Shep says, "This is really weird. We better decide on a mediator without fighting or we'll end up back in the Congo."

THE END

10

You look around and see that you are in your very own bedroom. "Hey, where are Shep, Mo, and Curly? What happened to all those goofy looking creatures?" Your heart is still pounding. All of a sudden, your alarm clock goes off. You look at the time. It's morning. Time to get up and meet your friends. You hope they don't argue about where to go. You don't want to end up in the Congo for real!

THE END

11

Settling Conflicts

You pass the creature and make it to the big boulder first. You have saved your life and the lives of your friends. All of the creatures gather around you. They have brought your three friends. They point to the sky and you look up and see a huge bubble floating downward. The bubble lands on the ground and a small little door on the bubble opens. The littlest creature motions for you to climb inside the bubble. You and your three friends climb inside. The creatures wave good-bye and shut the bubble door. Suddenly, you can see that the bubble is being lifted off the ground and is floating up into the sky. The creatures below get smaller and smaller. While you are in the bubble, you all agree on a different idea for what to do on your bikes when you get home. You agree to ride to the ice cream shop. When the bubble floats over your hometown, it lands in the exact spot where your bikes started to fly. You all climb out of the bubble and pedal to the ice cream shop.

THE END

12

Social Star

The gorilla starts to cry. He tells all of you about his family. He and the other gorillas in his home constantly disagreed. He says, "To this very day, we still can't settle a conflict." Pretty soon Curly, Shep, and Mo are crying too, because they feel badly about disagreeing so much. After telling the gorilla about the strategy called *combine your ideas,* he can't wait to find his brothers and sisters and try it. To express his appreciation, he shares the secret for how to get out of the Congo. He tells you that a man named Gilligan will be arriving on a nearby island with a boat to take you home. The gorilla swims to the island with the four of you on his back. He asks if you'll be his pen pal. An hour later, Gilligan arrives and you all head for home.

THE END

13

You feel like you are running in slow motion. The creature is so far ahead of you that you can barely see it. You hear a huge bird flapping as you run. Suddenly the bird lifts you off the ground a few inches and flies you closer and closer to the creature. You pass the creature and win the race. You thank the bird for its help. You are in the middle of your thank-you's when you feel yourself tumbling down a hole. Luckily, Curly, Shep, and Mo are with you. When you finally stop falling, you look around and realize that you are standing outside of your house. You smile and think about how nice it is to be home. You hope it's a long time before you have an adventure like that again.

THE END

14

Social Star

You start to walk through the thick bushes. You hold onto each other so you don't lose anyone. All of a sudden, you all slide down a muddy hill into a creek. The creek carries you downstream to a river. Your friends come floating down the river after you. You notice gold on the river's bed.

Everyone starts to gather gold nuggets and shove them into a sack. Fortunately, a canoe is by the side of the river, so you all climb in. The canoe won't float with everyone in it and the gold. Something will have to go. Everyone agrees (can you believe it?) to throw the gold overboard. You paddle the canoe down the river to the big blue ocean. The Coast Guard rescues you and takes you home.

THE END

15

Settling Conflicts

You give a loud shrill whistle to get your friends' attention. You say, "This arguing is ridiculous! First you argued about where to go on our bikes, and now you are arguing about how to get down from this tree. We've got more important things to do, like finding our way home! Each of you pick a coconut. We'll crack them open and see whose has the most milk. We'll let that person decide on a safe way to get down. This way everyone has an equal chance." Your friends agree, and each one picks a coconut. Curly's has the most milk. He decides you should all climb down one at a time. His plan works! If you all feel so happy to be down from the palm tree, that you...

Start singing, go to page 20.

Start laughing, go to page 9.

Start dancing, go to page 22.

16

You see something in the distance. It's not a plane, but a gigantic white goose with an elderly woman riding on its back. Could it be "you know who"? Yes, it's Mother Goose! She swoops down and picks up your friends and you. She says in rhyme,

"Agree to disagree,
An option that can be,
You know you'll be OK,
If you go your
   separate ways."

First she flies to the carnival and drops off Curly. Next she flies to the shopping mall and drops off Shep. After she takes Mo to the movie theater, she asks you where you want to go. You say, "Thank you, Mother Goose. I've learned enough about conflict for one day. I'd just like to go home."

THE END

Your friends have never heard of the song. When they ask how it goes, you say, "Well, I don't really remember. But I do know one way to work this out is to **combine your ideas**. It's early in the day or at least it was when we were back home. There's time to do all three things." Mo, Shep, and Curly agree. You're all so excited about this solution that no one sees the huge gorilla approaching. When you finally notice, you're speechless. All you can do is point at the gorilla as he gets closer and closer. He leaps, grabs all of you, and puts you into a large sack. You are bumped around as the gorilla drags the sack over rocks and tree roots. It seems you are squished in the sack for a long time. Finally, the gorilla stops walking and starts to open the sack. Shep whispers, "Pretend we're asleep." Curly whispers, "No, let's jump out of the bag and try to run away." Mo says, "Let's pretend we're gorillas too." Mo, Shep, and Curly are arguing again about what to do. You can't believe it!

If you explain to the gorilla that your friends often argue like this, go to page 13.

If you yell, "Stop arguing!" go to page 21.

18*

Social Star

You press the red button and the branches of the tree come alive and pick up the four of you. The branches begin swaying wildly. It is difficult to hold on. You look around and realize you're all wearing capes. The ninja rodents are now climbing the tree with a look of victory on their faces. "Fly!" you shout to your friends as the tree branches give a final shake. You are hurled from the branches and your capes catch the breeze. You realize you are flying. Soon you see your bikes and go in for a landing. You shed your capes, hop on your bikes, and cross the border. You pedal and pedal. Just as you think you can pedal no more, you smell a familiar smell. It's the fast food restaurant in your hometown. You all realize how hungry you are. You go inside and order some fries. You finish mediating where to ride bikes. You all agree to go to the carnival because today is the last day. You have a great time on the rides at the carnival, but they are not quite as exciting as your ride to the Congo!

THE END

You celebrate by singing, "If You're Happy and You Know It…" When the song is over, you say, "I'd sing again if we could find a way home and then agree on where to go on our bikes. If you can't decide between the mall, the theater, or the carnival, maybe we could all **agree on a totally different idea**?" Shep says, "There are all kinds of other places we could ride to. I'm sure we could find one we could all agree on."

As Mo and Curly nod in agreement, you notice 20 pairs of beady eyes staring at you from the bushes. You whisper to your friends, "We're being watched!" You all start to walk backwards slowly to get away from the beady eyes. All of a sudden, 20 strange looking creatures come walking out of the bushes. Mo, Shep, and Curly all faint. You stand there frozen as the creatures walk toward you. When the creatures are about five feet away, one of them says, "Wi walla bo tamra zoopa zoppa lubo." Even though you normally don't speak that language, you suddenly know that it means, "Please come with us. We want to have you for our dinner."

If you say, "Boo kila may, zimbo zay," go to page 4.

If you say, "Liko, biko, siko, gum noto pob," go to page 7.

20*

The gorilla doesn't like your yelling! He picks up the sack and swings it around his head about 20 times. He lets go and you feel yourselves landing on something hard. You also hear a splash and feel water leaking through the bag. You quickly kick loose the tie and discover you're on a raft made of logs. You float all day and when the sun starts to set, the raft drifts ashore. All of a sudden, there are cameras flashing and people clapping. You are back home! Even though there is no time left today to try your plan of going to the carnival, the movie theater, and the shopping mall, you know there will always be another day!

THE END

21

You dance for hours. You find yourselves doing dances you've never heard of before. You dance the jitterbug, then the waltz, and last but not least, you dance the twist. You decide to quit dancing because you are getting blisters on your feet. You say to your friends, "You know, opening coconuts worked great to decide how to get down from the palm tree. Maybe we could do something similar to help us decide what to do on our bikes when we get home. Maybe we could **draw straws or flip a coin**? Curly, Mo, and Shep think that is a great plan. You decide to draw straws, but the problem is that you can't find any straws in the Congo.

Go to page 25.

22*

Mo says, "This is no time for fairy tales! We have a serious problem here!"

You say, "Yeah! And so did the three little pigs! What I mean is that when the three little pigs couldn't agree on what to build their house out of, they decided to **agree to disagree**." Shep says, "I remember the story. When they couldn't agree, they didn't get angry with one another. They went their separate ways and each pig did its own thing." Curly suggests, "When we get back home, maybe we could agree to disagree and do different things today. We can ride bikes together another day."

Go to page 17.

23*

You notice that the glowing crystal ball changes color every few seconds. You walk closer and hear a deep voice. The voice says, "You will always have conflict in your life. You must learn how to deal with it in a positive way. Then you will hold the key to happiness in life. Now go forward knowing that you possess the skills to handle any conflict that comes your way." As the voice fades away, the cave is filled with a red foggy mist. You can't see around you. You feel very tired, so you lie down and then fall asleep. Three days later, you wake up and realize that you are sitting in a throne-like chair. The creatures are all around. You and your friends are now their leaders. You live happily ever after solving conflicts in the Congo.

THE END

24

Social Star

You decide to draw sticks instead. The person who draws the longest stick gets to pick where to go on the bikes. Mo draws a stick and it is very short. Shep draws a stick and it is medium-sized. Curly gets a big smile and starts pulling on the last stick. The stick is so long, it keeps coming and coming. Soon the stick extends up into the sky. The four of you decide to climb the stick. After everything that has happened, you wouldn't be surprised if you climbed up to find a castle in the sky, just like Jack and the Beanstalk. Well, you didn't find a castle, but you did find Peter Pan who flew you back home. Since Curly drew the longest stick, you all took Peter Pan to the carnival and had a great time.

THE END

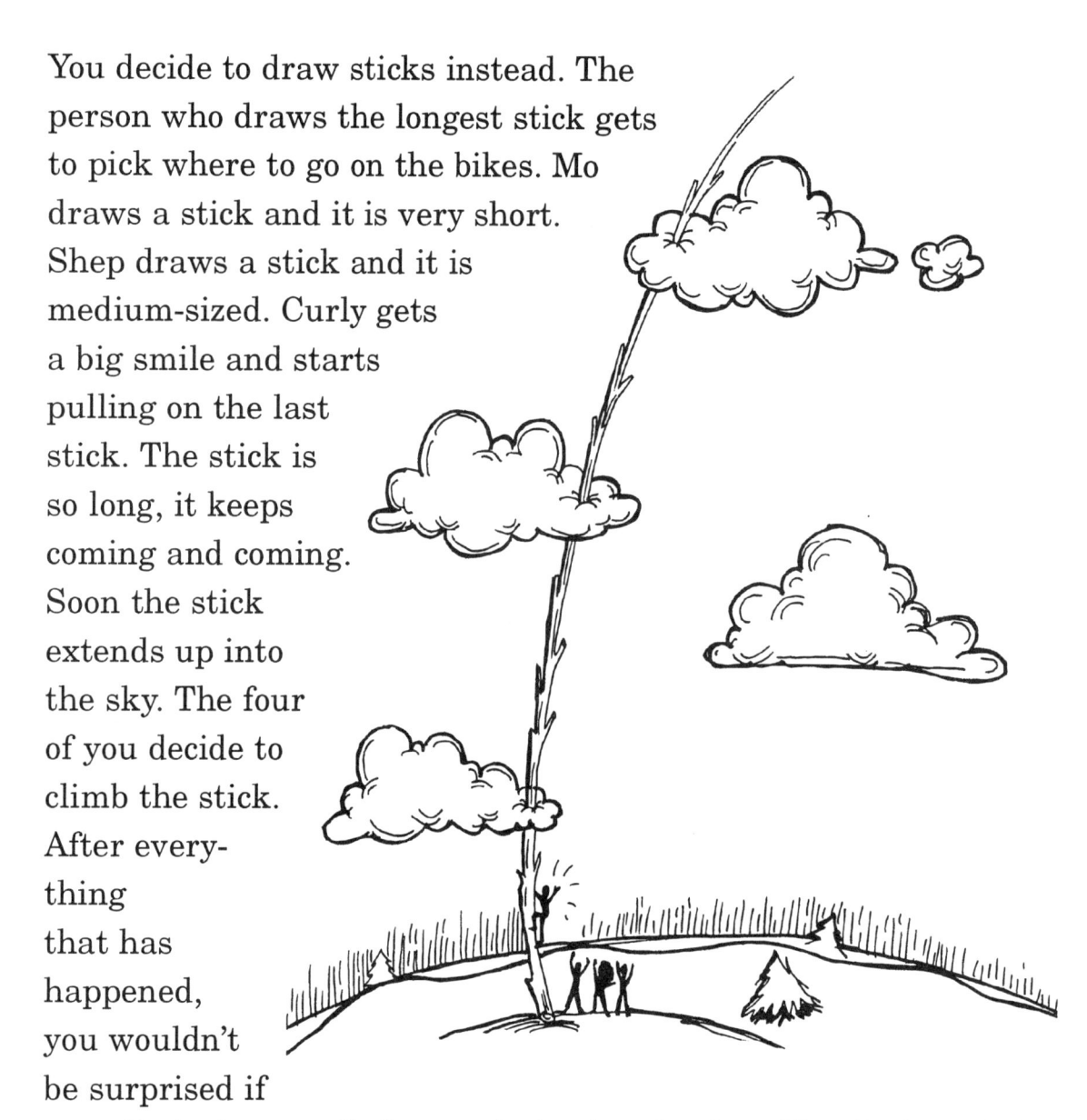

25

Settling Conflicts

Name _____

Six Ways to Settle a Conflict

1

6

2

Six Ways to Settle a Conflict

5

3

4

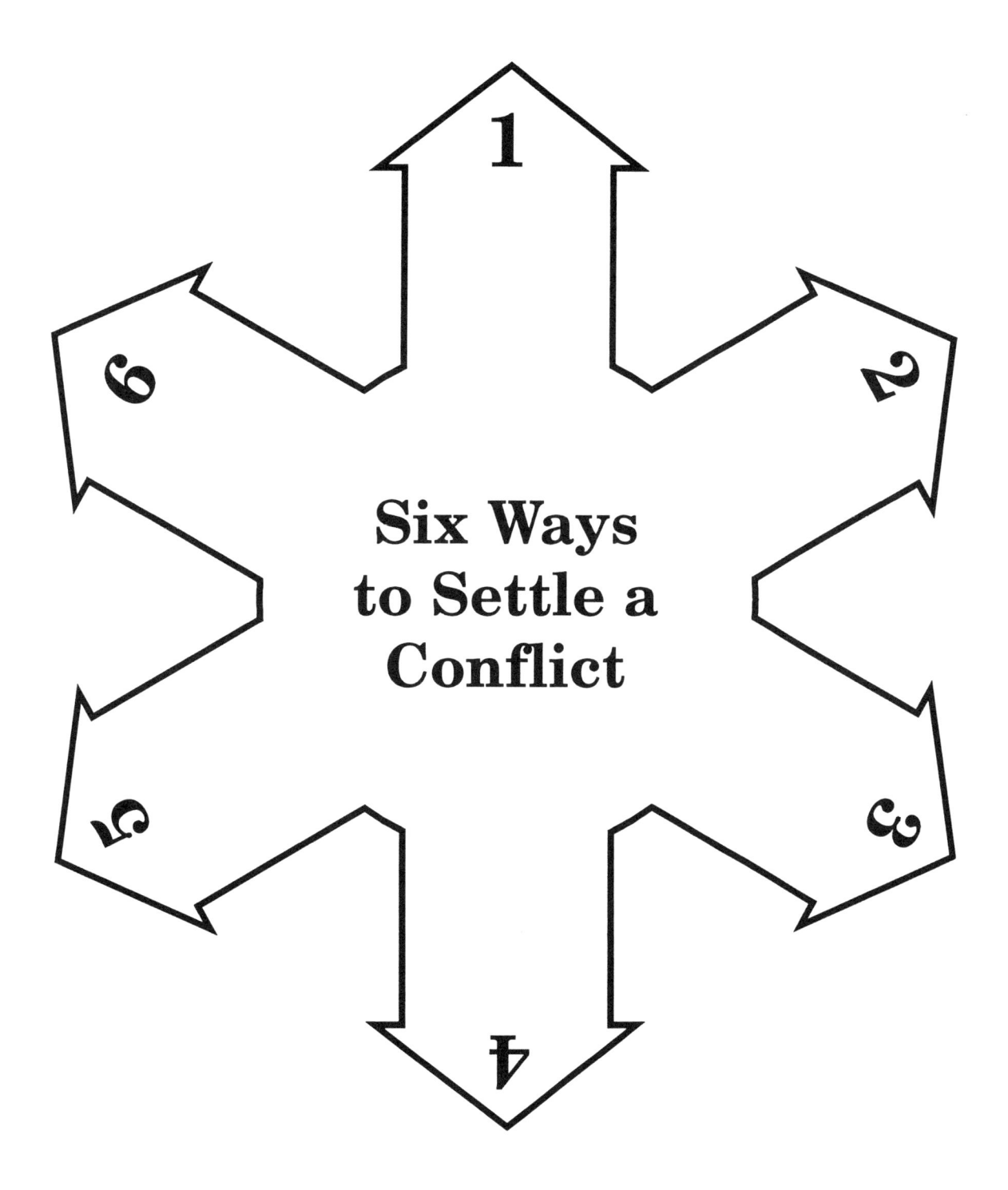

Flowchart

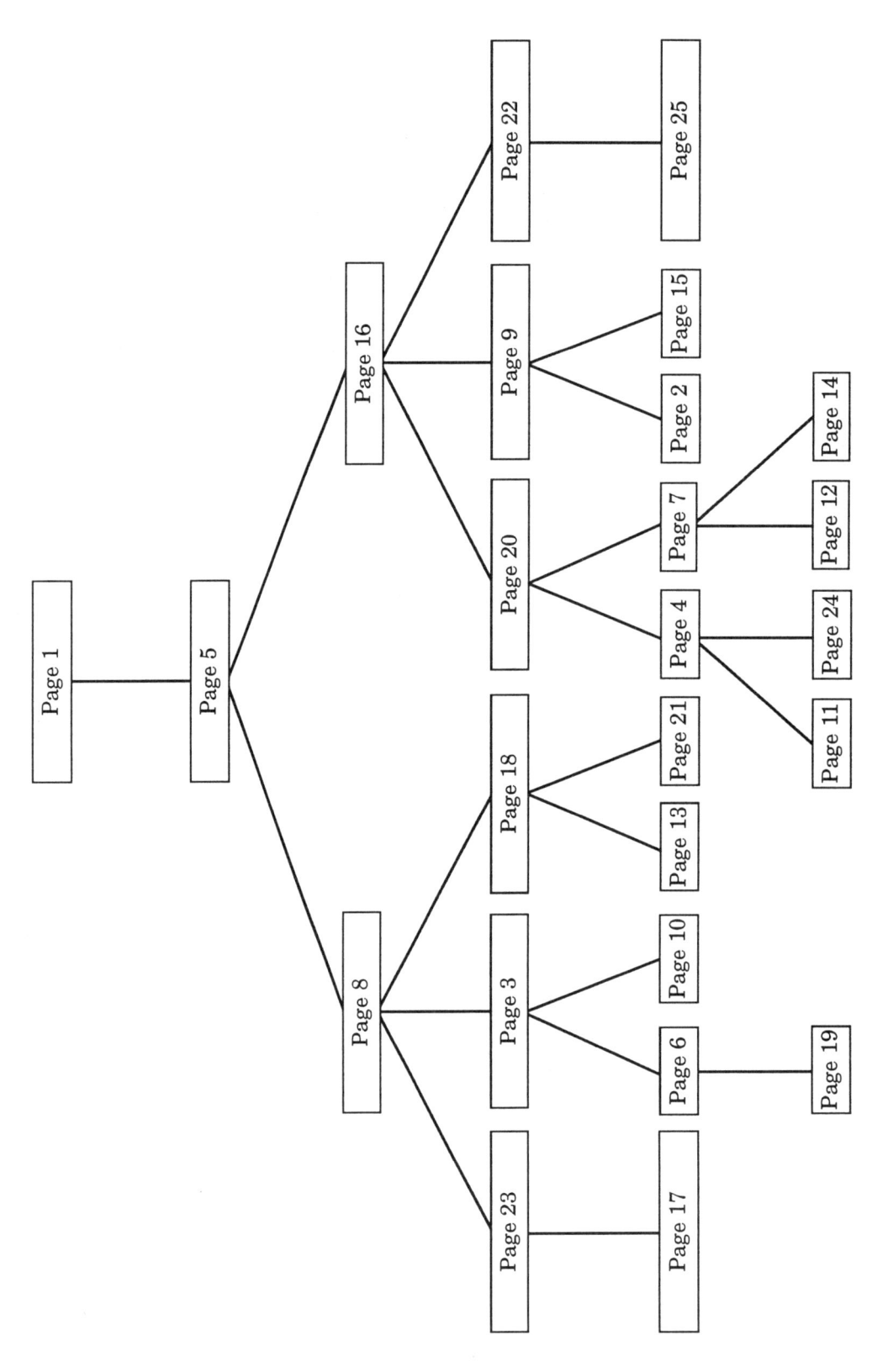

- Page 1 → Page 5
  - Page 5 → Page 16
    - Page 16 → Page 22
      - Page 22 → Page 25
    - Page 16 → Page 9
      - Page 9 → Page 15
      - Page 9 → Page 2
  - Page 5 → Page 20
    - Page 20 → Page 7
      - Page 7 → Page 14
      - Page 7 → Page 12
    - Page 20 → Page 4
      - Page 4 → Page 24
      - Page 4 → Page 11
  - Page 5 → Page 8
    - Page 8 → Page 18
      - Page 18 → Page 21
      - Page 18 → Page 13
    - Page 8 → Page 3
      - Page 3 → Page 10
      - Page 3 → Page 6
        - Page 6 → Page 19
    - Page 8 → Page 23
      - Page 23 → Page 17

Lesson C

EDUCATOR INFORMATION:

Designate six areas of the room as conflict stations. During this lesson, students will rotate through several conflict stations with a partner. Before the lesson, duplicate pages 327–340. Cut each page in half and place the halves together at a station.

OBJECTIVE:

To practice settling conflicts in a variety of contrived situations

MATERIALS:

1. *Settling Conflicts* classroom poster (See page 13.)

2. *Six Ways to Settle a Conflict* (Saved from Lesson B; one per student and one transparency.)

3. *Conflict Situations* (See pages 327–340; one copy of each page, cut in half.)

4. *Settling Conflicts Log* (See page 341; several per pair of students depending on how many stations pairs will rotate through; and one transparency.)

PREPARATORY SET:

Tell students that in today's lesson, they will practice settling several conflicts with a partner. Pair students using *Animal Sounds* (see Appendix P).

PLAN:

1. Review the definition and skill steps for settling conflicts by referring the class to the *Settling Conflicts* classroom poster.

2. Display and distribute the completed copies of *Six Ways to Solve a Conflict* that were saved from Lesson B. Briefly review the six strategies. Tell students they can refer to their sheets while they are working with their partners.

3. Tell student pairs that you will be assigning a conflict station for each of them to report to. Explain that when they get to their assigned station, each person should choose one of the two half-sheets located at the station. One person from each pair will receive a "Person A" half-sheet and one person will receive a "Person B" half-sheet. "Person A" and "Person B" are in a conflict and by reading both half-sheets the conflict will be discovered. (As an alternative, have students brainstorm the conflicts to be used in the scenarios at each station in place of those provided. A blank *Conflict Situation* form is provided on page 340.)

4. Distribute and display *Settling Conflicts Log*. Explain that after student pairs have read about the conflict at their assigned stations, they should work together to complete one copy of *Settling Conflicts Log* by writing their names, describing the conflict, brainstorming ideas for settling the conflict, and choosing an idea on which they can both agree.

5. Choose an assistant and model how the *Settling Conflicts Log* should be completed by using the half-sheets for Conflict Situation 1.

6. Assign each pair of students to a different conflict station and ask pairs to get started. Rotate pairs through as many stations as time allows or do this activity on more than one day.

———————— ★★★ ————————

Sweet are the uses of adversity.

William Shakespeare

Conflict Situation 1

Person A

You and your friend are ordering a pizza. You like pepperoni and onion, but hate green pepper.

Conflict Situation 1

Person B

You and your friend are ordering a pizza. You like pepperoni and mushroom, but hate onion.

Conflict Situation 2

Person A

Your family just got a black kitten. It has one white patch of fur on its stomach. You think the kitten should be named "Oreo."

Conflict Situation 2

Person B

Your family just got a black kitten. It has one white patch of fur on its stomach. You think the kitten should be named "Patch."

Conflict Situation 3

Person A

You are at your friend's house for the evening. At 8:00, you want to watch your favorite TV show on channel 3.

Conflict Situation 3

Person B

Your friend is at your house for the evening. At 8:00, you want to watch a movie on channel 12.

Social Star

Conflict Situation 4

Person A

You and your friend are going swimming. You want to go to the Weston pool because it has inner tubes.

Conflict Situation 4

Person B

You and your friend are going swimming. You want to go to the Kennedy pool because it has diving boards.

© 1996 Thinking Publications — Duplication permitted for educational use only.

Settling Conflicts

Conflict Situation 5

Person A

You and your brother or sister are riding in your family's car. You want the radio turned on.

Conflict Situation 5

Person B

You and your brother or sister are riding in your family's car. You want the radio turned off.

Social Star

Conflict Situation 6

Person A

Your family is going to donate a gift to a child during the holidays. The child likes crafts. You want to donate construction paper and markers.

Conflict Situation 6

Person B

Your family is going to donate a gift to a child during the holidays. The child likes crafts. You want to donate crayons and stickers.

© 1996 Thinking Publications — Duplication permitted for educational use only.

Conflict Situation 7

Person A

Your family is traveling and can make one "fast food" stop for lunch. You want a hamburger and French fries.

Conflict Situation 7

Person B

Your family is traveling and can make one "fast food" stop for lunch. You want a submarine sandwich.

Social Star

Conflict Situation 8

Person A

You and your friend are starting a new club. You think your club should be called "The Protectors" because you will be doing projects to protect the environment.

Conflict Situation 8

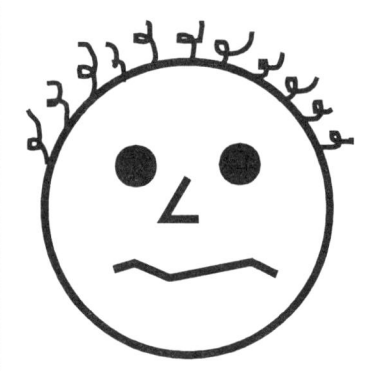

Person B

You and your friend are starting a new club. You think your club should be called "The Earth Savers" because you will be doing projects to help clean up the earth.

© 1996 Thinking Publications — *Duplication permitted for educational use only.*

Conflict Situation 9

Person A

You and your neighbor are disagreeing about what radio station is best. You prefer WSAW.

Conflict Situation 9

Person B

You and your neighbor are disagreeing about what radio station is best. You prefer WRIG.

Social Star

Conflict Situation 10

Person A

You and your friend want to hang out together on Saturday. You want your friend to come to your house.

Conflict Situation 10

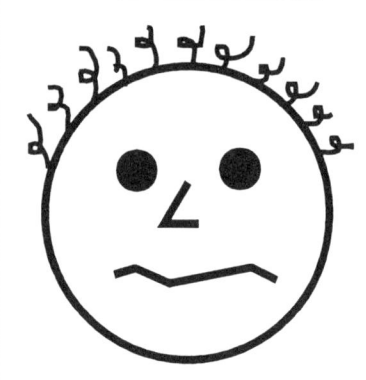

Person B

You and your friend want to hang out together on Saturday. You want you and your friend to go to the video arcade.

© 1996 Thinking Publications — *Duplication permitted for educational use only.*

Settling Conflicts

Conflict Situation 11

Person A

You think you should be able to play with your new toy and not share it with your brother or sister.

Conflict Situation 11

Person B

You want to play with your brother or sister's new toy. You almost always share your toys.

Social Star

Conflict Situation 12

Person A

You feel your friend is making fun of you. You are feeling hurt and you want the teasing to stop.

Conflict Situation 12

Person B

You are just goofing around teasing your friend in what you feel is a friendly way. You think your friend should be able to take a joke.

© 1996 Thinking Publications — Duplication permitted for educational use only.

Conflict Situation 13

Person A

You and your friend are playing a board game. You want to go first.

Conflict Situation 13

Person B

You and your friend are playing a board game. You want to go first.

Social Star

Conflict Situation

Person A

Conflict Situation

Person B

© 1996 Thinking Publications — Duplication permitted for educational use only.

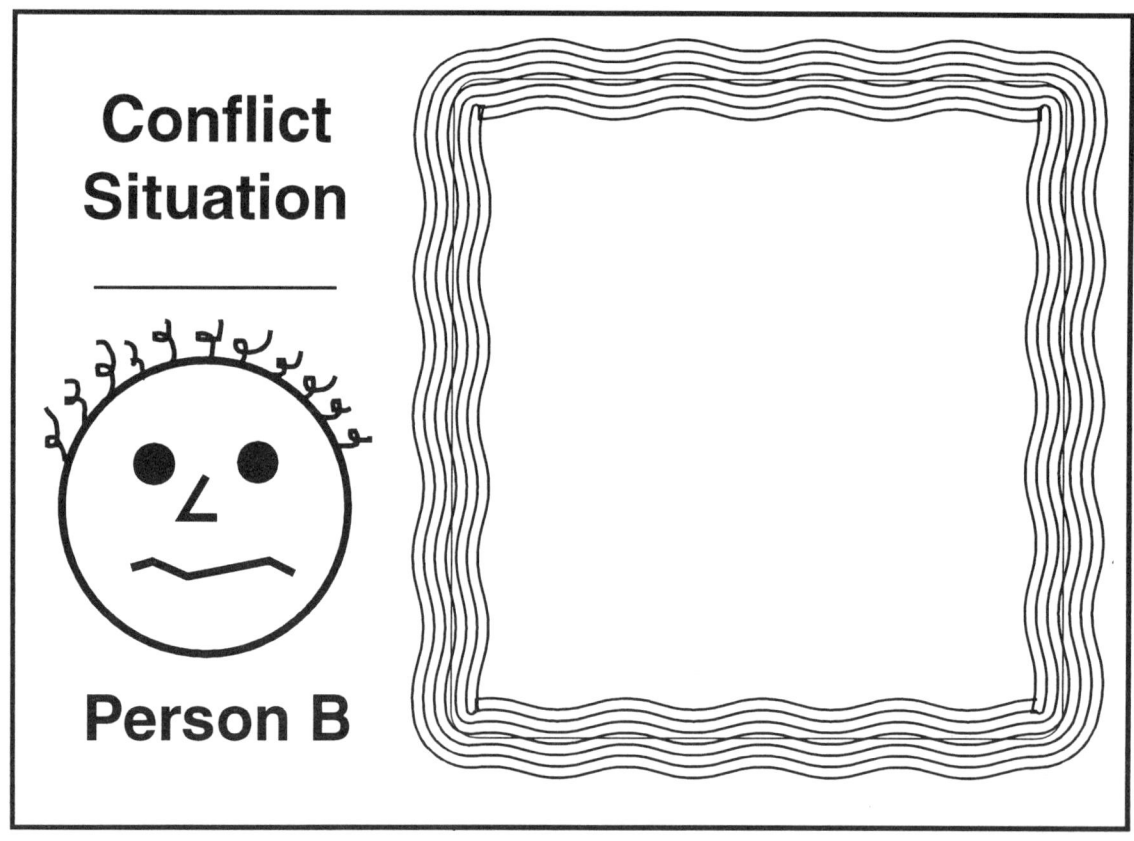

Settling Conflicts Log

Names: _____

_____

Conflict: _____

Brainstorming ideas:

_____
_____
_____
_____
_____
_____
_____

The idea we choose to settle the conflict:

_____
_____
_____
_____
_____
_____

Social Star

Lessons X, Y, and Z

Due to similarities in format, the final three lesson plans for each unit in *Social Star* are provided in *Appendix A*. Substitute the words "settling conflicts" whenever a "_____" appears in the lesson plans. Information specific to this unit follows.

LESSON X PREPARATORY SET:

Hand out *I Know*.... which was partially completed and then collected during Lesson A. Ask students to complete the "I Learned" column. After students have had the opportunity to record their responses, call on students to share them with the group.

LESSON Y PREPARATORY SET:

Darken the room, if you prefer, and ask the students to visualize themselves correctly using this social skill by reading the following script:

Let's take a few moments.... Make sure you are in a comfortable position.... Close your eyes if you feel like it.... On the count of three, take a very slow, deep breath. Remember to breathe in quietly through your nose. One...two...three.... Breathe in deeply.... Now breathe out slowly.... Remember to breathe out quietly through your mouth. Let your entire body relax.... Now imagine yourself settling a conflict you are having with your brother or sister. Picture yourself trying to work out a win-win solution. Imagine how positive it feels for both of you.

LESSON Z PLOT SITUATION:

Ask students to pretend that their family is experiencing a conflict about what to do with $100 given to the family as a gift.

LESSON Z ROADBLOCK EXAMPLES:

- Having a conflict with a person who is unwilling to consider negotiating or compromising

- Being under a time limit for settling a conflict

- Having a conflict about a situation that makes you feel very emotional

Settling Conflicts T-Chart

LOOKS LIKE...

using appropriate body talk

- facing the person
- using eye contact
- looking sincere

SOUNDS LIKE...

a sincere, calm tone of voice

an appropriate volume

brainstorming ideas to settle the conflict

saying

- "How could we compromise?"
- "We can agree on something."
- "Let's work this out."

SHOW TIME

HOME

Pretend you are having a conflict with your cousin about which video game to play. Show what you might say to settle this conflict in a win-win manner.

SCHOOL

Pretend you and the members of your group are having a conflict about the best colors to use on the poster you are completing. Show what you might say to encourage the group to find a solution that everyone can agree with.

COMMUNITY

Pretend your club needs money to replace a broken window in the clubhouse. A member's parent has agreed to purchase and install the window if the members can raise the $25 cost. The members are having a conflict about how to raise the money to replace the window. Show what you could say to suggest that the group settle the conflict in a positive way.

There are many ways to settle a Conflict

Conflict

Social Star

HOME-A-GRAM

Dear Family,

At school, we have been talking about the social skill called

SETTLING CONFLICTS

I learned that *settling conflicts* means working out differences with others in a way that is positive and agreeable to everyone. When I work to settle a conflict with others, I can suggest solutions that can be considered "win-win" solutions everyone agrees with. I can be proud when I do my best to use the following three skill steps when in conflict with others:

1. _____

_____

2. _____

_____

3. _____

_____

After I share with you the skill steps I've written, please sign my "Settling Conflicts" badge so I can return it to school and become a SOCIAL SUPER STAR this week.

From: _____

© 1996 Thinking Publications — Duplication permitted for educational use only.

Making an Apology

Social Star

UNIT GOAL:

To demonstrate comprehension and use of strategies for making an apology

EDUCATOR INFORMATION:

This unit was developed to teach students how to make apologies. Students identify situations when making an apology would be appropriate. They identify words they can say when apologizing and brainstorm other things they can do or say to demonstrate their apology is sincere.

RELATED ACTIVITIES:

1. Discuss reasons why some people might find it difficult to apologize.

2. Ask students to draw and color the phrase, "I'm sorry," in a decorative lettering style.

3. Ask students to research how to say "I'm sorry" in several different languages.

4. Ask students to create and then solve math story problems about apologizing (e.g., If you apologize to three people, and then each of those three people apologize to three others, how many people will have received an apology all together?).

5. Discuss historical events that may have been different if a person, or a team, or a country had offered an apology.

6. Discuss the cumulative effect on a relationship if people never apologize (e.g., a friendship ending, a marriage ending in divorce).

7. Discuss the negotiation process that might occur when neither side feels it owes an apology to the other. (Refer to the unit titled *Settling Conflicts*.)

8. Discuss the relationship between this unit on apologizing and the unit titled *Being Responsible*.

9. Sometimes when people accept an apology, they continue to hold a grudge. Discuss the idea that once they accept an apology, the incident should be viewed as over. Discuss how this concept relates to the idiom, "forgive and forget."

10. Invite adults from different cultures to talk to the students about how their cultures' conventions for apologizing compare with the strategies presented in this unit.

It is important for educators to provide opportunities for students to work in groups, so they can experience social skills in contexts where social communication is needed. Therefore, educators are encouraged to have students complete the Related Activities in small groups whenever possible. Educators trained in cooperative learning could incorporate the five components (see pages 33–34) into the group activity. An excellent resource for teaching students cooperative skills and building a sense of community is *Tribes: A Process for Social Development and Cooperative Learning* (1987) by Jeanne Gibbs.

RELATED LITERATURE:

Goodbye Chicken Little (1979) by Betsy Cromer Byars, Harper Collins. (103 pages)

Cassie Binegar (1982) by Patricia MacLachlan, Ill. by Charlotte Zolotow, Harper and Row. (120 pages)

The Big, Fat, Enormous Lie (1978) by Marjorie Weinman Sharmat, Ill. by David McPhail, Dutton. (32 pages)

SOCIAL SKILLS ALL DAY LONG:

Look for opportunities to teach social skills throughout the day (incidental teaching). Four ways to reinforce appropriate social skills and an example of each follow:

Encouragement

Mike, I've noticed that you've been very nice to Lee since you apologized for teasing him. Your actions are showing him that your apology was sincere.

Personal Example

I apologized to my daughter last night when I lost my temper and yelled. Next time I'll stay calm when I'm angry so she knows that I really meant what I said.

Prompting

Maria, you could choose to apologize to Dirk. You may have hurt his feelings when you laughed at his answer.

Corrective Feedback (must be positive, private, specific, and nonthreatening)

Jolisa, when you apologized to me, your tone of voice did not match the words you were saying. If you had used a polite tone of voice, your apology would have seemed more sincere.

———————— ★★★ ————————

To be wronged is nothing, unless you continue to remember.

Confucius

Lesson A

OBJECTIVES:

1. To state the meaning of *making an apology* and tell why it's important

2. To listen to the self-talk associated with appropriate use of the skill

MATERIALS:

1. *Making an Apology* (See page 352; one per student and one transparency.)

2. *Thought Bubble* (See *Appendix O*; one for educator use.)

3. A deck of playing cards (See *Appendix P* and step 7 of this Plan.)

4. *Checking Myself* (See *Appendix I*; one per student and one transparency.)

PREPARATORY SET:

Ask for your students' attention and then sign "Excuse me. I'm sorry," following the sign language illustrations that follow.

EXCUSE ME. FORGIVE ME.

Repeatedly brush the fingertips of the bent open right hand, palm down, across the palm and fingers of the upturned left hand.

Hint: Brushing the mistake aside.

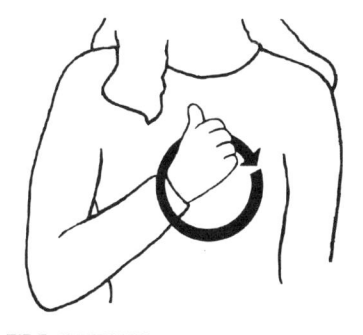

I'M SORRY.

Form a fist with your hand with your thumb facing up. Rub your fist, palm facing in, over the heart in a circular motion repeatedly.

Hint: Beating the heart in sorrow.

Ask if anyone knows what you just signed. If no one knows, explain that you just said, "Excuse me. I'm sorry." Provide time for students to practice making the signs. Use this activity to introduce this unit about making an apology.

PLAN:

1. Distribute and display *Making an Apology*. Discuss the definition. Explain the skill steps and the symbols next to them. Remind students that the symbols are there to help them visualize and remember the skill steps. Refer students to the body-talk symbol in the left-hand margin. Remind students that appropriate body talk is important when making an apology. (Discuss specific body language

that is important to remember when making apologies—appropriate posture, eye contact, etc.) Discuss the reasons for making an apology.

2. Model use of the skill steps for making an apology while thinking aloud. A scripted example follows:

Introduction

I am going to pretend to make an apology to my brother. I will show you how I make an appropriate apology and tell you the thoughts I'm having. When I hold up this Thought Bubble, *you'll know the words I'm saying are actually what I'm thinking.*

Actual Model

While holding up the *Thought Bubble* say, *I want to apologize to my brother. I'll use a sincere tone of voice, and I'll say something to demonstrate that I'm really sorry.* Put the *Thought Bubble* down and say, *I'm sorry I took your calculator without asking. I'll ask you first the next time I need a calculator.*

3. Read the story at the bottom half of *Making an Apology*.

4. Distribute and display the discussion guideline sheet called *Checking Myself*. Ask students to complete the goal statement with the words "think about an answer to each question," or use another classroom discussion goal more appropriate for your group (see pages 25–26). Tell students that you will be leading a discussion about the story they just heard. Explain that after you ask each question, it's important for them to think about an answer, even if they are not called on. Instruct them to draw a line between two dots on the star each time they think about an answer to a question. Provide enough "wait time" before calling on a student to orally answer each question.

Model use of the *Checking Myself* sheet while thinking aloud. A scripted example follows:

Introduction

I'm going to pretend to be one of you completing this sheet during the discussion we will be having. I will tell you the thoughts I'm having while I'm completing the sheet. When I hold up this Thought Bubble, *you'll know the words I'm saying are actually what I'm thinking.*

Actual Model

While holding up the *Thought Bubble,* say, *OK, the teacher just asked, "Why did Lee apologize to his grandmother?" I need to think of an answer.... OK, I know why he apologized. I'll draw a line between two dots on the star while I raise my hand, because I just thought of an answer to that question.* Put the *Thought Bubble* down and draw a line between two dots on the transparency.

5. Proceed with the actual discussion by asking the following questions. During the discussion, periodically remind students to think of answers to the questions and to mark their discussion guideline sheets.

   - Why did Lee apologize to his grandmother?

   - Why did Lee use a sad tone of voice when he apologized?

   - Why did Lee look at his grandmother when he apologized?

   - How do you think his grandmother felt after Lee apologized?

   - How do you think his grandmother would have felt if Lee's body talk didn't look like he was really sorry?

   - What actions did Lee take to demonstrate that his apology was sincere?

   - Should you only apologize when you get caught?

   After the discussion, have students complete the bottom of *Checking Myself*.

6. Process use of the sheet by asking the following questions or others more appropriate for your group:

   - Why is it important to stay on task by thinking of answers to questions during a discussion?

   - Why is it sometimes hard to stay on task and think of answers?

7. Pair students using the *Card Match* activity (see *Appendix P*). Ask student pairs to take turns telling each other the meaning of *making an apology* and why it's important to use the skill. Students could be reminded that the information they are to say is printed on *Making an Apology*.

   As an option to add structure to this activity, ask partners to come to an agreement about which person will be called "A" and which person will be called "B." After students have made their decisions, ask "A" to tell "B" the definition of *making an apology*. Next, ask "B" to tell "A" the definition. Ask students to use the same procedure to tell each other the reasons for making an apology.

   ──────── ★★★ ────────

   Life is an adventure in forgiveness.

   Norman Cousins

Social Star

Name _____

Making an Apology

MEANING OF MAKING AN APOLOGY:

Choosing words and actions that show you are sorry when you've done something wrong

SKILL STEPS:

1. Say, "I'm sorry for..."   "I'm sorry for..."

2. Ask myself: What else can I do to demonstrate I'm sorry?   What else?

REASONS FOR USING THIS SKILL:

When you say you're sorry, it may help you and others feel better. When you make choices that show you are sorry, people will believe your words.

DIRECTIONS: Listen to the story below. Look at the pictures of Lee and Mika Vue.

When Lee got home from school, he could see that his grandmother was upset with him. She said, "Lee, you didn't tell me that Mrs. Graham called last night. She said she left a message with you." Lee looked at her and said with a sad voice, "I'm sorry! I was going to write it down, but I forgot!" Later that night, Lee's grandmother found one of Lee's pens attached to a string hanging by the phone. She also saw a small spiral notebook labeled "Phone Messages."

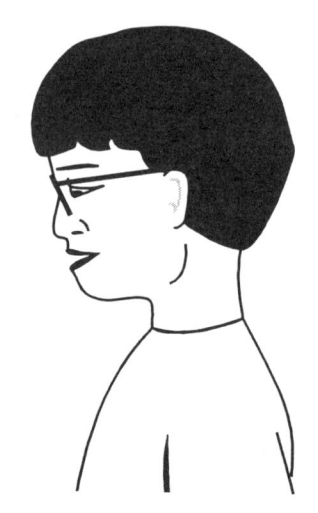

© 1996 Thinking Publications   Duplication permitted for educational use only.

Making an Apology

Lesson B

OBJECTIVE:

To identify actions or words to demonstrate to others that one is truly sorry

MATERIALS:

1. *Making an Apology* classroom poster (See page 13.)

2. *Apology Situations* (See pages 355–356; one set cut apart per pair of students and one transparency.)

3. *Dominoes* (See *Appendix T*; one set cut apart per pair of students and one set of transparency dominoes.)

PREPARATORY SET:

Ask a student (who has been prepared beforehand, so he or she knows what will happen) to tell the tale of *Goldilocks and the Three Bears* to the class. (For older students, ask someone to read *The Paper Bag Princess* [1980] by Robert Munsch.) While the story is being told, make several abrupt interruptions (e.g., asking questions, changing what the storyteller says) and follow each interruption with the words, "Oh, I'm sorry for interrupting, continue your story." After the story is over, ask students to tell the words you said to apologize when you interrupted the storyteller. Ask students, "Do you think I really was sorry?" (Lead students to an understanding that if you truly were sorry, you would not have continued interrupting.) Tell students that today's lesson will focus on skill step 2 for making an apology.

PLAN:

1. Review the definition and skill steps for making an apology by referring the class to the *Making an Apology* classroom poster.

2. Discuss the concept that our actions often speak louder than our words, particularly when making apologies. Tell students that it may be easy to say the words "I'm sorry," but it's much more difficult and important to choose actions or words to prove you are sorry. Display *Apology Situations*. After reading the first situation, ask students to brainstorm words or actions that could help to prove you are truly sorry. Discuss the remaining situations in the same way. (A blank situation card is provided for adding situations relevant to the students.)

3. Tell students they will be playing a game called "Apology Dominoes" using the situations they have just discussed.

4. Model specifically how to play traditional dominoes using an overhead and the *Dominoes* transparency.

5. Pair students (see *Appendix P*). Distribute one set of Dominoes and one set of *Apology Situations* cards to each pair. Ask student pairs to place their situation cards face down in front of them.

6. Ask students to proceed playing dominoes, but each time students match dominoes, have them pick the top *Apology Situations* card, read the situation aloud, and then tell words or an action that could be taken (beyond saying the words, "I'm sorry for...") to demonstrate that the person in the situation is truly sorry.

7. Ask student pairs to take turns telling each other the skill steps for making an apology. Follow the procedure described in step 7 of Lesson A. Next, ask students to work with their partners to think of a new ending to *Goldilocks and the Three Bears* in which Goldilocks follows the making an apology skill steps after waking up, instead of just running away. (Students might write a new ending for *The Paper Bag Princess,* in which the prince apologizes for his behavior toward the princess, if that story was read during the Preparatory Set.) Tell students that one or more pairs will be asked to share their new story endings.

———————★★★———————

Forgiveness is man's deepest need and highest achievement.

Horace Bushnell

Apology Situations

You accidentally spilled lemonade on your grandmother's tablecloth. You said, "Grandma, I'm really sorry that I made this mess."

You made a funny comment, but it hurt your friend's feelings. You said, "Juan, I'm sorry for hurting your feelings."

You lost your temper when your mother said you couldn't meet your friends at the arcade. You said, "I apologize for hollering at you, Mom."

You ran into the back of your friend's bike while you were riding behind her. You said, "Are you OK? I'm so sorry."

You said some mean things to your friend and now you are feeling bad. You call your friend and say, "I am very sorry about the mean things I said. Will you forgive me?"

You were late coming in from recess. Your group was waiting for you so they could start working on the group project. You said, "I'm sorry that I'm late. Thanks for waiting for me."

Apology Situations

You forgot to return a jacket that you borrowed from your friend. When you saw your friend, you said, "I forgot your jacket again. I am so sorry!"

Your dad spent a lot of time making you a costume for your play. When you saw it, you made a face. Your dad was very sad. You felt bad and said, "I'm sorry I made that face."

You used your sister's headset without her permission. You said, "I'm sorry I took your headset."

You were angry with your brother and kicked him. After you had calmed down, you said, "I'm sorry I kicked you."

When your friends were over, you told your sister she couldn't play with you. Later you said, "I'm sorry I didn't let you play. That was mean of me."

Lessons X, Y, and Z — Social Star

Due to similarities in format, the final three lesson plans for each unit in *Social Star* are provided in *Appendix A*. Substitute the words "making an apology" whenever a "_____" appears in the lesson plans. Information specific to this unit follows.

LESSON X PREPARATORY SET:

Share a story about a time when you wrote an apology note. Discuss times when someone may wish to apologize in writing.

LESSON Y PREPARATORY SET:

Darken the room, if you prefer, and ask the students to visualize themselves correctly using this social skill by reading the following script:

Let's take a few moments to relax.... Make sure you are in a comfortable position.... Close your eyes if you feel like it.... On the count of three, take a very slow, deep breath. Remember to breathe in quietly through your nose. One...two...three.... Breathe in deeply.... Now breathe out slowly and quietly through your mouth. Let your entire body relax.... Now imagine yourself feeling bad about arguing with your sister. You said some mean things. Picture yourself apologizing to her for what you said. Imagine how good you feel because you gave a sincere apology.

LESSON Z PLOT SITUATION:

Ask students to pretend their mothers force them to apologize to the neighbor boy for something they did not do.

LESSON Z ROADBLOCK EXAMPLES:

- Getting upset all over again when you're apologizing
- Thinking only "sissies" apologize
- Having the person start arguing when you're trying to apologize
- Having your apology rejected

Making an Apology T-Chart

LOOKS LIKE...

using appropriate body talk

- looking serious and sincere
- facing the person

doing or saying something afterwards (or the next time) to prove you're really sorry

SOUNDS LIKE...

a sincere tone of voice

an appropriate volume

saying

- "I apologize for..."
- "I'm sorry about..."
- "Next time I'll..."

SHOW TIME

HOME

Pretend you told your dad you'd clean your room after your favorite TV show but you didn't follow through. Show how to apologize sincerely to him. (What action can you take to show you are truly sorry?)

SCHOOL

Pretend you are at school. You accidentally run into someone when you are playing softball. Show how to apologize to the person. (What action can you take to show you are truly sorry?)

COMMUNITY

Pretend your dog digs a hole in your neighbor's lawn. Show how you will apologize. (What action can you take to show you are truly sorry?)

Saying You're Sorry + Showing You're Sorry

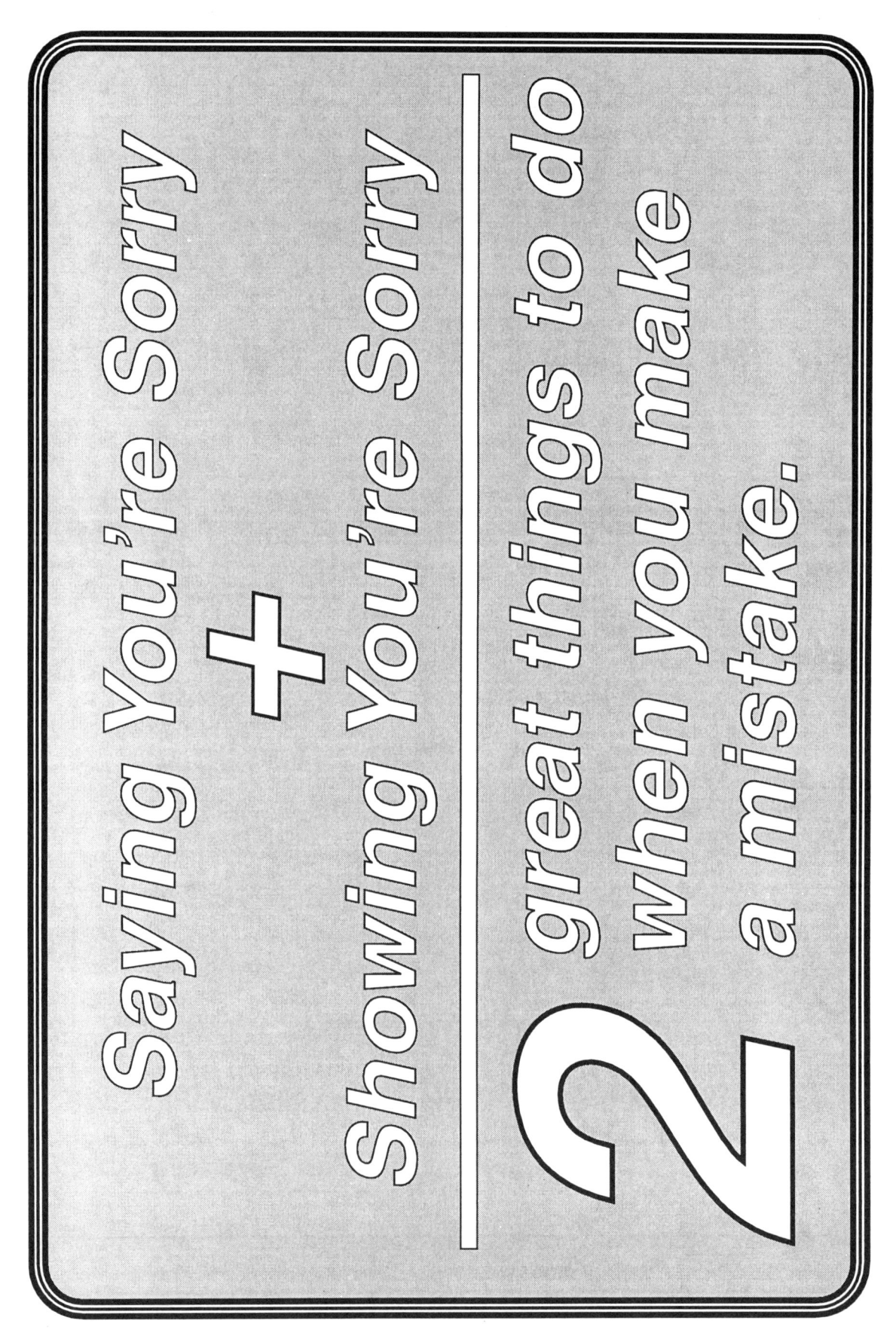

2 great things to do when you make a mistake.

HOME-A-GRAM

Dear Family,

At school, we have been talking about the social skill called

MAKING AN APOLOGY

I learned that *making an apology* means choosing words and actions that show I am sorry when I've done something wrong.

When I apologize to someone, I should begin by using the words, "I'm sorry about..." or "I apologize for...."

After I apologize, I ask myself, "What else can I say or do to prove I'm sorry?"

When I make an apology, it may help me and others feel better. When I make choices that show I am sorry, people will believe my words.

A situation at home when it might be important for me to apologize to someone is:

_____

_____

A way I could prove that I am sorry in that situation would be:

_____

_____

I will tell you the words and actions I could use to apologize in a situation that you describe to me. After I do, please sign my "Making an Apology" badge so I can return it to school and become a SOCIAL SUPER STAR this week.

From: _____

© 1996 Thinking Publications — *Duplication permitted for educational use only.*

Responding to Criticism

Social Star

UNIT GOAL:

To demonstrate comprehension and use of strategies for responding to criticism

EDUCATOR INFORMATION:

1. During this unit, students are helped to understand the importance of "constructive" criticism. They are taught that criticism can be helpful and need not be experienced as a negative event. Students learn that there is "helpful criticism" and "hurtful criticism." They are taught to use positive self-talk to help them respond to criticism and to look underneath hurtful criticism to decide if there is a useful suggestion for improvement.

2. During the unit, students create a book about criticism (including helpful tips for parents about giving criticism to their children) to take home.

RELATED ACTIVITIES:

1. Offer a parent workshop that provides suggestions for positive ways to give children criticism. Some resources include:

    Raising Self-Reliant Children in a Self-Indulgent World (1989)
    by H.S. Glenn and J. Nelsen
    Prima Publishing and Communications
    3875 Atherton Road
    Rocklin, CA 95765
    (916) 632-4400

    Siblings Without Rivalry (1987) and *How to Talk So Kids Will Listen and Listen So Kids Will Talk* (1987)
    by A. Faber and E. Mazlish
    Avon Books
    1350 Avenue of the Americas
    New York, NY 10019
    (800) 238-0658

    Successful Parenting (an audiocassette program) (1992)
    by C. Andreas
    NLP Comprehensive
    4895 Riverbend Road, Ste.A
    Boulder, CO 80301
    (800) 233-1657

2. As a current events activity, find examples in the media of criticism. Have students give their opinions as to whether the criticisms are helpful or hurtful.

3. Start a "Criticize Kindly" campaign with colleagues. For an entire week, pass out "a tip a day" of suggestions for giving students feedback or criticism in a positive way. (Strategies can be taken from the Parent Tips section in *A Book about Criticism for Kids and Parents* from Lesson C of this unit.)

4. Investigate the neurolinguistic programming technique for "responding resourcefully to criticism." An excellent resource is:

   Heart of the Mind (1989)
   by C. Andreas and S. Andreas
   Real People Press
   Box F
   Moab, UT 84532
   801-259-7578

   A simplified version of the technique follows.

   - In your mind, see yourself at a distance. (You may also wish to imagine a plexiglass shield between the "distant you" and the real you.)

   - See the "distant you" being criticized.

   - Have the "distant you" watch a movie of what the criticism is about.

   - Decide if you agree with any part of the criticism.

   - Decide how you will respond (e.g., tell the person you agree, tell the person you're sorry, give the person information to clarify your position, ask the person what you can do to change, tell the person you'll do it differently in the future, tell the person you disagree).

   - In your mind, rehearse doing your new behavior next time. Do this for several different examples.

   - Let the plexiglass melt and bring the "distant you" back into yourself.

5. Several times during this unit, students discuss a prehistoric character named Og who experiences "fight or flight" responses. As a science extension, investigate the adrenal gland and the adrenaline surges (causing blood to be diverted from our brain to other parts of our body) during "fight or flight," which is an automatic, physiological response to either real or perceived danger (Roger and McWilliams, 1991).

6. Do a vocabulary activity in which students define the term "constructive" as it relates to constructive criticism. Compare the terms "constructive criticism" and "helpful criticism." Have students define the terms "thoughtfulness" and "tact" and relate the words to the manner in which people give criticism.

7. Invite adults from different cultures to talk to the students about how their cultures' conventions for responding to criticism compare with the strategies in this unit.

It is important for educators to provide opportunities for students to work in groups so they can experience social skills in contexts where social communication is needed. Therefore, educators are encouraged to have students complete the Related Activities in small groups whenever possible. Educators trained in cooperative learning could incorporate the five components (see pages 33–34) into the group activity. An excellent resource for teaching students cooperative skills and building a sense of community is *Tribes: A Process for Social Development and Cooperative Learning* (1987) by Jeanne Gibbs.

RELATED LITERATURE:

Molly's Pilgrim (1983) by Barbara Cohen, Ill. by Michael T. Deraney, Lothrop. (32 pages)

The Ears of Louis (1974) by Constance Greene, Viking. (90 pages)

Bear's Picture (1972) by Daniel Manus Pinkwater, Dutton. (32 pages)

Officer Buckle and Gloria (1995) by Peggy Rothman, Putnam. (32 pages)

SOCIAL SKILLS ALL DAY LONG:

Look for opportunities to teach social skills throughout the day (incidental teaching). Four ways to reinforce appropriate social skills and an example of each follow:

Encouragement

Maria, I just gave you some constructive criticism about your dolphin report. You listened respectfully and then asked a few questions. You seemed genuinely concerned about improving your report.

Personal Example

My husband criticized me last night. He wanted me to turn off the lights in our house because I frequently leave them on after I leave a room. He said it in a mean way. I had to remind myself to stay calm, use positive self-talk, and not take it personally. Later I realized that he was right. I do leave the lights on too much!

Prompting

Mike, I'm going to give you some helpful criticism. You may want to look at the Responding to Criticism *poster to remind yourself of the skill steps you can use.*

Corrective Feedback (must be positive, private, specific, and nonthreatening)

Ann, just now when I started giving you some criticism, your body language changed. You got an angry look on your face and rolled your eyes. You gave a big sigh. You could have reminded yourself to stay calm and listen.

———————— ★★★ ————————

Find the grain of truth in criticism—chew it and swallow it.

D. Sutten

Lesson A

OBJECTIVES:

1. To state the meaning of *responding to helpful criticism* and tell why it's important

2. To listen to the self-talk associated with appropriate use of the skill

3. To describe the "fight or flight" response and how it relates to receiving criticism

MATERIALS:

1. A small collection of sports equipment (e.g., bat, ball, glove, soccer ball)

2. *Responding to Helpful Criticism* (See page 370; one per student and one transparency.)

3. *Thought Bubble* (See *Appendix O*; one for educator use.)

4. *Og* (See page 371; one transparency.)

5. *Numbered Stones* (See *Appendix P*; one set per pair of students.)

PREPARATORY SET:

Hold up examples of sports equipment while asking, "How many of you have ever been on a team with a coach? What is the coach's job?" Accept all responses (e.g., "The coach makes the schedule," "She makes out the plays"). Ask, "Do coaches ever offer team members suggestions for improvement?" Discuss the concept that athletes often improve their skills when they take suggestions from others. Use this discussion to introduce this unit about responding to criticism.

PLAN:

1. Distribute and display *Responding to Helpful Criticism*. Discuss the definition of *helpful criticism*. Explain the skill steps and the symbols next to them. Remind students that the symbols are there to help them visualize and remember the skill steps. Refer students to the body-talk symbol in the left-hand margin. Remind students that appropriate body talk is important when responding to helpful criticism. Discuss the reasons for appropriately responding to helpful criticism.

2. Model use of the skill steps for responding to helpful criticism while thinking aloud. A scripted example follows:

Introduction

I am going to pretend to be someone your age. I'll be responding to helpful criticism from my dad after I yelled at my brother. I will show you how I respond appropriately to helpful criticism and tell you the thoughts I'm having. When I hold up this Thought Bubble, *you'll know the words I'm saying are actually what I'm thinking.*

Actual Model

While holding up the *Thought Bubble* say, *Dad is talking about my yelling. I better stay calm and listen. He's saying I seem to be really crabby today. He notices that happens when I stay up too late. Tonight he thinks I should get to sleep on time. Do I agree with this criticism? I guess he's right. I am crabby! I am going to get to sleep earlier tonight.*

3. Read the story at the bottom of *Responding to Helpful Criticism,* then have students complete the directions.

4. Tell students that you will be reading them another story about something each of them has inside, but they may never have heard of it before. Display Og and read the following aloud:

One day a caveman named Og was walking cheerfully through the forest. Suddenly, he heard a loud roar. His body tensed up and he stood in a fighting stance. He was breathing quickly. All of a sudden, he saw a ferocious animal. Og knew he would have to fight or run to stay alive. He turned on his heels and fled as fast as he could. His heart was pounding so fast he thought it would burst. He was surprised how fast he was running. He had never run that fast before.

Fortunately, Og made it safely back to his cave. He spent the rest of the day taking a nice long nap. When he woke up, he was feeling much better.

Mo, Og's good friend, came to visit. Mo said, "Og, we've been friends a long time, so I feel I should talk to you about something. You need to bury your garbage sooner. We can smell it all the way over in our caves." Once again, Og's body tensed up. He was breathing rapidly and he was ready to fight or flee. Unfortunately, Og yelled, "Get out of here, Mo! I never want to see you again."

Today, we still have a small part of Og with us. Part of our brain called the "old brain" or "reptilian brain" still has what we call the "fight or flight" response. Whenever we sense danger, our brain automatically says, "I've got to fight or run." But, the fight or flight response can save our lives by making us stronger and quicker than normal, like the situation when Og saw the ferocious animal. Sometimes when someone gives us criticism, our brain automatically thinks "danger" even though there isn't really any danger.

Sometimes we're so concerned about fighting or running that we can't calmly concentrate on the criticism which offers a suggestion for improvement. That's why it's important to remind ourselves to be calm.

Ask students the following questions:

- What things happened to Og's body when he saw the ferocious animal?
- Why do you think this is called the "fight or flight" response?
- How did the "fight or flight" response help Og when he saw the ferocious animal?
- Why do you think Mo gave helpful criticism to Og?
- What things happened to Og's body when he received helpful criticism from Mo?
- How did the "fight or flight" response hurt Og when he received helpful criticism from his friend?
- How does this response relate to skill step 1?
- Have you ever been in real danger like Og? What happens to your heart and your breathing?
- Have you ever had that feeling when someone is criticizing you? What did you do?

Tell students that in the next lesson they will be learning about hurtful criticism. Knowing about their body's automatic "fight or flight" reaction can be helpful in responding appropriately to any type of criticism.

5. Pair students using *Numbered Stones* (see *Appendix P*).
6. Ask student pairs to take turns telling each other the meaning of *responding to helpful criticism* and why it's important to use the skill. Students could be reminded that the information they are to say is printed on *Responding to Helpful Criticism*.

As an option to add structure to this activity, ask partners to come to an agreement about which person will be called "A" and which person will be called "B." After students have made their decisions, ask "A" to tell "B" the definition of *responding to helpful criticism*. Next, ask "B" to tell "A" the definition. Ask students to use the same procedure to tell each other the reasons for responding appropriately to helpful criticism.

———————★★★———————

He has a right to criticize, who has a heart to help.

Abraham Lincoln

Social Star

Name _____

Responding to Helpful Criticism

MEANING OF HELPFUL CRITICISM:

Suggestions for improvement or change given in a respectful way

SKILL STEPS:

1. Stop, be calm, and listen

2. Respond politely

3. Think about the suggestion and decide if I agree

   IF YES,

4. Go ahead and follow the suggestion

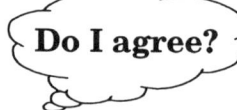

REASONS FOR USING THIS SKILL:

When you accept helpful criticism, you continue developing your skills. You feel proud inside knowing you're becoming an even better person. People who care about you feel good when they can help you improve.

DIRECTIONS: Listen to the story below. Then, underline the parts of the story where Ann follows the four skill steps for responding to helpful criticism.

Ann Olson plays soccer and Mr. Parra is her coach. During halftime, Coach Parra said to Ann, "Nice goal, Ann. Now listen, when you go in on defense, I want you to stay close to the goalie. Last week, you kept going too far downfield." At first, Ann felt a little upset, but she took a deep breath, listened to her coach, then said, "OK." Ann thought about last week's game and decided her coach was right. She stayed close to the goalie during the second half.

© 1996 Thinking Publications — Duplication permitted for educational use only.

Responding to Criticism

OG

Social Star

Lesson B

OBJECTIVES:

1. To state the meaning of *responding to hurtful criticism* and tell why it's important

2. To listen to the self-talk associated with correct use of the skill

3. To understand that when criticism is delivered in a hurtful manner, it still may include a worthwhile suggestion for improvement

MATERIALS:

1. A fresh pineapple hidden in a paper bag

2. A kitchen knife and a cutting board (For cutting the pineapple)

3. *Responding to Helpful Criticism* classroom poster (See page 13.)

4. *Responding to Hurtful Criticism* (See page 375; one per student and one transparency.)

5. *Thought Bubble* (See *Appendix O*; one for educator use.)

6. *Brain Voice* (See page 376; one transparency.)

PREPARATORY SET:

Hold up the paper bag containing the pineapple. Tell students that you will be giving them clues about what is inside the bag and that after all the clues have been given, they will have a chance to guess what is in the bag. (The clues will begin with somewhat negative, first impression characteristics of a pineapple from the outside, and end with the positive characteristics of the inside.) Read the following clues:

It is hard and brown. The outside is bumpy, rough, and prickly. It can hurt when I touch it. It is yellow inside. It tastes sweet and juicy. It is full of vitamin C.

Ask students to guess what is in the bag. If necessary, give additional clues. After they have guessed correctly, cut open the pineapple and allow students to taste a piece. As they sample the pineapple, tell students that in this lesson they will be learning about hurtful criticism. Have students brainstorm how hurtful criticism might be like a pineapple. (Underneath something that may not look or feel good, there may actually be some hidden good thing.)

PLAN:

1. Review the definition and skill steps for *helpful criticism* by referring the class to the *Responding to Helpful Criticism* classroom poster.

2. Pair students (see *Appendix P*). Ask student pairs to take turns telling each other the skill steps for responding to helpful criticism. Follow the procedure described in step 6 of Lesson A. Next, ask students to work with their partners to think of a time when it is important to respond appropriately to helpful criticism.

3. Distribute and display *Responding to Hurtful Criticism*. Discuss the definition. Explain the skill steps and the symbols next to them. Remind students that the symbols are there to help them visualize and remember the skill steps. (The symbol for skill step 3 will make better sense after completing step 6 of this Plan.) Refer students to the body-talk symbol in the left-hand margin. Remind students that appropriate body talk is important when responding to hurtful criticism.

4. Model use of the skill steps for responding to hurtful criticism while thinking aloud. A scripted example follows:

Introduction

I am going to pretend to respond to hurtful criticism. I will show you how I respond appropriately to the criticism and tell you the thoughts I'm having. When I hold up this Thought Bubble, *you'll know the words I'm saying are actually what I'm thinking.*

Actual Model

While holding up the *Thought Bubble* say, *The scout leader just said in a mean voice, "You never listen when I tell you to do something. You need to clean out your ears or you're going to get yourself into all kinds of trouble!" What a rude thing to say! I feel so angry I could scream. I better stop and take some slow deep breaths.... Remember, I'm a good person! I usually listen when she tells me something. Even though she was rude, I guess maybe I wasn't listening just now.*

5. Read the story at the bottom of *Responding to Hurtful Criticism*.

6. Ask students to process the story using the *Question, All Write* strategy (Harmin, 1995). This strategy maximizes the number of students who actually think about questions by asking all students to write answers before calling on them to respond. Ask students to write answers to the following questions before calling on students to answer them. (If all answers will be shared, this procedure may be time-consuming. As an alternative, some of the questions may be saved for discussion during another lesson.)

- Why did Mr. Aaron's criticism seem hurtful?

- What did Jolisa do to calm her "fight or flight" reaction to the hurtful criticism?

Social Star

- What positive self-talk did Jolisa use while responding to the hurtful criticism?
- Did Jolisa find a helpful suggestion under the hurt?
- Why do people give hurtful criticism?
- How is hurtful criticism like a pineapple? (E.g., within something that might not look or feel very good, there may actually be some hidden good thing.)
- What if you truly don't agree with any part of the criticism? What can you do? (E.g., not say anything, tell the person you don't agree and tell why.)
- Why is it important to stay calm when you're telling someone you disagree?

7. Display *Brain Voice.* Say:

You may already know that each of us has a brain voice inside of our head. Our brain voice is often talking to us. We call this "brain talk" or "self-talk." Jolisa used her brain voice in the story you heard earlier to remind herself how to respond appropriately to hurtful criticism. When you need to respond to hurtful criticism, it will be important to use positive self-talk. If you do, it will help you to be calm. Using positive self-talk will remind you that you are a good person. It will help you remember that even with hurtful criticism, there may be good advice.

8. Have student pairs take turns telling each other the meaning of *responding to hurtful criticism* and why it's important to use the skill. Follow the procedure described in step 6 of Lesson A. Students could be reminded that the information they are to say is printed on *Responding to Hurtful Criticism.*

———— ★★★ ————

To escape criticism—do nothing, say nothing, be nothing.

Albert Hubbard

Name _____

Responding to Hurtful Criticism

MEANING OF HURTFUL CRITICISM:

Suggestions for improvement or change given in a disrespectful way

SKILL STEPS:

1. Stop, calm down

2. Remind myself: Use positive self-talk

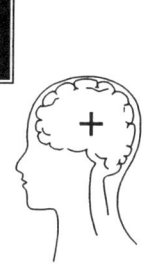

3. Ask myself: Is there a helpful suggestion under the hurt?

REASONS FOR USING THIS SKILL:

When you deal with hurtful criticism, you do not let it make you feel bad about yourself. You feel proud because you used the opportunity to make improvements.

DIRECTIONS: Listen to the story below. Look at the pictures of Jolisa and Mr. Aaron while you listen.

Jolisa had lots of fun during recess. She was laughing and talking loudly when she came back into McKinley School. Mr. Aaron walked up to her and said, "Jolisa, why are you always so loud? You better quiet down, or everyone's going to call you a bigmouth!" Jolisa's feelings were hurt. She almost yelled at Mr. Aaron, but told herself to count to 10 first. The counting helped her calm down. She used positive self-talk and thought, "I'm a good person and I'm not always loud. Even though Mr. Aaron spoke rudely, is he right? Yeah, I guess I was being too loud."

© 1996 Thinking Publications 375 *Duplication permitted for educational use only.*

Social Star

Brain Voice

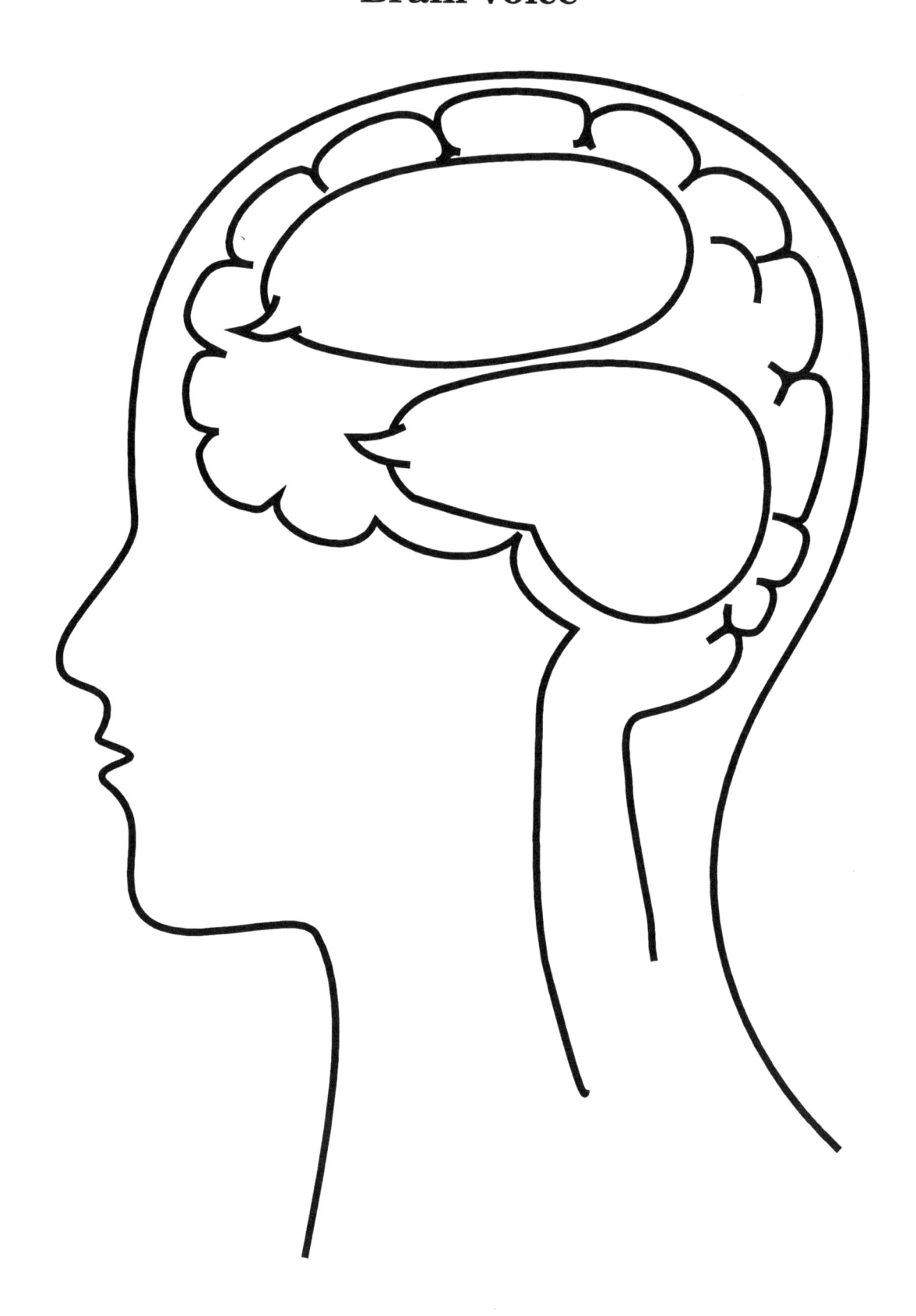

Lesson C

OBJECTIVES:

1. To distinguish between helpful and hurtful criticism

2. To create a booklet with tips on criticism for children and adults

MATERIALS:

1. *Og* (See page 371; one transparency saved from Lesson A.)

2. *Responding to Hurtful Criticism* classroom poster (See page 13.)

3. *Helpful or Hurtful?* (See page 379; one transparency.)

4. *Numbered Heads Together Spinner* (See *Appendix U*; one prepared for educator use.)

5. *A Book about Criticism for Kids and Parents* (See pages 380–384; one per student precut and stapled and one transparency.)

6. Crayons or markers (An assortment for each student)

PREPARATORY SET:

Display *Og* and say the following:

Do you remember our friend Og, the caveman? You'll be happy to hear that he's gotten his "fight or flight" response under control when he's criticized. He stays calm when someone gives him helpful criticism, and he doesn't want to run or fight anymore. Since he's been able to listen to criticism, Og has learned some new things. He's learned to make tools, to make fire, and to make wheels. Og wants you to remember that criticism can be very helpful!

PLAN:

1. Review the definition and skill steps for *responding to hurtful criticism* by referring the class to the *Responding to Hurtful Criticism* classroom poster.

2. Pair students (see *Appendix P*). Ask student pairs to take turns telling each other the skill steps for responding to hurtful criticism. Follow the procedure described in step 6 of Lesson A. Next, ask students to work with their partners to think of a situation at home, at school, or on the playground when it's important to respond appropriately to hurtful criticism. Tell students that one or more pairs will be called on to share their situations.

Social Star

3. Combine existing student pairs to form groups of four students. Display *Helpful or Hurtful* and cover numbers 4–12. Tell students that you will be reading examples of criticism to them. Say the following:

I will be reading several examples of criticism to you. Some of the situations are just plain silly, like #2. (Read #2 aloud.) *Some of the situations contain hurtful criticism and may or may not have a helpful suggestion under the hurt, like #1.* (Read #1 aloud.) *And finally, some of the situations contain helpful criticism, like #3.* (Read #3 aloud.) *You will be discussing the remaining statements in your group to decide which is which.*

4. Display #4 on the transparency *Helpful or Hurtful?* Read the situation aloud. Using the *Numbered Heads Together* structure (see pages 34–35) and the *Numbered Heads Together Spinner* ask students to work with their partners to decide whether the criticism in the situation is silly, helpful, or hurtful and be prepared to explain why. If the situation is an example of hurtful criticism, ask them to decide whether there is a helpful suggestion under the hurt. Then have students think about the positive self-talk that may be used to deal with the hurt. Proceed in the same manner with each of the remaining situations on *Helpful or Hurtful?*

5. Distribute and display *A Book about Criticism for Kids and Parents*. Read through the Kid Tips section with your students. Distribute the crayons or markers. Have students complete the writing and drawing activities as directed in that section. Tell students the Parent Tips section contains some information about criticism that their parents may find interesting. Collect the books to be redistributed during Lesson Z.

———————★★★———————

The rule in carving holds good as to criticism; never cut with a knife what you can cut with a spoon.

Charles Buxton

HELPFUL OR HURTFUL?

1. You little runt! You forgot to shut the dog cage. Now the dog is loose.

2. I've noticed that you often wiggle your second toe when it rains. It'd be better to keep it still.

3. When you write, you need to leave more space between words. It's easier to read your writing that way.

4. You've just made a threatening face at Joe. If you are upset with him, you could be assertive and tell him what's bothering you instead.

5. Hey, knock it off! You want to get yourself killed? Get down from that roof.

6. You're always the last one in from recess. Can't you hear the bell? Everyone else lines up right away. You're way out on the field looking around all the time. What can we do with you? Are you ever going to learn or am I going to have to get on your case all year long?

7. The next time your brother takes one of your toys, see if you can handle it yourself first. I know the two of you can solve a lot of these problems on your own.

8. Your gerbil cage seems like it's getting quite dirty. How often did we decide you need to clean it?

9. Stop running! Walk on the edge of the pool, please.

10. You're never going to be a great writer, but let's see if you can make this story a little more interesting.

11. You should have caught that pass at the end of the game. What were you thinking? You've got to get with it. I was so embarrassed.

12. I noticed you chew seven times before swallowing fruit and only six times before swallowing vegetables. You should be consistent.

A Book About Criticism for Kids and Parents

Kid Tips

(Responding to Criticism)

Criticism means:

_____
_____
_____
_____
_____
_____

Here's a picture of me listening to my _____ give me criticism.

2

✂ ---

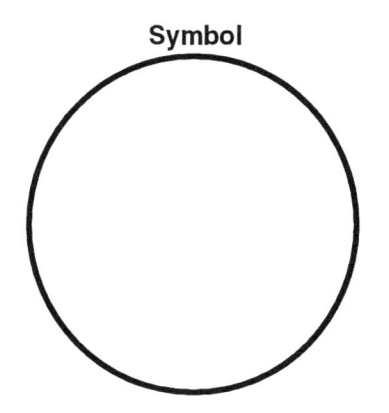

Symbol

Symbol

Symbol

★ People give me criticism because they want me to improve.

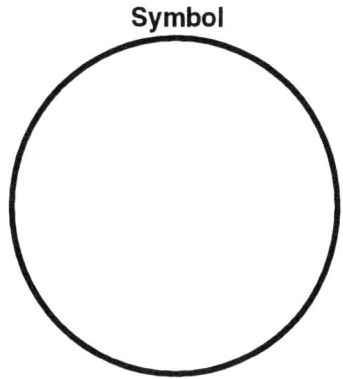

★ I spend time thinking about the criticism I receive.

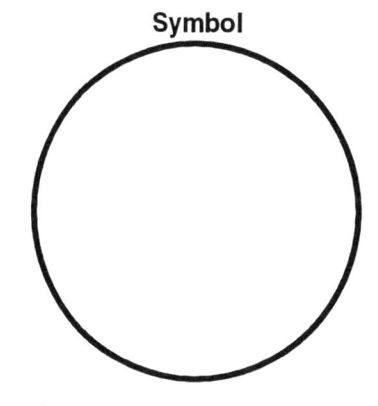

★ My positive brain voice reminds me I'm a good person.

4

Social Star

Criticism Tips

Directions: Draw a symbol to help you remember each criticism tip.

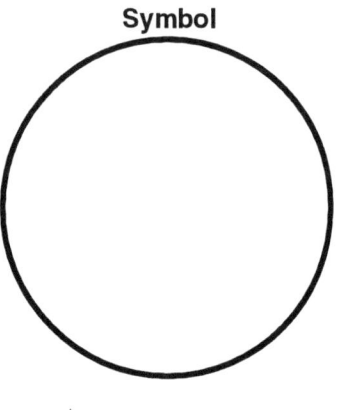

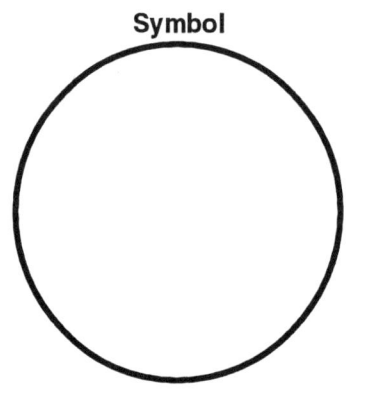

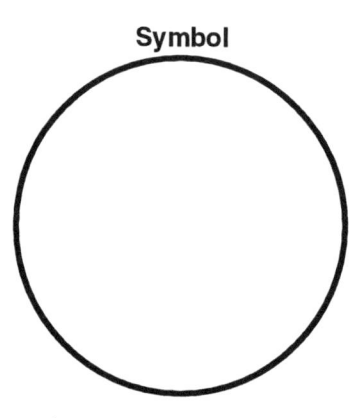

Symbol   Symbol   Symbol

( )   ( )   ( )

★ Stay calm!   ★ Use appropriate   ★ Remember,
                    body talk!   criticism
                                          can be
  • stand or sit straight   helpful!
  • listen and don't interrupt
  • have a serious face
  • use a pleasant tone of voice

3

My own story, poem, or drawing about
CRITICISM

5

© 1996 Thinking Publications   382   *Duplication permitted for educational use only.*

PARENT TIPS
(Giving Criticism)

Give a positive alternative to the criticism.

Examples:

1. "You said you'd do the dishes while I was gone. I'll bet you can get them done right now in 10.3 minutes."

2. "I don't think you remembered to throw your baseball shirt in the wash. Now it's dirty when you need it. After tonight's game you should come in the house and throw it in the hamper right away."

Use a neutral calm voice when giving criticism.

Kids will hear more. They'll be less likely to put up a defensive shield as often happens when criticism is given in an angry or sarcastic tone of voice.

Give your child a reason that explains why a behavior is unwanted.
(or better yet, have your child tell you the reason).

Examples:

1. "It's important to be quiet while I'm on the phone. I need to hear what the person on the phone is saying and sometimes I get very important calls."

2. "Can you think of some reasons why it would not be a good idea to pick your nose." (Elicit rationale from the child.)

Write a note to your child.
(Usually, writing a note gives you time to calm down so you can collect your thoughts to give criticism in a way that will be helpful.)

Example:

Maria,

You were supposed to be home by 5:00 last night. You were an hour late. I was worried that something happened to you. If you want me to continue to think of you as a responsible girl, don't let it happen again.

Love,

Dad

Assume that positive intentions are hidden under unwanted behavior.

Examples:

1. Child hits sister—"It looks like you're trying to give your sister an important message. Say it with words, not your hands!"

2. Kids fighting over a toy—"It looks like you two are really interested in playing with the same toy. You'll need to work out a way to share it in the next few minutes or I will become highly interested in that toy!"

Avoid globalizing words (e.g., "always," "never") when giving criticism.

Examples:

1. Instead of "You're always whining" (or "You're such a whiner") say, "You're whining right now. You're usually so cheerful."

2. Instead of saying "You never hang your coat up," say, "You forgot to hang your coat up. You've been doing such a nice job of remembering to do that lately."

7

Give criticism privately.

Examples:

1. Instead of reprimanding your child in front of other parents and kids at the open house, walk over to your child and state the criticism quietly.

2. If your child is acting up at home when the relatives are over, take the child into a different room to privately share your concerns.

Be specific. Don't make general comments.

Examples:

1. Instead of "You're being naughty," say, "Right now you are using a very sassy tone of voice in front of your aunt and uncle. You need to speak politely."

2. Instead of saying "This room is a mess," say, "Your room will be clean when you pick up your clothes, make your bed, and put your game away."

After giving criticism, let the person know you care about him or her.

Examples:

1. Use a pleasant, friendly tone of voice after using a serious tone to give the criticism.

2. After giving the criticism, smile and say something positive.

3. Sometime later in the day, tell your child you love him or her.

9

Lessons X, Y, and Z

Due to similarities in format, the final three lesson plans for each unit in *Social Star* are provided in *Appendix A*. Substitute the words "responding to criticism" whenever a "_____" appears in the lesson plans. Information specific to this unit follows.

LESSON X PREPARATORY SET:

Display *Og*. Say:

> *Og's son has been doing a poor job of caring for his pet dinosaur. The dinosaur's water dish is often empty. He doesn't polish the dinosaur's scales anymore. It's been a week since the dinosaur has had a walk around the watering hole. Og will be giving his son some criticism when he gets home from school.*

Ask students to list tips Og might follow when he gives the criticism to make it helpful rather than hurtful.

LESSON Y PREPARATORY SET:

Darken the room, if you prefer, and ask the students to visualize themselves correctly using this social skill by reading the following script:

> *Let's take a few moments to relax.... Make sure you are in a comfortable position.... Close your eyes if you feel like it.... On the count of three, take a very slow, deep breath. Remember to breathe in quietly through your nose. One...two...three.... Breathe in deeply.... Now breathe out slowly and quietly through your mouth. Let your entire body relax.... Now imagine yourself listening to your sister give you criticism about the way you eat.... You start to get upset, but you remember to stay calm.... You ask yourself if it's helpful or hurtful criticism.... You respond to her in a calm way. Think how proud you feel about responding to criticism appropriately.*

LESSON Z PLOT SITUATION:

You had two great teachers last year. This year, one of your teachers is mean and says things to you that make you sad.

LESSON Z ROADBLOCK EXAMPLES:

- Getting angry and not hearing what is said

- Having a person criticize you so often that you don't listen even when he or she has helpful criticism

Social Star

- Knowing that the person makes the same mistake he or she is criticizing you about
- Having a hard time using positive self-talk instead of negative self-talk
- Having someone criticize you about something you have no control to change

Responding to Criticism T-Chart

LOOKS LIKE...

using appropriate body talk

- facing the person
- looking at the person
- standing straight and tall

following the suggestion for change if you agree

staying calm

SOUNDS LIKE...

a respectful tone of voice

an appropriate volume

saying aloud

- "You're right. I'll do that."
- "That is a good suggestion."
- "OK. Thanks!"
- "I'll think about that."

saying to yourself

- "I'm a good person."
- "Is there a good idea for improvement in this criticism?"
- "I know I can do that."

SHOW TIME

HOME

Pretend your mother is giving you some helpful criticism about controlling your temper. Show how you would respond to the criticism.

SCHOOL

Pretend a lunchroom helper is giving you some helpful criticism about how loudly you speak in the lunchroom. Show how you could respond to the criticism.

COMMUNITY

Pretend an older girl in your neighborhood gives you hurtful criticism about walking across her lawn. Show how you might respond to the criticism.

Responding to Criticism

Criticism...

Remember It Can Be Helpful!

HOME-A-GRAM

Dear Family,

At school, we have been talking about the social skill called

RESPONDING TO CRITICISM

I learned that *responding to helpful criticism* means handling suggestions for improvement or change given in a respectful way. When someone gives me helpful criticism, I can tell myself to:

- stay calm and listen
- be polite and say something to the person
- decide if I agree with the suggestion for improvement or change. If I do agree, I can follow the suggestion.

I learned that *responding to hurtful criticism* means handling suggestions for improvement or change given in a mean way. When someone gives me hurtful criticism, I can:

- be calm and use self-talk to tell myself that I am a good person
- ask myself, "Is there a useful suggestion under the hurt?"

I know that most times people who criticize really do care and are trying to help me be the best person that I can be.

If I respond appropriately to criticism, I don't let it lead to negative thoughts or feelings about myself. If I think about the criticism I receive, then I won't miss any opportunities to improve.

I am bringing home a booklet called *A Book About Criticism for Kids and Parents*. After we have read through the Kid Tips part of the booklet together (the Parent Tips are just for you), please sign my "Responding to Criticism" badge so I can return it to school and become a SOCIAL SUPER STAR this week.

From: _____

© 1996 Thinking Publications — *Duplication permitted for educational use only.*

Helping My Community

Social Star

UNIT GOAL:

To demonstrate comprehension and use of strategies for helping in the community

EDUCATOR INFORMATION:

1. This unit is designed to help students recognize their role as a community member and to understand the importance of community. It discusses small, "random acts of kindness" students can do to brighten someone's day (e.g., smiling at someone, picking up trash in a neighbor's yard, doing the dishes without being asked). The unit also promotes larger, more organized efforts that can improve whole communities (e.g., keeping a neighborhood park clean, raising money to buy books for a library). Terms used interchangeably with "helping my community" in the research include *service learning, social responsibility, community service, social action,* and *citizenship participation.*

2. Berman (1990) identifies recent educational movements that have addressed social responsibility—cooperative learning, conflict resolution, multicultural education, moral development, global education, and environmental education. He stresses, however, that social responsibility is so important that it should be the core component of any curriculum. Berman (1990) is troubled to find that "young people in the United States are expressing a sense of powerlessness to affect constructive social or political change" (p. 75). Many students no longer live in small communities in which everyone feels a useful member of society. Berman (1990) cites the results of an annual survey of high school seniors. Each year since 1978, an average of approximately 45 percent of the students chose "mostly agree" or "agree" when responding to the statement, "I feel I can do very little to change the way the world is today."

3. Service learning provides opportunities for students to feel connected to their community. It intertwines learning and the child's community in a powerful manner. Duckenfield and Swanson (1992) share the following definition of *service learning* from The National Service and Community Act of 1990:

    > Students learn and develop through active participation in thoughtfully organized service experiences that meet actual community needs and that are coordinated in collaboration with the school and community. [Service learning] is integrated into the students' academic curriculum and provides structured time for a student to think, talk, or write about what the student did and saw during the actual service activity. [It] provides students with opportunities to use newly acquired skills and knowledge in real-life situations in their own communities. [It

also] enhances what is taught in school by extending student learning beyond the classroom and into the community and helps to foster the development of a sense of caring for others. (p. 7)

4. In 1994, Carol W. Kinsley, Executive Director of The Community Service Learning Center, in a speech to the National Society for Experiential Education, stated that "in our own century, John Dewey, and more recently, Ralph Tyler and Hilda Taba, have reminded us that students who actually do things, who engage in activities related to school subjects, learn more efficiently, and more effectively, and remember what they have learned much longer than students who don't" (p. 40). She went on to share that community service learning is directly related to the academic subject matter and it involves students making positive contributions to individuals and to community groups. Community service learning provides a way for students to complement and implement their learning. A key component of community service learning involves having students reflect on what happens and what it means.

5. Lewis (1991) sees many benefits in teaching citizenship participation. Most remarkably, as students reach out to help others, the process internalizes, and they learn to better control their personal lives. She feels this is especially important for "at risk" students, because they learn through experience that they can cause things to happen. "They don't just have to remain the receivers of actions. Self-esteem and personal worth sky-rocket as a result of this sense of power" (p. 49).

6. The Search Institute conducted a survey in 1989 and 1990 in which over 46,000 students in grades 6–12 were polled about their attitudes and behavior. In the analysis of survey results, there appeared to be noticeable differences between troubled teens and those teens who were leading productive, healthy, positive lives. The difference between the two groups was that the healthy teens possessed 30 behaviors/beliefs that were termed "developmental assets." The three developmental assets related most closely to the concept of "helping my community" are listed below (Benson, Galbraith, and Espeland, 1995):

    a. student places high personal value on helping other people;

    b. student reports interest in helping to reduce world hunger; and

    c. student cares about other people's feelings.

7. Becoming a socially responsible human being is a developmental happening. Every person develops a relationship to society and to the world (Berman, 1990). The concept of serving one's community should be introduced even before children reach school age to develop a lifetime of serving the community.

8. According to Duckenfield and Swanson (1992), service learning experiences can meet the following needs of elementary children:
   - belonging and group approval
   - a sense of self-worth
   - being accepted for one's uniqueness
   - a sense of personal competence
   - affection and acceptance
   - the opportunity to assume independence and responsibilities
   - challenging experiences
   - participating in creative, nonconforming activities

   Duckenfield and Swanson identify the following positive outcomes that occur as a result of service learning in each of the developmental areas listed below:

   Personal Growth

   (the development of characteristics related to self-improvement and self-actualization)

   - self-confidence and self-esteem
   - self-understanding
   - a sense of identity
   - independence and autonomy
   - openness to new experiences and roles
   - ability to take risks and accept challenges
   - a sense of usefulness and purpose
   - personal values and beliefs
   - responsibility for one's self and actions
   - self-respect

   Social Growth

   (the social skills that are necessary for relating to others in society)

   - communication skills
   - interpersonal skills
   - leadership skills
   - ability to work cooperatively with others
   - a sense of caring for others
   - a sense of belonging
   - acceptance and awareness of others from diverse and multicultural backgrounds
   - peer group affiliation

Intellectual Growth

(the cognitive skills necessary to enhance academic learning and acquire higher level thinking skills)

- application of knowledge, relevance of curriculum
- problem-solving and decision-making skills
- critical thinking skills
- skills in learning from experience
- use of all learning styles
- development of a positive attitude toward learning

Citizenship

(the responsibilities of participation in a multicultural society and of citizenship in a democracy)

- a sense of responsibility to contribute to society
- democratic participation (informed citizen, exercises voting privileges)
- awareness of community needs
- organizational skills
- social action skills (persuasion, policy research, petitioning)
- empowerment (belief in ability to make a difference)

Preparation for the World of Work

(the skills that help students gain work experience and make choices about possible career directions)

- human service skills
- realistic ideas about the world of work
- professionalism (dress, grooming, manners)
- ability to follow directions
- ability to function as a member of a team
- reliable working skills (punctuality, consistency, regular attendance)
- contacts and references for future job possibilities

Duckenfield and Swanson (1992) explain that the previously listed skills were acquired naturally in the past. Children were prepared for adulthood through real work experiences in factories or on the farm. However, in the present world, students may find few opportunities outside school to acquire these skills.

9. As a framework of what is developmentally appropriate, Duckenfield and Swanson (1992) illustrate the following progression of service learning activities from kindergarten through high school:

Primary (K–2nd)

- Make signs announcing a school recycling center.
- Help third graders sort and weigh recycled material.
- Pick up trash around the school grounds.

Upper Elementary (3rd–5th)

- Organize the school recycling center and arrange for collection.
- Assist primary students in making recycling signs and collecting recycled products.
- Write textbook companies and ask them to use recycled paper.

Middle School (6th–8th)

- Adopt a two-mile section of highway in front of the school to keep free of litter.
- Rake leaves and shovel snow for the local elderly population, or those with disabilities.
- Petition to ban styrofoam from the school district's lunchroom.

High School (9th–12th)

- Initiate a Community Beautification Committee with monthly meetings for new ideas and projects.
- Persuade the local government to set up regular recycling collection sites, or to improve existing ones.
- Organize a community-wide Adopt-A-Highway project.

10. Some excellent existing resources to expand your personal library about community service include:

 Learning the Skills of Peacemaking (1987)
 by Naomi Drew
 Jalmar Press
 2675 Skypark Drive, Suite 204
 Torrance, CA 90505
 310-784-0016

 The Peaceful Classroom: 162 Ways to Teach Preschoolers Compassion and Cooperation (1993)
 by Charles Smith
 Gryphon House
 10726 Tucker Street
 Beltsville, MD 20704
 800-638-0928

Kid Stories: Biographies of 20 Young People You'd Like to Know (1991)
by James Delisle
Free Spirit Publishing
400 First Avenue North, Suite 616
Minneapolis, MN 55401
800-735-7323

Girls and Young Women Leading the Way: 20 True Stories About Leadership (1993)
by Frances Karnes and Suzanne Bean
Free Spirit Publishing,
400 First Avenue North, Suite 616
Minneapolis, MN 55401
800-735-7323

RELATED ACTIVITIES:

1. Each day, ask a different student to read a page from *Acts of Kindness* (1993) by McCarty and McCarty or *Kid's Random Acts of Kindness* (1994) by Conari Press aloud to the class. Have students develop their own "random acts of kindness" book.

2. Have students research animals that have a sense of community (e.g., gorillas, wolves, geese, whales).

3. Ask students to write to service organizations requesting information about their causes. The names and addresses of national organizations can be found immediately following this introduction to the unit (see page 398). Be sure to consider local service groups (e.g., Optimist clubs, Jaycees, and school service groups).

4. Ask students to create banners to display or make morning announcements using quotes about service to others. A resource list of quotes can be found immediately following this introduction to the unit (see page 399).

5. Have students solicit the community's Chamber of Commerce (or other recognized agency) to sponsor a community event designed to promote service. The city of Wausau, WI has set aside an annual "Random Acts of Kindness Week." Information about this event can be obtained by calling the city's Chamber of Commerce 715-845-6231.

6. Invite adults from different cultures to talk to the students about how their cultures' conventions for helping in the community compare with the strategies presented in this unit.

It is important for educators to provide opportunities for students to work in groups, so they can experience social skills in contexts where social communication is needed.

Therefore, educators are encouraged to have students complete the Related Activities in small groups whenever possible. Educators trained in cooperative learning could incorporate the five components (see pages 33–34) into the group activity. An excellent resource for teaching students cooperative skills and building a sense of community is *Tribes: A Process for Social Development and Cooperative Learning* (1987) by Jeanne Gibbs.

RELATED LITERATURE:

Big Book for Our Planet (1993) edited by Ann Durell, Jean Craighead George, Katherine Paterson, Dutton. (136 pages)

Brothers: A Hebrew Legend (1985) by Florence B. Freedman, Ill. by Robert Andrew Parker, Harper and Row. (40 pages)

Wilfrid Gordon McDonald Partridge (1985) by Mem Fox, Ill. by Julie Vivas, Kane/Miller. (32 pages)

Chester (1980) by Mary Francis Craig Shura, Ill. by Susan Swan, Dodd Mead. (92 pages)

SOCIAL SKILLS ALL DAY LONG:

Look for opportunities to teach social skills throughout the day (incidental teaching). Four ways to reinforce appropriate social skills and an example of each follow:

Encouragement

It's really wonderful to have the privilege of working with students who find ways to be of service to their community.

Personal Example

When I was in high school, there were some kids who had a very difficult time in school. They were in a special class most of the day and did not have many friends. When a counselor approached the student council about the kids' need to feel more included, we began a "Circle of Friends" program. We all took turns spending time with the kids at lunch. It ended up being really fun and we made some new friends.

Prompting

When you are on spring vacation next week, look for things you can do to be of service to others.

Corrective Feedback (must be positive, private, specific, and nonthreatening)

Maria, just now when the others were discussing possible service projects, I heard you say, "There's nothing I can do that can make a difference." Try using powerful self-talk like, "I can make a big difference!"

Goodwill is the mightiest practical force in the universe.

Charles F. Dole

NATIONAL ORGANIZATIONS:

Amnesty International
322 8th Avenue
New York, NY 10001
212-807-8400

Save the Children
54 Wilton Road
Westport, CT 06880
800-243-5075

UNICEF
Three United Nations Plaza
New York, NY 10017
212-326-7000

The Hunger Project
15 E. 26th Street
New York, NY 10010
212-251-9100

The American Cancer Society
1599 Clifton Road, NE
Atlanta, GA 30329
404-320-3333

Special Olympics International
1325 G Street, NW
Suite 500
Washington, D.C. 20005
202-628-3630

Future Problem Solving Program
318 West Ann Street
Ann Arbor, MI 48106
313-998-7377

The Ecology Center
2530 San Pablo Avenue
Berkeley, CA 94702
510-548-2220

National Wildlife Federation
1400 16th Street, NW
Washington, D.C. 20036
800-477-5560

Animal Legal Defense Fund
1363 Lincoln Avenue, Suite 7
San Rafael, CA 94902
800-922-3764

Center for Marine Conservation
1725 DeSales Street NW
Washington, D.C. 20003
202-429-5609

The Oceanography Society
4052 Timber Ridge Drive
Virginia Beach, VA 23450
804-464-0131

World Wildlife Fund
1250 24th Street NW
Washington, D.C. 20037
202-293-4800

Earth Island Institute Dolphin
300 Broadway #28
San Francisco, CA 94133
415-788-3666

U.S. Environmental Protection Agency
External Relations and Education
Youth Programs (A-108)
401 M Street, SW
Washington, D.C. 20460
202-260-209

Paper Recycling Committee
American Paper Association
1111 19th Street Street, NW
Suite 800
Washington, D.C. 20036
800-878-8878

The Rainforest Action Network
450 Sansome
Suite 700
San Francisco, CA 94111
415-398-4404

Cousteau Society
301 Broadway, Suite A
Norfolk, VA 23517
804-441-4395

Greenpeace
1436 U Street, NW
Washington, D.C. 20013
202-462-1177

Tree People
12601 Mulholland Drive
Beverly Hills, CA 90210
818-753-4600

American Forestry Association
Save-A-Tree
P.O. Box 862
Berkeley, CA 94701
510-843-5233

American Forestry Association
Global Releaf Program
P.O. Box 2000
Washington, D.C. 20013
202-667-3300

These quotes were taken from *Positive, Motivational, Life-Affirming & Inspirational Quotations* (1993), compiled and arranged by John Cook. This book contains 7,341 quotations arranged according to 703 concepts. It is available from Rubicon Press, P.O. Box 310102, Newington, CT 06131-0102.

You don't live in a world all your own. Your brothers are here too.
　　　　　　　　　　　　　　　　　　　Albert Schweitzer

Everyone needs help from everyone.
　　　　　　　　　　　　　　　　　　　Bertolt Brecht

The service we render others is the rent we pay for our room on earth.
　　　　　　　　　　　　　　　　　　　Wilfred Grenvell

Maturity begins to grow when you can sense your concern for others outweighing your concern for you.
　　　　　　　　　　　　　　　　　　　John MacNaughton

Wherever there is a human being, there is an opportunity for kindness.
　　　　　　　　　　　　　　　　　　　Seneca

I expect to pass through life but once. If, therefore, there be any kindness I can show, or any good thing I can do for any fellow being, let me do it now... as I shall not pass this way again.
William Penn

Sharing what you have is more important than what you have.
Albert M. Wells, Jr.

Give what you have. To someone else it may be better than you dare to think.
Henry Wadsworth Longfellow

The only gift is a portion of thyself.
Ralph Waldo Emerson

We cannot hold a torch to light another's path without brightening our own.
Ben Sweetland

The habit of being uniformly considerate toward others will bring increased happiness to you.
Grenville Kleiser

Happiness...is only achieved by making others happy.
Stuart Cloete

The only ones among you who will be really happy are those who will have sought and found how to serve.
Albert Schweitzer

If you have not often felt the joy of doing a kind act, you have neglected much, and most of all yourself.
Seneca

Happiness...consists in giving, and in serving others.
Henry Drummond

The most satisfying thing in life is to have been able to give a large part of oneself to others.
Pierre Teilhard de Chardin

Lesson A

OBJECTIVES:

1. To state the meaning of *helping my community* and tell why it's important

2. To listen to the self-talk associated with appropriate use of the skill

MATERIALS:

1. *Community Rainbow* (See page 403; one per student and one transparency.)

2. Light-colored markers or colored pencils (An assortment for each pair of students)

3. *Helping My Community* (See page 404; one per student and one transparency.)

4. *Thought Bubble* (See *Appendix O*; one for educator use.)

PREPARATORY SET:

Display and distribute *Community Rainbow* and the markers or colored pencils. Tell students that the rainbow is the symbol for the first skill step in this unit called *Helping My Community*. Ask students to color in their rainbows. Explain that you'll collect their completed rainbows for use in the next lesson. Introduce the title for this unit and work as a group to answer the following questions:

- What is a community?

- Why are communities important?

- How do people form communities?

PLAN:

1. Distribute and display *Helping My Community*. Discuss the definition. Explain the skill steps and the symbols next to them. Remind students that the symbols are there to help them visualize and remember the skill steps. Refer students to the body-talk symbol in the left-hand margin. Remind students that appropriate body basics is important when helping in the community. Discuss reasons for helping in the community.

2. Model use of the skill steps for helping my community while thinking aloud. A scripted example follows:

Introduction

I am going to pretend to be someone your age who is looking for a way to help my community. I'll share the thoughts I'm having. When I hold up this Thought Bubble, *you'll know the words I'm saying are actually what I'm thinking.*

Social Star

Actual Model

While holding up the *Thought Bubble* say, *Random Acts of Kindness Week sure was fun. I'm glad our city celebrates it every year during the month of February. Even though the week is over, I still want to keep doing nice things for the people in my community. Let's see, what can I do this week? I know, I'll set a goal to help at least four people. There's Mr. Smith, our neighbor. I see he's picking up his newspapers for recycling. The papers have blown all over his yard. I'll go ask Mom if I can offer to help him.* Put the *Thought Bubble* down and say, *Mom, Mr. Smith has papers blowing all over his yard. Can I go over and offer to help pick them up?*

3. Pair students (see *Appendix P*). Read the story at the bottom of *Helping My Community*.

4. Ask students to process the story using the *Sharing Pairs* strategy (Harmin, 1995). This strategy maximizes the number of students who talk about their ideas and hear the ideas of others. Ask students to discuss answers to the following questions with their partners before you call on one pair to share their ideas with the whole class:

- What did Victor and Lee decide to do for their community service project?
- What evidence is there that the boys followed skill step 2?
- How might volunteering at the library help the boys' community?
- Victor and Lee will get the "outside reward" of a badge after volunteering. What "inside rewards" might the boys also get?
- Do Victor and Lee have to quit volunteering at the library after their two hours? Why or why not?
- If Victor and Lee lived here in our community, what could they do to help?

5. Ask student pairs to take turns telling each other the meaning of *helping my community* and why it's important to use the skill. Students could be reminded that the information they are to say is printed on *Helping My Community*.

As an option to add structure to this activity, ask partners to come to an agreement about which person will be called "A" and which person will be called "B." After students have made their decisions, ask "A" to tell "B" the definition of *helping my community*. Next, ask "B" to tell "A" the definition. Ask students to use the same procedure to tell each other the reasons for helping my community.

———————— ★★★ ————————

Service is the rent we pay for living.

Marian Wright Edleman

Name: _____

COMMUNITY RAINBOW

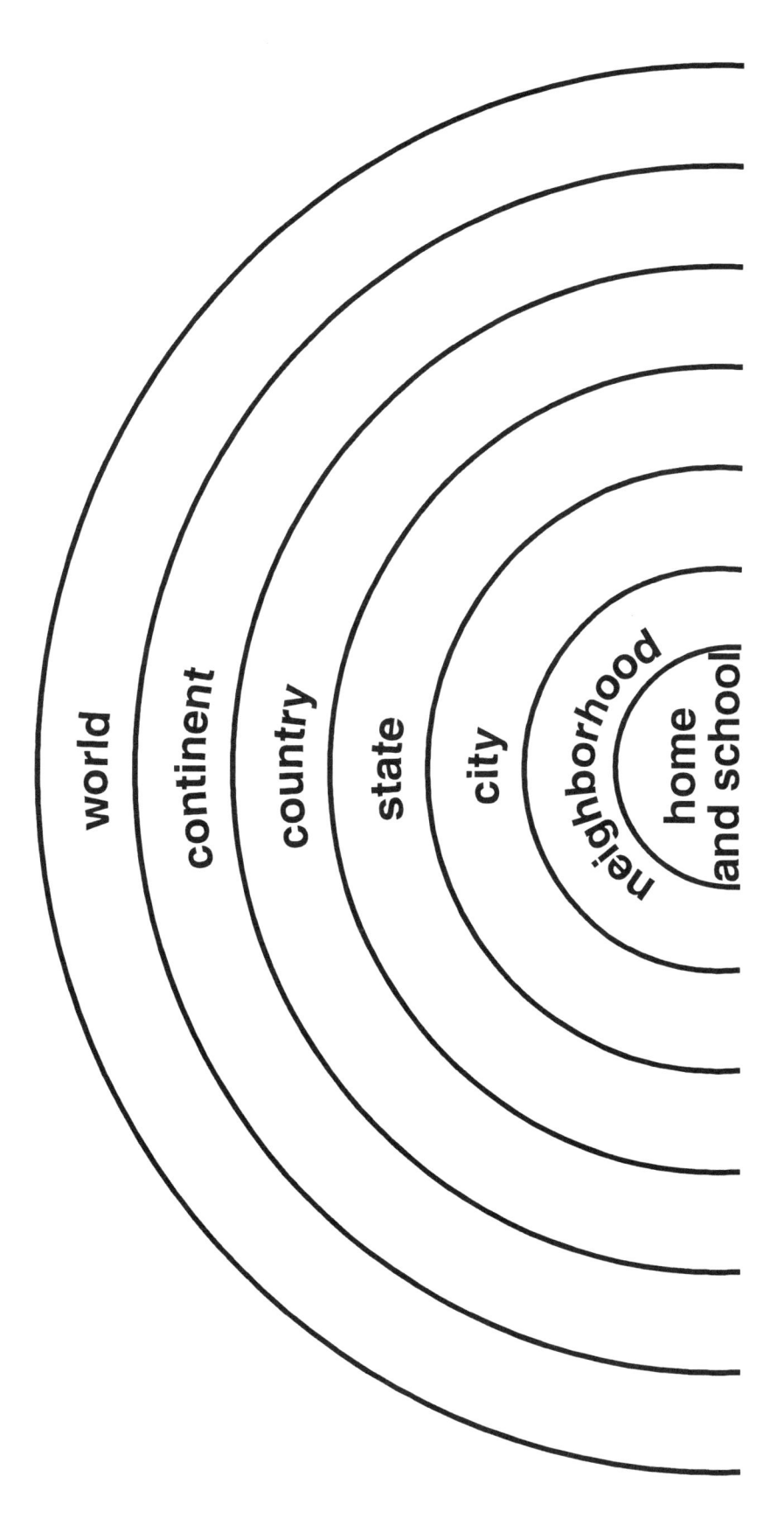

- world
- continent
- country
- state
- city
- neighborhood
- home and school

Social Star

Name _____

Helping My Community

MEANING OF HELPING MY COMMUNITY:

Identifying the needs of my community and doing my part to help

SKILL STEPS:

1. Ask myself: What can I do for my community?

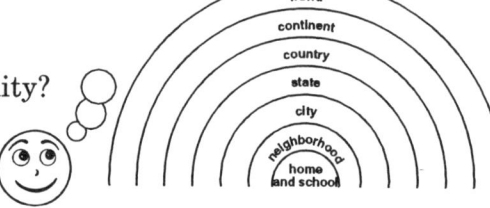

2. Tell myself: I'll set a goal and take action.

I will...

(rings labeled: world, continent, country, state, city, neighborhood, home and school)

REASONS FOR USING THIS SKILL:

When you help in your community, you will positively affect the lives of others.

DIRECTIONS: Listen to the story below. Look at the pictures of Victor and Lee while you listen.

Victor and Lee went to a Scout meeting together. They learned that one requirement for earning their next badge was to do at least two hours of community service. After the meeting, Lee asked Victor, "Have you heard about the reading program at our public library for preschoolers who are new to our country?" Victor answered, "Yes, I think so. Isn't that the program where volunteers read stories to kids to help them learn to understand and speak English?" "That's the one," said Lee. "Maybe we could volunteer to read for our two hours of community service." Victor said, "Good idea, let's go call the library right now."

© 1996 Thinking Publications   Duplication permitted for educational use only.

Lesson B

EDUCATOR INFORMATION:

During this lesson, students will hear about a variety of community service ideas. This format was chosen in response to Berman's (1990) contention that "it is important...to tell young people about the success stories of others,...students who have improved their school environment, and helped the homeless. They need to hear about the Mother Theresa's..., but also about people down the street who are doing what they can to improve the neighborhood" (p. 78).

OBJECTIVES:

1. To read a play about a group of students who work together to find a way to help their community

2. To interview others about community needs and brainstorm a list of service learning projects

MATERIALS:

1. *Community Rainbow* (See page 403; one transparency and students' colored copies saved from Lesson A.)

2. Black marker or crayon (One per student)

3. *Helping My Community* classroom poster (See page 13.)

4. *Social Star Club Meeting—Helping My Community* (See pages 408–411; one per student.)

5. Figures of Mr. Aaron, Mr. Walker, Ann Olson, Jolisa Walker, Mike Olson, Lee Vue, Maria Parra, and Victor Parra (See *Appendix F*.)

6. *Community Service Hunt* (See page 412; one transparency and one per student.)

PREPARATORY SET:

Display *Community Rainbow*. Distribute colored copies (saved from Lesson A) and a black marker or crayon to each student. Say, "Please use your marker/crayon to add the word "my" at the beginning of each band in your rainbow" (model how to do this for your students). "When you are finished, your rainbow should say, my home and school, my neighborhood, etc."

When students are finished, collect their rainbows for use during Lesson X. Ask students, "Why do you think I asked you to add the word "my" to each band on the rainbow?" Call on various students to share their ideas (lead to an understanding that if they each feel ownership, they'll feel more responsible for doing their part in their communities).

PLAN:

1. Review the definition and skill steps for *helping my community* by referring the class to the *Helping My Community* classroom poster.

2. Pair students using *Line up–Fold up* (see *Appendix P*). Ask student pairs to take turns telling each other the skill steps for helping my community. Follow the procedure described in step 5 of Lesson A. Next, ask students to think of a situation when it's important to help their community. Tell students that one or more pairs will be asked to share their situation.

3. Distribute *Social Star Club Meeting—Helping My Community*. Display the characters while reading the script. Assign roles for Scene One and read it as a class. Before reading Scene Two, ask students to respond to the following questions:

   - Have any of you heard or read about someone like Isis Johnson? (The full story of Isis Johnson can be found in *Girls and Young Women Leading the Way* (Karnes and Bean, 1993).

   - What roadblocks do you think she might have encountered while helping in her community?

   - Have any of you ever felt that "good feeling deep down inside" that Mr. Aaron talked about?

4. Assign roles for Scene Two and read it as a class. Before reading Scene Three, ask students to respond to the following questions:

   - What preparations will the Social Star Club need to make before going to clean their section of the park?

   - What safety factors will need to be discussed?

5. Assign roles for Scene Three and read it as a class. Ask students to respond to the following question:

   - What thoughts do you think the Social Star Club members had while hearing the letter from Ida B. Positive?

6. Ask students to pretend that Victor goes to their school. Share the following ideas that Victor might have:

   Surprise another classroom in our school by delivering a batch of cookies to them for a treat. Challenge them not to "repay" you, but to "pass the kindness on" by treating another class in a similar way and challenging that class to "pass it on."

Contribute to our school library by donating a new or used book on your birthday.

Set up a schedule to take turns working with classmates who have been ill and missed school. Classmates could help the student who has missed by preparing a "Welcome back—We missed you!" note, sharing information they missed, or by helping with work missed.

Pair each student with a resident of a local Senior Center and plan a monthly art project that the students could work with their partners to complete.

Organize a winter clothing drive and raise funds to mail the winter articles to those in need nationally or internationally.

Ask, "What other ideas do you think Victor might have shared?"

7. Display and distribute *Community Service Hunt* and read the directions for its completion with students. Discuss the example provided. Ask students to complete this assignment before the next lesson. Tell students that during the next lesson, they will be sharing the community needs they found.

---★★★---

Most teachers enter the profession because they care about children and care about the world. Teaching is our vehicle for making a difference in this world. This vision offers all of us an occasion for seeing our work as part of the world we hope to create.

Sheldon Berman

Social Star Club Meeting

Helping My Community

Characters:	Narrator	Mr. Aaron
	Ann Olson	Jolisa Walker
	Mike Olson	Lee Vue
	Maria Parra	Victor Parra
	Mr. Walker	

Scene One: **The Social Star Club Meeting**

Narrator: The Social Star Club is about to start their meeting.

Mr. Aaron: Welcome to this week's meeting of the Social Star Club. Lately, I have read and heard stories about kids your age who have done things to help others in their communities. I'd like to tell you about one of those true stories: An eight-year-old girl named Isis Johnson felt sad after she and her grandmother watched a TV program about hungry children in another country. She took action! Isis and her grandmother went to her neighbors asking for food donations for the poor and hungry. In a short time, one thousand canned items were collected. Isis was not able to send the food to the children in the far-off country, but her local Salvation Army helped her with a plan to get the food to people in her city who needed it. She continued her work and ended up helping dozens of families.

Lee: Wow! That must have taken her a long time to get all that food!

Ann: My mom was telling me about a boy who started a project sort of like that in his town. Instead of collecting food, they collected winter coats.

Victor: Can we do something like that?

Mr. Aaron:	I was hoping you'd ask! During today's meeting, I thought we'd talk about our community right here in Socialville and about ways that we might help.
Jolisa:	That's a great idea. I've seen stories about poor people before too. I just never thought I was old enough to do anything for them. Did you say Isis was only eight years old?
Mr. Aaron:	Yes!
Mike:	My dad helps in the community. He drives elderly people to their doctor's appointments. He says he feels good about helping others. It would be neat if our club could think of a way to help.
Lee:	If Isis can do it, we can too!
Mr. Aaron:	It sounds like you are all interested in finding ways to help out right here in Socialville. That is important, because this community belongs to each and every one of you.
Ann:	Last year there was a day called "Make a Difference Day." My Mom read about it and our family planted flowers in a vacant lot. It wasn't a big thing. It only took us a few hours, but lots of people said they enjoyed the flowers.
Maria:	My aunt lives in Wausau, Wisconsin. On a 100 degree day, a family handed out cold soda to workers coming off their shift and getting into their hot cars to go home. A national newspaper told about the story.
Victor:	Boy, I wish I'd get a free pop. That would be great! So what did those people get for doing all those nice things?
Mr. Aaron:	Good question, Victor! Does anyone want to answer?
Mike:	Well, they probably didn't get money or anything like that. But I bet they felt proud about helping.
Mr. Aaron:	You're right, Mike. They had a good feeling deep down inside. There's a quote that says, "Anything done for another is done for one's self." What that means is, we really help ourselves when we help others.
Narrator:	Mr. Aaron looked at his watch.
Mr. Aaron:	Well, our meeting time is almost up. Let's talk more about what our club can do when we meet again next week.

Social Star

Scene Two:　　The Next Week

Narrator: The Social Star Club is about to start their next meeting. They are curious, because Mr. Walker, from the Parks Department, is there.

Mr. Aaron: Welcome to the Social Star meeting. It's so nice to see such a large turnout. What a great bunch you are! Last week we talked about people who have found ways to help their communities. At the end of the meeting, you said you wanted our club to find a way to help our community.

Jolisa: I went home and told my family about our meeting. My dad said he really could use our help. That is why he is here.

Mr. Walker: I'm very glad to be here today. I hope you'll be interested in what I have to say. As many of you know, I work for the Socialville Parks Department. Our department has always been proud because we keep our parks very clean.

Mr. Aaron: Yes, our parks really are very nice!

Mr. Walker: A few months ago, the county board decided to cut four people from our staff. With less people on our staff, we aren't able to pick up the litter that is thrown around. We really need help. We'd like to divide the parks into small sections and ask groups like yours to "adopt" sections and keep it picked up.

Mike: Don't they do the same thing with highways? I've seen signs along some roads.

Mr. Walker: Yes, they do. That's where we got our idea.

Lee: So we would take care of a section of the park?

Mr. Walker: Sure! I was thinking of a section of Nicetime Park.

Maria: Sounds like fun! We could each have our own trash bag.

Victor: When can we start?

Mr. Walker: You can start as soon as you want. Boy, it's great to have a group as excited as you are. It will really help keep our parks as nice as they've been in the past.

Mr. Aaron: Great, it sounds as if everyone's in favor of adopting a section of Nicetime Park. We'll have to make some decisions about how often we'll go to the park. Let's have a round of applause for our guest speaker!

Scene Three: Six Months Later

Narrator: It is now six months later. The Social Star Club is about to start their meeting.

Mr. Aaron: Welcome to another meeting of the Social Star Club. It was quite a while ago that we adopted part of Nicetime Park in Socialville. Jolisa has an update on our project.

Jolisa: My dad has been excited about how nice we are keeping our section of the park. Believe it or not, other people have noticed too. Listen to this letter my dad got.

Dear Park Supervisor,

I live near Nicetime Park. I take my dog for a walk there. I never really thought about how nice the park is until yesterday. I started talking to a person who just moved here from another city. She talked about how beautiful the parks are here. She said the parks in her old town were full of litter. Her story helped me appreciate how beautiful Nicetime Park is. Thank you so much!

Sincerely,

Ida B. Positive

My dad wanted us to hear this letter. He knows our parks stay so clean because of help from groups like ours.

Maria: Cool letter. You know, I really have fun when we pick up the park. It doesn't seem like work at all!

Lee: Me too!

Victor: I have an idea for another way we can help our community.

Ann: What is it?

Narrator: The group listened to Victor. They agreed that besides taking care of the park, their club could take on another community project.

Social Star

Name _____

Community Service Hunt

DIRECTIONS: Ask adults you know if they are aware of needs in your community. Record their ideas on the chart below. Look at the example.

WHO	THINKS THERE IS A NEED FOR...
★ 1 Mr. Aaron	*Keeping the school's restroom floors free of paper towels and litter.*
★ 2	
★ 3	
★ 4	

© 1996 Thinking Publications — Duplication permitted for educational use only.

Lesson C

EDUCATOR INFORMATION:

During this lesson, students are asked to brainstorm community service needs. The lesson lays the groundwork for actually doing a real service project which may take an extended period of time to plan, organize, and implement. The educator is encouraged to remind students of the possible levels of community service including the needs within their classroom or school.

Berman (1990) states that it is important to consider that the form community service takes matters less than whether children see it as important and choose it for themselves. Therefore, depending on your students' levels of interest, step 2 of this lesson may or may not be completed.

For groups who do choose to do a community service project, consider Berman's advice that "whether it is having students help each other...or [having them] participate in their local community, students need coaching from adults" (p. 78). The key is to allow students to feel ownership of the project while being there to guide them.

OBJECTIVES:

1. To brainstorm community service needs
2. To choose one or more service projects to actually carry out (optional)

MATERIALS:

1. A gift-wrapped scrapbook or three-ring binder (Prepared before class by attaching the following message to its cover and gift wrapping it: *Inside this book is a lasting reminder of service that we or others have given to our community.*)
2. *Thinking Skills Web* (See *Appendix S*; one transparency.)
3. *Helping My Community Planning Guide* (See page 415; one transparency.)

PREPARATORY SET:

Present the gift-wrapped scrapbook or three-ring binder to the students. Ask a student representative to unwrap the gift and read the message included. Tell students that one dictionary's definition of *community* is "people with common interests living in the same area." With that definition in mind, challenge them to think of their home as a community, their school as a community, their neighborhood as a community, their city as a community, their state as a community, their country as a community, their continent as a community, and their world as a community.

PLAN:

1. Display *Thinking Skills Web*. Write the heading "Needs in our community" in the large circle in the middle. Ask students to name needs they discovered by completing *Community Service Hunt* or needs they can think of themselves. Write their responses on the transparencies outside lines. If students express a genuine interest in carrying out one of the brainstormed ideas, proceed to step 2 of this Plan. If not, encourage students to bring in written examples (e.g., newspaper clippings) of service projects to add to the scrapbook or three-ring binder.

2. Once a project has been selected, display *Helping My Community Planning Guide*. (This guide is adapted from the *Brownie Girl Scout Handbook* [Sparks, et al., 1993].) Utilize the guide during the planning and implementation stages that occur as the project unfolds.

———————— ★★★ ————————

Happiness...consists in giving, and in serving others.
Henry Drummond

Helping My Community Planning Guide

It may be helpful to follow these steps when planning your project:

1. Name the problem or need.

2. Gather information about the need.

3. Talk about actions and think of solutions.

4. Pick a solution that will work best.

5. Decide how to do the project. Think carefully about the following:

    a. What will be done?

    b. Will it cost money?

    c. When will it be done?

    d. Is it too hard to do? Can we divide the project into smaller parts?

    e. Who will help us? Can we get other people in the community to help?

    f. How much time will we need?

6. DO IT!!

7. Think about what we accomplished.

8. Share what we did with others.

Lessons X, Y, and Z

Due to similarities in format, the final three lesson plans for each unit in *Social Star* are provided in *Appendix A*. Substitute the words "helping my community" whenever a "_____" appears in the lesson plans. Information specific to this unit follows.

LESSON X PREPARATORY SET:

Pair students (see *Appendix P*). Distribute the colored copies of *Community Rainbow* (saved from Lessons A and B), scissors, tape or glue, and string. Ask students to work with their partners to cut out their rainbows, tape or glue them together so they become two-sided. Finally, ask them to attach a length of string to the top of their rainbow and hang it as a mobile in the classroom. Review the significance of the rainbow with students. Remind them that they are a part of their community at every level, extending from their own home and school all the way up to the level of the world.

LESSON Y PREPARATORY SET:

Darken the room, if you prefer, and ask the students to visualize themselves correctly using this social skill by reading the following script:

> *Let's take a few moments.... Make sure you are in a comfortable position.... Close your eyes if you feel like it.... On the count of three, take a very slow, deep breath. Remember to breathe in quietly through your nose. One...two...three.... Breathe in deeply.... Now breathe out slowly.... Remember to breathe out quietly through your mouth. Let your entire body relax.... Now imagine yourself creating a plan and setting a goal for helping your community. Imagine how positive it feels to do your part in your community.*

LESSON Z PLOT SITUATION:

Ask students to pretend they are part of a group that has committed to a community project. Now that the project is underway, many members of the group are not working cooperatively to implement the plan they agreed upon.

LESSON Z ROADBLOCK EXAMPLES:

- Noticing the people you want to help feeling embarrassed for taking help or receiving charity
- The project costing more than you thought it would
- Encountering difficulties that you did not expect

Helping My Community T-Chart

LOOKS LIKE...

using appropriate body talk

- having a pleasant facial expression while helping others
- looking at the people you are helping or at those you are working with
- using an alert and friendly posture
- having good hygiene when helping others

helping without being asked

SOUNDS LIKE...

an appropriate volume

an appropriate tone of voice

saying aloud

- "Sure, I'd be glad to help."

asking

- "Is there any way I can help?"

saying to yourself

- "Wow, they really needed our help. They really appreciated it."

SHOW TIME

HOME

Pretend you want to help your neighbor who is picking up newspapers that got blown all over her yard. Show how you could ask for permission from a parent.

SCHOOL

Pretend there is a group of students in your school helping at the recycling center. You would like to help too. Show how you could ask one of the students how you can get involved.

COMMUNITY

Pretend you are helping your community by volunteering at a nursing home. Show how you could politely begin and end a conversation with one of the residents.

Helping My Community

Social Star

HOME-A-GRAM

Dear Family,

At school, we have been talking about the social skill called

HELPING MY COMMUNITY

I learned that *helping my community* means identifying things that need to be done in my community and making sure that something is done about those needs.

I learned that there are things I can do to help my community. I can remind myself to be on the lookout for ways to help in my community. When I find a need, I should set a goal and take action.

When I help my community, I am making a difference in a way that cannot be measured. My actions, even small ones, may have effects that ripple off in many directions.

On the lines below, I have written down some things that I could do to be helpful in my community. I would like to talk with you about my ideas.

_____

_____

_____

_____

If possible, let's choose one of the ideas, set a goal, and take action. After we talk, please sign my "Helping My Community" badge so I can return it to school and become a SOCIAL SUPER STAR this week.

From: _____

© 1996 Thinking Publications — Duplication permitted for educational use only.

Appendix A

Lesson X

Social Star

OBJECTIVE:

To observe the appropriate use of _____ in a home, school, or community role-play

MATERIALS:

1. _____ classroom poster (See page 13.)

2. _____ T-Chart (One per student and one transparency of page within the unit) or *Blank T-Chart* (See *Appendix L*; one per student and one transparency.)

3. _____ *Show Time* (One transparency of page found within the _____ unit)

4. *Thought Bubble* (See *Appendix O*; one for teacher and student use.)

PREPARATORY SET:

Follow the Preparatory Set described for Lesson X within the _____ unit.

PLAN:

1. Quickly review the definition and skill step(s) for _____ by referring to the _____ classroom poster.

2. Distribute and display the _____ *T-Chart*. Tell students it is a chart showing what a person looks and sounds like when appropriately using the social skill of _____. Review the information listed in the chart and encourage students to make additions. Although time-consuming, T-Charts can be used more effectively by having students create their own with your help and then compiling the information on a single T-Chart for all to see. If you choose this option, use the *Blank T-Chart*.

3. Display _____ *Show Time*. Discuss each situation and explain that everyone will be role-playing these situations during the _____ *Show Time* activity in the next lesson. Today will be a rehearsal for their _____ *Show Time*.

4. Model each situation and verbalize self-talk using the *Thought Bubble*. (Remind students that use of inappropriate body talk can sabotage any social skill.)

5. Choose a student to role-play one of the situations twice (see pages 18–20). The first time, the student should verbalize self-talk using the *Thought Bubble*. The second time, the student should not verbalize self-talk.

6. Remind students that the next lesson will be _____ *Show Time*.

Appendix A—*Continued*

Lesson Y

Social Star

OBJECTIVE:

To demonstrate use of ____ in a home, school, or community situation

MATERIALS:

1. ____ *Show Time* (One transparency of page found within the ____ unit)

2. ____ *Show Time* sign (One or more per student; found in ____ unit immediately after ____ *Show Time*.)

3. Markers or crayons for each student

PREPARATORY SET:

Ask students to visualize by reading the script provided for Lesson Y within the ____ unit.

PLAN:

1. Display ____ *Show Time*. Review the home, school, and community situations which students will be role-playing during today's ____ *Show Time* activity.

2. Distribute markers or crayons and a copy or copies of the ____ *Show Time* sign to each student. Tell students that you will be calling on them to role-play the ____ *Show Time* situations. While they are waiting their turns to role-play, students should decorate their ____ *Show Time* signs so that they can be hung in predetermined locations throughout the school during Lesson Z. Encourage students to avoid interrupting so that you may observe the ____ *Show Time* role-plays.

3. Students may be called to role-play individually or in pairs. (For additional information on role-playing, see pages 18–20.) If a pair is role-playing, one person can be the observer while the other student role-plays with the educator. The students should then switch roles. It is important to provide feedback to students. (For additional information on feedback, see pages 20–21.)

4. If time allows, ask students which previously learned social skills they have used successfully. Have students identify how they feel when they use their social skills appropriately. Ask students which social skills they might like to improve.

5. Collect ____ *Show Time* signs to hang during Lesson Z.

Appendix A—*Continued*

Lesson Z

Social Star

OBJECTIVES:

1. To review and practice cognitive planning techniques

2. To identify and discuss _____ roadblocks

3. To prepare an activity to transfer use of _____ into the home

MATERIALS:

1. *Cognitive Planning Formula* chart (See page 12.)

2. *Secret Formula Pages* (See *Appendix N*; one of the two pages per student.)

3. *Self-Management Sheet* (See *Appendix H*; one of the 10 choices per student and one transparency.)

4. *Roadblock Sheet* (See *Appendix Q*; one per student and one transparency.)

5. _____ *Home-A-Gram* (See page found in the _____ unit; one per student and one transparency.)

6. _____ badge (See *Appendix R*; one per student.)

7. *Social Super Stars* display (See page 13.)

8. Completed *Show Time* signs (Colored during Lesson Y)

PREPARATORY SET:

To foster internalization of the cognitive planning steps called STOP, PLOT, GO, SO, ask students to participate in a "Beat the Clock" activity (see pages 55–56).

PLAN:

1. Display the *Cognitive Planning Formula* chart and remind students that they can use the four steps to solve problems they may have in their lives. As an option to reinforce this concept, have students complete one of the two *Secret Formula Pages* by addressing a real-life problem they need to solve or just recently solved. (These pages do not need to be used in every Lesson Z but should be used occasionally. They may also be used at any time when a student is trying to solve a problem. This shows the usefulness of the STOP, PLOT, GO, SO strategy across all areas of daily living.)

2. Review STOP with students by reminding them that STOP means stay calm and use self-control. Review what *self-control* means and why it's important. Ask students to practice one of the strategies for staying calm and using self-control by reading one of the six scripts on pages 50–51.

3. Review PLOT by reminding students that in whatever situation they find themselves, they should:

    - Decide exactly what the problem is
    - Brainstorm choices
    - Think about what might happen after each choice (consequences)
    - Pick a choice
    - Think about social skills needed

4. Have students practice the five steps to PLOT by asking them to pretend that...(use the plot situation described for Lesson Z within the _____ unit). Students can work individually, with partners, in small groups, or as a whole class.

5. Review GO by reminding students that after they pick a choice, they need to actually go ahead with the plan by doing it.

6. Review SO by reminding students that after they use their choice, they should ask themselves "So, how did my plan work?" If the plan worked well, they could praise or reward themselves. If the plan did not work, they could think about why it didn't work or what they would do differently next time.

7. Bring the discussion back to the specific social skill of _____. Tell students it's important for them to check how they are doing at using _____ during and outside of class. Distribute the chosen *Self-Management Sheet* and give directions for its use. (See pages 24–25 for a general discussion of self-management strategies.)

8. Distribute and display the *Roadblock Sheet*. Tell students that it will sometimes be difficult to use _____ because of roadblocks. Explain that a roadblock is something that may get in the way of successful use of a social skill. Remind students not to become discouraged if use of their social skills does not always turn out right. Suggest to students that when a roadblock occurs, they may need to take a "detour" rather than give up. Make students aware that a roadblock situation is an opportunity for them to use the SO step of STOP, PLOT, GO, SO. They could ask themselves questions such as how they did, what might have gone wrong, and how the roadblock could be dealt with in a more positive way next time. Examples of _____ roadblocks are described in Lesson Z within each specific social skill unit. Give students the opportunity to think of additional roadblocks that may occur.

9. Distribute the _____ *Home-A-Gram* and a _____ badge to each student. Have students complete the *Home-A-Gram* as directed (see page 23).

10. Point to the *Social Super Stars* display. Remind students that their badges will be added to the display once their *Home-A-Grams* are signed.

11. Distribute the completed _____ *Show Time* signs and ask students to hang them in the predetermined location(s).

Appendix B

| Social Communication Skills Rating Scale | Social Star |

(Adult Form—Conflict Resolution and Community Interaction Skills)

Name of Student: _____ Grade: _____

Age: _____ Date rating scale completed: _____

Name of person completing rating scale: _____

Relationship with student (e.g., parent, case manager, regular education teacher):

_____

DIRECTIONS: Rate this student on how well he or she uses the following social skills. Circle:

1—if the skill is **SELDOM** used appropriately.

2—if the skill is **SOMETIMES** used appropriately.

3—if the skill is **ALMOST ALWAYS** used appropriately.

For example, a student who rarely asserts himself or herself would be rated as follows:

BEING ASSERTIVE—speaks up for himself or herself in a confident ①　2　3
and respectful way.

Please give examples or comments when appropriate (e.g., if you give a low rating for taking charge of anger, explain if the student hurts himself or herself, other people, or property; tantrums frequently, etc.)

RATING

SOCIAL COMMUNICATION SKILL	SELDOM	SOMETIMES	ALMOST ALWAYS
1. TAKING CHARGE OF FEELINGS—Identifies how he or she is feeling and takes charge of those feelings by expressing them in a responsible way.	1	2	3

Comments:

© 1996 Thinking Publications　　　*Duplication permitted for educational use only.*

Appendix B: Social Communication Skills Rating Scale

RATING

SOCIAL COMMUNICATION SKILL	SELDOM	SOMETIMES	ALMOST ALWAYS
2. BEING ASSERTIVE—Speaks up for himself or herself in a confident and respectful way. Comments:	1	2	3
3. BEING RESPONSIBLE—Chooses to do what he or she feels is right. Comments:	1	2	3
4. TAKING CHARGE OF ANGER—Takes charge of angry feelings by dealing with them in responsible ways. Comments:	1	2	3
5. RESISTING PEER PRESSURE—Is not led by others into doing what he or she feels should not be done. Comments:	1	2	3

© 1996 Thinking Publications *Duplication permitted for educational use only.*

RATING

SOCIAL COMMUNICATION SKILL	SELDOM	SOMETIMES	ALMOST ALWAYS
6. SETTLING CONFLICTS—Can find a way to work out disagreements, so that everyone involved feels OK. Comments:	1	2	3
7. MAKING AN APOLOGY—Chooses words and actions that show he or she is sorry after doing something wrong. Comments:	1	2	3
8. RESPONDING TO CRITICISM—Accepts helpful suggestions for improvement or change when given in a respectful way. Comments:	1	2	3
9. HELPING MY COMMUNITY—Identifies what others need in the community and does his or her part to help. Comments:	1	2	3

Appendix C

Student Social Skill Summary Form

Social Star

STUDENT'S NAME:	Identified as a strength	Identified as problematic	Skill has been taught in class		
1. Taking Charge of Feelings					
2. Being Assertive					
3. Being Responsible					
4. Taking Charge of Anger					
5. Resisting Peer Pressure					
6. Settling Conflicts					
7. Making an Apology					
8. Responding to Criticism					
9. Helping My Community					

© 1996 Thinking Publications *Duplication permitted for educational use only.*

Appendix D

Class Summary Form

Social Star

Mark social skills identified as strengths with a "+" and those identified as problematic with a "–".

SOCIAL SKILLS:	STUDENTS' NAMES									
1. Taking Charge of Feelings										
2. Being Assertive										
3. Being Responsible										
4. Taking Charge of Anger										
5. Resisting Peer Pressure										
6. Settling Conflicts										
7. Making an Apology										
8. Responding to Criticism										
9. Helping My Community										

Appendix E

Socialville Buildings

Social Star

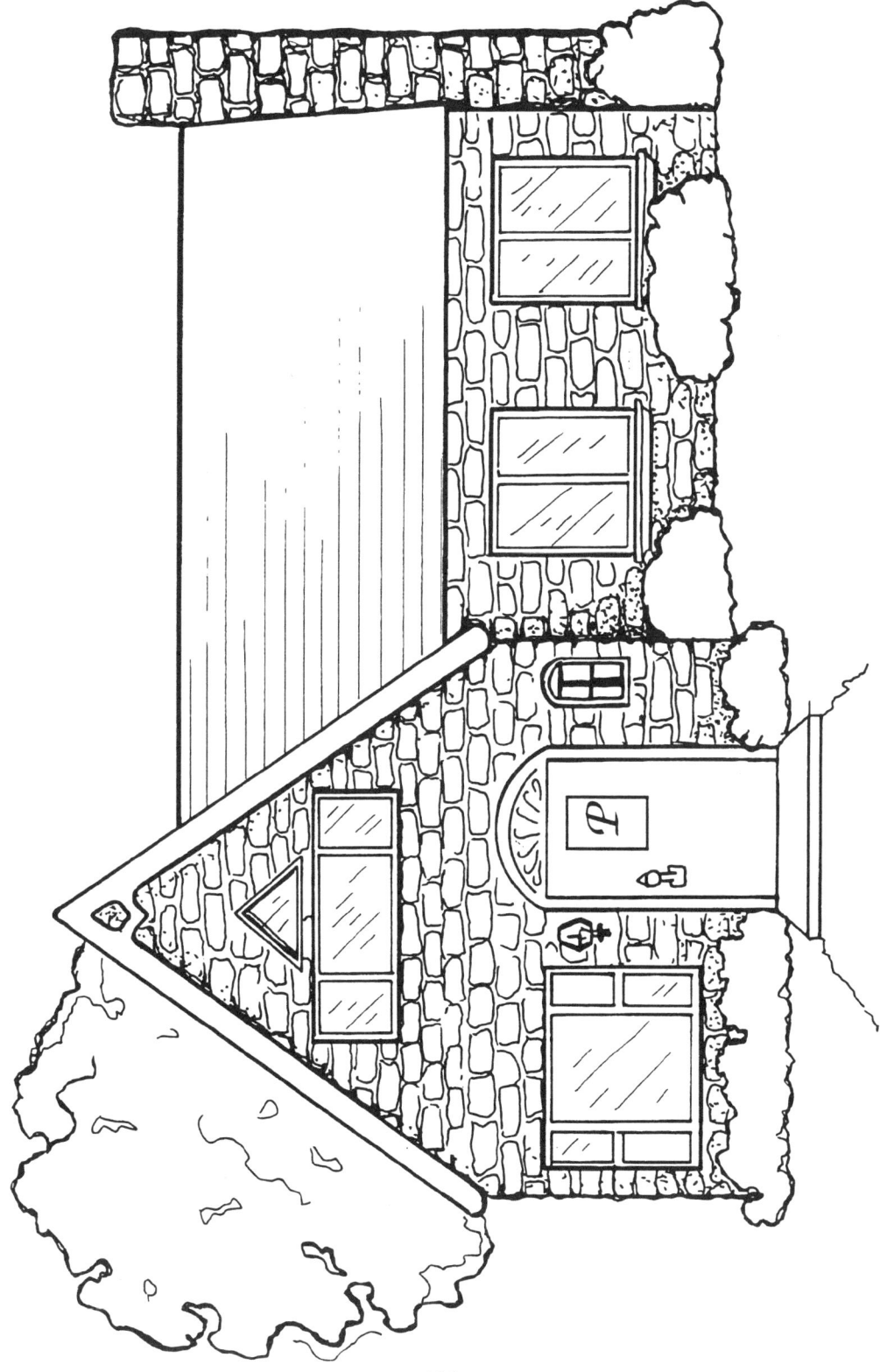

© 1996 Thinking Publications   431   *Duplication permitted for educational use only.*

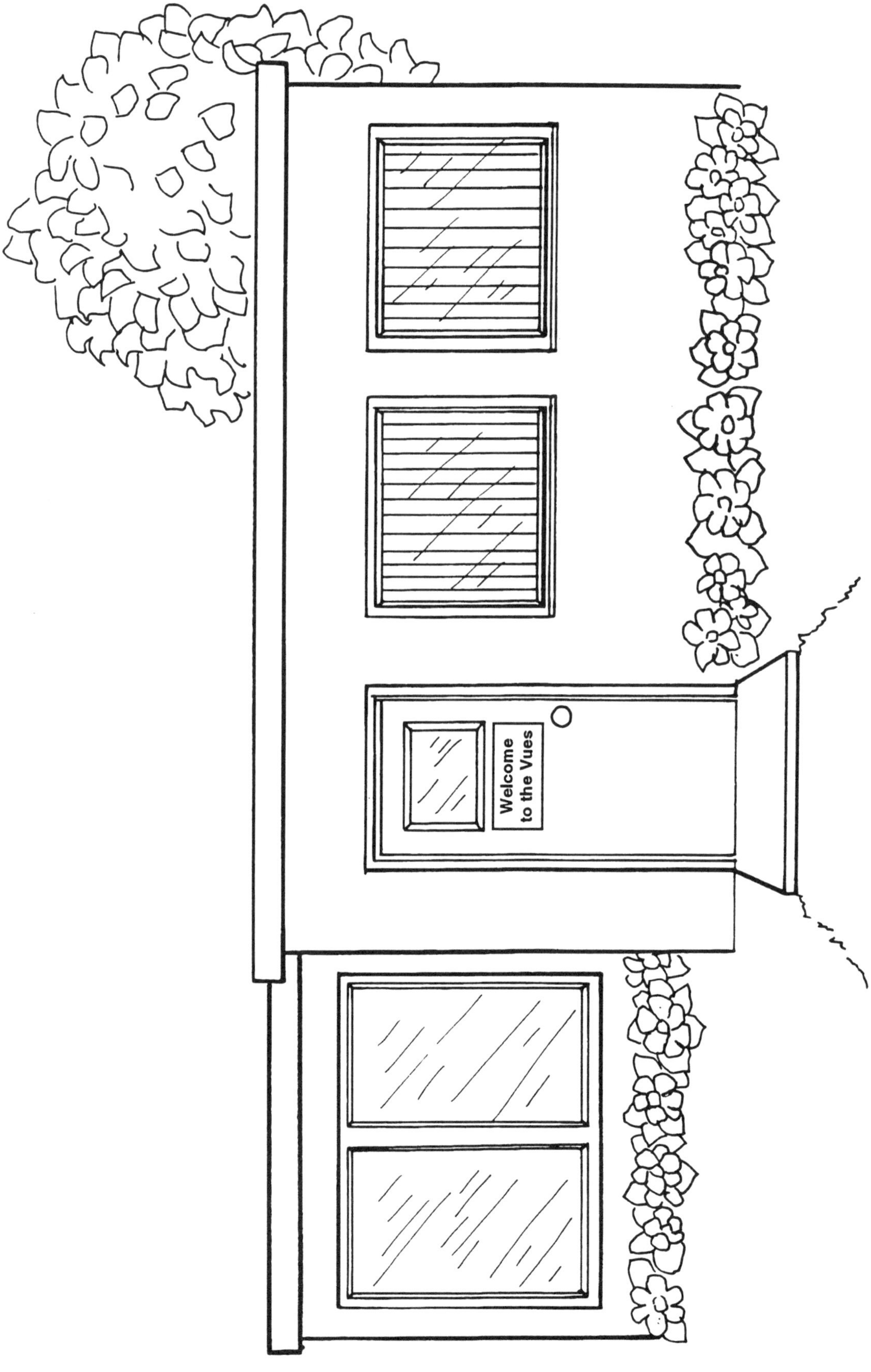
Welcome
to the Vues

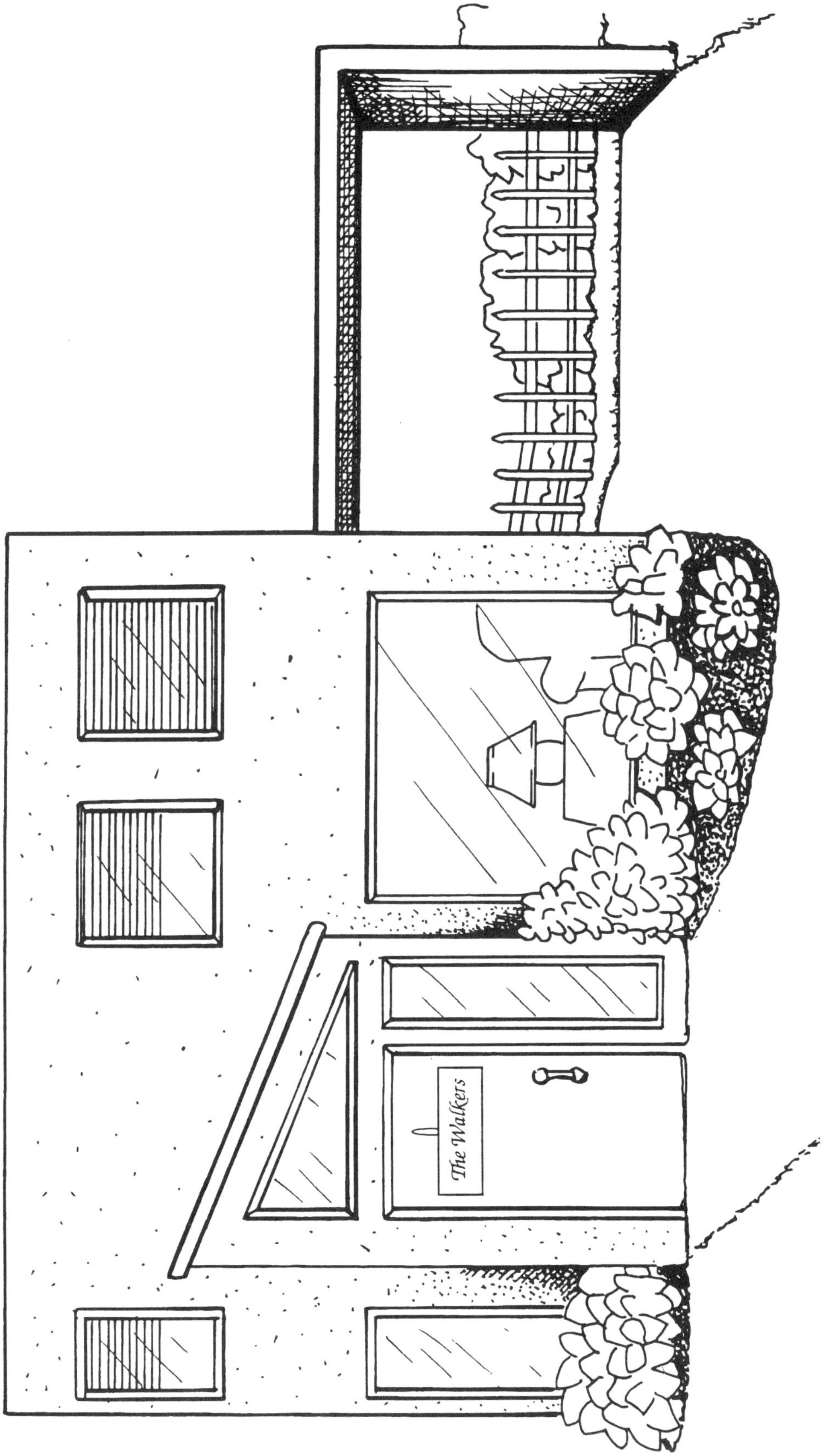
The Walkers

Social Star

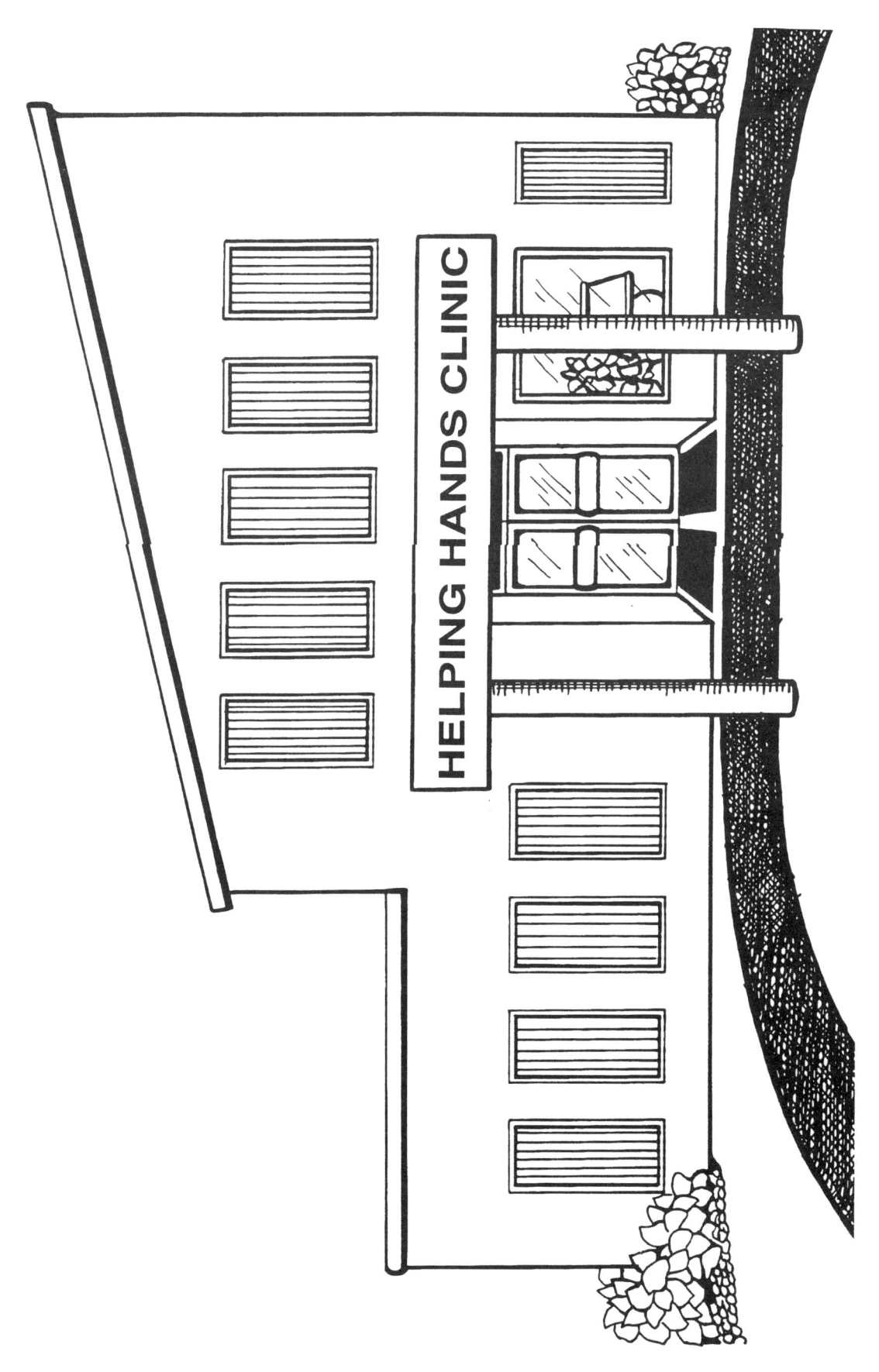

Appendix E: Socialville Buildings

Social Star

Get Along Toy Factory

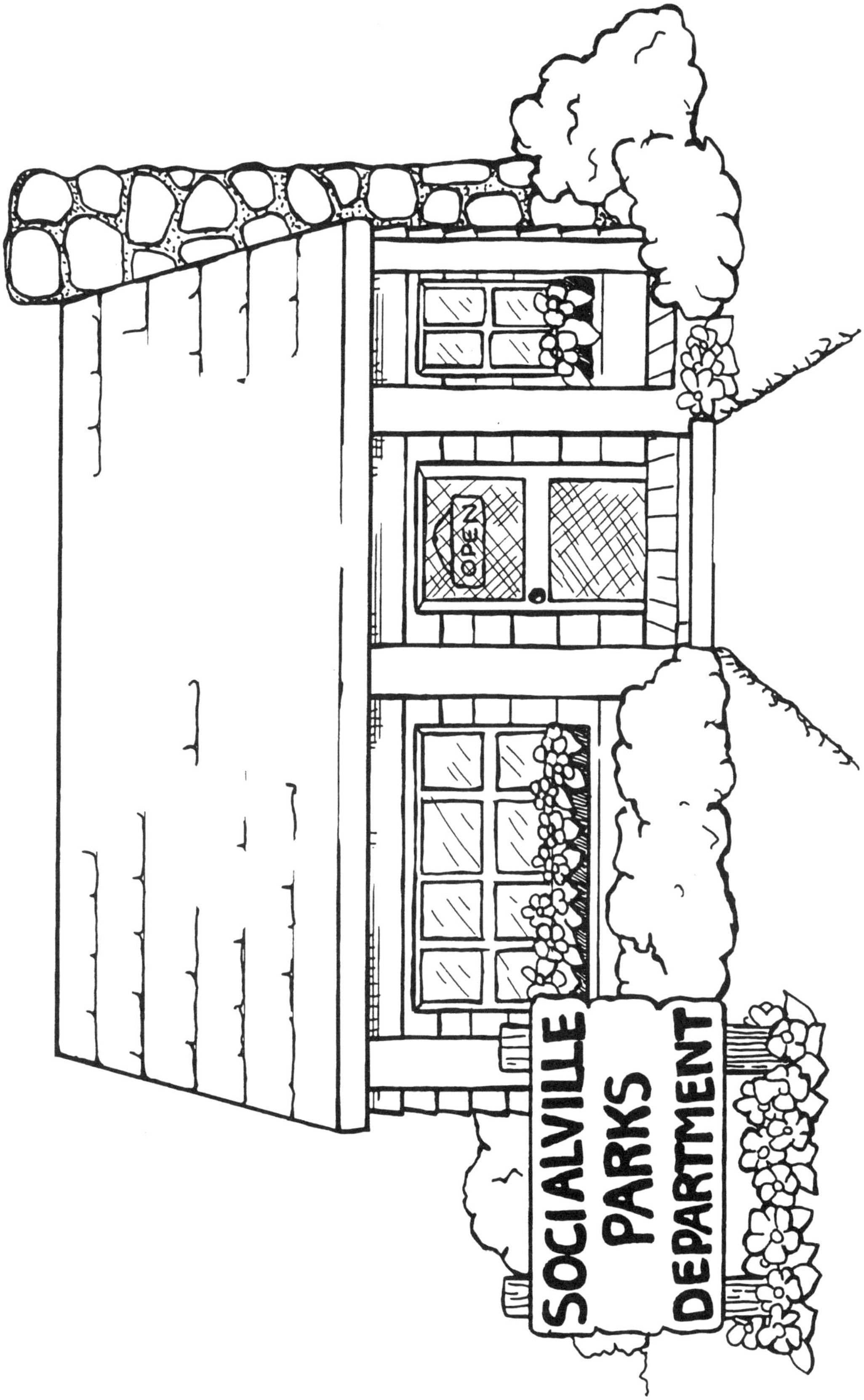
OPEN
SOCIALVILLE
PARKS
DEPARTMENT

Good Meals-Good Manners Restaurant

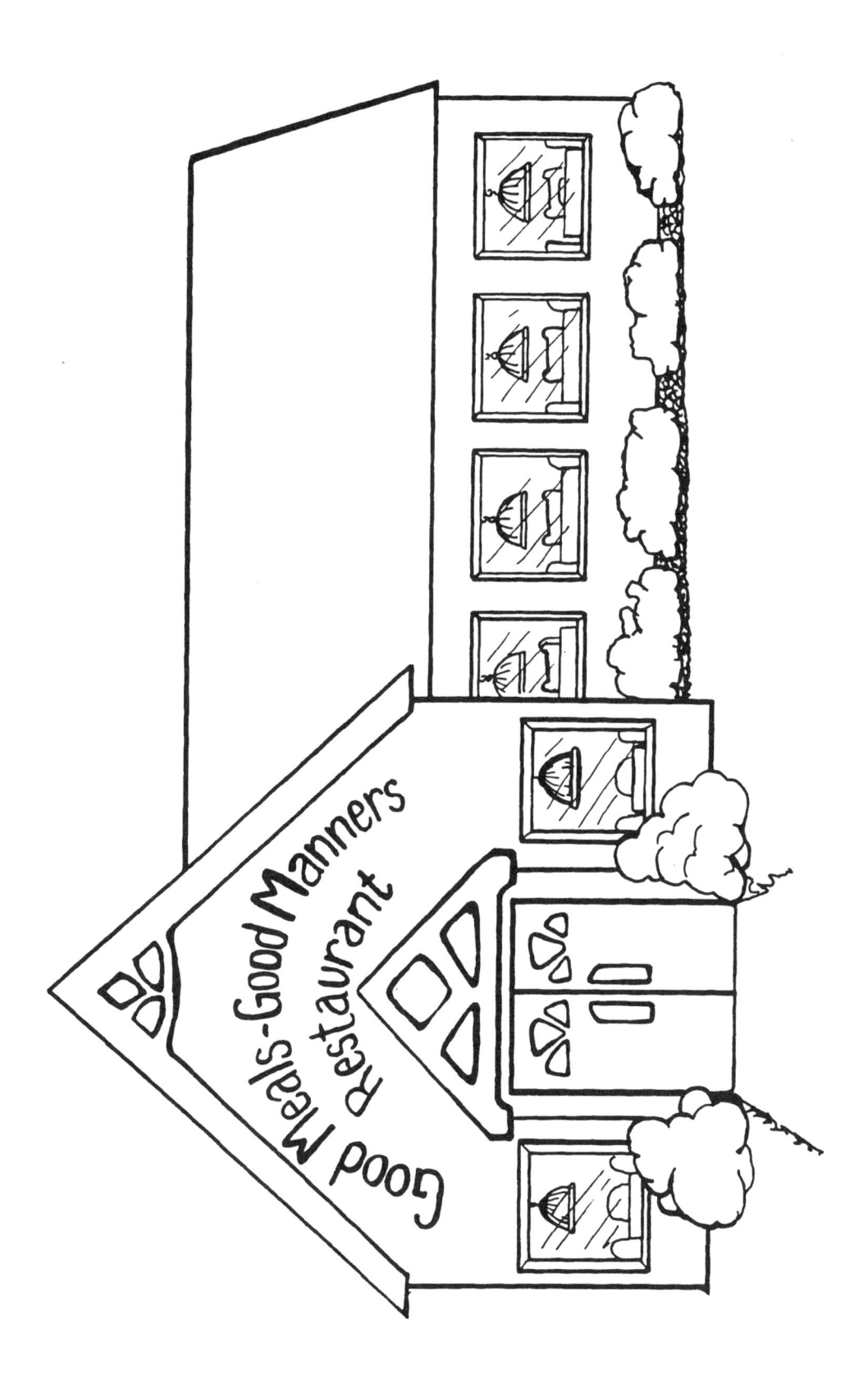

Appendix E: Socialville Buildings

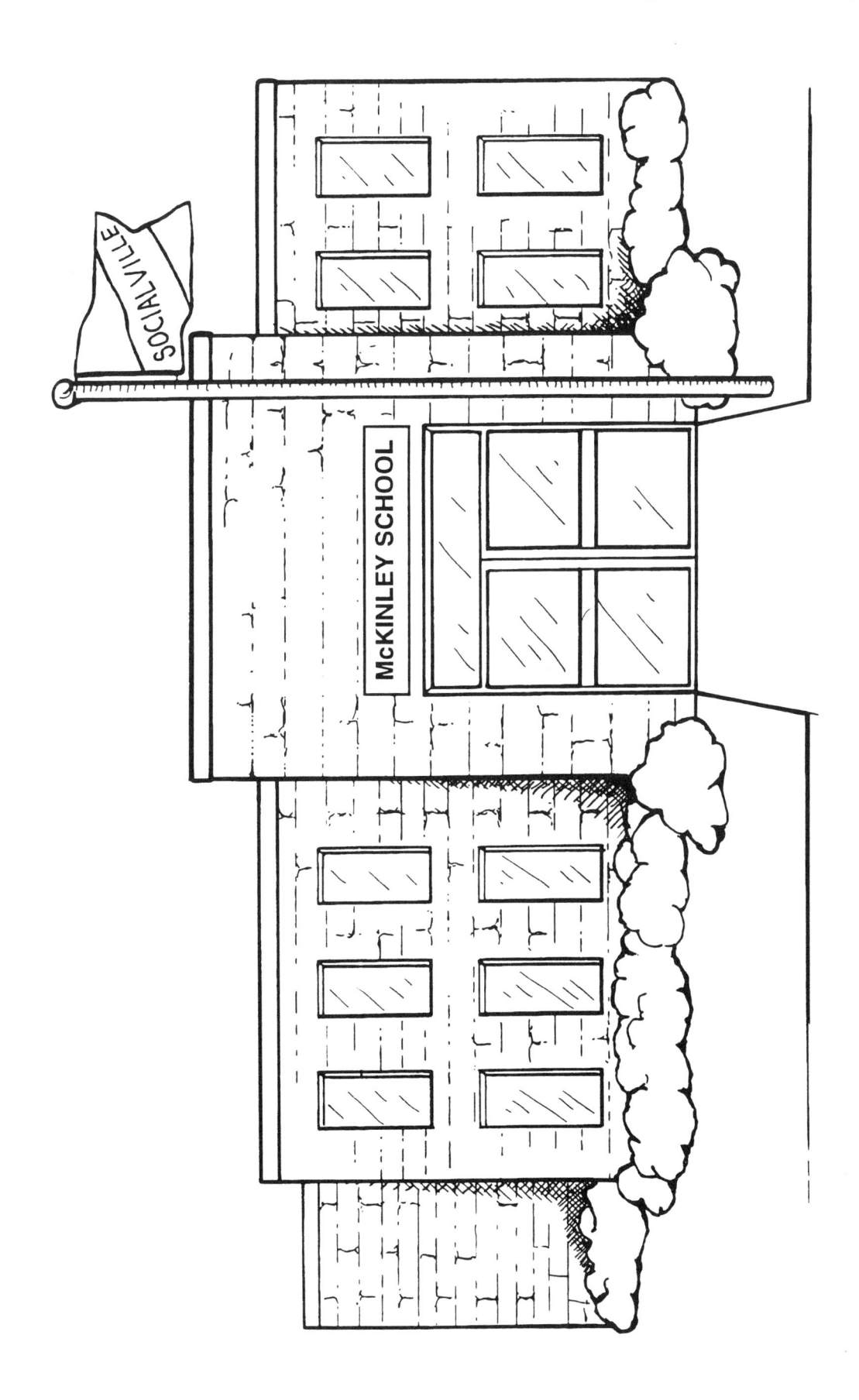

McKINLEY SCHOOL

SOCIALVILLE

© 1996 Thinking Publications · 439 · *Duplication permitted for educational use only.*

Appendix F

Socialville Characters

Social Star

JOLISA WALKER

LEE VUE

© 1996 Thinking Publications · Duplication permitted for educational use only.

Appendix F: Socialville Characters

JESSE WALKER

CORIN WALKER

© 1996 Thinking Publications · *Duplication permitted for educational use only.*

Social Star

MIKA VUE

HO VUE

© 1996 Thinking Publications — 442 — *Duplication permitted for educational use only.*

Appendix F: Socialville Characters

JOE JACKSON

MARY JACKSON

© 1996 Thinking Publications 443 *Duplication permitted for educational use only.*

Social Star

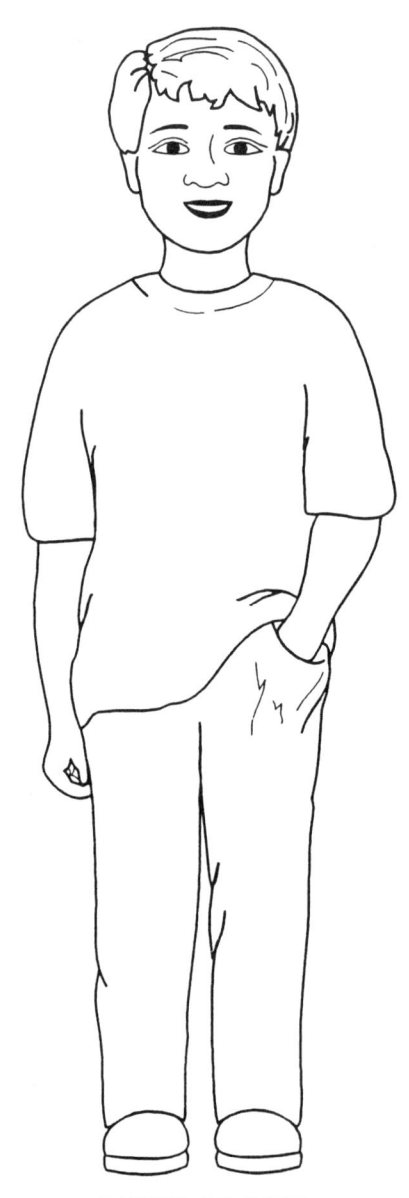

ANN OLSON   **MIKE OLSON**

Appendix F: Socialville Characters

RICARDO PARRA

DR. JUANITA PARRA

© 1996 Thinking Publications — *Duplication permitted for educational use only.*

Social Star

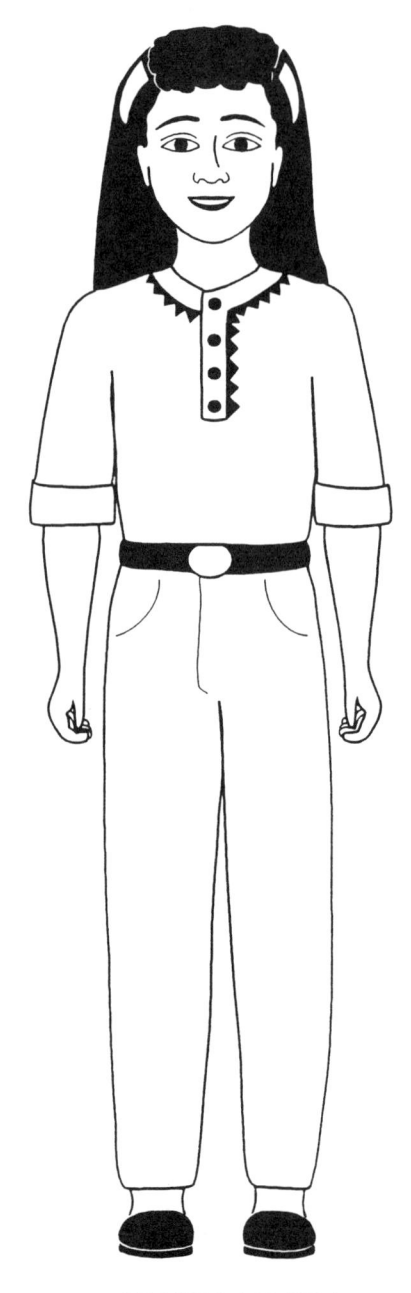

MARIA PARRA **VICTOR PARRA**

MRS. CORA MARRERO   **MR. MARCUS AARON**

Social Star

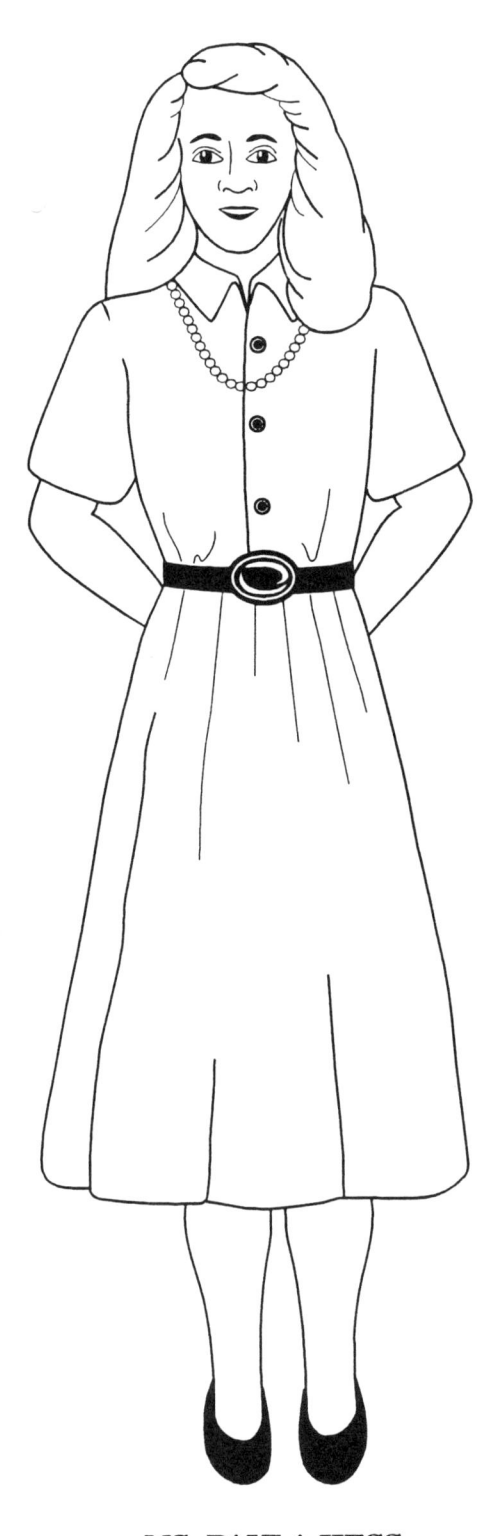

MS. PAULA HESS

Appendix G

Parent Letter

Social Star

Dear

Your child will be participating in a social skills class. The purpose of the class is to teach children social skills which will help them get along better with others and feel better about themselves. A list of social skills that will be taught during class is attached.

Each social skill taught is broken down into small steps with symbols to make them easier to learn. For example, the social skill of *being responsible* has the following skill step and symbol:

1. Ask myself: How can I be responsible?

During class, your child will participate in a variety of activities that teach and provide practice for each social skill. In addition to these activities, it is critical that the skills be practiced in other settings including at home.

At the end of each social skill unit, your child will be bringing home a note called a *Home-A-Gram* and a *Social Super Star* badge. The *Home-A-Gram* will provide you with information about the skill. It will also describe an activity related to the skill for your child to complete at home with your participation and supervision. When the activity is successfully completed, please sign the *Social Super Star* badge and have your child return it to school. Returned badges will be displayed in the classroom.

I look forward to working together with you to expand your child's skills for getting along with others. If you would like further information about the class, please contact me any time. In addition, if you have any questions, concerns, or suggestions, I will be glad to discuss them with you.

Sincerely,

© 1996 Thinking Publications *Duplication permitted for educational use only.*

Appendix H

Self-Management Sheets

Social Star

EDUCATOR DIRECTIONS: Fill in the name of a social skill and a description of the time during which it is to be evaluated (e.g., during science, during free time, during lunch) before making copies for student use.

DIRECTIONS: Rate yourself. Circle either "great," "OK," or "needs improvement." Write your comments if you want. Ask your teacher to rate you too.

SOCIAL SKILL	MY RATING	THE TEACHER'S RATING
_____ **EVALUATED DURING:** _____	GREAT OK NEEDS IMPROVEMENT Comments: _____ _____ _____ _____	GREAT OK NEEDS IMPROVEMENT Comments: _____ _____ _____ _____ _____ *Teacher's Signature*

© 1996 Thinking Publications — Duplication permitted for educational use only.

Appendix H: Self-Management Sheets

EDUCATOR DIRECTIONS: Fill in the name of a social skill and a description of the time during which it is to be evaluated (e.g., during a meal, while playing with friends) before making copies for student use. Send the self-management sheet home with the student. Attach any necessary information for the students' parent(s) concerning use of the sheet.

DIRECTIONS: Rate yourself. Circle either "great," "OK," or "needs improvement." Write your comments if you want. Ask a parent to rate you too.

SOCIAL SKILL	MY RATING	THE PARENT'S RATING
_____ **EVALUATED DURING:** _____	GREAT OK NEEDS IMPROVEMENT Comments: _____ _____ _____ _____	GREAT OK NEEDS IMPROVEMENT Comments: _____ _____ _____ _____ _____ *Parent's Signature*

© 1996 Thinking Publications   *Duplication permitted for educational use only.*

Social Star

EDUCATOR DIRECTIONS: Before making student copies of either self-management sheet below, fill in where you want them to be turned in (e.g., on your desk, in a box, in your hand). Write the name of a specific social skill on the blank line or let the students write the name of any social skill they want to tell you about.

DIRECTIONS: Write your name below. Put this sheet _____ _____. As soon as possible, I'll come and ask you to tell me all about it.

Hey! I want to tell you about when I correctly used the social skill of:

_____

NAME

DIRECTIONS: Write your name below. Put this sheet _____ _____. As soon as possible, I'll come and ask you to tell me all about it.

Just wait till you hear! I did a great job with:

_____

NAME

© 1996 Thinking Publications · Duplication permitted for educational use only.

Appendix H: Self-Management Sheets

EDUCATOR DIRECTIONS: Fill in the name of a social skill and its skill step(s) on either self-management sheet below before making copies for student use.

DIRECTIONS: Draw a smile on one of the faces each time you use this social skill correctly. Then, IN YOUR MIND shout "Good Job!"

SOCIAL SKILL OF:

_____

SKILL STEP(S):

_____

_____

_____

NAME

DIRECTIONS: Mark a Social Star each time you use this social skill correctly. Then, picture yourself jumping up and down cheering for yourself.

SOCIAL SKILL OF:

_____

SKILL STEP(S):

_____

_____

_____

NAME

© 1996 Thinking Publications   *Duplication permitted for educational use only.*

Social Star

EDUCATOR DIRECTIONS: Before copying either self-management sheet below for student use, fill in the name of a social skill, or let students write the name of any social skill they have previously learned about.

DIRECTIONS: Fill in the blanks.

Great Job!

I did a great job using the social skill of:

_____

When: _____

Who with: _____

I praised myself by: _____

_____

_____

NAME

DIRECTIONS: Fill in the blanks.

I used the social skill of:

_____

When: _____

Who with: _____

So? How did I do? _____

_____

_____

NAME

© 1996 Thinking Publications   454   *Duplication permitted for educational use only.*

Appendix H: Self-Management Sheets

EDUCATOR DIRECTIONS: Fill in the name of a social skill and its skill step(s) on either self-management sheet below before making copies for student use.

DIRECTIONS: Each time you do a good job using this social skill, circle the next number below. (Start with 1.)

Social Skill: _____

Skill Step(s): _____

_____

_____

NAME

1 2 3 4 5 6 7 8 9 10 11 12

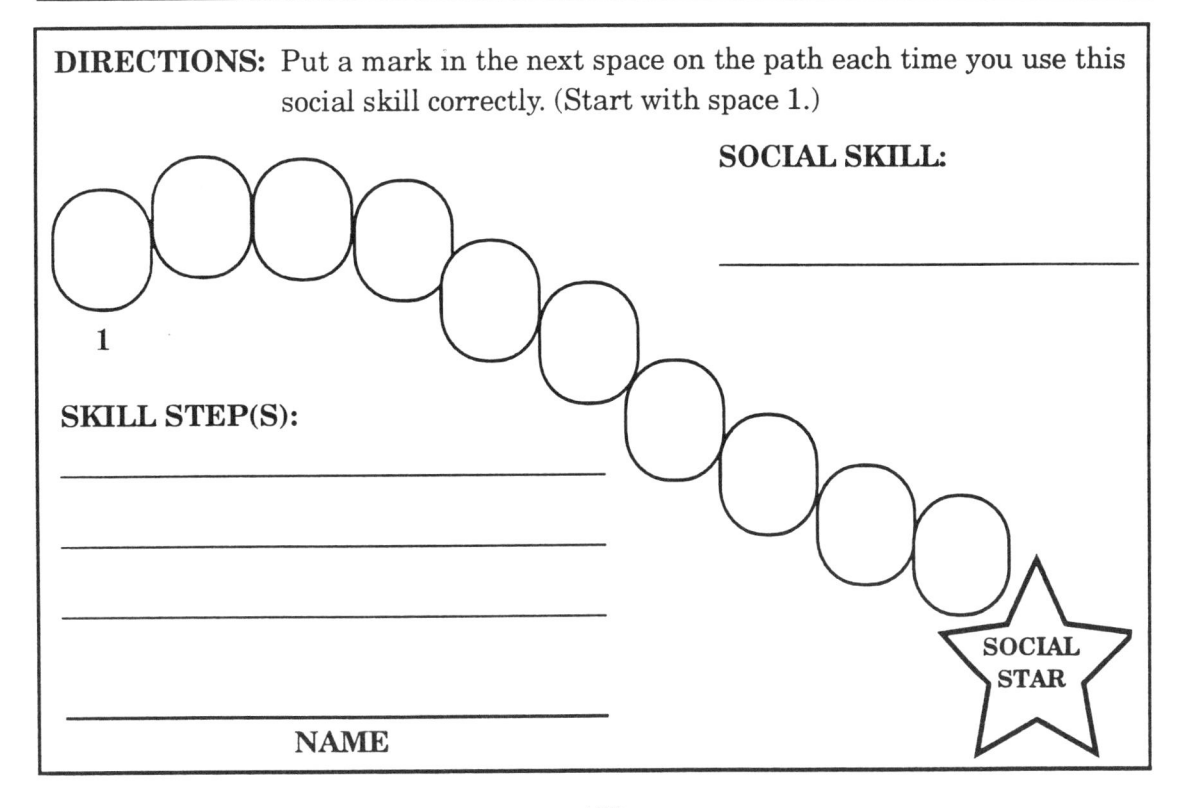

DIRECTIONS: Put a mark in the next space on the path each time you use this social skill correctly. (Start with space 1.)

SOCIAL SKILL: _____

SKILL STEP(S):

_____

_____

_____

_____

NAME

SOCIAL STAR

© 1996 Thinking Publications   455   *Duplication permitted for educational use only.*

Appendix I

Checking Myself

★ Social Star

Name _____

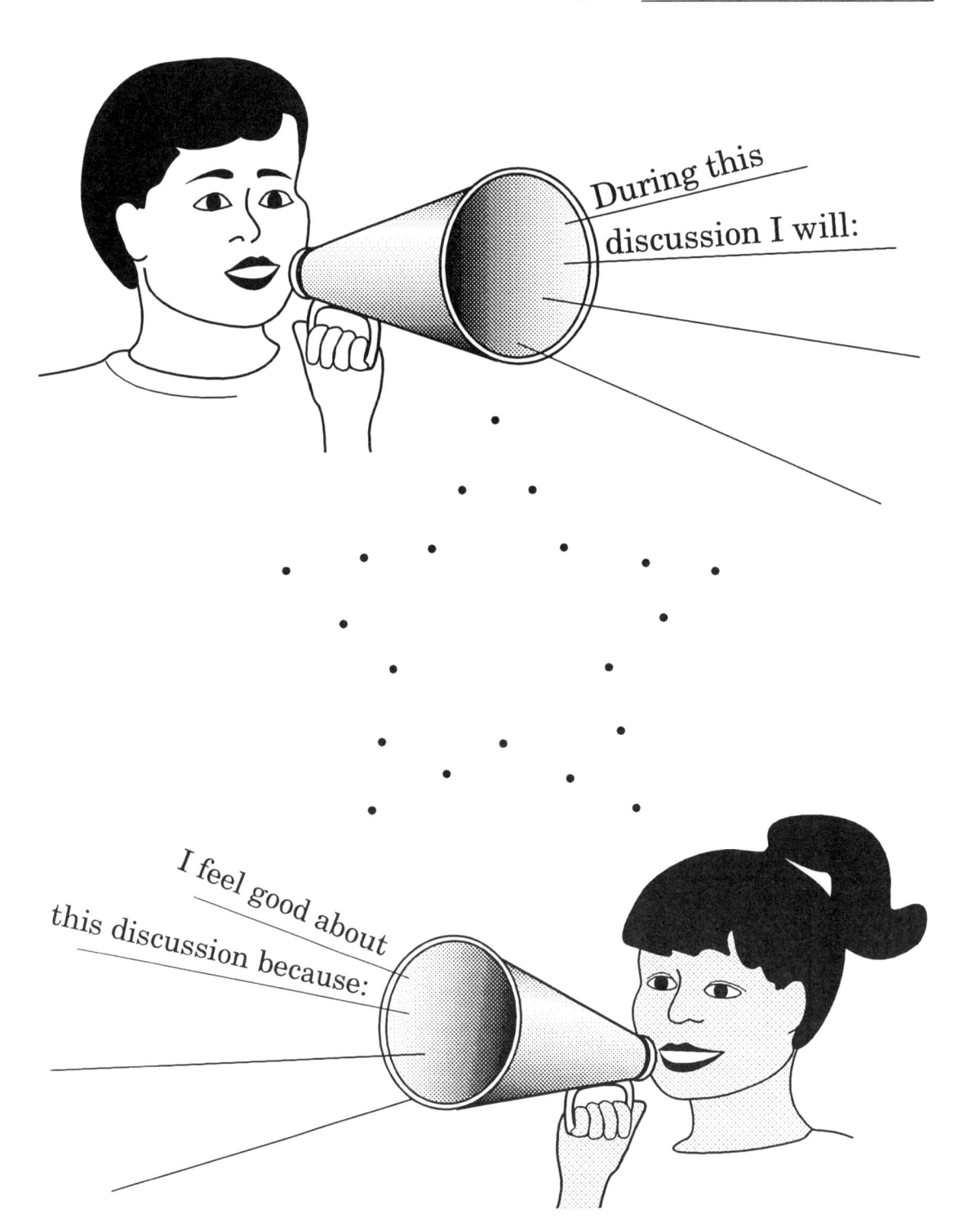

During this discussion I will:

· ·

I feel good about this discussion because:

© 1996 Thinking Publications   456   *Duplication permitted for educational use only.*

Appendix J

Social Gram

Social Star

SOCIAL GRAM

_____,

you did a great job using the social skill of

_____

when _____

_____

_____

_____

_____
Signature

Appendix K

Great Coupon Caper

Social Star

COUPON

NAME: _____

REASONS: _____

_____

_____

_____

Signature

COUPON

NAME: _____

REASONS: _____

_____

_____

_____

Signature

COUPON

NAME: _____

REASONS: _____

_____

_____

_____

Signature

COUPON

NAME: _____

REASONS: _____

_____

_____

_____

Signature

COUPON

NAME: _____

REASONS: _____

_____

_____

_____

Signature

COUPON

NAME: _____

REASONS: _____

_____

_____

_____

Signature

© 1996 Thinking Publications — *Duplication permitted for educational use only.*

Appendix L

Blank T-Chart

Social Star

Social Skill: _____

LOOKS LIKE...	SOUNDS LIKE...

Appendix M

Relaxation Scripts

Social Star

RELAXATION SCRIPT FOR YOUNG CHILDREN

MATERIALS:

One sponge (or piece of a sponge) for each child

PLAN:

Pass out a sponge to each child. Say the following to students in a slow, calm manner.

1. Look at the sponge you have in your hands. Take the sponge and scrunch it up tight like mine. (Show the scrunched up sponge.)
2. Now, let go of your sponge very slowly. See how the sponge opens back up.
3. Try it again. Squeeze your sponge tightly. Now let go slowly.
4. Now I'd like to collect your sponges. (Collect sponges.)
5. Pretend that you are a sponge. Scrunch up your body tightly. Hold it.
6. Let your body out slowly just like when you let go of the sponge.
7. Your body should feel relaxed.
8. Try it again. Scrunch up your body. Take a deep breath.
9. Now, slowly let your body relax. Feel how nice your body feels.
10. Sometimes when you get angry, your body tightens up. You can act like a sponge and relax your body. This will help you stay in control.

A good resource for other relaxation activities is *Lazy Dogs and Sleeping Frogs* (1988) by Darrel Lang and Bill Stinson, Coulee Press, LaCrosse, WI.

PROGRESSIVE RELAXATION SCRIPT FOR OLDER CHILDREN

MATERIALS:

None

PLAN:

The following script should be read in a slow, calm manner:

1. We are going to learn a way to relax our bodies. When we keep our bodies relaxed, it is easier to have self-control.
2. Sit in your chair with your feet flat on the floor. Let your arms hang loosely at your sides.

3. You may close your eyes if you wish.
4. Take a slow, deep breath. Breathe in, two, three and out, two, three. In, two, three and out, two, three.
5. Keep breathing deeply and slowly.
6. Make your hands into tight fists. Keep making tight fists. (Pause for a few seconds.)
7. Now slowly open your hands again. You are teaching your muscles how to relax.
8. Now tighten your arms and your hands. Keep them tight. (Pause for a few seconds.)
9. Slowly relax your hands and then your arms.
10. Keep breathing deeply and slowly.
11. Now tighten your feet. Keep them tight. (Pause for a few seconds.)
12. Slowly relax your feet.
13. Now tighten your feet and your legs. Keep them tight. (Pause for a few seconds.)
14. Slowly relax your feet and legs.
15. Let's move up your body to your neck and face.
16. Scrunch up your face real tight. Keep it scrunched. (Pause for a few seconds.)
17. Let the muscles in your face slowly relax.
18. Keep breathing deeply and slowly.
19. Let your head slowly tilt forward so that your chin almost touches your chest.
20. Now slowly bring your head back up.
21. Let your head slowly tilt backward.
22. Slowly bring your head back up.
23. Tilt your head slowly from shoulder to shoulder. (Pause a few seconds.)
24. Take a slow, deep breath. Breath in, two, three, and out, two, three.
25. Just sit quietly for a few seconds. Think about how relaxed your body feels. (Pause for five to ten seconds.)
26. You can use this way of relaxing whenever you want. Remember, people who are more relaxed have better self-control.

Appendix N

Secret Formula Pages

Social Star

Name _____

★ ★ SECRET FORMULA ★ ★

STOP

I can stay calm by:
_____
_____
_____
_____

PLOT

My problem is: _____
_____

Choices: Consequences:

1. _____ → _____
2. _____ → _____
3. _____ → _____

My choice: _____

Social skills I need: _____
_____

GO

What I can say or do so I actually use my plan:
_____
_____
_____
_____

SO

How did my plan work?
_____
_____
_____
_____

© 1996 Thinking Publications — Duplication permitted for educational use only.

Appendix N: Secret Formula Pages

Name _____

★★★★ SECRET FORMULA ★★★★

STOP

I stayed calm by:
_____
_____
_____
_____

PLOT

My problem was: _____
_____

Choices: Consequences:
1. _____ → _____
2. _____ → _____
3. _____ → _____

My choice was: _____
_____

Social skills I needed: _____
_____

GO

What I said or did so I actually used my plan:
_____
_____
_____
_____

SO

How did my plan work?
_____
_____
_____
_____

© 1996 Thinking Publications — *Duplication permitted for educational use only.*

Appendix O

Thought Bubble

Social Star

Appendix P

Pairing Activities

Pairing activities are fun activities for getting students into pairs. These activities increase the amount of socialization students do while learning new social skills. (Students cannot practice newly learned social skills if they are continually working by themselves.)

Each unit in *Social Star* includes several opportunities for students to work in pairs. Sometimes a specific pairing activity is suggested and other times the educator is asked to choose a pairing activity from the list that follows (or to develop a new one). Some of the pairing activities require prior preparation (e.g., copying, laminating, cutting). These materials are meant to be reused.

The pairing activities often require that students mingle and communicate with one another while forming pairs. Learning to work with several different people, despite personal preferences, is a critical skill. Before using pairing activities in the classroom, discuss with the students that the partner they work with may or may not be someone they were hoping for. Explain that they will be working with a variety of partners in class and that they need to cooperate and respect individual differences while working together. Students must learn to use body language that doesn't show disappointment. You may wish to demonstrate the body language (e.g., facial expression, voice tone, posture, proximity) students could use when they find their partners. It is helpful to demonstrate this in a humorous, exaggerated manner (e.g., use a huge smile, shake hands, say, "I'm so glad to be your partner").

SHOE MATCH

Have students remove one shoe and place it on a pile. Hold up two shoes from the pile. Have the owners retrieve their shoes and become partners.

ANIMAL SOUNDS

Before this is used, duplicate two copies of the *Animal Cards* (see page 468). Choose one pair of animal cards for every two students (e.g., two pigs, two cows). Distribute one animal card to each person. Have students walk around the room and make the animal sounds on their cards. When they find another student making the same animal sound, have them become partners. For a variation, have students close their eyes during this activity.

LINE UP–FOLD UP

Ask students to cooperatively form a line in a specific order (e.g., according to the months of their birthdays, the first letters of their first or last names, their heights). After telling students the chosen criteria for forming a line, have them interact and line up. Give minimal assistance. As a variation, instruct the students not to talk and thus to find alternative methods of communicating with one another. After the students have formed a line, have the line fold up. Have the two students at opposite ends become partners. Ask the students who are second from each end to become partners and so on towards the center of the line.

PICTURE PUZZLE

Before this activity is used, choose a variety of pictures. (These pictures can be drawn by students or cut from magazines.) Cut the pictures in half in "puzzle-piece" fashion. Choose one set of puzzle pieces for every two students. Give each student one puzzle piece. Have students find partners by locating other students whose puzzle pieces match theirs.

INSIDE-OUTSIDE CIRCLE

Ask half of the group to form a circle. Have the remaining students form an outside circle around the first circle. Tell the students to rotate in their circles in opposite directions until they are instructed to "stop." The inside circle should then face outward and the outside circle should face inward so that the students are looking at one another. Have the students be partners with the person each one is facing.

PICK-A-CARD ANY CARD

Write the name of each student on a separate card. Choose the top card, read the person's name, and ask that person to draw a card from the deck. Have the person named on the card chosen be the partner. Proceed in this manner until each student has a partner.

OPPOSITES MATCH

Before this activity is used, duplicate *Opposites Match—A* and *B* (see pages 469–470). Choose one pair of opposite cards for every two students (e.g., black/white, short/tall). Give one card to each student. Have each student find a partner by locating the person who has a card with a picture that is the opposite of the student's picture.

GO TOGETHER CARDS

Before this activity is used, duplicate *Go Together Cards—A* and *B* (see pages 471–472). Choose one pair of *Go Together Cards* for every two students (e.g., fishbowl/fish, beach/beach ball). Give one card to each student. Have students find their partner by locating the person who has a card that "goes together" with theirs. You may choose to make additional sets of matching cards related to concepts in the classroom. For example, matching states with state capitals, lowercase with uppercase letters, clock faces with numbered times, coins with numbered values, faces of famous men or women with descriptions of their accomplishments, song titles and composers.

NUMBERED STONES

Before this activity is used, gather one stone for each student. On each pair of rocks write the same number (e.g., two rocks would have the number one, two rocks would have the number two). Choose one pair of rocks for every two students and place the rocks in a bag. Ask each student to draw a rock from the bag. When all of the rocks are distributed, have the students find their partners by looking for the rock number that matches.

CARD MATCH

Using a deck of playing cards, choose one matching pair of cards for every two students (e.g., two fours, two kings). Give a card to each student. Have the students find their partners by locating the card number that matches.

Social Star

ANIMAL CARDS

BEES "Buzz-z-z-z"	**BIRD** "Tweet-tweet"	**CAT** "Meow"	**COW** "Mooo"
DOG "Woof-woof"	**DONKEY** "Hee-haw"	**DUCK** "Quack-quack"	**FROG** "Ribbit"
HORSE "Neigh"	**LION** "Roar"	**OWL** "Whoo"	**PIG** "Oink"
SHEEP "Baa"	**SNAKE** "S-s-s-s"	**ROOSTER** "Cock-a-doodle-do"	**TURKEY** "Gobble-gobble"

Duplication permitted for educational use only.
© 1996 Thinking Publications

OPPOSITES MATCH—A

NEAR	COLD	BOY	DOWN
OUT	SHORT	WHITE	NARROW
QUIET	SLOW	HARD	DECORATED
UNDER	SUMMER	SMOOTH	FULL

Social Star

OPPOSITES MATCH—B

FAR	HOT	GIRL	UP
IN	TALL	BLACK	WIDE
LOUD	FAST	SOFT	PLAIN
OVER	WINTER	ROUGH	EMPTY

Appendix P: Pairing Activities

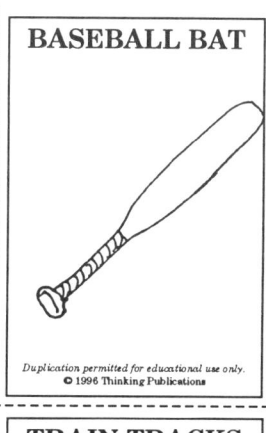

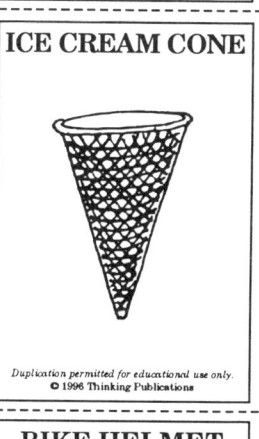

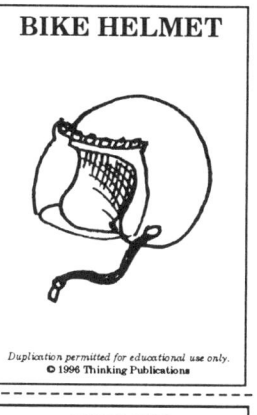

GO TOGETHER CARDS—A

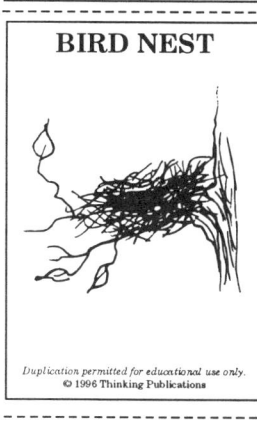

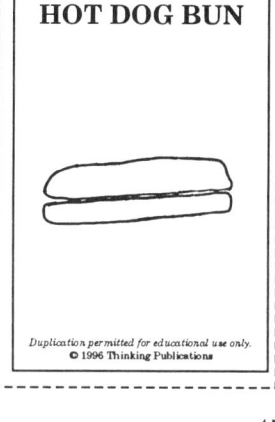

BABY BOTTLE	FISHBOWL	BASEBALL BAT	BEACH
HAMBURGER BUN	TOOTHPASTE	TRAIN TRACKS	ICE CREAM CONE
STAR	RAINCOAT	POT OF GOLD	BIKE HELMET
BIRD NEST	HOT DOG BUN	FLOWER PETAL	CHALK

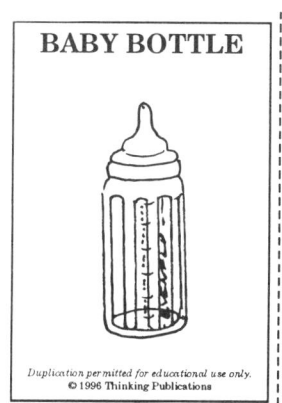

471

GO TOGETHER CARDS—B

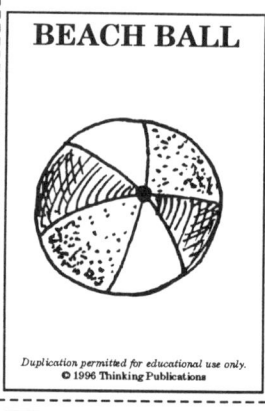

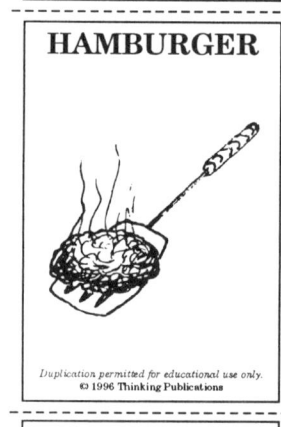

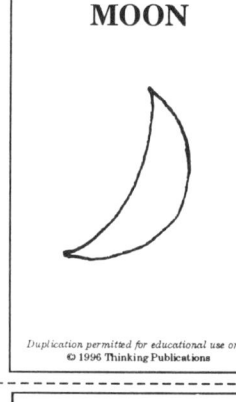

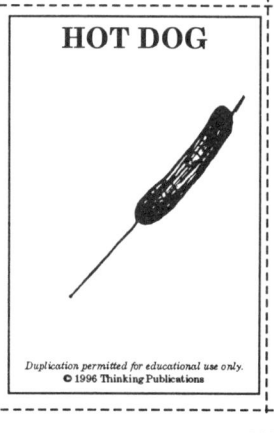

BABY	FISH	BASEBALL	BEACH BALL
HAMBURGER	TOOTHBRUSH	TRAIN	ICE CREAM
MOON	RAIN BOOTS	LEPRECHAUN	BIKE
BIRD	HOT DOG	FLOWER STEM	CHALKBOARD

Appendix Q

Roadblock Sheet

Social Star

Social Skill

Alternative Route

ROADBLOCKS

1.
2.
3.
4.

© 1996 Thinking Publications — 473 — Duplication permitted for educational use only.

Appendix R

Social Super Star Badges

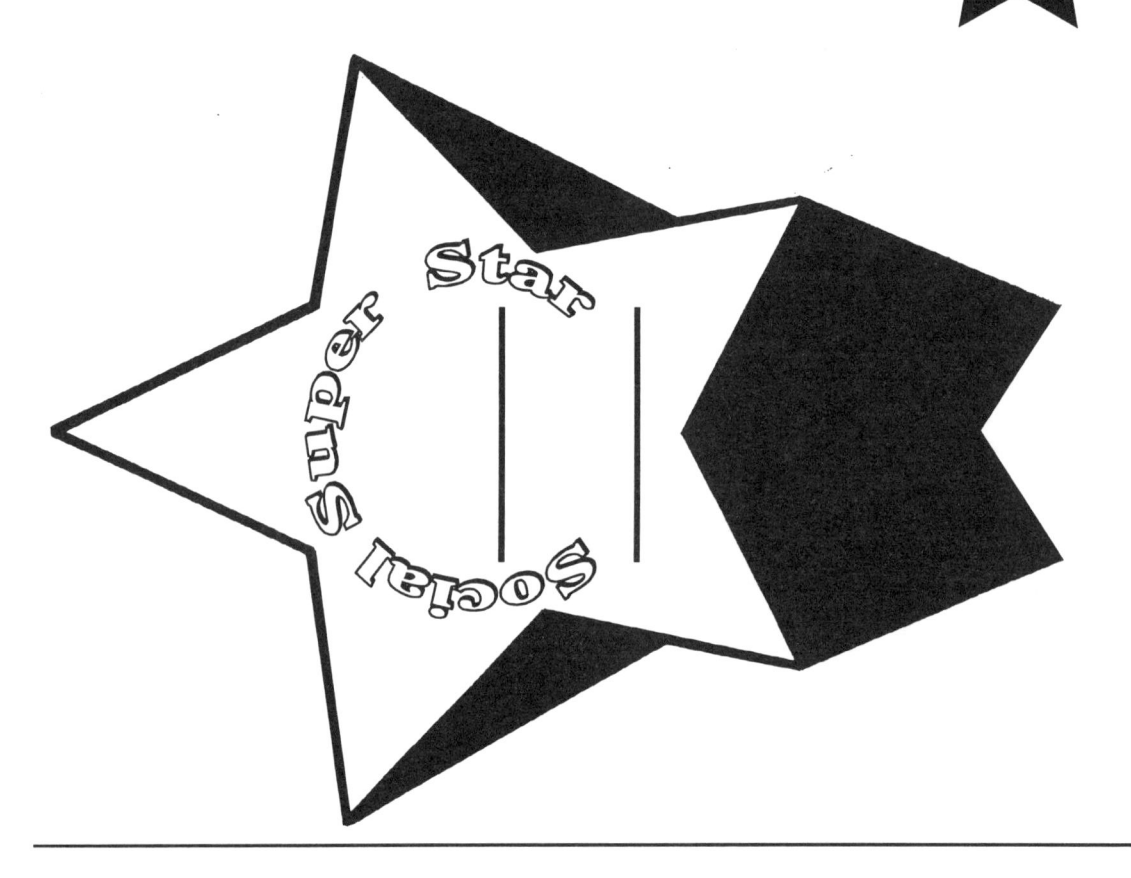

Appendix R: Social Super Star Badges

Social Super Star

Social Super Star

© 1996 Thinking Publications 475 *Duplication permitted for educational use only.*

Appendix S

Thinking Skills Web

★ Social Star

Names _____

© 1996 Thinking Publications — Duplication permitted for educational use only.

Appendix T

Dominoes

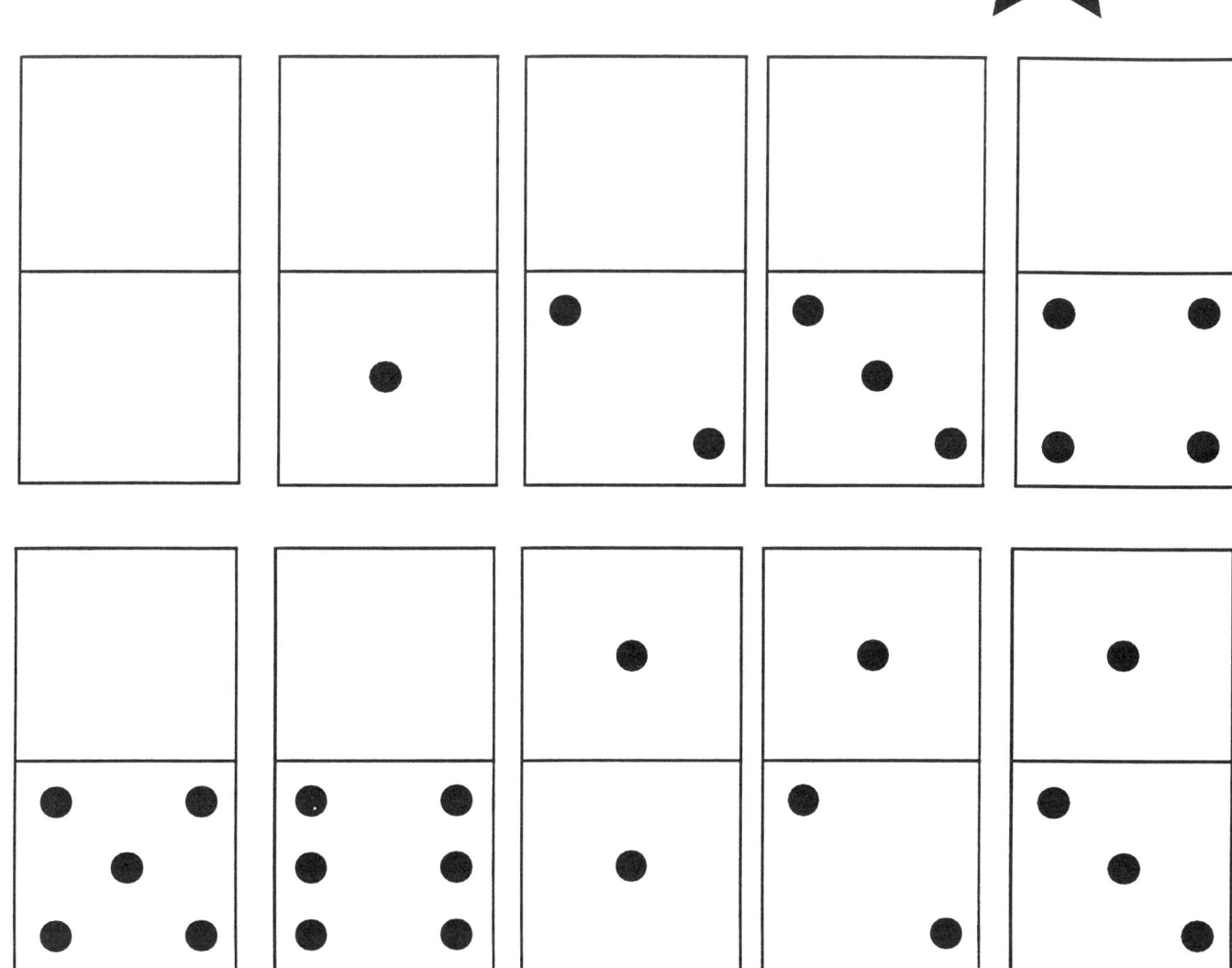

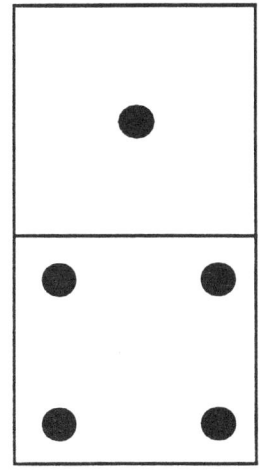

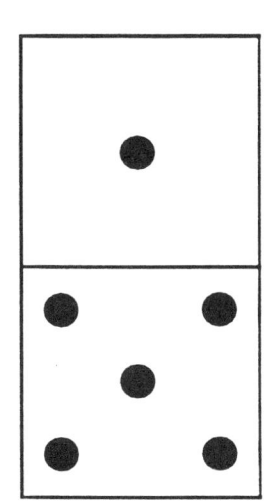

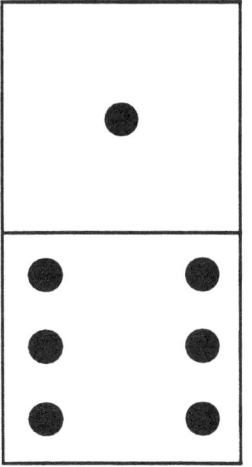

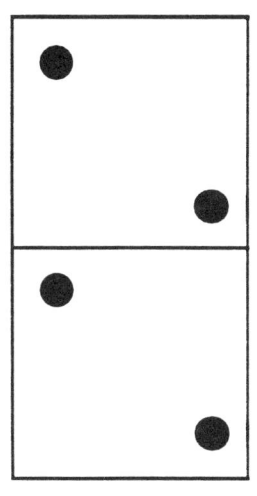

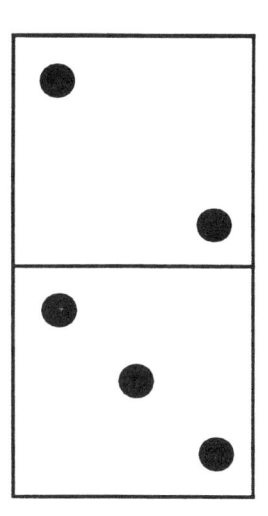

Social Star

© 1996 Thinking Publications — 477 — *Duplication permitted for educational use only.*

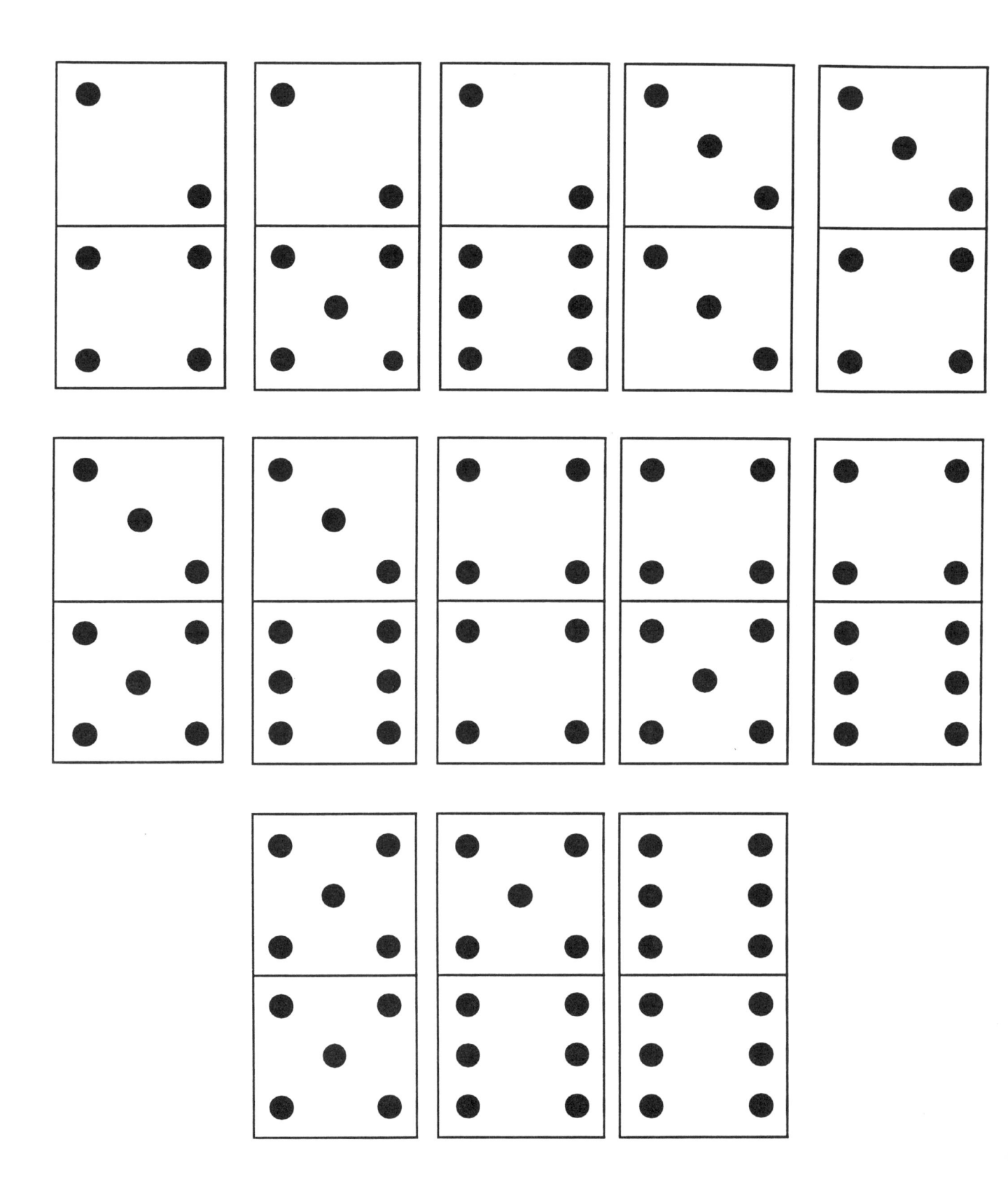

Social Star

Appendix U

Numbered Heads Together Spinner

Social Star

EDUCATOR DIRECTIONS:

Make a transparency of the illustration below. Insert a spinner into the center of the illustration on the transparency. (Spinners are available at most learning stores, or you can develop your own using an arrow and a brass fastener.) When you are at the point in the *Numbered Heads Together* structure that you need to ask students with a certain number to raise their hands, display the transparency and spin the spinner so students watch to see which number is chosen. This adds a new element of fun to the group structure. If students are in groups of two, use the inner circle, with groups of three, use the middle concentric circle, and with groups of four, use the outer concentric circle. A ready-made *Numbered Heads Transparency Spinner* can be purchased from Spencer Kagan, Kagan Cooperative Learning, 27134 Paseo Espada, Suite 303, San Juan Capistrano, CA, 92675, 1-800-933-2667.

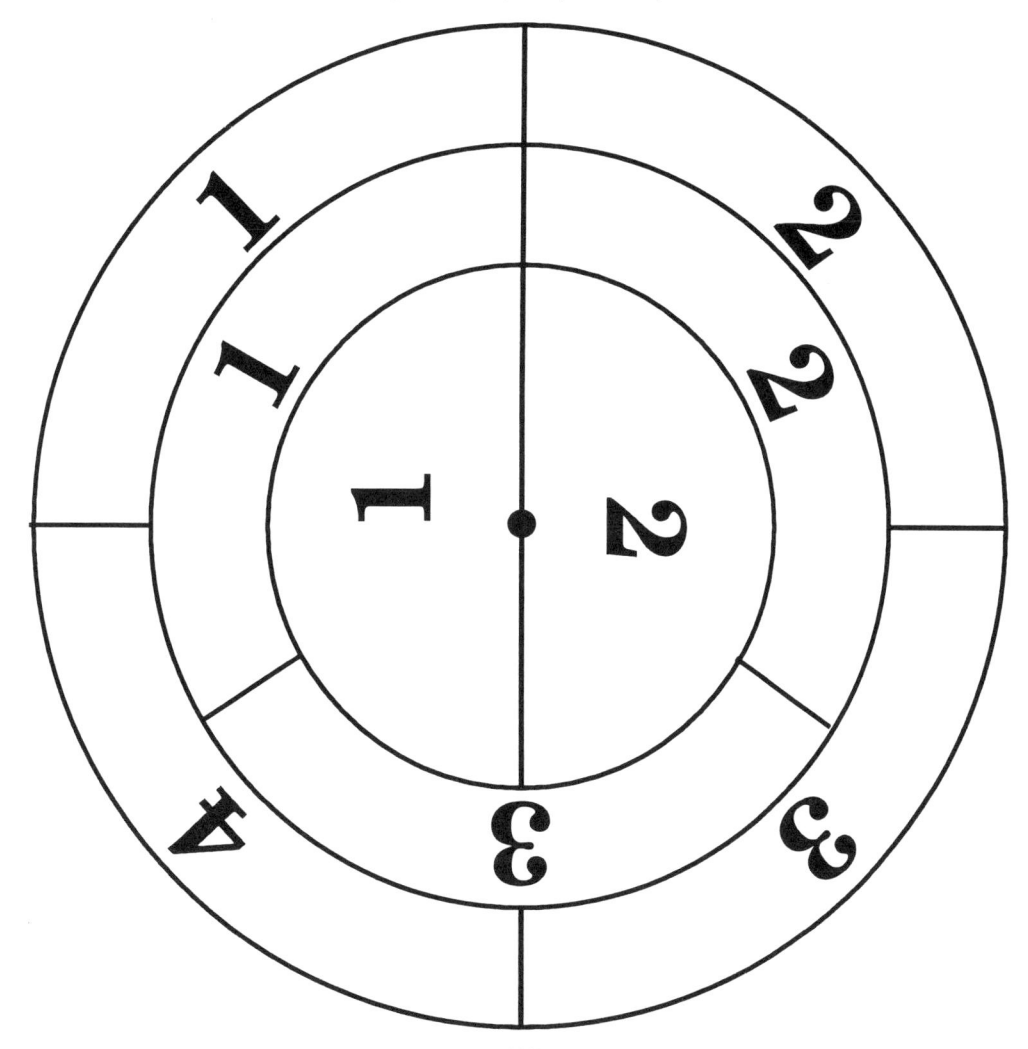

© 1996 Thinking Publications   479   *Duplication permitted for educational use only.*

Appendix V

I Know....

Social Star

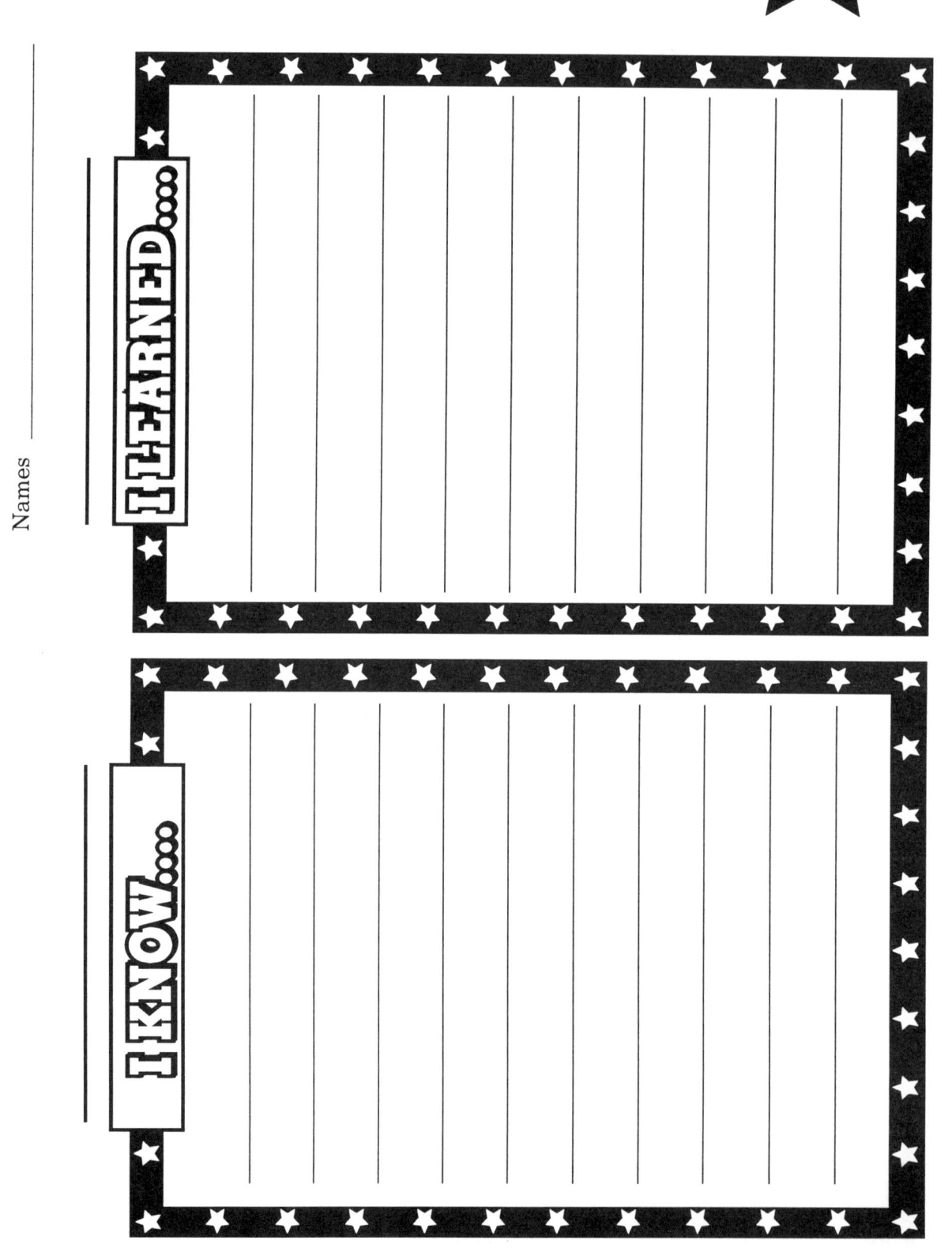

Names _____

I LEARNED....

I KNOW....

© 1996 Thinking Publications — Duplication permitted for educational use only.

MORE SOCIAL SKILLS FOR ELEMENTARY STUDENTS!

Item #5201-BP

Item #5202-BP

SOCIAL STAR:
General Interaction Skills (Book 1)

provides the same interactive format for teaching social skills as **Social Star: Conflict Resolution and Community Interaction Skills (Book 3)** but focuses on 15 *general interaction* skills for instruction. The following skills are presented:

- Eye Contact
- Volume
- Tone of Voice
- Facial Expression
- Posture
- Personal Space
- Hygiene
- Body Talk
- Manners
- Listening Basics
- Staying on Topic/Switching Topics
- Conversations
- Interrupting
- Right Time and Place
- Being Formal or Casual

SOCIAL STAR:
Peer Interaction Skills (Book 2)

builds on the skills taught in **Social Star (Book 1)**. If your students have intact general interaction skills, **Book 2** emphasizes an additional 12 skills essential for successful *peer interaction*:

- Dealing with Teasing
- Giving and Receiving Compliments
- Playing Cooperatively
- Being a Friend
- Respecting Differences
- Optimism
- Building a Positive Reputation
- Getting into a Group*
- Giving Put-ups*
- Participating*
- Staying on Task*
- Disagreeing Politely*

* These units address collaborative group skills. Educators versed in cooperative learning or those looking for a teaching tool to promote successful group interaction will be delighted with these units in **Social Star: Peer Interaction Skills (Book 2)**.

Turn the page for tools used to reinforce the social skills taught in *Social Star* Books 1, 2, and 3 and for order information!

Reinforce Elementary Social Skills —Boldly and Brightly!

Use brightly colored **Reinforcement Certificates, Stickers,** and **Note Pads** to send special compliments to your social super star students!

Social Skill Reinforcement Certificates include 30—8" x 5" certificates per pad. Choose from one of five designs:

Social Super Star (Book 1 skills)	Item #6020-BP
Blastoff! (Book 2 skills)	Item #6021-BP
Genuine Social Skills (Book 3 skills)	Item #6022-BP
Terrific Social Skills	Item #6023-BP
Excellent Social Skills!	Item #6024-BP

Colorful **Social Star Stickers** will be proudly worn by your students. Each pack of 150 stickers corresponds to **Social Star (Book 1), (Book 2),** or **(Book 3)** social skills. **Social Star Stickers** include 15—1⅝" stickers per sheet; 10 sheets per set.

Social Star Stickers

Set 1 (Book 1 skills)	Item #6001-BP
Set 2 (Book 2 skills)	Item #6002-BP
Set 3 (Book 3 skills)	Item #6003-BP

Social Skill Note Pads can deliver special messages to parents or students on two different note pad designs. Note pads are 5½" x 4¼".

Social Skill Note Pads   Item #6010-BP
(Includes two pads; each of a different design.)

Social Star Classroom Posters can be constant reminders of the skill steps students need to use. Each colorful poster has skill steps for a social skill boldly printed. Posters measure 17½" x 22½" and are available in sets corresponding to the skills in **Social Star (Book 1), (Book 2),** and **(Book 3)**.

(Book 1) 15 posters	Item #5301-BP
(Book 2) 12 posters	Item #5304-BP
(Book 3) 10 posters	Item #5305-BP

Our **Cognitive Planning Formula Chart** provides a quick reminder for your students to think "Stop, Plot, Go, So" as they discover how useful this cognitive strategy is in their daily lives. The multi-colored chart measures 24" x 36" and is printed on heavy stock.
Item #5302-BP

Have a special place to display **Social Super Star** badges to help your students feel proud! The **Social Super Stars Badge Display** measures 17½" x 22½" and is just the focal point you need to culminate each **Social Star** unit.   Item #5303-BP

To order or to request more information, call **1-800-225-GROW**

THINKING PUBLICATIONS®
A Division of McKinley Companies, Inc.

424 Galloway Street • P.O. Box 163
Eau Claire, WI 54702-0163
FAX 1-800-828-8885
E-MAIL custserv@ThinkingPublications.com